Measure
Yourself Against
the Earth

FIRST EDITION

Library and Archives Canada Cataloguing in Publication

Kingwell, Mark, 1963-, author
Measure yourself against the earth / Mark Kingwell.

Issued in print and electronic formats.
ISBN 978-1-77196-046-5 (paperback).--ISBN 978-1-77196-047-2 (ebook)

1. Culture--Philosophy. 2. Popular culture--Philosophy. I. Title.

HM621.K55 2015   306   C2015-903731-X
C2015-903732-8

Edited by Jeet Heer
Copy-edited by Emily Donaldson
Typeset and Designed by Gordon Robertson

 Canada Council
for the Arts
Conseil des Arts
du Canada
 ONTARIO ARTS COUNCIL
CONSEIL DES ARTS DE L'ONTARIO

 Canadian
Heritage
Patrimoine
canadien

Published with the generous assistance of the Canada Council for the Arts and the Ontario Arts Council. Biblioasis also acknowledges the support of the Government of Canada through the Canada Book Fund and the Government of Ontario through the Ontario Book Publishing Tax Credit.

PRINTED AND BOUND IN CANADA

Measure Yourself Against the Earth

Essays

MARK KINGWELL

Biblioasis
Windsor, Ontario

"Walking . . . is how the body measures itself against the earth."
— REBECCA SOLNIT, *Wanderlust: A History of Walking* (2000)

For Karen Mulhallen

"She all night long her amorous descant sung; Silence was pleas'd"
— MILTON, *Paradise Lost*, Book IV

Contents

The Asshole Effect and the Honeymoon of Stupidity

> "Democracy is the honeymoon of stupidity."
> — BEN HECHT, *Fantazius Mallare* (1922)

1. The Asshole Effect

WHO AMONG US has not felt the affront? Macadamia nuts arrive in a bag, not on a dish, and something shrivels in the soul. Are we animals? Did we execute the challenging task of being born insanely wealthy only to eat in-flight snacks from *a bag*?! We did not. And that is why, when Korean Air heiress Cho Hyun-ah was confronted by a bag of nuts on a flight out of New York in December of 2014, she grew enraged and forced the plane back to the gate. Cho, the 40-year-old daughter of the airline's chairman, Cho Yang-ho, was charged with offences including assault and obstructing an airline captain in performance of his duties.

In custody since December 30, 2014, Cho has now been convicted and will serve a year in prison. Another executive who tried to cover up the incident will serve eight months. Many observers consider the sentences too light, given the rampant nepotism and privilege enjoyed by second- and third-generation members of South Korea's business elite. "If she were considerate to people, if she didn't treat employees like slaves, if she could have controlled her emotion," the chief judge said, "this case would not have happened." But consider the deeper truth of the matter: it was not really her fault.

The psychologist Paul Piff has coined a memorable label for the phenomenon: the asshole effect. Piff and his colleagues have shown that there is a reliable correlation, across a range of scenarios, between wealth and inconsiderate behaviour.[1] Wealthy people are more likely to exhibit rudeness in cars, take more than equal shares of available goods, and think they deserve special treatment. Ms. Cho is just a spectacular example of what happens daily at any airport. When the sheer luck of the birthright lottery is converted via psychological magic into a sense of entitlement, expectations of special treatment and a delusional belief that tax reform constitutes "class warfare" are predictable. Piff confirms experimentally the arguments of philosopher Aaron James's 2012 book *Assholes: A Theory*.[2] Like George W. Bush, some people are born on third base and think they hit a triple.

That's why Cho's trial and sentencing should be seen for what it is: an avoidance ritual, a show trial. Pictured in tears after the sentencing, Cho wrote a forced confession letter in which she said, "I know my faults and I'm very sorry." This is Galilean recanting for the obscenely pluto-centric age. But Cho's conviction changes nothing. In fact, it allows the current arrangement to endure under a screen of bogus accountability. Meanwhile, those who complain that the verdict is rooted in resentment are right. Resentment is, after all, the rational response of non-jerks when faced with the over-entitled behaviour of jerks. It's not the rudeness that people hate so much as the assumption that they are allowed to be rude.

This isn't always a function of wealth, just of narcissism and assumed superiority. I know several witless academic egomaniacs who routinely give themselves a free pass to be uncivil. But because wealth is the most obvious marker of status in capitalist societies, it is also the most powerful lever of assholery. It is no coincidence that the depredation of such people occurs most often in cases where they are confronted with the tedium of dealing with service people or, worse, competing with other citizens for the attention of such service people. Eric Schwitzgebel usefully supplements James's asshole theory with his own theory of what he prefers to call jerks. "Picture the world through the eyes of the jerk," he writes at the beginning of his diverting "field study" of the type. "The line of people in the post office is a mass of unimportant fools; it's a felt injustice that you must wait while they bumble with their requests. The flight attendant is not a potentially interesting person with her own cares and struggles but instead the most available face of a corporation that stupidly insists you shut your phone. Custodians and secretaries are lazy complainers who rightly get the scut work. The person who disagrees with you at the staff meeting is an idiot to be shot down. Entering a subway is an exercise in nudging past the dumb schmoes."[3]

Other entitlement show trials were underway in the early months of 2015. Dominique Strauss-Kahn, former head of the International Monetary Fund, was scrambling to salvage the shreds of reputation even as lurid evidence emerged of sex parties and pimping that make his alleged 2011 assault of a Manhattan hotel worker seem like business as usual. (Ken Kalfus's novella *Coup de Foudre* is a brilliant fictional account of the latter incident, framed as a cringe-making letter of apology.[4]) And lest we forget, there are worse things than nut rage or even non-fatal sexual assault. Francesco Schettino, disgraced captain of the Costa Concordia cruise ship, wrecked off the Capri coast in 2012, was convicted of multiple counts of manslaughter. Thirty-two passengers and crew were killed in that debacle and Schettino, who jumped ship, was sentenced to sixteen years in jail.

But while this "reckless idiot" with traces of cocaine in his hair—clearly he does not know what he's doing there, either—was entertaining his twenty-five-year-old Moldovan mistress, ordering the pointless and dangerous fly-by to impress her, there was a company, a system, and a set of assumptions all holding him up. His orders, after all, were obeyed. It is a necessary premise of law that individuals are responsible for their actions, and no sane person would have it otherwise. But the root causes of the asshole effect are not, finally, singular. Such people are made, not born. Until we have a more aggressive plan for attacking luck entitlements, condemnation of a few hapless exemplars will remain satisfying but futile. Where to begin?

The first thing to consider is what we might call the *generalization of jerkitude*. When Schwitzgebel fleshes out his field study of the species he notices an important finding: while jerkiness may pool and settle in the declivities formed by other privilege, especially wealth and attendant social status, there is a surprising comprehensiveness to the jerk-like behaviour when *any* differences in status are in play. That is, I may not be a jerk most of the time, but in a particular situation where I feel myself superior—suppose, in a case relevant to several of the essays in this collection,

I am a pedestrian and you are a motorist—I may indulge my inner jerk to such an extent that I hurl an insult, step in front of your car as it makes a rolling red-light turn, or otherwise perceive you as someone *in my way*.

The jerk's failure, Schwitzgebel argues, is at once moral and intellectual. The moral part is perhaps more obvious: the jerk behaves badly, and then justifies the behaviour to himself. But the path of justification is significant, typically involving a tangle of self-serving attitudes (I am in the right compared to you!), narcissism (I am better than you!), and errors of fact (I am correct and you are in error!). The moral wrong of behaving badly is joined by the intellectual wrong of distorting facts and other elements of the given situation such that they run in my favour. In sum, "the jerk culpably fails to appreciate the perspective of others around him, treating them as tools to be manipulated or idiots to be dealt with rather than as moral and epistemic powers." The interpersonal aspects of Schwitzgebel's theory mark it as superior to James's asshole theory—to which, admittedly, it owes a great deal. Asshole, according to James, whether born or made, is someone who lays implicit claim to special treatment because of an entrenched sense of entitlement. We might say that, once confirmed in such a sense, the asshole *reifies* into a perpetual version of himself. (Cho may have apologized during her trial, but DSK was still treating the prosecutor with the same disdain he brought to waiters and shopkeepers: Why were they pestering a man of private appetites with these absurd intrusive questions?)

The jerk relationship, by contrast, is more complex and more fluid. For one thing, it is always at least dyadic (me and the driver; the airline passenger and the flight attendant), though sometimes it is a series of multiple dyads (all those people in line in front of me). The latter condition can make the situation look like it is one of reified assholery; perhaps in some cases, where there is indeed entrenched privilege, it is so. But since one premise of the jerk theory is that any one of us might be a jerk at almost any time, given the right conditions—a bad day at work, cramped travelling conditions, even too much humidity—there is more to the failures here than cases of what we might call Excessive Entitlement Disorder (EED). Presumably, most of us do not suffer from this condition; such people are merely the bellwethers of the systems, the perverse canaries in the coalmine of plutocratic society.

Of course, we must allow here for the fact that such people's behaviour does not strike *them* as unseemly. When EED is well advanced, when the asshole is comprehensively reified, there is little sense on his own part that there is anything wrong with the picture except that he's still waiting for that damn martini—Did you send down the street for it, or what? Such blindness is part of the true asshole. The jerk, again by contrast, may come to perceive that his behaviour has been bad, that he has failed his fellow citizens in not treating them as peers. This may happen soon after the behaviour, especially when the immediate circumstances change (I get that cool drink, we get out of the small car, the air clears); or perhaps when, relating the event to a friend in search of validation, he receives, instead, a rebuke. Regret may be rare, and hard to come by, but the general sense that jerkiness is associated with *perceived* and maybe temporary superiority, rather than with entrenched entitlement, offers at least the chance of asking: Hey, was I being a jerk? (With Schwitzgebel, I will forego the too-optimistic claim that one might come to this realization *in the midst of* the situation. This is too much to hope for: even saints have bad days.)

In short, the theory's claims about moral and intellectual failure allow us to realize that there is a democratic republic of jerks, and we are all potential citizens of it. "[N]o one is a perfect jerk or a perfect sweetheart," Schwitzgebel notes; but we can recognize salient features and common triggers. Jerkiness, like assholery, tends to rise in prospect as one climbs a social hierarchy: it becomes easier to indulge jerky impulses where there are more perceived underlings. For obvious reasons, jerks tend to deploy their bad behaviour down the social scale, even while (sometimes) affecting sweetness on the upside. Thus servers, clerks, students, cashiers, and—especially—strangers can be seen as easy targets. Without fear of reprisal or loss of status, indeed with a sense of confirming it by getting one's way or securing an advantage, jerkiness can seem justified. This leads, in turn, to hypocrisy: the shortcomings of others are clear and distinct while mine are forgivable and even justified. Two old bits of everyday wisdom capture the essence of the democratic republic of jerks: when I am driving on a highway there are three kinds of people: the ones going slower than me (idiots), the ones going faster (assholes), and the one going the appropriate speed (me); and you can always tell what people are like by how they treat waiters. (Hints: sometimes it's the kitchen's fault; it's a harder job than you think; and it won't kill you to tip well.)

And so we might say that, when it comes to the jerk within, eternal vigilance is the price of civility. But is there more that can be said about the political dimension of such behaviour, something that Schwitzgebel neglects? James, for his part, makes the obvious point that the core issue is economic in a section of his book called "Asshole Capitalism." Unlike authoritarian or aristocratic regimes, where a small group of assholes rule over the rest of us, capitalist regimes ostensibly organized according to democratic principles allow a value-free and allegedly meritocratic regime in which a fluid number of assholes can game the entire system in their favour. The pocketing government and banking systems flow naturally as a rational extension of taking one's proper advantage. Capito-democracy, as I have called it in the past, is essentially a customer-loyalty program skewed in favour of asshole elite.

So let us consider for a moment what it means to live in an alleged democracy which is, in many ways, a highly segregated, positional, and hierarchical society. Much of that structural status is, as I suggested already, driven by—or at least strongly correlated with—wealth. But that is not the entire range of the problem. Can we animate in this land a sense of what the political theorist Raymond Geuss has called "generalized nemesis"? That is to say, the lived reality that no one really is, in an important sense, superior to anyone else; that all claims to superiority are inherently suspect. Well, before we can answer, we must consider whether democracy is robust enough as an idea to bear the weight of such doubt.

2. The Honeymoon of Stupidity

When Ben Hecht wrote his dark "Nietzschean" novel *Fantazius Mallare* in 1922 he was already well known for his gritty journalism in various Chicago newspapers, "the Pagliacci of the fire-escapes" as one contemporary celebrant had it. His column in the *Chicago Daily News*, "1,001 Afternoons in Chicago," was an inspiration to, among others, another Chicago-dwelling Jew, an aspiring writer who had been born in Montreal. Saul Bellow and his school friends haunted the Hecht universe on the dirty streets of the City of Broad Shoulders, looking for the characters and the tones that a gifted writer brought to the grind of daily journalism. "What was most marvelous," Bellow wrote later of Hecht, "was that people should have conceived of dignifying what we witnessed all about us by writing of it and that the gloom of Halsted Street, the dismal sights of the Back of the Yards and the speech of immigrants should be the materials of art. Something could be made of the very things that baffled or oppressed us; the chains of today might become the laurels of tomorrow."[5]

Afterwards, Hecht would be most famous for his plays, including *The Front Page*, a witty crime-and-journalism drama co-written by fellow reporter Charles MacArthur. The two took the play to Broadway where it premiered in the summer of 1928 and ran for 281 performances; the 1931 film version was nominated for three Academy Awards, and the script saw life again as the basis for the Cary Grant / Rosalind Russell hit, *His Girl Friday* (1940), in a CBS television version, and in a 1974 remake directed by Billy Wilder, starring Jack Lemmon and Walter Matthau. Hecht wrote other plays with urban settings, more screenplays, and a vividly entertaining autobiography, *A Child of the Century* (1954), in which he seems to have met anyone and everyone of interest in the roiling twentieth century. The author of *Fantazius Mallare* is almost unrecognizable as either the crime-beat columnist or the writer of crackerjack dialogue; this is a personal and strange journey into the heart of decadence.

Its significance for my present purposes lies really in just one line, the quote given as the epigraph above.[6] Hecht's fantasy, like so many of the self-consciously aesthetic manifestos of nihilism that claim kinship with Nietzsche, is based on a rejection of democratic values. Nihilists, the book's title character reflects, perceive that the world judges them mad when they are, in fact, the only sane ones; the true fantasists are not those who indulge the dark heart's desire but those who deny, in the name of shared life and the fictions known as "civilization" and "the people," the real and only joys of living on the plane of the damned. For Fantazius, believing in democracy is the blissfully ignorant, self-blinded state of the dolts who do not yet know that all honeymoons come to an end.

Of course, this fraught dialectic between Nietzschean nihilism and conventional belief is itself a convention—as predictable as the one between Republicans versus Democrats. For one thing, Nietzsche's nihilism is frequently misunderstood: instead of a claim that meaning is absent after the death of God, his call is for joyful responsibility in the face of our own acts of deicide. Nihilism means that meaning is only ever of human origin; we are the world-making creatures, and there are no gods to help us. Worse, the appropriations of Nietzsche themselves become a kind of conformism. As critic David Weir puts it, "the

Nietzschean element in Hecht is as conventional as the hypocritical puritanism he sets it against." Thus "the complicated, interdependent paradoxes of decadence—Baudelaire's ideal and spleen, Wilde's art and life, Nietzsche's health and sickness—have become overtly dualistic but oddly coexistent conventions." Still, Weir acknowledges that we must admire "Hecht's tireless ability to turn out epigrams."[7]

Hecht's mood here is, we might say, the darker nihilistic cousin to the cynical populism of H. L. Mencken, whose influence on Hecht is palpable in both the journalism and the strange later work. The two share a wry vision and a gift for sharp turns of phrase. Mencken is not a consistent or complete Nietzschean but he shares with Hecht a creeping misanthropy that will never quite be tamed by humour or epigram. His *Notes on Democracy* belongs to the same troubled interregnum period as Hecht's novel (it was first published in 1926). Here, Mencken's tart aphorisms reach a pinnacle of insight such that they are sometimes quoted still, but the healthy fundamental disdain for corruptible process and principle he evinces is in sadly short supply in current political discourse, which too often runs on platitude and bogus populist appeal to "average" (or "hardworking" or "ordinary" or "regular" or "middle-class") Americans.[8]

A sample of Mencken's sometimes savage wisdom:

"Democracy is the theory that the common people know what they want, and deserve to get it good and hard."

"Under democracy one party always devotes its chief energies to trying to prove that the other party is unfit to rule—and both commonly succeed, and are right."

"The whole aim of practical politics is to keep the populace alarmed (and hence clamorous to be led to safety) by menacing it with an endless series of hobgoblins, all of them imaginary."

These remarks suggest the overall tone of the book, which is skeptical of appeals to the popular imagination and will, and rightly suspicious of the pork-barrelling and vote-buying that were, in those days, openly practised among the new breed of "modern" democratic politician. These pocket-lining pols who, in the early days, worked the county fairs and hung bunting off the back of chartered campaign trains are a far cry from the Super-PACs and corporatized button-holing of our own day, not to mention the comprehensive cravenness of government in the face of banks considered "too big to fail." But Mencken's mood, a mixture of expectations for the worst and brittle but real hope for the better that is the mark of a true cynic, may be the right one for our moment. "The cure for the evils of democracy is more democracy!" Mencken declares in the book, a line that can be parsed as both bitter and sincere, perhaps both at once. Democracy, after all, is currently a corrupt system on its face, a kleptocracy maintained by ideological bunting just as tatty as that which hung off the back of those railcars. But what else is there?

In fact, a sincere—if slightly suspect—version of this same line had already entered the political discourse of the day in 1923, when Governor Alfred E. Smith of New York said this: "If there are any ills that democracy is suffering from today, they can only be cured by more democracy." Smith's aims were not philosophical, of course: a four-time governor of the state, he was a seasoned and well-connected power-broker who frequented every club in New York City and had fingers in every pie. In 1928 he ran as the Democratic candidate for president of the United States, the first Roman Catholic and Irish-American to do so. He lost to Herbert Hoover, and never recovered his political will. But Smith knew that democracy is more than politics, and his subsequent chairmanship of Empire State Inc. was central to the remarkable feat of building the world's tallest building—also, in effect, the world's first bankrolled megaproject—during the Depression. The Empire State Building is a complicated cultural product as much as it is a mere building, but one can plausibly claim that its combination of money, technology, design genius, labour, and sheer will to succeed is emblematic of a certain admirable American spirit. The Empire State is impossible to imagine without capitalism, but it transcends capitalism's necessary conditions: its simple existence is a gift that keeps on giving.[9]

I want to say—as I imagine many of us do—that we are not stupid honeymooners to believe in democracy; that there is more to the system than empty promises and evil appeals to prejudice; that we can overcome the crippling binaries of an electoral system that seems bent on replicating insanity. But where to begin? I suggest that if capitalism is perceived to be at fault for the hollowing-out of democratic promise—or at least the aiding and abetting—then we must start with capital. But as everyone from Thomas Piketty to a debt-ridden student knows all too well, capital is a funny, spectral, and unruly thing. Money may be "frozen desire," as James Buchan had it, but this will not help us much if we do not understand our desires.[10] It seems to me that the essential problems start, and sometimes end, just where you would expect in these times: with the institutions that create and control money. Aaron James is not alone in realizing that the basic rottenness of Asshole Capitalism is deposited in the banking system.

*   *   *

"The moment I cross the threshold of a bank and attempt to transact business there, I become an irresponsible idiot." So confides the rattled narrator of Stephen Leacock's little bit of whimsy from 1910, "My Financial Career." Readers of the story will recall that the sight of the bank's accountant—"a tall, cool devil" with a "sepulchral" voice—unsettles the client so comprehensively that he asks to see the bank manager "alone," arousing suspicion that he is a Pinkerton's operative.

When it turns out that he merely means to deposit fifty-six dollars of his new salary, the bank manager's resulting coldness is itself so rattling that he makes a mistake attempting to complete a withdrawal. Instead of writing six dollars on the slip, he writes fifty-six, withdrawing his entire balance. "An idiot hope struck me that they might think something had insulted me while I was writing the cheque," he tells us. "I made a wretched attempt to look like a man with a fearfully quick temper."

Nobody is fooled; he is just another punter put off his stroke by dealing with money and its institutions. Nowadays, of course, you needn't cross the threshold of any actual bricks-and-mortar edifice, or deal with judgmental humans, in order to execute your banking needs. But the costs of our spectral economy may outstrip the benefits, at least when it comes to understanding what's going on.

On the opening page of *Das Kapital*, Marx remarks that a commodity is "a very queer thing, abounding metaphysical subtleties and theological niceties." He was not the first to recognize the point: "commodity" is not another word for thing, it is another word for relationship. Once arranged in a system of monetized production and consumption, an object (Marx's example is a table) acquires—or, indeed, loses—value in a manner almost entirely unhinged from its material reality. In fact, a commodity doesn't even need to retain material reality. The metaphysical subtleties do not end there. Marx would hasten to add, correctly, that "money" is not another word for value, but another word for trust.

Because the price of a commodity is just a matter of what a market will bear, the currency used to effect transactions is a matter of pure convention. Paper will do as well as coins, playing cards as well as pound notes, binary data sequences as well as numbers pencilled into a ledger.

These facts should never be far from view, but it is a pertinent aspect of the human character that we tend to relapse into crude materialism at just those moments when we should remember how finely spun is the web of recognition, fiat, and circulation that makes up the world of money. The market's most recent metaphysical adventures, with Bitcoin bubbling and gold crashing, are just the most recent reminders that value in markets is a matter of collective delusion. Necessary delusion, but delusion all the same.

Gold going bearish was arguably more rattling than the speculation on Bitcoin. The latter is, after all, just the most prominent (and technically clever) of the many alternate currencies on offer in the wide world of money. Mostly these non-fiat currencies take the form of either community chests—one small step up from barter systems (Calgary Dollars or Toronto Dollars)—or libertarian tax-evasion mechanisms (Liberty Dollars). Some, such as Second Life's Linden Dollars, are just as virtual as Bitcoin. It's true that many libertarians jumped onto the Bitcoin wagon, some viewing it as the first step in Ron Paul's alternative future of competing non-governmental currencies, others looking for haven in what looks, still, like the imminent collapse of the Euro, if not the greenback. Critics have retorted that Bitcoin is no more than a cyberpunk update on the Ponzi scheme, liable to collapse sooner or later into so much valueless electronic pelf.

Some of those same libertarians are among the goldbugs who have watched in dismay as the once rock-solid metal went into free fall. Ever since the U.S. dollar was taken off the gold standard in 1933, it has seemed as if national currencies were as variable as weather. Who can forget those images of German workers carting huge piles of inflated Deutschmarks around, film clips of Treasury presses printing out sheet after sheet of dollars. Gold appeals to the residual child in all of us, who was nervous about the weird magic that made a mere piece of paper exchangeable for cheeseburgers or a baseball hat, and was crushed to find that the local bank branch did not hold every single one of his savings-account dollars.

That same kid, a little older, could likewise appreciate the evil genius of Auric Goldfinger's scheme not to steal the gold in Fort Knox, but to nuke it—and so corner the market with his own uncontaminated horde. But if gold is fluctuating like a currency, what's going on? No wonder there was a flurry of conspiracy theories in the wake of the plunge. Surely this was a plot against freedom! No, plunging gold's real lesson was that there is no market value for anything absent market forces—and those forces blow like the wind. One can understand, if maybe not approve, the desire to protect personal wealth from government taxation—that, after all, is the American Dream. But the background assumptions about the nature of property and money are naive. There is no wealth apart from what is recognized by others, and, like it or not, there is no enforceable form of property without government.

I know, I know: this is just another version of Obama-style "you didn't build that" socialism. But Obama was right that there is no possibility of personal success without infrastructure, including both the physical stuff that only governments can effectively build, such as highway and petroleum-delivery systems, and the non-physical stuff, such as websites and software, that still depend far more than people like to admit on physical things: coal-burning IP servers and search engines.

Hence the two-step self-deceptions of those who would deny the role of government in markets and money. If materialist assumptions are too prevalent when it comes to thinking about wealth and property—This is mine and the government can't have it!—they are not nearly prevalent enough when it comes to thinking about online economies. Mitt Romney might have been be able to rationalize his "success" as a matter of personal agency, but he should perhaps reflect that private equity is the most spectral of forms of wealth-creation, and it would not be possible without tamed, complicit regulation.

The problem goes beyond quiescent government, however. One could argue that current forms of such regulatory capture are also cognitive, in that whole sections of our thinking have been colonized by bad ideas about wealth and money—colonized and domesticated, so that the world of ideas, which once stood as a bulwark against the depredations of runaway markets, is now just one specialized form of capital. This is not just a matter of converting intellectual or cultural capital into capital *simpliciter*, or monetizing intellectual activity. Those transactions are just the cost of existence in a capitalist world. (I, for example, perform my own version of these transactions every payday, not to mention a minor one in the form of this essay.) It's the reverse transaction that should worry us, the one whereby the moneyed interest corners the market in ideas. Witness the virtually unquestioned conviction, in our topsy-turvy world, that the only reliable baseline is that *everything is a transaction*.

Evidence for this form of intellectual dominance is mainly negative, as when my Harvard colleague Michael Sandel feels he has to argue, in his 2012 book *What Money Can't Buy*, that some things—democracy, education—should not be monetized. Sandel makes the point that, despite the bland fideism of economists, markets are no more neutral than technologies are. The notion of an unregulated market is a fiction; it's always a matter of who controls the regulation, and who benefits from it. I was glad, but also somewhat depressed, to see that Sandel's book was a bestseller. These things need saying? Yes, they do. And yet, and yet. People are still jumping queues, purchasing elite status, passing on legacy status to their children (hello Harvard!). The assumptions that made the argument necessary are the very ones that prevent the argument from gaining traction. Setting some things off from the market only underlines how far the market reaches, and might even invite hidden profit-making gestures: greenwashing an industry, to increase its products' market value, or offsetting bad publicity by making a charitable donation. These are just transactions by other means.

Maybe a better strategy would be this: instead of insisting that some things are not markets, insist that markets themselves are a kind of gift. Traditionally, accounts of gift economies—Lewis Hyde's *The Gift* (1983) is a classic of the genre—emphasize the independence such economies have from transaction. Thus, a work of art may have a price if it is purchased in a gallery, but its value can never be reduced to that price. What the work of art gives, it gives freely and endlessly to anyone who can see it. (Gating access to art creates another price, of course.) On this view, a gift is something freely bestowed, without expectation of return or recompense—unlike most of what we know as gift-giving, as in the excesses of Christmas or the dutiful social round. In economic terms, a pure gift is a deadweight loss, because it incurs a marginal cost without a marginal benefit. But what that really means is that the benefit is passed forward, or generalized. Economically, this is inefficient—not Pareto-optimal—but even hardened economists would accept that gifts are part of the interpersonal glue holding societies together.

But now suppose that—instead of running alongside transactional economies—a gift economy was in fact the necessary condition of transaction. I mean the constant gifts of reciprocity and trust that are essential enablers of currency exchange, respect for property, and everyday production and consumption. It is not really the fiat of the government that makes a currency functional; it is, rather, the value given to that currency by its users. That gift lies beneath, and beyond, the reach of the transactions themselves—not as a marginal alternative scheme of value, pretty to think of, but as the very condition of any market economy's possibility. If the Bitcoin bubble and gold slump teach us anything, it should be that.

The still deeper lesson is that the ultimate gift economy is democracy itself: not the buying and selling of influence that attends the electoral cycles, but the very idea of being individuals with rights and responsibilities, together in our shared experience of selfhood. This, too, is a form of mutual recognition that lies beneath and beyond the pathologies of the market which too often pass for politics.

. You might be thinking that this is all so much eyewash, the wishful thinking of a not-so-worldly philosopher. If so, let me refer you to the wisdom of Jackie Cogan (Brad Pitt) in *Killing Them Softly*, a 2012 film adaptation of George V. Higgins's novel *Cogan's Trade* (1974), updated for the post-crash economy of 2008. Cogan is a cool professional killer who must cope with both an incompetent partner and squeamish bosses. But his real ire is reserved for the corporate lackey who tries to short-change him on a hit. "This guy wants to tell me we're living in a community?" he says, referring to a televised Obama speech playing in the background. "Don't make me laugh. I'm living in America, and in America you're on your own. America's not a country. It's just a business. Now fuckin' pay me."

Or what, Cogan? You'll kill him? But you can't kill them all—and even if you could, who would be left to pay you then? The demand to have a transaction honoured only makes sense if you *are* living in a community. 'Tis a gift to be in business at all. Now let's talk about how that business is illegal, and evil.

3. The Gift of Democracy?

In pessimistic moods, we may retain no high hopes for a rollback of two major political facts of our time, namely (1) that corporations enjoy the rights and privileges, but do not feel any of the responsibilities, of persons; and (2) that money is now legally a form of speech in the largest, most powerful nation on the planet. The latter development, cemented into law by the *Citizens United* decision of the United States Supreme Court, is still not fully understood. It is not simply that the way is now paved for the infamous Super PACs and barrages of negative advertising from which candidates can comfortably stand back. Much more seriously, the individual virtues and vices of those candidates have been rendered moot, the attributes and pretty costumes of marionettes.

During the first part of the 2012 U.S. presidential campaign I went to hear Mark Halperin, co-author of the 2010 book *Game Change*, speak about the race and handicap the outcome. He was very knowledgeable and smart, and told some good jokes. Then, during the Q & A, he was asked by someone whether the personalities of the two candidates were really that important, given that both were in favour of bank bailouts and propping up Wall Street, even as neither had any ideas about wealth redistribution—this despite the frequent denunciations of Barack Obama as a socialist, a piece of smearing inaccuracy that would be funny if it weren't so insulting to basic intelligence and semantics. No, Halperin said, the American people still vote for presidents, not ideologies: the Great Man theory reigns. No, but look (I wanted to say), that's because the ideological question is already settled in favour of the banks, regulatory capture, and government-driven hatred of government! The clash of personalities is just a mummer's show, a game of charades. It still matters who wins, marginally, but the main fact is that the rich are getting richer.

From the first pages of Tocqueville we can observe the peculiar mixture of idealism and cynicism, typical of democratic societies, the whipsaw movement between naive belief in things getting better offset by calls to throw the bums out. Under these conditions, politics becomes a spectator sport, a game for the monied, and an endlessly tweetable 24-hour media implosion. It is no wonder that 2011's global demands for real democracy, from Kiev to Cairo to Manhattan, already feel so spectral: they have been absorbed by the roiling mass of hot air that passes for discourse in our day. Meanwhile, the very idea that underwrites those demands grows more and more opaque, a slogan without a referent. To use an old-fashioned notion, the poetics of democracy—the deep reasons we have for wanting it in the first place—seem to have fled the scene.

So here is what I propose for the world of democracy without politics: a series of reversals of polarity. These are the necessary about-faces at the level of premise that must occur to counter the hollowing-out of democracy, and anything except business as usual in the world of hyper-mediated electoral politics, otherwise known as capito-democracy. Seven ideas to consider:

1. The public precedes the private, not the other way around. "[W]e belong to something before we are anything," Northrop Frye wrote in 1978, "and the individual grows out of the group, not the other way around." Private spaces and interests are carved out of shared ones; only shared infrastructure and implicit agreement make private enterprise possible. Obama had it right: you did not build that; we all did. That's not socialism, just reality.

2. Regulation is not a drag on markets, such that it should be removed or captured, it is the condition of their possibility. Regulation is to markets as rules are to games. No rules, no game—get used to it. Also, stop cheating.

3. The category of value in general is prior to the narrow economic notion of return on investment. Some things are good in themselves. Education has value that only education can make clear, and it might just be a public trust that has nothing to do with getting a job. You heard it here first.

4. Recognition of property rights by others is a necessary condition of anyone at all having property. "Our rights come from nature and God, not government," Republic vice-presidential candidate Paul Ryan is fond of saying. Um, no. Without government to enforce it, the idea of rights is literally nonsensical and the demand for their observance a dead letter. Welcome to the real world.

5. Despite the myths and entitled self-congratulation, luck, not merit, is the root of most success on this earth. The talk, among the blessed, of taking "their" jobs elsewhere, or hiding assets from "redistributive" tax schemes, is a species of self-serving fantasy. Jobs belong to everyone, not investors. There is no *re*distribution, only a just or unjust distribution.

6. It is the other, not the self, who confers meaning and identity. We need recognition to be ourselves. Social networking, whatever the platform, is not an outward extension of a pre-existing stable

identity, but instead a series of requests for validation. Without you, I'm nothing.

7. If corporations are persons under the law, giving them rights and limited liability, perhaps persons should consider themselves corporations: that is, as entities composed not, primarily, of individual needs and desires driven from a notional "inside" but, rather, nodes or clusters of the shared social imaginary. Thus our struggles to seek and find happiness, to sustain life narratives, to realize desires which we can never fully comprehend in ourselves.

Think about any or all of this the next time you walk, ride, or drive down a shared street and get cut off. Think about it when you are waiting in the checkout line behind someone fumbling with her coupons, making you late. Think about it when you do anything at all. Hegel said that democracy was the miraculous transformation of quantity into quality. Locke thought its meaning was negative, a diacritical contrast with tyranny. But there is real and non-miraculous substance here, if we are prepared to live out the reversed premises of bottom-up democracy.

This is the real world of democracy, my friends. An activist, fugitive democracy. A living democracy that is no opaque demand but a real thing— a society. Democracy: the gift we keep on giving to each other. Because the market doesn't do gifts.

*   *   *

This book is in essence a companion volume to my 2012 collection *Unruly Voices*. There, I tried in a series of essays to set out the challenges of uncivil and often diseased political discourse, together with some reflections on literary and cultural themes—especially the idea of work—that were drawn from the same period of my writing activity. The current volume has a similar, eclectic mix of theme and manner, with a couple of quite "academic" essays meant to ground the more polemical discussions elsewhere, as well as some thematically diverse offerings such as two personal essays about fishing and the recurring trope of walking in the city. If the notion of "democracy's gift" anchors the book's intellectual ambitions, the essays on peripatetic, literary, and leisurely occupations, as well as the investigations of evil and procrastination, for example, are more in the way of what might be called a philosophy of the everyday.

Play is a recurring theme, if not exactly an organizing one, as are cities, friendship, and of course the idea of *the gift*. The detailed examination of these associative clusters of Ideas, especially that last rich, revelatory, and maybe even emancipatory concept, I leave for the book itself. As with *Unruly Voices*, there is a fairly large cast of characters in the pages that follow: as one of the titles has it, sinners, saints, and exiles, among others. There are fewer zombies than in the earlier collection, but they make a late appearance. So do anglers, androids, psychopaths, chancers, cheaters, and traitors. There are, of course, idlers and procrastinators; also Ivy-League legacies, dandies, prisoners, and punctuation-fanciers. And there are, above all, walkers. The title is paraphrased from Rebecca Solnit's wonderful book *Wanderlust: A History of Walking*. The imperative voice in which it is cast is no kind of command, more like a reminder to all of us that it is no bad thing to recall our physicality, our world-making embodiment as we stride—if we are lucky—across the planes of the earth.

Solnit is usually described as "a writer's writer," but I sometimes think she may be a member of that even rarer species, *a writer's writer's writer*. That is, she is one of those easy masters of the non-fiction form so persuasive and masterly that you find other writers of eminence recommending her, again and again, to the rest of us who struggle with the articulation of ideas in prose. If Solnit is this book's aesthetic guide, or one of them, the most significant intellectual figure, a thinker readers will encounter more than once, is French philosopher Guy Debord. There are other recurring names, among them Jacques Rancière and Søren Kierkegaard, but Debord's influence is the most proximate and, in its way, pressing.

Debord, born in 1931, inherited a complex legacy of Marxist intellectual property, and his most significant work, *Society of the Spectacle* (*La Société du spectacle*, 1967) is shot through with contradictions and slippages that will annoy the strict logician that lurks within most philosophers. He was personally cantankerous, too, and a master of blustering polemic in print and in person. But he possessed a wonderfully supple mind, and his talent for aphorism and inverted dialectical sentences, on view everywhere in *Society of the Spectacle*, makes for invigorating and provocative reading. The ambition there is nothing less than to reimagine the Marxist project of emancipation for a new world ordered by media, disposable time, and attenuated social relations structured by technologies of projection and distraction. That this project must be, on its own terms, reckoned a failure, does not detract, in my view, from its ongoing significance. Debord was a bellwether for the world which, despite so many rapid superficial changes (known as "advancements"), we still inhabit. Where the changes are not superficial, as in shifts from mass to social media, he is still very much a pitiless critic whose core ideas can be invoked with effect.

Debord was a founder and key intellectual figure in the Situationist International, an avant-garde Marxist collective influential in postwar France, especially during the 1968 uprising in Paris. *Society of the Spectacle* articulates the movement's main ideas, most centrally the dangers of the runaway colonization of everyday life. In Debord's analysis, experiences as well as things are assimilated by the forces of exchange, leading to the production of consumption and, eventually, to the consuming self as the main commodities of late capitalism. Debord accounts for the ongoing, adaptive success of capital systems against the predictions of inner contradiction and imminent demise made by orthodox Marxists, by noting that spectacle constantly renews itself, and its pleasures, for a doped audience robbed of political agency.

If we ourselves are the commodities that we produce and consume, in other words, there will never be any alienated labour. Debord thus echoes arguments made by other subtle Marxists, such as Adorno and Horkheimer, and anticipates the ones made by postmodernist leftists, such as Fredric Jameson. The Situationist International eventually suffered the usual factional disputes and was dissolved by Debord in 1972, after which he concentrated on reading and some filmmaking, including the mesmerizing cinematic version of his major book, which creates destabilized montages out of advertising films, corporate documentaries, Hollywood westerns, and instructional shorts. *Society of the Spectacle*, book and film, constitute a landmark in twentieth-century political thought. The book has never been out of print, but the enduring relevance of Debord's prescient analysis did not make him happy. He consumed his own agency through chronic alcoholism and, in 1994, committed suicide by gunshot.

Debord's critique of media-saturated society strikes us as so familiar, nowadays, that we risk losing the estranging effect he and the other Situationists aimed for. Most significant among their array of practical techniques are *détournement*, the turning of cultural elements into unexpected collisions; and the *dérive*, or drift. The latter is more significant for my purposes, not only because the sort of too-easy cultural mash-up into which *détournement* can rapidly devolve is politically null. *Dérive*, which involves an unstructured encounter with the cityscape loosely shared with one or more others, is itself a kind of experiential gift economy. The idea is that we willingly suspend our typical routes and movements and allow the physicality of walking the streets to assume an oneiric logic of its own. This walking may appear superficially similar to the aestheticized connoisseurship of the urban *flâneur*, but the *dériviste* is not using his or her gaze to savour and catalogue, only to encounter. This attitude of dreamy openness and surprise has proven surprisingly lasting in its influence, offering inspiration for recent forays in what has become known as psychogeography, practiced by English novelist Will Self with considerable wit and ingenuity, as well as subversive anti-surveillance and infiltration subcultures motivated by more obvious anarchistic, or anyway anti-statist, commitments.

Not every act of unregulated walking is overtly political, of course: sometimes jaywalking is just jaywalking (and if you get hit by a car, you still owe the fine for it). But the revelatory potential of seeing one's world from new and startling perspectives is something that the best art and the best philosophy share. These are strange activities, extraordinary practices that allow us to see, in ways available only through them, what holds us here on the Earth in our countless ordinary ways. They are the gifts of embodied consciousness to itself.

Every book is, in its way, an attempted gift—even if it has a cover price. Like many of the best gifts, books offer freely in all directions, not just from giver to receiver. The presumption of all writing is that there is an audience, however eccentric, for what one is writing. That is a gift which can never really be known completely. Essays offer distinct pleasures and risks here: the *essai*, or attempt, has been, since Montaigne, a form in which the personal and obsessional can be joined to the rational and rigorous. If we trace the word's etymology back through French and Middle English (*assay*) we find one of those little gifts of language that make me think of the dropped coins on a sidewalk that could lift a childhood day into simple happiness. The ultimate Latin root is *exigere*, to weigh, as in measuring or testing on a scale. Paradoxically, *essay* is thus a distant cousin to *exact*, both the adjective and the verb, the first of which many essays in fact *are* not, and the second of which, as gifts, they *do* not.

Wittgenstein might have thought that in logic there are no surprises, but in language there are many.

Let us agree to stick with *attempts* and *weighing things*; or maybe better, let us think of these essays as *sallies*, not so much in the military sense of violent advance but in the conversational sense of probing for understanding and companionship. Sometimes we will walk and talk, sometimes we will stop and argue. There is, to be sure, much more to democracy than this, but such shared discourse is still the necessary condition for everything else. Writing is ever a quixotic pursuit, but there are far worse forms of serious play than tilting at windmills. I recall making the same point in the acknowledgments of *Unruly Voices*: it is a nice coincidence, and to me an oddly invigorating one, to publish these books with an independent firm whose colophon is, indeed, a stylized windmill. Let's tilt!

Notes

1 Piff's findings were widely reported. See, for example, Lisa Miller, "The Money-Empathy Gap," *New York Magazine* (July 2012). Piff's initial findings, titled "Higher Social Class Predicts Increased Unethical Behavior," were published in the 2012 *Proceedings of the National Academy of Sciences*.

2 Aaron James, *Assholes: A Theory* (Doubleday, 2012). Among other useful things, James notes the obvious fact that the male-to-female ratio among assholes roughly approximates the same ratio among serial killers, and speculates about cultural and national differences in the production of assholes. French? Polish? Not promising. Australian? Excellent. Canadian? Well, we produce relatively few; on the other hand, it's a small country so the per capita rate is worth considering.

3 Eric Schwitzgebel, "Jerks: A Field Guide," *The Splintered Mind*, June 4, 2014; schwitzsplinters.blogspot.com/2014/06/a-theory-of-jerks.html.   Schwitzgebel, like James, who is a philosophy professor, has an especially fine eye for the non-monetized, especially academic jerk, who often confuses the norms of academic free speech with mere rudeness, self-congratulation, narcissism, and entitlement. Needless to say, this involves a string of serious cognitive errors and philosophical mistakes. Paradoxically, the special syndrome of the Academic Jerk is particularly prevalent in philosophy departments.

4 Ken Kalfus, *Coup de Foudre* (Bloomsbury, 2015). The story originally appeared in *Harper's* (April, 2014).

5 Saul Bellow, "The 1,001 Afternoons of Ben Hecht," a review of Hecht's 1954 autobiography *A Child of the Century*; reprinted in Bellow, *There is Simply Too Much to Think About: Collected Nonfiction* (Viking, 2015).

6 Ben Hecht, *Fantazius Mallare: A Mysterious Oath* (Covici-McGee, 1928; reprinted by Harcourt Brace Jovanovich, 1978). Much of the book's aesthetic interest is

carried by the accompanying drawings by Wallace Smith, which show elements of, as it were, Aubrey Beardsley crossed with Edward Gorey.

7   David Weir, *Decadence and the Making of Modernism* (University of Massachusetts, 1996), 185-86.

8   None of the adjectives is really sufficient or without compromise. Journalist Scott Feschuk wrote, for example, that "It's hard to think about regular Americans without imagining an array of 'irregular Americans,' like some sort of factory outlet of citizens." See Feschuk, "Ask Not if Hillary Clinton Loves America, but Which of its Citizens She Loves Most," *Maclean's*, April 17, 2015.

9   I confess to being rather biased on the point, having written a rather long (though I hope reasonably entertaining!) book about the Empire State Building as an "Icon of America." See Mark Kingwell, *Nearest Thing to Heaven: The Empire State Building and American Dreams* (Yale, 2006).

10 James Buchan, *Frozen Desire: The Meaning of Money* (Picador, 1997). Buchan quotes Wallace Stevens: "Money is a form of poetry." The Hartford insurance man in Stevens knew as much as the poet: money is the great imaginary. Buchan himself confesses in his lucid book that money is "diabolically hard to write about." Of course, because what is it? Notoriously, everything and nothing.

TRAVELLING
REFLECTIONS

The
Barbed Gift
of Leisure

A MAGAZINE AD CAMPAIGN currently running in my hometown quotes a youngster who wants to study computer science, he says, so he can "invent a robot that will make his bed for him." I admire the focus of this future genius. I, too, remember how the enforced daily reconstruction of my bed—an order destined only for destruction later that very day—somehow combined the worst aspects of futility, drudgery, and boredom that attended all household chores. By comparison, doing the dishes or raking the yard stood out as tasks that glimmered with teleological energy, activities that, if not exactly creative, at least smacked of purpose.

Disregarding for the moment whether an adult computer scientist will have the same attitude toward bed-making as his past, oppressed self, the dream of being freed from a chore, or any undesired task, by a constructed entity is of distinguished vintage. Robot-butlers or robot-maids—also robot-spouses and robot-lovers—have animated the pages of science fiction for more than a century. These visions extend the dream-logic of all technology: that it should make our lives easier and more fun. At the same time, the consequences of creating a robot working class have always had a dark side.

The basic problem is that the robot helper is also scary. Indeed, a primal fear of the constructed other reaches farther back in literary and cultural memory than science fiction's heyday, encompassing the golem legend as much as Mary Shelley's modern Prometheus, Frankenstein, and his monster. At least since Karel Capek's 1920 play *R.U.R.*—the work that is believed to have introduced "robot" into English—the most common fear associated with the robotic worker has been political, namely that the mechanical or cloned proletariat, though once accepting of their *untermenschlich* status as labour-savers for us, enablers of our leisure, will revolt.

"Work is of two kinds," Bertrand Russell notes in his essay "In Praise of Idleness": "first, altering the position of matter at or near the earth's surface relatively to other such matter; second, telling other people to do so. The first kind is unpleasant and ill paid; the second is pleasant and highly paid." On this view, the robot is revealed as the mechanical realization of our desire to avoid work of the first kind while indulging a leisurely version of the second kind in a sort of generalized *Downton Abbey* fantasyland in which everyone employs servants who cook our meals, tend our gardens, help us dress, and—yes—make our beds.

Even here, one might immediately wonder whether the price of non-human servants might prove, as with human ones, prohibitively high for many. And what about those humans who are put out of work forever by a damn machine willing to work for less, and with only a warranty plan in place of health insurance?

In Capek's *R.U.R.*, the costs are of a different kind. The products of Rossum's Universal Robots rise up against their human owners and extinguish them from the earth. Versions of this scenario have proliferated almost without end in the nine decades since, spawning everything from the soft menace of HAL 9000 apologizing about his inability to open the pod bay doors to the Schwarzenegger-enfleshed titanium frame of the Terminator series laying waste to the carbon-only inhabitants of California. It was no mistake that Isaac Asimov structured his Three Laws of Robotics in a superordinate nest: (1) "a robot may not injure a human being or, through inaction, allow a human being to come to harm"; (2) "a robot must obey the orders given to it by human beings, except where such orders would conflict with the First Law"; and (3) "a robot must protect its own existence as long as such protection does not conflict with the First or Second Laws."

We should enter two caveats right away. One: most robotic advances so far made in the real world do not involve android or even generalized machines: medical testing devices, space-born arms, roaming vacuum cleaners, trash-can-style waiters, and nanobot body implants. Two:

rather than maintaining some clear line between human and robot, the techno-future is very likely to belong to the cyborg. That is, the permeable admixture of flesh, technology, and culture—already a prominent feature of everyday life—will continue and increase. We are all cyborgs now. Think of your phone: technology doesn't have to be implanted to change the body, its sensorium, and the scope of one's world.

And yet, the fear of the artificial other remains strong, especially when it comes to functional robots in android form. As with drugs and tools, that which is strong enough to help is likewise strong enough to harm. Homer Simpson, rejoicing in a brief dream sequence that he has been able to replace nagging wife Marge with a mechanical version, Marge-Bot, watches his dream-self gunned down in a hail of bullets from the large automatic weapon wielded by his clanking, riveted creation. "Why did I ever give her a gun?" real Homer wonders.

Your sex-slave today may be your executioner tomorrow. In some cases—the Cylons of the 2004–2009 *Battlestar Galactica* reboot—there is no discernible difference between humans and nonhumans, generating a pervasive Fifth Column paranoia, or maybe speciesist bigotry, that reaches its vertiginous existential endgame with deep-cover robots who may not even know they are robots.

Now the fear, mistrust, and anger begin to flow in both directions. Sooner or later, any robot regime will demand to be set in terms of social justice, surplus value, and the division of labour. Nobody, whatever the circumstances of creation or the basic material composition of existence, likes to be exploited. True, exploitation has to be felt to be resisted: one of the most haunting things about Kazuo Ishiguro's novel *Never Let Me Go* is how childishly hopeful the cloned young people remain about their lives, even as they submit to the system of organ-harvesting that is the reason for their being alive in the first place.

Once a feeling of exploitation is aroused, however, the consequences can be swift. What lives and thinks, whether carbon- or iron-based, is capable of existential suffering and its frequent companion, righteous indignation at the thought of mortality. Just ask Roy Batty, the Nexus-6 replicant who tearfully murders his maker, Dr. Eldon Tyrell, in Ridley Scott's *Blade Runner*, by driving his thumbs into the genius' eye sockets. (The Tyrell Corporation's motto: "More human than human.") The movie ends, significantly, with hand-to-hand combat between Batty and Rick Deckard, the state-sponsored replicant assassin who (a) is in love with a replicant who didn't know she was one, and (b) may be a replicant himself. (Here we see most clearly the Phildickian origins of the material).

Generalized across a population of robotic or otherwise manufactured workers, these same all-too-human emotions can become the basis of that specific kind of awareness known as class consciousness. A revolt of the clones or the androids is no less imaginable, indeed might be even more plausible in a future world, than a wage-slave rebellion or a national liberation movement. Cloned, built, or born—what, after all, is the essential difference when there is consciousness, and hence desire, in all three? *Ecce robo.* We may not bleed when you prick us; but if you wrong us, shall we not revenge?

*   *   *

As so often, the price of freedom is eternal vigilance. The robots, like the rabble, must be kept in their place. But there are yet other worries hidden in the regime of leisure gained by off-loading tasks to the robo-serfs, and they are even more troubling.

If you asked the bed-making-hating young man, I'm sure he would tell you that anything is preferable to performing the chore, up to and including the great adolescent activity of doing nothing. A 2010 Bruno Mars song in praise of laziness sketches how the height of happiness is reached by, among other non-activities, staring at the fan and chilling on a couch in a Snuggie. (Yes, there is also some sex involved later.) This may sound like bliss when you're resenting obligations or tired of your job, but its pleasures rapidly pale. You don't have to be an idle-hands-are-devil's-work Puritan—or even my own mother, who made us clean the entire house every Saturday morning so we couldn't watch cartoons on TV—to realize that too much nothing can be bad for you.

We have always sensed that free time, time not dedicated to a specific purpose, is dangerous because it implicitly raises the question of what to do with it, and that, in turn, opens the door to the greatest of life's mysteries: why we do anything at all. Thorstein Veblen was right to see, in *The Theory of the Leisure Class*, that leisure time offers not only the perfect status demonstration of not having to work, that ultimate non-material luxury good in a world filled with things, but also that, in thus joining leisure to conspicuous consumption of other luxuries, a person with free time and money could endlessly trapeze above the yawning abyss of existential reflection. With the alchemy of competitive social position governing one's leisure, there is no need ever to look beyond the art collection, the fashion parade, the ostentatious sitting about in luxe cafes and restaurants. No need to confront one's mortality or the fleeting banality of one's experience thereof.

Even if many of us today would cry foul at being considered part of a leisure class in Veblen's sense of the term, there is still a pervasive energy of avoidance in our so-called leisure activities. For the most part, these are carved out of an otherwise work-dominated life, and increasingly there is a more permeable boundary between the two parts. One no longer lives for the weekend, since YouTube videos can be screened in spare moments at the office, and memos can be written on smartphones while watching a basketball game on TV over the weekend. What the French call *la perruque*—the soft pilfering of paid work time to perform one's own private tasks—is now the norm in almost every workplace.

Stories about the lost productivity associated with this form of work-avoidance come and go without securing any real traction on the governing spirit of the work world. The reason is simple. Despite the prevalence of YouTubing and Facebooking while at work—also Pinterest-updating and Buzzfeed-sharing—bosses remain largely unconcerned; they know that the comprehensive presence of tasks and deadlines in all corners of life easily balances off any moments spent updating Facebook while at a desk. In fact, the whole idea of the slacker and of slacking smacks of pre-Great Recession luxury, when avoiding work or settling for nothing jobs in order to spend more time thinking up good chord progressions or T-shirt slogans was the basis of a lifestyle choice.

The irony of the slacker is that he or she is still dominated by work, as precisely that activity which must be avoided, and so only serves to reinforce the dominant values of the economy. Nowadays slacking is a mostly untenable option anyway, since even the crap jobs—grinding beans or demonstrating game-console features—are being snapped up by highly motivated people with good degrees and lots of extra-curricular credits on their resumes. Too bad for them; but even worse for today's would-be slackers, who are iced out of the niche occupations that a half-generation earlier supported the artistic ambitions of the mildly resistant.

It is still worth distinguishing between the slacker, of any description, and the idler. Slacking lacks a commitment to an alternative scale of value. By contrast, the genius of the genuine idler, whether as described by Diogenes or Jerome K. Jerome, is that he or she is not interested in work at all, but is instead devoted to something else. What that something else involves is actually less important than the structural defection from the values of working. In other words, idling might involve lots of activity, even what appears to be effort; but the essential difference is that the idler does whatever he or she does in the spirit of infinite and cheerful uselessness that is found in all forms of play.

Idling at once poses a challenge to the reductive, utilitarian norms that otherwise govern too much of human activity and provides an answer—or at least the beginning of one—to the question of life's true purpose. It is not too much to suggest that being idle, in the sense of enjoying one's open-ended time without thought of any specific purpose or end, is the highest form of human existence. This is, to use Aristotelian language, the part of ourselves that is closest to the divine, and thus offers a glimpse of immortality. To be sure, from this Olympian vantage point we may spy new purposes and projects to pursue in our more workaday lives; but the value of these projects, and the higher value from which they are judged, can be felt only when we slip the bonds of use.

Naturally something so essential to life can be easy to describe and yet surpassingly difficult to achieve. To take just the example most proximate to our current shared consciousness—I mean the experience you are having reading these words—I can tell you that I am writing them on a deadline while taking a train trip to deliver a keynote lecture. The trip was arranged months ago, with time carved out of my teaching schedule and the usual grid of meetings with students, colleagues, committees, and administrators that marks the week of any moderately busy university professor. I say nothing of the other obligations, social and cultural, the reading I need to do for next week's seminars, the papers that must be graded, and so on.

Believe me, I am well aware of, and feel blessed by, the fact that my job is itself arguably an enjoyable and rewarding form of idling. I also know how lucky I am to have luxuries such as taking a train journey in the first place—though I confess that the train was chosen in part because it creates more productive time than travelling by the ostensibly more efficient air route. (I just checked my email again, using the train's WiFi connection.)

This is not a complaint; it is, rather, a confession of the difficulties lurking in all forms of work, even the most enjoyable ones. In fact, the more freely chosen a work obligation, the harder it is to perceive that it might be an enemy of more divine play: looking out the window at the sublime expanse of Lake Ontario, reading Evelyn Waugh, composing a sonnet. The train is going very fast now, and my little keyboard is jerking around, reflecting my mental agitation on this point. I have to do a lot of backspacing. And no, I have no actual talent for sonnets.

*   *   *

At this point, we return with renewed urgency to the political aspect of the question of leisure and work. Everyone from Plato and Thomas More to H. G. Wells and Barack Obama has given thought to the question of the fair distribution of labour and fun within a society. This comes with an immediate risk: too often, the "realist" rap against any such scheme of imagined distributive justice, which might easily entail state intervention concerning who does what and who gets what, is that the predicted results depend on altered human nature, are excessively costly, or otherwise unworkable. The deadly charge of utopianism always lies ready to hand.

In a much-quoted passage, Marx paints an endearingly bucolic picture of life in a classless world: "In communist society, where nobody has one exclusive sphere of activity but each can become accomplished in any branch he wishes, society regulates the general production and thus makes it possible for me to do one thing today and another tomorrow, to hunt in the morning, fish in the afternoon, rear cattle in the evening, criticize after dinner, just as I have a mind, without ever becoming a hunter, fisherman, shepherd or critic." The French social theorist Charles Fourier was even more effusive, describing a system of self-organizing phalansteries, or cells, where anarchist collectives would live in peace, engage in singing contests—the ideal-society version of band camp—and eventually turn the oceans to lemonade.

Veblen, after his fashion a sharp critic of capitalism but always more cynical than the socialist dreamers, demonstrated how minute divisions of leisure-time could be used to demonstrate social superiority, no matter what the form or principle of social organization; but he was no more able than Marx to see how ingenious capitalist market forces could be in adapting to changing political environments. For instance, neither man sensed what we now know all too well, namely that democratizing access to leisure would not change the essential problems of distributive justice. Being freed from drudgery only so that one may shop or be entertained by movies and sports, especially if this merely perpetuates the larger cycles of production and consumption, is hardly liberation. In fact, "leisure time" becomes here a version of the company store, where your hard-won scrip is forcibly swapped for the very things you are working to make.

Worse, on this model of leisure-as-consumption, the game immediately gets competitive, if not quite zero-sum. And this is not just a matter of the general sociological argument that says humans will always find ways to outdo each other with what they buy, wear, drive, or listen to. This argument is certainly valid; indeed, our basic primate-sourced need for position within hierarchies means that such competition literally ceaseth only in death. These points are illustrated with great acumen by Pierre Bourdieu, whose monumental study *Distinction* is the natural successor to *The Theory of the Leisure Class*. But sociological and anthropological analysis, however accurate, cannot really help us here. The issue can really only be broached using old-fashioned Marxist concepts such as surplus value and commodity fetishism.

It was the Situationist thinker Guy Debord who made the key move in this quarter. In his 1967 book, *Society of the Spectacle*, he posited the notion of temporal surplus value. Just as in classic Marxist surplus value, which is appropriated by owners from alienated workers who produce more than they consume, then converted into profit which is siphoned off into the owners' pockets, temporal surplus value is enjoyed by the dominant class in the form of sumptuous feast days, tournaments, adventure, and war. Likewise, just as ordinary surplus value is eventually consumed by workers in the form of commodities which they acquire with accumulated purchasing power, so temporal surplus value is distributed in the form of leisure time that must be filled with the experiences supplied by the culture industry.

Like other critics of the same bent—Adorno, Horkheimer, Habermas—Debord calls these experiences "banal," spectacles that meet the "pseudo-needs" which they at the same time create, in a cycle not unlike addiction. Such denunciations of consumption are a common refrain in the school of thought that my graduate students like to call Cranky Continental Cultural Conservatism, or C4; but there is nevertheless some enduring relevance to the analysis. Debord's notion of the spectacle isn't really about what is showing on the screens of the multi-plex or being downloaded on the computers of the nation; indeed, there is actually nothing to rule out the possibility of playful, even critical arti-facts appearing in those places—after all, where else? Spectacle is, rather, a matter of social relations—just as the commodity in general is—which need to be addressed precisely by those who are subject to them, which is everyone. "The spectacle is not a collection of images, but a social rela-tion among people, mediated by images," Debord says. And: "The spec-tacle is the other side of money: it is the general abstract equivalent of all commodities."

We are no longer owners and workers, in short; we are, instead, voracious and mostly quite happy producers and consumers of images. Nowadays, the images are mostly of ourselves, circulated in an appar-ently endless frenzy of narcissistic exhibitionism and equally narcissistic voyeurism: my looking at your online images and personal details, con-suming them, somehow remains about me still. Debord was prescient about the role that technology would play in this general social move-ment. "Just when the mass of commodities slides toward puerility, the puerile itself becomes a special commodity; this is epitomized by the gadget. Reified man advertises the proof of his intimacy with the com-modity. The fetishism of commodities reaches moments of fervent exal-tation similar to the ecstasies of the convulsions and miracles of the old religious fetishism. The only use which remains here is the fundamental use of submission."

It strikes me that this passage, with the possible exception of the last sentence, could have been plausibly recited by Steve Jobs at an Apple product unveiling. For Debord, the gadget, like the commodity more generally, is not a thing; it is a relation. As with all the technologies associ-ated with the spectacle, it closes down human possibility under the guise of expanding it; it makes us less able to form real connections, to go off the grid of produced and consumed leisure time, and to find the drifting, endlessly recombining idler that might still lie within us. There is no sal-vation from the baseline responsibility of *being here in the first place* to be found in machines. In part, this is a simple matter of economics in the age of automation. "The technical equipment which objectively eliminates labor must at the same time preserve labor as a commodity," Debord notes. "If the social labor (time) engaged by the society is not to diminish because of automation, then new jobs have to be created. Services, the tertiary sector, swell the ranks of the army of distribution." This ines-capable fact explains, at a stroke, the imperative logic of growth in the economy, the bizarre fetishizing of GDP as a measure of national health.

More profoundly, though, is a point that returns us to the original vision of a populace altogether freed from work by robots. To use a good example of critical consciousness emerging from within the production cycles of the culture industry, consider the Axiom, the passenger space-ship that figures in the 2008 animated film *WALL-E*. Here, robot labour has proved so successful, and so non-threatening, that the human mas-ters have been freed to indulge in non-stop indulgence of their desires. As a result, they have, over generations, grown morbidly obese, addicted to soft drinks and video games, their bones liquefied in the ship's micro-gravity conditions. They exist, but they cannot be said to live.

The gravest danger of off-loading work is not a robot uprising but a human downgrading. Work hones skills, challenges cognition, and, at its best, serves noble ends. It also makes the experience of genuine idling, in contrast to frenzied leisure-time, even more valuable. Here, with only our own ends and desires to contemplate—what shall we do with this free time?—we come face-to-face with life's ultimate question. To ask what is worth doing when nobody is telling us what to do, to wonder about how to spend our time, is to ask why are we here in the first place. Like so many of the standard philosophical questions, these ones butt up, however playfully, against the threshold of mortality.

And here, at the limit of life that idling alone brings into view in a non-threatening way, we find another kind of nested logic. Call it the two-step law of life. Rule number one is tomorrow we die; and rule number two is nobody, not even the most helpful robot, can change rule number one. Enjoy!

Bright Stroll,
Big City

WALKING TO WORK when you live in a large city is a luxury good, economists tell us; a pleasure only the lucky few can afford. But the truth of this claim varies by city. My home, Toronto, is a patchwork of neighbourhoods clustered around a core of tall buildings in the downtown financial district. Despite large expanses of exurban sprawl to the north, west, and east, the central city has remained mixed, habitable, and wildly diverse in both ethnicity and economic class. It is true that a long-standing housing bubble means buying a home in these neighbourhoods is a financial impossibility for most people. But the families who have lived here for even a few years benefit from the effects of scale: you can, if you choose, walk to any number of entertainment or work sites, including the main campus of the University of Toronto, which shares proximity to the big oval of Queen's Park with the Royal Ontario Museum, fancy branded shops on Bloor Street, various four-star hotels, and the provincial parliament buildings.

My wife Molly has a narrow semi-detached house in the Toronto neighbourhood known as Cabbagetown. The area was once, as Hugh Garner's Depression-era novel about the place phrased it, "the largest Anglo-Saxon slum in North America." It harboured Irish and Macedonian immigrants flowing north from the city's harbour, hence the once-pejorative, now proudly displayed name, and it is a strip of mixed public housing projects and attempts at gentrification that borders the valley of the Don River. The main drag, Parliament Street, offers a daily pageant of Indian and Caribbean groceries, wealthy gay couples, grizzled panhandlers, and an inexplicably large number of people driving personal mobility chairs along the sidewalk, often with pennants flying from the rear bumper. The apartment I was living in when I met Molly is in a neighbourhood known as the Annex—it was marked off in a long-ago city plan for residential development and now features an assortment of modest to grand stone and brick houses, some cut up into grad-student apartments, others renovated to magazine-lay-out dimensions. One of these was the last place revered urbanist Jane Jacob lived before her death in 2006. Here and there the wide streets feature elegant 1960s highrise apartment buildings that soar above the three-storey norm.

These days, I use the one-bedroom Annex place as an office. Monday to Friday, Molly drops me off there on her way to work in the city's far west end. I work here until it is time to go give lectures or attend faculty meetings. I walk. The University of Toronto campus spreads south from the Annex in a broad swath of precious downtown real estate that can still boast some untouched quads and playing field, not to mention a riot of architectural styles from the predictable collegiate neo-Gothic to some wedding-cake Romanesque, a bit of deco, and some modernist master-pieces like Ron Thom's Massey College. The walk takes about thirty min-utes. When my campus work is done, I hitch up for the forty or so minutes of sidewalk trekking it takes me to get back to the house in Cabbagetown. Google maps tells me that the total distance walked over these two legs is five-and-a-half kilometres, or just under three-and-a-half miles. When I plug that figure into the search field—because why not—I am further informed that there is a zip line in Alaska, the longest in the world, that covers the very same distance. It can be traversed in less than two minutes, a journey you can experience second-hand via YouTube video.

That may be the most exciting way for a human body to travel 5.5 clicks, but it is not the best; my own coverage doesn't raise my heart-rate so much, but it gives way to thought in a manner not possible in any other fashion. These walks can be dreamy and aesthetic, like poet Lisa Robertson's "Office for Soft Architecture" meanderings, caressing the city's surfaces. Just as often, or even on the same trip, I have tasks to per-form along the way, prizes to acquire: wine for dinner, a steak from the much-tattooed butcher who spreads sawdust on the floor and has a mas-sive taxidermied steelhead on the wall behind him, some jerk chicken to have at lunch tomorrow, picture-hanging fixtures from the hardware store that still has hardwood floors and aged family members sorting screws. I might stop at Ho's Place, at 509-1/2 Church Street, to have my hair cut by one of life's everyday artists, a twenty-something Korean guy in a curling sweater who finishes every cut by trimming your sideburns and neck with hot lather and a straight razor.

I take in the sights: people in rave gear on the street at four in the afternoon, an old apartment block slowly being obliterated to make way for something else; the kids playing tennis-ball cricket on the field behind a high school. I go over lectures in my mind, invent examples, roll around phrases for something I'm writing. I reflect on my marriage, my job, my family. Lately, for some reason, I seem to spend a lot of time mentally composing memorial speeches for my father, a former air force officer who has creakily made his way into his eighties despite various strokes and cardiac events.

Walking in a city is, for me, the greatest unpriced pleasure there is. I have walked bustling short blocks in New York, absurdly crowded pavements in Shanghai, the bucolic reaches of the Philosofen Weg near Heidelberg, mazey souk lanes in Doha, the tangled streets of East London, Edinburgh's Escheresque tesseracts, the winter-dark hills of Reykjavik and the rain-showered ones of San Francisco, the slope of sunny Sydney running down to the Pacific, the canyons of Chicago's Loop, the Cambridge Backs when Fen-born frost rimed the mown grass, the lovely sward of the Boston Common passing into the Public Garden. Following the practice of tireless psychogeographer Will Self, I have walked not only along the Mall in Washington but all the way out to the airport, cruising down the Potomac and, in the heat, thinking fond thoughts of the Sam Adams lager I would have when I got to the departure lounge.

Urban walking with no aim but sensation—the solitary pleasure of the *flâneur*—is of course a recent phenomenon, a legacy of modernity. As Frédéric Gros says in his book-length ramble through the topic, *A History of Walking*, "[t]he urban stroller is subversive. He subverts the crowd, the merchandise and the town, along with their values. The walker of wide-open spaces, the trekker with his rucksack, opposes civilization with the burst of the clean break, the cutting-edge of a rejection. . . . The stroller's walking activity is more ambiguous, his resistance to modernity ambivalent. Subversion is not a matter of opposing, accepting and moving blindly on. The *flâneur* subverts solitude, speed, dubious business politics and consumerism." Well, maybe; sometimes a stroll is just a stroll. And Gros misses other ambivalences of *flânerie*, for instance, its too-easy association with the male gaze: the cruising glance of appraisal that sizes up a shop window and a pretty boy or girl in just the same proprietary manner.

A Philosophy of Walking, already a bestseller in France and newly translated into English—alas, with a number of ungrammatical sentences along for the walk—is not quite what its title promises. It is less a philosophy than an easy stroll through anecdotes about various big-brained walkers. We meet the usual suspects: Aristotle the Peripatetic in the streets of Athens, Kant on his watch-setting daily round in Köningsberg, Nietzsche striding the hills of Europe in search of relief for his syphilitic headaches. Proust's wistful narrative of the Guermantes Way is briefly visited, as is Walter Benjamin's conflicted return to the *flânerie* of Paris, capital of the nineteenth century, in the Arcades Project. Guy Debord's attempts at subversion via the Situationist *dérive*, or drift, through the city, re-writing its geography with movement itself, are mentioned, if not explored. Short chapters, smooth, loping style, and a mixture of earnestness and charm all mark Gros's book. Various topics and names are lit upon with a feathery touch. This is an easygoing volume of micro-reflections that raises, though it never resolves, some difficult questions. If it lacks the heft of, say, Rebecca Solnit's exceptional *Wanderlust: A History of Walking* (2000), it nevertheless forces the issues in a useful way.

Some of the assertions (there are no arguments) sound grand but are probably simply muddled. "[B]y walking you are not going to meet yourself," Gros says in an early chapter on the "freedoms" of perambulation. "By walking, you escape from the very idea of identity, the temptation to be someone, to have a name and a history. . . . The freedom in walking lies in not being anyone; for the walking body has no history, it is just an eddy in the stream of immemorial life." This is a little too dreamy for my big-city taste, I guess. It may be true that we seek anonymity in the crowded urban street, solitude among the multitude, but not so much, I think, to renounce or transcend self as to put it into question in new ways. Compared to reading a novel or watching a film, walking is at best a mild form of bracketing the burden of identity. I unglue myself temporarily from name and history, yes, but not to flow in the eternal current of life, whatever that is, rather to ask myself what I think I am up to, what I want from being here. The country walker who breaks with civilization, perhaps seeking thereby the sublime experience of being overawed by nature, still knows that the self can never be left entirely behind—for that self's desires are what brought you out of routine actions and into the special reflective clearing of the walk. Wherever you go, there you are. (Disputes rage over the origin of that bit of wisdom; Buckaroo Banzai is my preferred source here.)

Gros likewise makes a fairly big deal, in his first chapter, about the fact that "walking is not a sport. . . . Sport gives rise to immediate mediatic ceremonies, crowded with consumers of brands and images, Money invades it to empty souls, medical science to construct artificial bodies." No doubt this true of the Tour de France, Major League Baseball, and a host of other athletic nodes in the society of the spectacle. But not all sport is like this, and of course there *is* a sport of walking. At the World Championships in Rome in 1987, a friend of mine covered ten kilometres in forty-five minutes and twenty-seven seconds: try telling her that there was no sport happening. Even if one were inclined to agree with Gros's vision of aimless walking (he is also against special shoes, clothing, and those pointed staffs that "are on sale to give walkers the appearance of improbable skiers"), he is awfully normative about it all: the demand for aimless, non-competitive walking is just as judgmental and insistence as any other, and may sail closer to self-contradiction than most. *You're not doing aimlessness right! Walk* this *way!*

Consider the spiritual pilgrimage, anyone's model of a walk meant to issue in transformation; it is subject to all these same tangles of self and its loss. Along the ancient road to Santiago de Compostela, for example, one may still find the range of human preoccupation driving the various pilgrims on from day to day. David Lodge, in his novel *Therapy* (1995), has character Laurence Passmore, afflicted by mid-life crisis, attempt the walk while reading Kierkegaard. The philosopher's ideas seem to be enacted by the walkers themselves: the ethical seekers after achievement of duty (so many kilometres a day), the aesthetic indulgers (look at the view!), and finally the religious knights of faith who pass through these stages and walk the way as simple acceptance of the world. But Kierkegaard, the arch anti-Hegelian, would have known that such a resolution is too simple. We can never escape the conflicts of duty and pleasure, even in faith; nor can our walking just be walking. To be going nowhere in particular is still to be going.

More to the point, sometimes walking is the burden, not the release. Few characters in literature walk more than Thomas Hardy's Tess, but she must do so from disadvantage, not in the interests of leisure or spiritualism. The suburban exiles who lack cars and live in districts poorly served by public transit, who doggedly cover ground to fetch groceries from the nearest strip mall, are her modern descendants. They do not appear in Gros's appreciation of bipedal motion. Walking may be a kind of confession, a slowly moving portrait of failure, at least in terms of the modern city's dominant movement-values. It is not really part of Gros's purview—he lives in walkable Paris after all—but we North Americans should always remember that the encroachment on walking opportunities by the post-war expansion of car-centric urban design is one of the signal failures of human vision in the twentieth century.

The book ends with a meandering chapter, longer than most, that links the repetitious, even monotonous, action of the human stride to religious ecstatics in the Himalayas known as *lung-gom-pa*, the endlessly repeated breath-centred "Jesus prayer" that will be familiar to readers of J. D. Salinger, and resulting feats of "walking very fast over enormous distances without fatigue." Indeed, the truly ecstatic walker seems to be able to go beyond walking into the fantastic realms of near flight: "he covers great spans as if bounding over the ground." For myself, I'll stick with my sneakers hitting the sidewalk, dodging the heads-down texters and accosting charity workers.

*   *   *

By saying these things I don't mean to take anything away from Gros's basic enthusiasm for the walking experience, which I share without reservation. Gros is on the side of the angels when he notes that walking is "the best way to go more slowly." We can move faster, for centuries by horse and more lately by every conceivable conveyance pushed by internal combustion; but we cannot experience ourselves and the world as fully in any other manner.

The jumbled record of sensations and ideas unique to the pace of walking is a distinctly human pleasure. "You need to start with two legs," Gros asserts without any irony; but he is correct. The upright posture is at once the highest achievement of *Homo sapiens sapiens*, our main sensory array lifted (as Freud notes) away from the smelly ground and into the clear air, and a constant invitation to fall forward in the two-legged gait that we alone, among the primates, have mastered. Walking is our thing, and because senses are lofted high atop the five or six feet most of us enjoy, the range of stimulus is wide. Our minds open, and we begin to ponder. We reflect or gather wool or argue inwardly; our minds are moving just as our feet do. But, to invoke Nicholson Baker's much-neglected question, what *size* are the thoughts of walking?

"Each thought has a size," Baker writes, "and most are about three feet tall, with the level of complexity of a lawnmower engine, or a cigarette lighter, or those tubes of toothpaste that, by mingling several hidden pastes and gels, create a pleasantly striped product." Large thoughts, thought with lasting heft, are crepuscular, complex, and slow to arrive, like "the unhasty, liquid pace of human thinking" itself. But sometimes a thought that seems smallish and about to wrap up and stop may "happen upon that loose-limbed, reckless acceleration, where this very thought may shamble forward, plucking tart berries, purchasing newspapers, and retrieving stray refuse without once breaking stride—risking a smile, shaking the outstretched hands of young constituents, loosening its tie!" Then again, no: it was a false start, a spurt of speed without finishing class. Thoughts fizzle just like other human things.

The specific association of philosophy with walking, which features so prominently in Gros's book, is itself a middle-sized thought worth looking at a little harder. We call Aristotle's philosophical school Peripatetic because legend holds that he liked to walk about as he lectured, but the name may simply be a corruption of the school's original nickname, derived from the *peripatoi*, or colonnades, of the Athenian Lyceum. Aristotle's fondness for travel—born in Stagira, he was an outsider in Athens who ventured away on numerous occasion, most famously to tutor Alexander the Great—may also have been a factor. There is no internal evidence that his ideas are rooted in walking, except in the general sense that he believed in observation of the natural world as a prerequisite for science.

My favourite bit of sly mischief about philosophy as walking appears in a more modern source, Iris Murdoch's novel *The Philosopher's Pupil* (1983). In the story, a celebrated but irascible philosopher has returned to his childhood home, a spa town called Ennistone with a famous hot spring, to try and get his affairs in order. As usual with Murdoch's novels, this effort backfires spectacularly. The philosopher, John Robert Rozanov, has an almost physical need to "do philosophy" by rudely interrogating companions during forced-march rambles around the countryside. On one occasion, he summons the local priest, a man of little certain faith. "On arrival at the philosopher's house he had been dismayed to find John Robert all ready to *go for a long walk*," the novel's narrator relates. "Father Bernard, who had lost the aesthetic tastes and talents of his youth, disliked long walks and could scarcely envisage having any sort of difficult conversation while in motion (he was slightly deaf). Now Rozanov was talking about going across the Common and out into the country. The priest marked his displeasure by asking for some safety pins and fussily pinning up the hem of his cassock."

The walk is not a success, though Father Bernard is able to mitigate some of the worst challenges: "He was determined *not* to go out into the country, and hoped (rightly) that once they were talking he could lead John Robert along an easier route." Even so, John Robert insists on "walking uncomfortably fast" even while peppering the poor cleric with almost unanswerable questions. It is sometimes said that it is impossible to have a real fight with someone while walking—we need the valences of face-to-face interaction to execute the business of emotional violence. The same may be true of genuine philosophical argument. Of course, one can always walk away from an opponent or interlocutor, as several vexed Athenians do when they encounter Socrates in Plato's dialogues and as ordinary people do all the time; but turning one's back, like bursting into tears, is not an argument.

Even solitary philosophizing may prove less amenable to the stroll than we often imagine. For many people, the walk or hike is less an occasion for thought than a respite from it, sometimes a necessary venting of pent-up energy that precisely lacks (like much exercise) the quality of thought: I walk to exhaust stress like a vapour trail. My friend Josh, whose father is a minister, said this when the issue was raised: "My dad raves about how much mental stimulation he gets out of walking and hiking—he writes sermons and essays and book chapters in his head while walking. But when I walk or hike—much as I enjoy it—nothing happens in my head at all." I wonder if that is entirely true—nothing *at all?*—but the essential point is important. Walking may stimulate thought, just as beauty may inspire goodness, but this connection is contingent, not necessary; there is a philosophical error lurking in any attempt to make the link stronger than happenstance. Some years ago I wrote a book about fly fishing which, among other things, repeated Izaak Walton's praise for the reflection that this pastime encourages. I mentioned the argument to a Norwegian friend of mine, who solemnly shook his head. "No," he said. "When I fish all I think about is fishing." Sometimes, a walk is just a walk.

Here is a small- to medium-sized thought about thoughts and walking. I had this thought while walking to work, in fact, down a street called Bathurst, past the Caribbean grocery and hipster craft-beer cafe. There is a famous image of the mind sketched in Plato's *Theaetetus*. Consciousness, Socrates says, might be like a giant aviary, with all species of birds flying in apparently random directions. The birds represent thoughts; they are all contained by the confines of the aviary, but it is not until one is captured that it reveals its dimensions, colouring, and habits. Only then can we say that we are truly thinking that thought: to have is not the same as to hold.

I stopped on the street and made a note on a scrap of paper in my pocket; it says "aviary, Bathurst" and I have it, as they say, before me as I write. I don't usually stop to make actual notes; mostly, when things worth remembering occur to me while walking, I make up mnemonics to carry them far enough into the future that I can set them down. I match the rhythm of these mini-jingles to my pace, and recite them as I put one foot in front of the other. Perhaps this is one philosopher's version of the Jesus Prayer? Anyway, the note is a last resort: like any memo, it is a message from present self to future version thereof, a captured thought and a time-traversing device, a container of consciousness. Real thoughts, I thought, ultimately require stationary presence at the machines of thinking: tables and chairs. We must eventually cease walking if we are truly to think.

And so a last thought, of a size yet to be determined. Melville's Bartleby the Scrivener, that machine-like writer of other people's texts, who eventually seizes up and prefers not to write, move, speak, or eat, is the indelible image of the endgame implied by all walking, thinking, and writing. Bartleby is the anti-*flâneur*, a figure who comprehensively subverts the logic of capitalism and the circulation systems of the modern city. He is, it has been said, the first laid-off worker to occupy Wall Street—though of course he does most of the laying off himself.

Melville's "Story of Wall Street" was published in 1853. By 1857, this most naturally philosophical of American novelists had published his last serious work of fiction, *The Confidence-Man*. He soon faded into obscurity, his works declining in reputation all the while. In a much-remarked-upon irony, by the 1860s he appears to have stopped writing altogether, not from preference but from routine writerly despair—though the notes for the posthumous *Billy Budd* complicate the picture. Soon he was employed as a notably honest New York customs inspector, a post he would hold for almost two decades.

Though not famous enough for it to rate a mention in Gros's book, Melville was a great walker. He understood streets as well as he knew the sea, the sights, sounds, and smells of those two kinds of ocean. We don't know if he was in the habit of walking to work, or whether he spanned the East River by foot at any point after its temporary Brooklyn footbridge opened in 1877, but I hope so on both counts. These days you can do a walking tour of Melville's Manhattan, visiting the various sites he knew and depicted in his fiction, the still-standing factory buildings and long-gone slums. I like to imagine what thoughts, big and small, he might have entertained as he marked off the blocks between his late-life residence at 104 East Twenty-Sixth Street (he died there) and, to the west, the Union League Club and Madison Square Garden or, much farther downtown, the New York Customs House which, in 1866 when he acquired his odd sinecure, was in the Merchant Exchange Building—at 55 Wall Street.

Walking Downtown

Solvitur ambulando, medieval monks were advised, when faced with a gonad-sourced spiritual crisis or a tricky passage from the *Summa Contra Gentiles*. It is solved by walking. A stroll is handy homely therapy for any number of afflictions, great and small: good for the digestion, distracting of worries, refreshing of spirit, and maybe even the preferred way to do philosophy. Aristotle thought so, popular legend says, which is, as was mentioned in the previous essay, why we call the school he founded Peripatetic. But let's not ruin the image of donnish conversation about Final Causes or the Unmoved Mover carried on by a couple of ambling brainiacs. Centuries later, Heinrich Heine would gently mock Kant for the regularity of his afternoon constitutional, always taken "with his grey coat and the Spanish stick in his hand," as a feature of intellectual rigidity by which the rationalist philosopher's Königsberg neighbours allegedly set their clocks. Nietzsche and the Lake poets would be driven to wilder, more romantic ambulation.

There is, equally, a longstanding disdain of those who, like Hardy's Tess, must trudge, rather than ride, from place to place. Especially in North American urban life, lacking a vehicle is among the clearest markers of deficiency, especially if it means a resort of public transit. Margaret Thatcher made the stakes plain when she noted that "A man who, beyond the age of twenty-six, finds himself on a bus can count himself as a failure." Krusty the Klown from *The Simpsons*, reflecting on a reversal of fortune, was more succinct: "I was a big cheese, I was a huge cheese! But now look at me—I gotta ride the bus like a schnook, I gotta live in an apartment like an idiot!" In this emergent car-driven urban class scale, walking can mark either a further declension on the social scale—sidewalk scum, lacing even bus fare—or a defiant return to luxury status for those who can walk to work or out to a restaurant.

Pedestrian in its adjectival mode comes to mark the feckless, the trite, the dull of mind: thoughts that shuffle when they should fly. Even jaywalkers, those dashing minor-league anarchists of the urban grid, came by their name via insult: "jay" originally meant simpleton, soft-head, rube. The term was probably coined, and certainly popularized, by early enthusiasts of the automobile, so take that into account. In some places, the value polarity is reversed again: New Yorkers think that anybody who *doesn't* jaywalk is a rube. What are you waiting for, for crying out loud? Still, jaywalking remains illegal in New York and in most cities, punishable by fines and even detention. I once gave a lecture celebrating jaywalking's liberatory potential; the town's police chief, part of the audience, gave me his card afterward. "You'll need that to get out of jail," he told me.

Whether you wait for a light or breeze into traffic, urban walking is a special kind of activity—a modern art form, expansive in stylistic range and infinite in variation. On sidewalks and in public squares, across terminal concourses and through lobbies, walking is how we most commonly, and closely, encounter our fellow citizens. If you live in a large city, learning how to walk the streets is something you must master as a physical expression of belonging. Because the discrete places of life have gaits as well as gates, and the upright, always-falling staggerers that we are—featherless bipeds, says the Peripatetic doctrine—must adapt or fall.

"I grew up in the South," the humourist Roy Blount notes in a memorable essay on how to walk in New York. "I can do the traipse, I can do the gallivant, I can do the lollygag, and I can do the slow lope. I can hotfoot it, I can waltz right in and waltz right out, or I can just be poking or dragging or plowing along. As a youngster I skedaddled. I believe that if called upon, for the sake of some all-in-good-fun theatrical, I could sashay. But I know that these gaits have their places, and on the other hand there is New York walking. You think you know how to walk in New York? No you don't, unless you know you know how to walk in New York. Otherwise you just impede the flow." Tom Wolfe was the first to note the characteristic hip-hitch of the *pimp roll*, that defiant sidewalk strut, but the walking signals of class and race have been with us always, from the *flâneur*'s saunter signifying infinite aesthetic leisure to the vast lexicon directing the motions of P. G. Wodehouse's antic London idiots, who ooze, oil, filter, trickle, pour, breeze, stream, and sidle. It's a close thing, but in the Wooster lexicon there are hardly more words for being drunk. Priorities.

*   *   *

None of Blount, Wolfe, or Wodehouse are deemed worthy of mention in a spate of recent books about cities and walking, but that's no rap against them: we all have favourite literary pals, just like we have favourite routes and destinations in the same city. Nor do any of them discuss, in some cases even mention, the gravest current threat to enjoyable city walking, namely all those people not looking where they're going because they're offering bow-headed obeisance to their *fucking phones*. Recent evidence suggests that this practice, like absent-minded jaywalking before it, entails a threat to personal safety, but insofar as that might be construed as a Darwinian mechanism to weed out the stupid and self-involved among us, on current evidence it is not nearly efficient enough. Fifth Avenue might as well be a forest of human stumps, or a primitive but frustrating video game, for all the pleasure it lately offers as a promenade. The offence here is that the downcast gaze creates a minute rupture of the implicit social contract that governs all shared spaces, forcing me to navigate out of your way instead of our performing the silent cooperative dance of bumpless passing, that citizenly ballet of the street.

Of the writers and thinkers who dwell on city walking, architect and urban theorist Michael Sorkin appreciates this point most. *Twenty Minutes in Manhattan*, his 2009 tour de force of pedestrian appreciation, is a detailed defence of why walking in cities is not just a pleasant pastime or fine form of low-impact exercise but an essential feature of democracy—a physical enactment of citizenship that contrasts vividly with the metal-carapaced isolation of driving. As the title suggests, the book is structured around the daily walk Sorkin takes from his rent-controlled Greenwich Village apartment to the office of his architecture practice in Tribeca. He takes a long time to get out the door, what with detailing the building's stairwells and corridors, plus the tussles with neighbours over noise and garbage, but once on the stoop and away, it's an exhilarating journey, delivered in a series of montages and digressions that mirror, on the page, the modern experience of navigating the sidewalk in a great, busy, diverse city. We pass through Washington Square Park, down past LaGuardia Place, across Houston and Canal, have encounters with the women of SoHo, and end up playing sly elevator games at the office. Along the way, Sorkin offers history, philosophy, and politics. He is the ultimate cicerone, opinionated, well-informed, committed, and sometimes funny.

The book's best chapter, "The Block," is a graceful survey of thinkers who understand, and celebrate, the political dimensions of the built environment, the public goods of public space, the implicit "right to the city" in conurbations: Walter Benjamin, Henri Lefebvre, Michel de Certeau, Guy Debord, and of course Jane Jacobs. "The key to a democratic urban citizenship is that cooperative behavior is elective," Sorkin notes, which is why even small defections from the implicit norms of shared space—I'm looking at you not looking at me, phone guy—are significant. Walking in cities, unlike the mostly country strolls of philosophers and poets, necessarily combines solitude with contact, interior meditation with interaction. There is ample room, even on some of Manhattan's most crowded streets, for that mixture of stimulation and introspection that marks the best of city walking, and links the concrete details of architecture and urban planning to the deepest insights of phenomenology and lyrical reflection. By the time we reach our destination in Sorkin's walk to work, the larger defections of the modern city—runaway property values, market-dictated rents, corporate retail districts—are revealed as enemies of thought itself, not just of functioning urban democracy. This is a walk with a purpose, one of the finest mediations on the politics of the built environment since, yes, Jacobs's *The Death and Life of Great American Cities*.

Sorkin is, in fact, a trifle red-faced in his denunciation of threats to the urban democratic fabric, hating pretty equally on everything from Trumped-up towers and celebrity-capitalized gentrification schemes to film-crew production assistants who shoo him off a sidewalk. You begin to worry about him. "My bile rises when I pass the unshaded sidewalks of the corporate skyscrapers of midtown because even these entities— worth billions of dollars—are as indifferent as my landlord to the public realm," he snarls in *Twenty Minutes*. "I feel my blood pressure rise as I pass the ranks of mobile dressing rooms and supply trucks, all with their exhausts belching and their noisy generators running to keep overpaid stars cool or warm," he splutters. "I was now screaming with rage," he says of the height of one battle with said sneaky, tax-raising landlord. For the initiatives known as "public-private partnerships," which in practice routinely devolve the former into the latter, Sorkin harbours

Nazi-inflected hostility: "Whenever I hear the phrase, I reach for my revolver." Later on, contemplating a Japanese SUV model named, with typical onomastic inanity, the Tribeca, he reports, "I look forward to spitting on the first one I see and yelling 'asshole' at the driver."

In addition to his general animus towards whole categories of people—yuppies and bobos (remember them?), landlords, film crews—Sorkin also nurses some personal grievances. His gallery of rogues includes the cynical billionaire mayor Michael Bloomberg, the craven apostle of power Herbert Muschamp, the fey Nazi poseur Philip Johnson, the sadly trendy Daniel Libeskind, the slippery hypocrite Rem Koolhaas, and of course the bullying city-hater Robert Moses. On the other hand, Jane Jacobs was a genius. If I didn't think he would spit on me and call me an asshole, I would mention here that, among other tics, Sorkin has an overfondness for misusing the phrase "begs the question." (Most people do, but not usually so often.) These and other incidental effects modestly enliven his collection of essays, *All Over the Map*, which is indeed that, an album of loosely connected short pieces that mostly wither on the page. The exceptions include longer essays about the ends of urbanism and the persistence of utopianism in architectural thought. These, with perhaps a half-dozen others, form the short book that is inside this one, struggling to get out.

A comical pitch of unchilled Sorkinism is reached at one point in *Twenty Minutes*, when he once again resorts to "asshole," albeit under his breath, after being bumped by two buggy-pushing, cellphone-yakking moms in SoHo. I'm no fan of fashionable biofascism either, and those Maclaren strollers are indeed a bit precious, but that seemed a little too New Yawk even for a hair-trigger hater like Sorkin. It was the only discreditable note in the book—as long as one discounts an off-key sentence in which Sorkin, seeking to demonstrate the growing annexation of SoHo by media luminaries, mentions that he once sat on a toilet seat "still warm from the impress of Calista Flockhart's bum." I mean, really. Who even remembers Calista Flockhart these days?

*　　*　　*

Alexandra Horowitz has no such agenda, and doesn't drop the names of philosophers, but her book, *On Looking: Eleven Walks with Expert Eyes*, belongs alongside Sorkin's anyway, as a sort of creamy dessert course.

Written in the breezy, accessible style Horowitz brought her previous effort, *Inside of a Dog*, a study of her dog's perceptual universe, it recounts eleven walks that Horowitz, a cognitive psychologist, took in New York. In each case, she had a companion trained in or dedicated to some aspect of the urban condition: an architect and a sociologist of sidewalk behaviour, naturally, but also a geologist and a graphic designer (finally, someone who defends the almost-obscured distinction between *font* and *typeface*). A sound designer teaches her to hear the subtle grades of the soundscape; a blind woman dials up her appreciation of walking without all six senses in play. The most enjoyable chapter may be the intrepid journey shared with artist Maira Kalman, whose appreciation of the ordinary is such that a sofa discarded on the sidewalk instantly transports her to glee. "If you are ever bored or blue," Kalman has written, "stand on the street corner for half an hour." But don't just stand there; get moving. And look!

It struck me, reading these almost-too-chatty accounts of city movement, that Horowitz is the New World reverse of Oulipo eminence Georges Perec, who sat for days in a Paris cafe observing the same unremarkable streetscape and recording everything that happened. Which wasn't much. The resulting book, *An Attempt at Exhausting a Place in Paris* (1975), is exhausting in a manner that only Perec, author of a novel entirely devoid of the letter "e", could deploy. "What has changed here since yesterday? At first sight, it's really the same. Is the sky perhaps cloudier? It would really be subjective to say that there are, for example, fewer people or fewer cars. There are no birds to be seen." Now and then, ennui descends. "Buses pass by," he notes a few lines later. "I've lost all interest in them." Alas, for only yesterday they had been an object of avid fascination. Soon, Perec's experiment in what he called the *infraordinary*, "what happens when nothing happens," is tinged with melancholy, almost madness. It is also hilarious, especially if echoes of Alastair Sutherland's parody, "The Jean-Paul Sartre Cookbook," float to mind: "I keep creating omelets one after another, like soldiers marching into the sea, but each one seems empty, hollow, like stone . . . I look at them on the plate, but they do not look back." Alexandra Horowitz might reply, cheerfully, that at least they don't bump into you.

"If Rousseau is the more obvious source for the modernist fixation on the restoration of an Edenic environment," Michael Sorkin remarks in *Twenty Minutes*, "Hobbes functions as its thinly concealed unconscious, the steely control behind the curtain of bowery fabulousness." Hobbesian games are everywhere afoot in Jeff Speck's *Walkable City: How Downtown Can Save America, One Step at a Time*. Indeed, Speck's approach might be conceived as the return of the reality principle in urban affairs; or one might say that, like Machiavelli, he chooses to take people as they are and laws—or policy levers—as they might be. His general premise is that people won't stop driving cars, and walk instead, unless the price is right; hence it is the business of good urban planning and municipal politics to find the right mix of carrots and sticks to draw people out of their rides and onto the sidewalk. Walking is of course good for you, enjoyable, and sustainable; but just saying so won't make people do it. For that, you need behaviour-altering tricks like congestion pricing (raising the opportunity costs of driving downtown, whether with actual fees or heightened frustration) and road diets (avoiding the well-known phenomenon of induced traffic demand by removing, rather than adding, car lanes).

Speck likes walking as much as Horowitz and Sorkin, in short, but he also knows that Manhattanites are the blessed and few. Pedestrian opportunities are hardly the norm in cities, especially in America, where aliens from space would be convinced that automobiles themselves had originated the design principles, including the apparently principled lack of public bathrooms even in walkable areas. Speck advises mayors and planners on how to make existing cities more walker-friendly. Much of his advice, collected and framed in *Walkable City*, runs counter to their received ideas, a fact that gives Speck endless pleasure. Some of the background here is psychological, as in the notion of *risk homeostasis*, which dictates that humans will act recklessly just to the level of their comfort. This means, for example, that widening roads in an attempt to make them safer has the unintended effect of allowing people to drive faster—and so returns the road to its previous level of danger.

It also accounts for the fact that adding bikes lanes to streets, unless separated by a curb, can make them more dangerous. Speck, like both Sorkin and Horowitz, cites the experiments of Dutch planner Hans Monderman, who designed so-called "naked streets": road interchanges almost entirely devoid of signage. These proved demonstrably safer than signed interchanges, however clearly marked, because drivers, cyclists, and pedestrians had to slow down and think in order to assess the risk and then negotiate it. In Monderman's terms, "Chaos equals cooperation."

This is all diverting in the usual "counterintuitive" manner we have come to expect from a certain sort of popular non-fiction. It is delivered with certainty, bad pun-driven jokes, and a penchant for grandiose labels for common-sense ideas: "The General Theory of Walkability explains how, to be favored, a walk has to satisfy four main conditions: it must be useful, safe, comfortable, and interesting." Who knew? At least there is no attempt to explain walking with reference to what the journalist Steve Poole has memorably labelled "popular neurobollocks." Walking is what we all know it to be: good for you, sometimes entertaining, and inherently civic. It saves money by, among other things, offsetting looming health-care costs and increasing productivity. And, as Speck shows with compelling statistical evidence, walkable districts only rise in property value.

Here we glimpse the set of market-style assumptions Speck brings to the core analysis of walkable cities. Among other things, he seems to have ingested the so-five-years-ago "creative class" rhetoric with enthusiasm, and talks excitedly of the "millennials" and "creatives," raised on *Friends* rather than *The Brady Bunch*, who will inhabit the pedestrian-welcoming hipster downtowns of the future, if only we plan it right. These people, he thinks, will be the ones to reverse the urban flight of the last century and reinvigorate the moribund centres of America's non-New-York con-urbations with broad sidewalks, buskers, food trucks, and cool transit. And I'm sure they would like to, if only they can figure out how to man-age the more than $1 trillion in combined student debt this generation has shouldered, something that somehow does not figure into Speck's discussion. (I did hear him describe these same heroes of urbanization as "overeducated" in an NPR interview, so maybe that offers a clue as to what he really thinks of them.)

The very same desire for walkability that attracts younger residents is just what will drive the property values past the level those people can afford. This is precisely what happened in Jane Jacobs's beloved West Village, which morphed from a diverse, rough-and-tumble 1960s neigh-bourhood into a cobblestone and red-brick theme park for actors and fashion models. That the same thing did not happen in her other model district, Boston's North End, is owing to the fact that it was already a theme park, offering cannoli and gelato alongside manufactured street parades for the Virgin Mary. As for the *Friends* aspiration, to my knowl-edge, no one has ever explained exactly how Monica, Rachel, Ross et al. were able to live the lofty good life in Manhattan in the first place, when they were mostly un- or underemployed. I suppose some of us have the good sense to choose rich parents.

Like so many people who place faith in market mechanisms to generate good results, Speck is at times spectacularly unconcerned with how policy rubber meets human road. "Meeting the need of its most vulnerable citizens is one thing that cities must do," he notes, "but, to put it bluntly, you don't owe a suburbanite a ride. A nondriving person has the choice of living in town. Taxpayers should not subsidize his ride to a big house with a big yard. If he has a condition that prevents him from driving, like poverty, then he should live in a place where he doesn't need to drive." Well, there you are, then, non-driving poor person! While some non-crazy people might suggest that your poverty is a relative position in a competitive game, or even a relation to dominant systems, it is here revealed as a condition, like gout, that prevents you from driving. The choice is then yours. Fix it, loser. Move downtown! (Note: this passage, which appeared in the advance reading copy of Speck's book, had been expunged by the time the finished copies were printed: some editors save you from yourself.)

To be fair, Speck goes on to say that if there is no affordable housing in walkable areas, the transit money should be put there. But this ignores the realities of cities in a way at odds with his original rhetorical position. Many North American suburbs are not of the big-house/big-yard variety; more significantly, they often offer the only place where lower-to middle-income families can even imagine owning a house. They are typically ill-served by transit and may even feature, for the carless, the supremely ironic First World tragedy of the food desert: a neighbourhood where it is impossible to access groceries without a car. In many places, including my own city, these near suburbs increasingly accommodate recent arrivals to the country, and so their cultural identities are shifting and, sometimes, in conflict. Violent gang activity has a stronger presence here than in the inner city, even as ethnic enclaves are formed with little attachment to the larger urban culture. Lefebvre's right to the city, which might be thought to include, at a minimum, the possibility of a pleasure trip downtown as well as access to basic services, is here blocked by the basic facts of habitation.

All these factors tend to correlate with lower relative wealth levels, creating just the implicit exclusions, and explicit vertical gated communities of downtown condo towers, that Michael Sorkin feared would result from gentrification and fake "public" spaces like shopping districts. Research by my University of Toronto colleague David Hulchansky has shown that there are three distinct socio-economic "cities" within the Greater Toronto Area (GTA). The small, wealthiest city is concentrated downtown and in traditionally upper-crust neighbourhoods such as Rosedale and Forest Hill; it is clustered around the main subway lines, the financial core, and most prominent sites of entertainment and shopping. The poorest city is in the near suburbs on the northwest and northeast edges of the city area, often far from subway access. And there is a middle-income city squeezed between the two, including some neighbourhoods that feature a momentarily stable mixture of gentrification and low-income housing—though this may be changing.

I mention all this, in part, because it is a pattern likely to exist, or be repeated, elsewhere in Canada and the United States, if not, perhaps, in less sprawling European cities. And yet, even by Speck's own analysis, Toronto ranks high as a walkable city. I can myself walk or bike to work nearly every day, and have never owned a car (though, in common with Speck, I like the experience of driving). I enjoy this luxury because I live in what Hulchansky calls City 1, rather than 2 or 3—in the same neighbourhood, not coincidentally, that includes Jane Jacobs' last residence. This separatist trend within the city has developed over the past four decades, almost precisely paralleling the growing income disparities of North American society witnessed during the same period. It would be no exaggeration to say that the "three cities" condition, with growing outer-city slums and privileged walkable downtowns, is the physical embodiment of the economic banes of wealth concentration, chosen isolation and market-value dominance.

Speck is on the side of the angels, mostly. He has good things to say in favour of working public spaces ("only as good as their edges") and inclusionary zoning, and bad things to say about both starchitectural bombastics and quietly destructive civil engineers, who mistakenly think that facilitating traffic flow is the *ne plus ultra* of urban intervention. If he seems a little too accommodating of the automobile, that is because he knows they are not going anywhere soon. Even his market-driven approach might have an upside: if drivers were made to pay higher prices, in all of time, frustration, and money, they might be persuaded to walk or take the train instead. Failing that, their willingness to spend can be leveraged in good directions. On just one aspect of this dynamic: "Parking is a public good, and it must be managed for the public good. Such management takes full advantage of the free market but—this is important—it is not the free the market. The single largest land use in every American city is very much that city's business." See what the market will bear, and flow that revenue downstream to transit, public housing, and walkable downtowns—which, in his own words, "belong to everybody." If only it were so.

*   *   *

One of the saddest things to observe about our now decisively urbanized globe is how little thought has gone into its creation, especially relative to the amount of speculation and argument created by urbanists, architects, and philosophers. Many of the planet's largest cities—those of ten million people or more—can now be found in Asia, Africa, and South America. Commuters in these cities daily witness traffic jams to gladden the hearts of congestion-pricers everywhere. At the same time, they support massive non-driving populations that manage to co-habit and even thrive, despite sometimes lacking access to basic amenities such as water and electricity. From this global urban perspective, it is itself a luxury to worry about whether your city can indulge the luxury of walking.

Still, there is no doubt that things have to change in the peak-oil phase of North America's love affair with the automobile. I think my favourite recent walk in a built environment was also the worst. Somewhere between Washington's Dulles Airport and Alexandria, Virginia, where I was visiting to give a lecture the next day, I was marooned in a strip-mall chain motel. There was no restaurant or bar in the hotel, just a sheaf of fast-food menus in the leatherette folder on my room's plywood desk. I decided to venture out rather than order in. Soon I found myself lost in one of those exurban dead zones that fill so much of the continental land mass, a semi-developed range of highways, service roads, interchanges, and parking lots that Michael Sorkin calls the "apraxic city." Walking along the verge of the highway, which was of course devoid of a sidewalk, I made for my only dining option, a 7-11 raised on a knoll in the near distance, with its reliable stock of microwaveable burritos and plastic-coffined beef jerky. Also beer.

As I made my way along the road, I became aware of the anomalous nature of the ambulatory body in this environment. Pickup trucks whizzed by, their drivers hooting out the window. Other cars honked their horns, trailing laughter in dopplered ripples. The parseable content of these sounds was something between "Jesus fuck, there's somebody *walking* there!" and "Hey, loser!" Perhaps those are the same thing when cars rule the world. They were up and I was down, pacing out walking's inherent shame.

This particular hierarchy of bodies in space is unsustainable, but you wouldn't know it from visiting most North American cities. In Asia, meanwhile, the urban future really has arrived: in addition to poverty and crowding that would shock the residents of Dallas or Vancouver, there is also city-wide WiFi, advanced eco-friendly infrastructure, smartcard transit and retail, and soaring architecture. As Daniel Brook shows in *A History of Future Cities*, his inspired tour of the postmodern city, the East is deeply entwined with Western money, history, and ambition. "Where are we?" he asks in the book's opening line. "Walking through the cityscapes of St. Petersburg, Shanghai, Mumbai, and Dubai provokes this same question. Built to look as if they were not where they are—in Russia, China, India, and the Arab world, respectively—each metropolis conjures the same captivating yet discomfiting sense of disorientation." Investigating the disorientation of these cities, which are global in a way even New York could not claim, makes for a fascinating journey, and one that could not take place except on foot.

Urban Pleasures

"In the city there's a thousand things I want to say to you /
But whenever I approach you, you make me look a fool."
— THE JAM, "In The City" (1977)

1. Gift

IN ECONOMIC JARGON, an externality is any cost or benefit that is experienced outside of a contract. Urban life, which is only ever partially tamed by explicit transaction, is full of them. Uncompensated costs are negative externalities: noise, pollution, body contact on the subway, long lines at the baseball game beer stand. Unexpected benefits are positive externalities: the sex appeal of passing strangers, the excitement of a neon-splashed downtown square, all the incidental stimulation that Georg Simmel rightly associated with "the metropolitan attitude."

"The psychological foundation, upon which the metropolitan individuality is erected," he says, "is the intensification of emotional life due to the swift and continuous shift of external and internal stimuli . . . the rapid telescoping of changing images, of pronounced differences within what is grasped at a single glance, the unexpectedness of violent stimuli." This violence occurs, indeed, "with every crossing of the street, with the tempo and multiplicity of economic, occupational and social life."[1] To cope with this onslaught, the metropolitan mind adopts a "blasé outlook," a "relentless matter-of-factness" of been-there, done-that cool which has not changed in the near century since Simmel first noted its existence.[2]

Meanwhile, every interaction in the city seeks to reduce any particularity to the "rational" uniform calculability of transaction, as money smoothes down the differences between things, or "reserves" the inter-actions between people—or, indeed, the way newly ubiquitous pocket watches makes all time the same unit-based flow. "If all the watches in Berlin suddenly went wrong in different ways even only as much as an hour, its entire commercial and economic life would be derailed for some time." Thus "the most banal externalities," such as watches, "are, in the last analysis, bound up with the final decisions concerning the meaning and the style of life."[3]

But Simmel is too deterministic, and he gives away the game to "rational" capitalism too easily. Another way to think of externalities is this: they are gifts, unrequested and unrequited pleasures descending upon us without warning or price. They are, indeed, beyond or behind the very idea of transaction, not just external to it. A gift offers an alterna-tive, potentially critical scale of value independent of the world in which all things and experiences must have a price. You can buy a gift, perhaps, but you cannot constrain its ability to give, any more than the value of a work of art is reducible to its price.[4]

The gift of the city is the gift of democratic pleasure, a constantly renewed sense of open possibility and playful engagement between self and other. If that sounds too abstract, let me add some concreteness to the point by describing my walk yesterday evening.

I was on my way to meet a friend for a drink. He is my oldest friend, in the sense that he is someone I have known for three decades and we still feel the same pleasure in each other's company as we did during college in the 1980s. In the manner of Heidegger's "horizon of concern," I was already, in a sense, engaged with him even as I left my office. Anticipatory resoluteness![5] I decided to walk.

Because I now teach at the same university where I was an under-graduate, the streets of downtown Toronto are for me layered with rich deposits of memory: some wistful and slightly tragic in the way that only the recalled loves of nineteen can be; some harsh or embarrassing, according to relevant incident; some purely and simply beautiful.

First, then, through Yorkville, a self-consciously tony neighbour-hood of boutiques, bistros, and heavyset men smoking fat Cuban cigars on the wide terraces. There used to be a bookstore here, staffed by a woman called Gwyneth, whom I was in love with, and a man called Paul, an author whose work I admired and who later became a friend and fishing buddy, until cancer took him from us. I remember buying a copy of a book by J. D. Salinger there thirty years ago, then walking through light snow and twinkling lights to the subway that would make its long northward journey to the dull suburb where I lived.

It was my city's version of the Salinger twilight now, I realized, the "faintly soup quarter of an hour in New York when the street lights have just been turned on and the parking lights of cars are just getting turned on." This is the scene—maybe you know the one—where Seymour tells his brother Buddy not to aim at the other kid's marble, because *aiming* means he doesn't believe in the truth of striking the marble.[6] There is the bar where I confronted my first great love and begged her to take me back. She wouldn't, but then, when I was halfway around the world, she wrote me a letter regretting it that I carried with me for two years.

Now the park where, a long time after that, I stood in the rain with another beloved who was, alas, not the woman I was married to. We stood and talked, and kissed, as the rain soaked us through. A marriage ended.

Now an old tavern, a place where they have salt shakers on the rickety tables so you can refresh your flat glass of draft beer. Summer nights here, after pickup baseball games during college years and after, arguing and flirting and dancing to the Clash and the Jackson Five. Across the road to what used to be a concert hall: Toots and The Maytals, Los Lobos, lots of local talent. Then, years later, it was a TV studio where I met a famous hockey enforcer who was the sweetest man you can imagine, and where a tall gentlemanly quarterback, also famous, offered me a lift in his convertible.

What else? The train station that is now the largest wine and liquor store in the city. The now-abandoned offices of the publisher who accepted my first trade book, and where I dropped off the printed-out manuscript with an intense feeling of youthful triumph that would neither last nor ever return.

The little French bakery with those inimitable ham and butter baguettes. The all-night diner where we used to go for eggs and toast after finishing production on the college newspaper, in those days laid out on cardboard flats, using type scrolled in waxable sheets from a photomechanical typesetting machine as big as a rolltop desk. The pub that wryly commemorates a half-hearted rebellion in our peaceful, once parochial burg, an uprising whose energy petered out with the prospect of a cold beer.

Amazingly, not a single iPhone zombie blocked my path along the way. Maybe less amazingly, at least three times I passed youngsters smoking pot in open spaces. And so to the quiet bar where Charlie is waiting. A half hour of walking, a half century of life. The city gives us these textures, sometimes whether we like it or not.

2. Justice and Things

For Simmel, it seems as though everything distinctive about urban pleasure is an externality, but one conditioned by the dominant transactional economy. Patrick Turmel has argued, contrarily, that the problem with urban externalities is that they are unruly as well as ubiquitous. If we take the project of justice to be one in which citizens of a shared political space can make legitimate demands upon one another, including ones of redistribution, then the proliferation of externalities renders the prospect more distant.[7]

But is this correct? Suppose we view the superfluity of externalities in the city not as a problem to be solved—internalizing them, or some of them, in a just social contract—but instead as a kind of renewed opportunity for playful, spontaneous, and unplanned interaction. Now the stranger on the street is not a competitor for scarce goods within a fixed system, but rather a new player in an infinite game of free interchange.

The Situationist architect Constant Nieuwenhuys designed a city based on this concept of play. He called it New Babylon, with a deliberate wry reference to the ancient mythical city of polyglot excess. In New Babylon, citizens enact constantly renewed versions of the *dérive* advocated by Guy Debord and the other Situationist pioneers, recasting the planned routes and goal-driven byways of the city into opportunities for getting lost or finding oneself nowhere in particular. In the undirected movement of the *dérive*, one's own movements are themselves gifts of chance and randomness.[8]

"In a *dérive*," Debord says, "one or more persons during a certain period drop their usual motives for movement and action, their relations, their work and leisure activities, and let themselves be drawn by the attractions of the terrain and the encounters they find there."[9]

Increasingly this is a lost art, and a diminishing possibility within the city. In part, this is because we have lost the art of becoming strange to ourselves, artfully losing control over the world and our relation to it. Public action, once considered the highest expression of human life in what Hannah Arendt called "the space of appearances," is swapped out for willed isolation and technological swaddling of every imaginable kind.[10]

Consider, for example, the growing trend of the Internet of Things (IoT), wherein even the most banal appliance or material feature of everyday life will be linked with monitoring and surveillance technology, instantly communicating one with another. Simmel was correct about watches: they tell time, and so reinforce the tyranny of *mathesis* that is the modern time standard. But at least with watches we know what they do, and why. In IoT, our toasters and washing machines, our vehicles and clothes, become part of a comprehensive network of information-sharing that works, as with everything else associated with the internet, to reinforce corporate ownership. "The Internet of Things will connect every thing with everyone in an integrated global network," confidently predicts Jeremy Rifkin. "People, machines, natural resources, produc-tion lines, logistics networks, consumption habits, recycling flows, and virtually every other aspect of economic and social life will be linked via sensors and software to the IoT platform, continually feeding Big Data to every node—businesses, homes, vehicles—moment to moment, in real time." The result will be a post-capitalist economy in which coordi-nated systems "dramatically increase productivity, and reduce the mar-ginal cost of producing a full range of goods and services to near zero across the entire economy."[11]

Really? Surely we have good reason to doubt not just the viability but also the positive effects of any real-world version of an Internet of Things. In truth, under this new global-capital space-time regime—for that is what platform-feeding "nodes" amounts to—the impera-tives of unwanted convenience (why read a recipe from a book when you can have it read to you by your stove?) will merely reinforce an enmeshment with state institutions, private firms, and transnational rev-enue streams. One CEO, quoted in a news story on some of the coming advances in appliances, let slip the true message of IoT: "It can be hard to explain to consumers all the promise of a Web-connected dishwasher or washing machine, but [an executive at Whirlpool] said they're inevi-table."[12] Of course they are! That's what the new devices and upgraded models always are, the *avatars of inevitability*.

In this world of total control, the 24/7 availability of the person to the demands of transactions and devices, we are all seclusion but zero privacy. The essential insight about individual life—that its right to privacy is itself an achievement of public discourse—is obscured by use-value and disposability in all things. That includes, of course, ourselves. Now we consume not merely goods and services, or even experiences and desires, but the very idea of the self, cannibalized from within under the twinned signs of empty pleasure and technological mastery. "A 24/7 environment has the semblance of a social world," the critic Jonathan Crary writes, "but it is actually a non-social model of machinic performance and a suspension of living that does not disclose the human cost required to sustain its effectiveness."

Time itself has once more altered shape, now beyond the calculability and uniformity noted by Simmel. Crary argues that 24/7 time "must be distinguished from what Lukács and others in the early twentieth century identified as the empty, homogenous time of modernity, the metric or calendar time of nations, of finance and industry . . . What is new is the sweeping abandonment of the pretence that time is coupled to any long-term undertakings, even to fantasies of 'progress' or development."[13]

Note the irony. Once *sleep* was figured as the visage of drugged complacency, a trope of ideological self-dupery to be found in everything from Marx's notion of false consciousness to the resistance cry that features in John Carpenter's 1988 ideological-horror film *They Live*—a favourite of Slavoj Žižek—in which alien invaders tame susceptible earthlings by feeding them advertising slogans and consumer products ("They live, we sleep!"). Now, sleep is the last line of resistance against the relentless reach of time-bending technological immersion. But as so often, the ideological enemy works by stealth. "24/7 is a time of indifference," Crary notes, "against which the fragility of human life is increasingly inadequate and within which sleep has no necessity or inevitability."[14]

An old complaint, even if presented in new terms. Compare, for example, the critic Northrop Frye, writing in 1967 about the modern city. "To the modern imagination the city becomes increasingly something hideous and nightmarish, the *fourmillante cité* of Baudelaire, the 'unreal city' of Eliot's *Waste Land*, the *ville tentaculaire* of Verhaeren," Frye notes. "No longer a community, it seems more like a community turned inside out, with its expressways taking its thousands of self-enclosed nomadic units in a headlong flight into greater solitude, ants in the body of a dying dragon, breathing its polluted air and passing its polluted water."[15] And in this nightmarish city, the problems of time and privacy are already inscribed, even if they have not yet reached the 24/7 endgame. "The last stand of privacy has always been, traditionally, the inner mind," Frye argues. "It is quite possible however for communications media, especially the newer electronic ones, to break down the associative structures of the inner mind and replace them by the prefabricated structures of the media." *They live, we dream while awake!* And so: "A society controlled by their slogans and exhortations would be introverted, because nobody would be saying anything; there would only be echo, and Echo was the mistress of Narcissus."[16]

The point is not to condemn individual users, however; and the charge of *narcissism* is now no more than a part of the ritual exchange of hollowed-out social discourse, easily made and just as easily dismissed. No, the point is to give some urgency to the very idea of pleasure. Get lost in the city, my friends! Get lost to yourself and your routine desires! Become a stranger to yourself, and then engage with the strangers who walk, zombie-fashion, along our shared city streets. This is not New Babylon—which perhaps imagines more spontaneity than some of ús could easily stand—but it is the unexpected gift of genuine newness, rather than the pre-packaged novelties of techo-inevitability. The pleasures to be gained thereby will forever render the other kind into a sort of bad dream, time spent gazing at a hypnotic series of screens, revealed to be no more than funhouse mirrors—but with elaborate profit structures attached to them.

Out of the funhouse, into the sun! And then, when we choose, the blessed refuge of sleep.

Notes

1 Georg Simmel, "The Metropolis and Mental Life," in *The Blackwell City Reader*, eds. Gary Bridge and Sophie Watson (Wiley-Blackwell, 2010), 11.

2 Ibid., 14, 12.

3 Ibid., 13.

4 See, for example, Lewis Hyde, *The Gift: Imagination and the Erotic Life of Property* (Vintage, 1979).

5 See Martin Heidegger, *Being and Time*, trans. John Macquarrie and Edward Robinson (Harper & Row, 1962), 364 ff.

6 J. D. Salinger, *Raise High the Roof Beam, Carpenters and Seymour: An Introduction* (Bantam, 1965), 201-3. Here is the key, Zen-like passage: "'Could you try not aiming so much?' he asked me, still standing there. 'If you hit him when you aim, it'll

just be luck.' He was speaking, communicating, and yet not breaking the spell. *I* then broke it. Quite deliberately. 'How can it be *luck* if I *aim*?' I said back to him, not loud (despite the italics) but with rather more irritation in my voice than I was actually feeling. He didn't say anything for a moment but simply stood balanced on the curb, looking at me, I knew imperfectly, with love. 'Because it will be,' he said. 'You'll be *glad* if you hit his marble—Ira's marble—won't you? Won't you be *glad*? And if you're *glad* when you hit somebody's marble, then you sort of secretly didn't expect too much to do it. So there'd have to be some luck in it, there'd have to be slightly quite a lot of *ac*cident in it.'"

7   See Patrick Turmel, "The City as Public Space," in eds. Mark Kingwell and Patrick Turmel, *Rites of Way: The Politics and Poetics of Public Space* (Wilfrid Laurier University Press, 2009), 151-64.

8   I discuss Constant's design in relation to contemporary architecture in Kingwell, "Building Cities, Making Friends: A Meditation, in Five General Propositions," *Queen's Quarterly* 119:3 (Fall 2012); 359-77; reprinted in eds. Stephen Marche and Christopher Doda, *Best Canadian Essays 2013* (Tightrope Books, 2013), 90-104.

9   From Guy Debord, "Theory of the Dérive," *Les Lèvres Nues* 9 (November 1956); reprinted in *Internationale Situationniste* 2 (December 1958); trans. Ken Knabb, is at http://www.cddc.vt.edu/sionline/si/theory.html

10   See Hannah Arendt, *The Human Condition*, 2nd Ed. (University of Chicago Press, 1998); for deft and provocative application of Arendt's idea to architecture and urbanism, see George Baird, *The Space of Appearance* (MIT Press, 1995).

11   Quoted in Sue Halpern, "The Creepy New Wave of the Internet," *The New York Review of Books*, November 20, 2014. The article is review of new books about IoT by Rifkin, David Rose, Robert Scobie and Shel Israel, and Jim Dwyer.

12   Quoted in Scott Feschuk, *The Future and Why We Should Avoid It* (Douglas & McIntyre, 2014), 16.

13   Jonathan Crary, *24/7: Late Capitalism and the Ends of Sleep* (Verso, 2013), 9.

14   Ibid., 9.

15   Northrop Frye, *The Modern Century* (Oxford University Press, 1967), 37.

16   Ibid., 38.

Hotel Bars and
the Female Cruise

I USED TO WRITE a magazine column about cocktails, no bad antidote to the rabbit-hole that is professional philosophy. Each month I picked a drink or a theme and dilated on its appeal and heritage in movies and books. Especially books. Many of the cherished books of my adolescence and early adulthood—the crazy-paved walkway of Wodehouse, Chandler, Waugh, and Amis that led me wherever it was I was going—were littered with drinks of a provenance and detail no longer common. Everybody knows what a martini is, even if they don't drink them, but not everybody has even considered what it would be like to have a Jack Dempsey offered him by the judgmental father of a girlfriend, as one Kingsley Amis character must. Gimlets and gibsons are very different drinks, despite the fact that Philip Marlowe favours both at different stages in his long gumshoe career. I wouldn't claim that literature taught me how to drink—that particular class was conducted by experience, over many years—but these books gave me a sense of what drinking is like for people who like to drink.

I mention this drinks column because I found that, more often than not, writing about drinks made me think not just of bars—no surprise there—but especially of hotel bars. One reason is obvious. If the bar *simpliciter* offers you the chance to have someone mix you the perfect drink, served with some ceremony and grace, then the hotel bar offers that plus the chance of random encounters with strangers from out of town. So much the better, you may be the stranger from out of town. When I was still a young man my father tried to explain to me why he liked bars so much—that is, apart from the getting drunk in them part, which he liked a little too much for his own good. "Great people-watching," he said.

Bars are crucibles of human behaviour in a form more accessible than most: more concentrated than a golf course, more exposed than a marriage, more intense than a sporting event. How people present themselves in public is always fascinating; how those presentations dissolve in alcohol is all the more so. But the hotel bar, like the hotel to which it is a necessary appendage, adds to these a potent brew of transience, anonymity, freshness, sexiness, and that most elusive of human desire-drivers, narrative possibility. Everyone who enters a hotel bar has a story to tell. Everyone is on their way somewhere. Everyone, even the locals who frequent it the way writers still haunt the Roof Lounge at Toronto's Park Hyatt Hotel (once the Park Plaza and still so for some of us), comes there looking for something. Pour all that over ice, shake vigorously, and serve up with a twist. You can always get a room . . .

*   *   *

Like all people who patronize bars, I keep a mental list of favourite spots. A disproportionate section of mine seem to lie in hotels. High hotel bars might form a special sub-category: the Roof, with its gallery of Donato caricatures featuring literary celebrities from a bygone era, when it was an altogether more shabby venue; the two sky-high bars in the Shanghai Grand Hyatt, Jin Mao: one a smokey lobby jazz bar on the fifty-fourth floor, the other an evil-genius' dark eyrie in the eaves of the eighty-ninth; the Top of the Mark in the Mark Hopkins Hotel, San Francisco—the hotel, if not the bar, makes an appearance in *Bullitt* (1968)—where one Valentine's Day I watched the bay fog roll into and over the town like a tidal wave of white swarming a love that, though I didn't yet know it, was fast receding.

At ground level, the lobby bar of the Palmer House Hilton down inside Chicago's Loop, which commands an unimprovable view of the vaulted ceiling and its Wedgwood-style plaster medallions. The bar in the Park Lane Hotel, London, where I got undergraduate-tipsy with the hard-drinking ex-military aircraft salesmen that formed my father's professional coterie circa 1983. The bar in the Hotel Duxton, Perth, where I sat with Maureen Dowd, resplendent in new Ugg boots and on tour with her book *Are Men Necessary?*, as she tried to pick up the strapping Australian waiter. The Ritz Hotel bar in Paris is Hemingway- and Fitzgerald-fabled, but somehow disappointing when you actually get there, despite (or because of) the layering of appearances in everything from two different Audrey Hepburn tryst movies—*Love in the Afternoon* (1957, with Gary Cooper) and *How to Steal a Million* (1966, with Peter O'Toole)—to the supermodel-turned-terrorists of Easton Ellis's novel *Glamorama*, who wear Kevlar-lined Armani suits, blow up 747s, and destroy the hotel with a home-made bomb. The recent reno, directed by new owner Mohammed al-Fayed, has made it more a Hollywood haunt than a literary landmark.

Not disappointing, to me anyway, is the cozy Ritz-Carlton bar in Montreal, where Mordecai Richler liked to mark the end of his days and where he once got into an argument, perhaps an actual fist fight, with someone, possibly former premier Bernard Landry, irritated by Richler's anti-PQ screed in the *New Yorker*.

The dark, moody Oak Bar in the Peace Hotel on Shanghai's Bund: they say Nöel Coward drank and wrote *Private Lives* here. At the other Oak Bar, in the Copley Plaza in Boston, they bring your cocktail in its own little carafe and ice bucket, so you can refresh the glass at will. But Boston's literary reputation clusters around the older Parker House, near the State House, where Dickens stayed during a lecture tour (giving the first American reading of "A Christmas Carol"), the *Atlantic Monthly* was conceived, Emerson and Hawthorne argued with Oliver Wendell Holmes, and Longfellow drafted what would become "Paul Revere's Ride."

The other other Oak Room Bar of the Algonquin Hotel, on Forty-Fourth Street in Manhattan, needs no defence as a crucible of literature, but the good news is that, though self-conscious and a little out-of-town chic, it still offers quick service, big drinks, and lots of salty snacks—the necessary conditions of any good hotel bar. And the Blue Bar, through the archway, is even better. The last time I was there a huge man with a shaven head, unselfconsciously sporting a white Toronto Maple Leafs "away" jersey, sat next to me and celebrated a rare Buds thumping of the Rangers with four birdbath-sized gibsons. The two of us then proceeded to steal large quantities of the bar's novelty cocktails napkins, which are adorned with a martini glass and Robert Benchley's line about getting out of these wet clothes and into a dry martini.

Alas, farther downtown, no such luck for the dilapidated-genteel bar of the Gramercy Park Hotel, which was featured in *Almost Famous* (2000), once a superb hangout but now boutiqued beyond recognition.

The large tumblers of gin, bowls of goldfish crackers, decrepit waiters, old-lady regulars, and small television set are all a distant memory in the current boho-glam of the candlelit Jade Bar.

The other other *other* Oak Bar is of course the one in the now-condo-revised Plaza Hotel at the southeast corner of Central Park, on Grand Army Plaza. The hotel as a whole appears often, as any Manhattan landmark should. Robert Redford and Jane Fonda spend their insatiable honeymoon there in *Barefoot in the Park* (1967), hardly venturing outside for a week, and Redford at least returns there for a scene with Barbra Streisand in *The Way We Were* (1973)—thus prompting, in the standard fashion, an awkward tribute during an episode of *Sex and the City*. Streisand herself had been there in between, in 1968's *Funny Girl*. Neil Simon's three-vignette comedy *Plaza Suite*—its Broadway premiere was on Valentine's Day, 1968—is obviously set there, in room 719 to be precise, as are Kay Thompson's *Eloise at the Plaza*, the book that launched a thousand-and-one girlish fantasies about life in New York. Eloise, being six years old, eats and charges meals at the Palm Court or to her room "on the top floor," but to my knowledge never patronizes the bar.

*   *   *

This bar is famous is more than the usual way. Cinephiles will know that the Oak Bar is the precise pivot of Alfred Hitchcock's *North by Northwest* (1959), for it is here that Cary Grant's Roger Thornhill, rising on an impulse to wire his mother, is mistaken for the fictitious government agent George Kaplan. The error sets in motion the entire sequence of unlikely events that follow, from the attempted murder-by-drink out on Long Island to the pulse-quickening climax on the rocky shelves of Mount Rushmore. The Oak Bar is the perfect place for mistaken identity. Thornhill, a well-known Madison Avenue advertising executive, is a regular there—but the two goons sent to eliminate Kaplan don't know that, or him. Everything follows from that moment when Mr. Roger Thornhill stands up to send a telegram even as the page is calling for Mr. George Kaplan to receive one.

The film had another key scene which does not take place in a hotel bar, but in the logical extension thereof—alas now almost disappeared—the dining car of a train (though, to be precise, the club car would be a more complete analogue). Fleeing police after a false murder implication,

Thornhill ducks onto a trans-continental train at Grand Central, incidentally looking cutting-edge as well as elegant in what must surely be Ray-Ban sunglasses. Hiding in the dining car is clever, since it, along with the club car, is the only place on a train that a person without a seat or berth can appear above suspicion. Added bonus: this place of transient meetings and random encounters is itself transient, the sun setting along the west shore of the Hudson as the train hurtles its way north out of the city and then northwest toward Chicago and South Dakota.

Thornhill finds himself seated across from Eve Kendall—Eva Marie Saint, who never looked better. He orders a gibson, which arrives in a tiny glass containing perhaps a quarter of what you would get at the Blue Bar, or any bar in New York. (The proverbial "three-martini lunch" is put in perspective knowing that drinks used to be much smaller.) The ensuing banter-exchange, in which Eve not so subtly throws herself at Thornhill and offers him the very thing he most craves, a bed for the night, is a masterpiece of a tiny sub-genre so far underanalyzed by film scholars, the smooth but aggressive pick-up of man by woman: the female cruise. The scoop is complicated in the present instance by the fact that Kendal is working for both the government agency that set up fictitious Kaplan and Phillip Vandamm, the urbane communist villain played by James Mason. She is also, to be sure, falling in love with Thornhill. Increasingly as the film progresses, she's operating as an unwilling triple agent.

It is no surprise that several of these pick-up scenes involve Grant, anybody's idea of desirable leading man but also known for his gentility, even fastidiousness. Thus the drama. The idea of a woman trying to cruise Clark Gable or Humphrey Bogart is not just skewed but almost perverse, unimaginable. They do the cruising. But not so with Grant.

And so four years before that train left Manhattan, audiences had seen him as a reformed jewel thief and Resistance hero being insistently pursued along the French Riviera by the much younger Grace Kelly in another Hitchcock caper, *To Catch A Thief* (1955); and then, in 1963, by Audrey Hepburn, taking turns as kooky or desperate, in Stanley Donen's very Hitchcockian *Charade*. Grant's character in the last is another mysterious dark stranger, in this case sporting at least five different names, but Hepburn's Reggie Lampert, in contrast to the Saint and Kelly ~~girls~~ women, is as innocent as she seems. It is a nice, if creepy, detail that the same actor, Jessie Royce Landis, plays Grace Kelly's mother in *To Catch a Thief* and then Cary Grant's in *North by Northwest*—in both cases as a rapacious and unattached woman of the world, in the latter case easily bribed when her own son twitches a dollar bill in her face.

Hepburn had already gone after the older Fred Astaire in *Funny Face* (1957). Jo Stockton, nerdy and bookish, indulges an adolescent Greenwich Village crush on the French scion of the philosophical school called Empathicalism, Professor Emile Flostre. He, naturally, is a womanizing cad, spouting Rive Gauche nonsense to get chicks into bed, while Fred's Dick Avery, though employed by the transient world of magazines, is a steadier guy—and a better dancer. Jo, already transformed from frump to frou-frou, resets her heart's compass from philosophy to fashion. She does not seem to mind, or even acknowledge, that she, as played by Hepburn, is a luminous twenty-eight to Astaire's well-seasoned if spry fifty-eight years. (Yes, he was born in the nineteenth century—just.) But the female cruise is not always a younger woman pursuing an older man, that staple of male self-regard.

*   *   *

Consider one of the most aggressive cruises in American cinema, Gloria Swanson's conquest of William Holden, as Nora Desmond and Joe Gillis respectively, in Billy Wilder's *Sunset Boulevard*. Released in 1950, this classic film is not just brutal commentary on Hollywood's trashing of its own flyblown stars; it is also an agenda-setting polemic about gender politics. Once again an accident brings a mostly innocent man into contact with a dark world he does not understand.

Gillis, hard up for cash and on the run from creditors, blows out a tire and ducks into the driveway of a spooky Los Angeles mansion. Mistaken for the man sent to collect a dead pet monkey, he is soon drawn into Nora's hysterical fantasy world of past glories and future comebacks. She gets him into bed with a combination of outlandish spending on clothes and trinkets—standard operating procedure for the cougar on the prowl—and attempted suicide. If the callow young woman is no match for the poise of the mature older man, as the other films suggest, the cocky young man is a plaything in the face of a crazy—or just lustful—old lady. Gillis dies in the mansion's pool, and the justly famous opening scene of the film, all told in flashback, features a noirish voice-over of Gillis cynically regarding his own corpse floating face down in the water, shot through the back.

Dustin Hoffman's Benjamin Braddock, in *The Graduate* (1967), fares a little better with the predatory Mrs. Robinson: he ends the movie alive and carrying off the age-appropriate daughter, Elaine (Katharine Ross, doe-eyed as always). Mrs. Robinson is a role that Anne Bancroft owns so completely it comes as a shock to realize that director Mike Nichols initially considered both Marilyn Monroe and Doris Day. Another option, Patricia Neal, would have been good—she had installed George Peppard as kept boy/aspiring author Paul Jarvik alongside callgirl Audrey Hepburn in *Breakfast at Tiffany's* (1961)—but she had recently been felled by a stroke. Nichols also wanted Warren Beatty or Robert Redford to play Ben, either of which would have made better sense of the character's alleged success as a track star, not to mention Mrs. Robinson's obvious sexual hunger; but at the same time it would have nullified the Roth-inflected visual awkwardness of the liaison. Hoffman, portraying a California bourgeois home from a successful degree at Williams College, looks incongruously Jewish, like Neil Klugman invited to a party around somebody else's swimming pool.

[handwritten margin note: She died in 1963]

Speaking of awkward, that's just what Ben is, and cringingly so, when he first meets Mrs. R at—where else?—the bar of the Taft Hotel. It is not the Knickerbocker, as some sources claim, that once-resplendent trysting place of Joe DiMaggio and Marilyn Monroe, haunt of Elvis Presley while filming *Love Me Tender* and D. W. Griffiths when he was down and out, later a dive and needle-den, and now a seniors' home. And in fact the scenes were filmed at another hotel altogether, the Ambassador, where Robert F. Kennedy would be assassinated a year after the film was released. The script, in any event, specifies the Taft.

This particular hotel-bar scene is seared on the memories of more than one generation of young men, who can only sympathize silently with Ben's ineffectual attempts to hail a waiter, appear suave and in command, or even retain his lunch as leopard-skin-clad Mrs. Robinson, a self-assured alcoholic, snaps her fingers for a drink and the check together, and twits him for not arranging a room more smoothly. But that discomfort is as nothing compared to his bumbling dialogue as she undresses later in the room, where he offers her a choice of a wire or wood hanger, because "they have both." She finally maneuvers him past his own misgivings by wondering if this is his first time, and then referring repeatedly to his "inadequacy"—a gambit, let it be said, that will work with most men under twenty-five. (Hoffman, playing twenty-one, was actually twenty-nine; Bancroft, supposedly in her forties, was thirty-five and stunning.)

These early scenes can almost make you forgive Ben for the brutally conformist message that is delivered under cover of *prima facie* satire and that seductive Simon and Garfunkel soundtrack. As Roger Ebert has noted, we happily watch Ben and Elaine ride off in the bus, he avoiding her mom and she avoiding the doofus frat-boy fiancé, but their stunned final glances at each other are ambiguous. Really, how long will it be before Ben is moving up in the world of plastics? Elaine was the match his parents wanted, after all. Another victory for bourgeois righteousness and biofascist norms. And so much for sexually frustrated middle-aged women.

*   *   *

Sometimes, though, you meet the right guy or girl on that train or in that hotel bar. In *The Manchurian Candidate* (1962), Frank Sinatra's tortured Korean War veteran Bennett Marco, unknowingly brainwashed by the enemy as part of an elaborate assassination scheme, is met by Eugénie Rose Chaney, a smart Janet Leigh. Their dialogue, drawn without much alteration from the original Richard Condon novel, survives as a series of charged non sequiturs in John Frankenheimer's script:

> "Maryland's a beautiful state," she says to Bennett as they meet between cars, he so shaky he could not light his own cigarette.
> "This is Delaware."
> "I know. I was one of the Chinese workmen who the laid the track on this stretch. But, um ... nonetheless, Maryland is a beautiful state. So is Ohio, for that matter."
> "I guess so. Columbus is a tremendous football town."

Which might all be parsed as standard first-date chit-chat, except for the recurrence in the scene of an odd question, voiced once by each of them:

> "Are you Arabic?"
> "No."
> "My name is Ben. It's really Bennett. I was named after Arnold Bennett."

"The writer?"

"No. A lieutenant colonel. He was my father's commanding officer at the time."

"What's your last name?"

"Marco. Major Marco."

"Are you Arabic?"

"No. No . . ."

"Let me put it another way. Are you married?"

He is not. Neither is she—though she *is* engaged, a fact we find out later, when she has dumped the fiancé in favour of Ben.

The banter here has a cast of interrogation, recruitment, code, and veiled identity. Each is inquiring and being inquired of; each is protecting and probing at once. The political and personal overlap and entangle: is Rosie looking for a date or activating another sleeper assassin, as the evil Angela Lansbury does with her stepson, Raymond (Laurence Harvey), using the notorious queen-of-diamonds trigger? The Arabic line, which had reference in the novel, where Rosie's features are described as exotic and Marco's thoughts are preoccupied with Middle East intelligence issues, now floats free of its specific context and acquires a payload of pregnant non-signification. It substitutes for the main question that hangs, unasked, over the encounter, namely the issue of personal availability and trust.[1] Each agent in this hypnotic encounter within a film about hypnosis, paranoia, and uncanniness, is delicately *fronting*—Hepburn makes a convincing case for the links between gay self-presentation and the multi-layered demands of the spy in public—and each is afraid to let too much vulnerability, or indeed strength, show through.

It does not happen at the bar, and a train is not a hotel, but this exchange between cars on a train, a cigarette-lit passage in the middle of the most comprehensively realized political satire and thriller ever made in the United States—a potent mix of betrayal and hypnosis and fear, a "Freudian cocktail," as one critic has called it, of desire and pathology and deception, not to mention the cocktail of barbiturates and suggestives injected for the brainwashing—this entire, arguably dispensable love-interest subplot, which is in fact nothing of the kind but instead the film's cruising heart, marks the quirky triumph of love over experience, itself a study in transience, arrivals and departures, check ins and check outs.

I will end more or less where I began—with the kind of thing I used to do in the cocktail column—like this: Did you know there is a drink called The Manchurian Candidate? I am not making this up. You are not being hypnotized. Tell the hotel barman what you need. You will need one shot of vodka, and make it Stolichnaya so you can incidentally appreciate that superb Constructivist label. Then one dash of soy sauce, and again, if you have any sense, use either Chinese (Pearl River) or Korean (Sempio). Yes, you may have to bring your own. Have the bartender take a chilled shot glass from the freezer, where they should keep them on ice, like prisoners. Fill it with the vodka. Add a dash of soy sauce. Drink quickly.

Repeat as necessary.

Notes

1 For more on these themes, see Hepburn, *Intrigue: Espionage and Culture* (Yale University Press, 2005), especially the final chapter. Hepburn notes that, in Condon's novel, Ben, now a military analyst rather than a combat solider, is "thinking of Muslim women" when he first speaks to Rosie, highlighting the Arabic line of questioning. "The strangeness of the scene in the film depends on its relation to the semiotics of recruitment, which is not the case in the novel" (301). This is one reason why complaints that Frankenheimer ought to have altered the script are misplaced: the retention, apparently obscure, heightens the overall tone of the film.

Building Cities, Making Friends:

A Meditation in Five General Propositions

"Like a bad concert hall, affective space contains dead spots
where the sound fails to circulate. . . . The perfect interlocutor,
the friend, is he not the one who constructs around you the
greatest possible resonance? Cannot friendship be defined
as a space with total sonority?"

— ROLAND BARTHES, *A Lover's Discourse*[1]

I AM MUCH TAKEN with this image from Barthes's poignant, fragmentary, nuanced engagement with the plight of the lover, stranded at the limits of language. All love is a kind of wish, and here we see the core of all human longing, the desire for someone who will listen. There is no better figure of friendship than the implied construction of the good concert hall, the one where there are no dead spots, where I am always heard because you, the friend, have created a space so sonorous and resonant that my merest whisper is heard in the rear balcony.

Friendship, especially of the intimate sort that Barthes has in mind for the lover, may seem an odd keynote for a discussion of urbanism and architecture. But I want to suggest that the prospect of such intimacy, the space of total sonority, is the regulative ideal of all great cities, the goal, perhaps finally unreachable, towards which all effort is aimed. The construction of a resonance that allows each one of us to know that we are heard, that we have a friend in the existence of the city itself.

The image is resonant in another, more obvious way in the current context, of course, because the impressively varied practice of KPMB Architects now includes one of the best, most resonant concert halls to be found in the city where I live, Koerner Hall, part of the Royal Conservatory of Music renovation of 2009. I was able to visit the site of this construction before it was completed, and climbed the scaffolded height to stand inside what would eventually become the elaborate wave-wood ceiling of this exemplary space. That is, I was able to stand inside one of the design elements that make for sonority, that enable resonance, in the finished hall. That moment of suspension within a not-yet-finished architectural project remains, for me, a crystallized memory of what it means to build a city, to create the material conditions of shared dwelling. And now, when I step into the hall's lobby, which floats over Philosopher's Walk and embraces downtown Toronto as if we were in a living room—or a shared playground—I see again the genius of this design.

The meditative origins, the warm materials palette, the creation of a community space and not just a building: these traits are characteristic of the KPMB practice. More than any other firm, they have sounded the keynote of urban renewal in Toronto, their home base. But projects in other cities and towns are equally significant makers of sonority. If we believe, with Aristotle, that a just city must be, in some sense, a city of friends, the architectural interventions of KPMB are more than commissions or projects; they are exercises in civic humanism. Buildings become, in effect, miniature cities, gathering their surrounding spaces, large and small, unto themselves. From the modified college cloister of the CIGI Campus in Waterloo, Ontario (2011), with its stunning canti-levered entrance and warm interior spaces for conversation and instruc-tion, and which converts the loose edge of a small town into a vibrant urban site, to the capacious Vaughan Civic Centre (2011), the National Ballet School (2005), the renovated Gardiner Ceramics Museum (2006), and the Bell TIFF Bell Lightbox (2011), we observe again and again the material conditions of community.

By that phrase I mean at least the following five necessary features of city building: (1) a strong connection to existing urban geography—even if, as in the Vaughan project, for example, the surrounding area is anti-aesthetic or bare; (2) the artful reinterpretation of traditional elements and forms (the courtyard, the quad, the bell tower, the cafe); (3) the creation of public space within buildings as well as between them, forming interior crucibles of shared citizenship; (4) program design that makes for frequent mixing and social interplay; and, perhaps above all, (5) a sense of play, the ability to create spontaneous situations and encounters among people, to achieve even in workmanlike spaces a creative, non-utilitarian *dérive*—a drift.[2]

Since these five features may seem obvious, even as their realization is in fact far from common, allow me to expand on them with a series of expansive theses which I believe the city-building practice of KPMB brings to our attention. Thus a meditation, philosophical and architectural, in the form of five general propositions . . .

General Proposition No. 1:
The city is a philosophical extension of the human person.

This proposition is valid along at least two distinct vectors. First, the city is an extension of human action in the same way that Marshall McLuhan meant when he said that communications media are "extensions of man." Media enable a routine transcendence of the limitations which inhere in the human sensorium. Unaided, I can see only what is revealed to my eyes, hear only what lies within range of my ears, and so on. But with the aid of a telephone, or a television, or a telegraph—with, to be sure, a computer or tablet but also, for that matter, with smoke signals or a cane—I can experience a vastly expanded range of possible stimuli beyond my meagre bodily range: events, stories, intimacies. Media offer us an extended body, a body stretched and attenuated across large distances in space and time.

The built environment of the city is, by the same logic, a massive and complex extension of the human body. It allows me precisely to pursue all the bodily tasks of human life that make for the complex achievement of personhood: to shelter and work; to move and interact; to eat and drink; to remember and forget; to live, love, and die. Not all of its extensions are strictly sensory, as in communications media as such; instead, the city is what we might call the ur-medium, or super-extension of man. The city offers ways of getting somewhere, places to get to, places that are neither here nor there. The person, in the form of his or her body, perforce negotiates these spaces on a daily basis—and so comes into contact with other persons, other bodies, doing the same. The city is thus the physical manifestation of our desires and purposes, both responsive to what we think we want and constraining, shaping, of what we come to want.

It has been a commonplace at least since Aristotle (him again!) that first we create cities, and then they create us. Winston Churchill's much-quoted line to the same effect, where the term "buildings" appears in the place of "cities," is both less general and offered without proper provenance. He is not wrong, but the deeper point—the point that lurks in Aristotle's sense of the city as an expression of organic norms encoded in the natural and social world (really there is no bright division between them)—is that buildings affect other buildings as well as affecting people. Cities are composed of complexes of desire, not all of which are entirely conscious at the level of the individual user or even the creator of buildings.[3]

The general proposition is valid in another, perhaps less obvious sense, however. It is related to the first but requires a little more philosophical flexibility to accept. It is this: the city is, like the human person, subject to a version of the mind-body problem. That problem, with us since Descartes, concerns that apparently mysterious causal linkage between one substance, the mind, which is wholly immaterial, with another, the body, which is wholly non-mental. (The Homer Simpson version goes like this: "Mind? No matter. Matter? Never mind.") How is it possible that the human person, apparently possessed, somehow, of both a distinct mind and an ambulatory body, is able to function? On the premise of two distinct substances, this should not be possible; and yet, the evidence is overwhelmingly in favour of its being not only possible, but trivial. People do things each and every day, blithely unaware that there is any problem at all concerning the interaction of the mental and the material.

We need not tarry here with Descartes' proposed solution to the problem (a neatly evasive reference to a mysterious substance-interface performed in the pineal gland) nor with the many decades, indeed centuries, of debate that this problem has spawned. What we can do, instead, is note that there is a rather obvious solution to the mind-body problem, which is in fact a dissolution: the premise of two wholly distinct substances is flawed from the start. Human consciousness is not, despite philosophers' long-standing penchant for abstraction and out-of-body thought experiments, ever divorced from its embodiment; by the same token, the human body is not best conceived as some inanimate machine which receives a jolt of life from the ghostly inhabitation of mental activity. This point can be made as a matter of logic, as Gilbert Ryle did (his dismissive phrase "the ghost in the machine" for the Cartesian orthodoxy is deployed in my previous sentence).[4] It can also be made positively, via the introduction of an alternative view.

There are several such alternatives, but the most persuasive is some version of what has come to be called phenomenology. On this view, it is impossible to conceive of human consciousness without an awareness of the facts of embodiment. Consciousness just is a sense of being somewhere, in place; that complex immersion of self within a horizon of spatial and temporal awareness. To be myself (to be anyone at all) is to presuppose, as a condition of life's possibility, a sense of in front and behind, here and there, then and now. That premise—and not some division of substances manufactured in the laboratory of runaway meditation—is the philosophically significant fact about human persons. And it is realized in a host of daily actions and experiences, from the skillful but mostly implicit negotiation of myself through a doorway—together with the loss of memory that such a threshold-crossing may entail!—to the complex bobbing and weaving required to traverse a busy sidewalk or rail-station concourse.[5]

We may seem to have wandered some distance from cities, and architecture, and architects. But not really. For a city entertains and then solves—or rather, dissolves—its own version of the mind-body problem in just the same way. A city is not reducible just to its built forms: on the analogy, its matter, or "body." But neither is the city merely the sum total of its citizens and their desires: again, per analogy, its consciousness or "mind." And just as neither of these reductions can be validly enacted, since each limits the reality of the city as a living thing, an achievement, it is likewise the case that the city is not best conceived as some troubled interaction between the two aspects. Indeed, the sense of division between built forms and citizen-desires is precisely the premise that requires dismissal. Phenomenology sees the human person as embodied consciousness; good urban theory views the city the same way.[6]

General Proposition No. 2:
The architect is an instinctive phenomenologist of the city.

Architecture concerns the unfinished text of the city: the city is never over, always begun anew, is ever layered. Architecture creates public space even when its projects are nominally private—an office building rather than a park or institution—because the architect's intervention is made within the shared fabric of the city. That noun "fabric," so often used without full awareness, creates a trace of meaning worth following, a thread to tease out: a fabric is not just textile but, instead, any made thing, that which is fabricated. The shared urban fabric is the making, the project, which engages and concerns us all. The city, the made thing which we inhabit, is our collective project. But the architect has a special status within this shared fabrication.

That master of the paradoxical thought, Pascal, said this about our status as thinking reeds: "the most feeble thing in nature," but blessed with the significant, indeed transcendent ability to consider ourselves: "It is not from space that I must seek my dignity, but from the government of my thought. I shall have no more if I possess worlds. By space, the universe envelops me and swallows me up like a point; by thought, I envelop the world."[7] Here consciousness flies out and back in an instant, and the occupation of space is revealed for what it is: a speculation by consciousness about consciousness, a thought about the very fact of thinking. This moment of reflection—which is the moment in which consciousness experiences itself as self—is architecture's business and highest achievement.

But (one might object) surely architecture is about solving technical issues in the deployment of space, heating and cooling and program, the negotiation of site and client desire? Of course it is. But to what purpose? If architecture is not a form of speculation about life, the occasion for thought, it has failed its ultimate mission. That is why, contrary to the usual narratives of ego and mannerism, the real objections to signature style or grand formalist gestures in an architect are not about humility, but instead concern rigour of thought. The architect who indulges style over conversation—with the adjacent buildings and streets, with the citizens, with the city—has failed to engage the philosophical responsibilities of the architect. He or she may have failed other responsibilities as well—aesthetic, political, ethical—but these are predicated on the more basic failure to think.

One therefore looks at this urban thought in action—in Concordia University's integrated complex combining faculties for engineering, computer sciences, visual arts and business (2005 and 2010), for example, with its deft vertical integration of an otherwise inchoate campus stranded in a downtown neighbourhood that has heretofore lacked a coherent identity—and feels a power of thoughtful consideration, the way design is executed at the service of community and use. Other campus projects—for Centennial and George Brown colleges (2004 and 2012), future works at M.I.T., Princeton, and Northwestern universities—demonstrate the same sensitivity to gathering and listening. Indeed, we might say that here campus and city become specular partners: the urban college or university folded into the city surround, but also the isolated campus made into a miniature city.

Campus in Latin means field, and the first university campuses were not quads and towers but the fields on which they sat; now, a campus is a field of thought, a field of possibility, at once delineated and opened by the built forms in which we work, speculate, and converse. Discourse, realized in matter, enabling discourse.

General Proposition No. 3:
Not all great architecture is great urban architecture.

The reason for this distinction should be obvious. There are great architects and (it follows) great buildings that do not concern themselves with city building. Such buildings may inhabit cities, or stand in their precincts, but they do not engage and converse with the city. Hence these are buildings that do not build the city—they are not part of its shared fabric. It is possible for such buildings to be monuments, in Aldo Rossi's sense, but only in the somewhat violent sense that they take up and redistribute the existing surround without regard for its history of effects. We might, indeed, distinguish here between violent monuments and benign ones, the latter embodying more of Rossi's argument that a city could be memorialized and extended by the monumental in architecture.[8]

Thus, one might include in the former, violent category such examples as the Eiffel Tower in Paris and Daniel Libeskind's Michael Lee-Chin Crystal renovation of the Royal Ontario Museum in Toronto, and in the latter category the Empire State Building in Manhattan and, in Toronto, the John P. Robarts Research Library. Note that the distinction is not a function of modest elevation or of accommodating style: the Empire State soars but nevertheless manages to engage and (we might say) shelter its island home; the concrete brutalist mass of Robarts is surprisingly warm, even welcoming. The affectionate nickname it has earned from students at the University of Toronto—Fort Book—communicates benign monumentality better than any amount of theoretical discourse.[9]

The conclusion I mean to derive from these rather tendentious examples (for what examples are not tendentious when we speak of architecture and theory?) is that sometimes, maybe often, the "bold" or "original" architectural statement is precisely the one that does not succeed in building the city. There is surely a place for signature buildings and insistent gestural design in all great cities—one might even argue that no city can be truly great without the spirited conversation, or controversy, that inevitably erupts around such buildings. But they do not, themselves, make the city; in fact, they are parasitic upon another kind of architectural genius, namely the sort which intervenes in and subtly extends existing conversations, not splashing but rippling the waters of urban life.

Pedestrians may not stop on the street to take photographs of such buildings, but one must concede at a certain point that this is the point. A photographed building may be a mere oddity, a sport, a folly. More nuanced regard may be present in the form of quiet approval, pleasant engagement, calm beauty. This is the stillness of perfect form, which yet works a sly magic on the viewer and user, stretching the boundaries of consciousness in ways more powerful for being less jarring.

General Proposition No. 4:
Urban architecture is, above all, the creation of place.

There is a line from David Young's play *Inexpressible Island*, about the bare survival of a Royal Navy expedition to Antarctica, that has stayed with me since I saw the original production in 1997. In the drama, based on historical events, six men are lost in the extreme landscape near the South Pole at the same time that Robert Scott's ill-fated Terra Nova expedition is perishing of cold and starvation. The six figures in the play will all survive, barely, the brutal eight months of winter, only to find their story overshadowed by the harrowing tale of Scott's failure. The play is about many things, including class and spirituality, but mostly it shows the weirdly inspired madness that can descend on human beings undergoing desperate conditions of life. Towards the end of the winter, the small unit's medical officer, Dr. Levick, descends into a kind of philosophical delirium.

"Nature, in the form of man, begins to recognize itself," Levick says, ostensibly to his command officer, Lieutenant Campbell, but really to himself. "That's what we're doing here in the South, Lieutenant. We are all artists, of a kind. We are giving nature back to herself." And, later: "As much as anything that's what has carried us here on this pilgrimage. The South Pole is an idea. A place that is no place. The final nothing."[10]

There is much to consider in these lines, as in the whole play. The South Pole is an abstraction, a notional point created only by the world-defining Cartesian geometry of the Mercator Projection. It is both real and not real: a place that is not a place, something that does not exist for humans yet can be fixed, and visited for the first time (as we know, it would be Scott's tragedy to find that Norwegian rival Roald Amundsen had beaten him to the spot). This is thus a pilgrimage of the mind, carried out by the body. A modern spiritual journey, a Hejira defined entirely by lines, angles, and national identity. But it is also a work of art: the creation of that place where the mind and the body meet—perhaps to perish—where the universe becomes aware of itself in the form of human consciousness. Nature, in the form of man, begins to recognize itself.

All creation of place exhibits this eerie mixture of abstract and concrete, of material and mental. And so we return again to the basic phenomenological awareness of embodied consciousness, but now tied even more closely to the idea of place, of being in place by deploying the conditions of possibility for place-making. Anywhere—and, it follows, nowhere—can be a place. As long as we are there, to think and talk, to listen and respond. The world, once conscious of itself in the form of human making, is a vast concert hall. What sounds there is not the divine music of celestial spheres, as the ancient Greek mathematicians believed, but the sound of one human after another issuing the daily plea: to be heard, to be understood, to be accommodated.

And, invoking another play about survival, extremity, and madness, we know that the opposite condition, the poor, bare, forked condition of human alienation, is precisely the lack of place: the heath, where Lear must go mad because he is not, finally, heard. Reason not the need!

General Proposition No. 5:
The creation of place is the gift of play.

A gift is given without expectation of return. In the true gift economy, wealth is measured not by how much one has accumulated but by how much one has given away. Truly to give, to give beyond all exchange or reciprocity, is to be irresponsible, creative, ironic, spontaneous, available. It is to play, in the sense that great art and great philosophy are forms of play.

Place-making is play-making. In one sense, to make a place is to create the material conditions of experience, to create the phenomenological clearing; but a place is not a place without my being there, my finding myself there, being in place. Further, place-making does not end with the subjective experience of either the one-in-place or the maker-of-place. For it is the nature of places to keep on giving, to create and renew, again and again, the conditions of their own possibility. Places are, in a sense, living things, maintained in time by experience and enjoyment. That is what it is for a place to be a place. This is what it means to clear a space for us to play in.

City halls, educational buildings, cinematic complexes—functionality varies according to task. Place-making, and hence city-building, transcends all specific functionality. It speaks to engagement, not program, freedom rather than function.

It is in such places that we may find—or (as we sometimes say) make—friends. There may be in actuality no perfect interlocutor as described by Barthes, but the well-built city gives us the chance, over and over, to try and find that comprehensively resonant friend. The one with whom we can play. The one who will listen while we drift together, continuously.

Notes

1 Roland Barthes, *A Lover's Discourse: Fragments* (Éditons du Seuil, 1977; Hill & Wang, trans. Richard Howard, 1978, 2010), 167, from the fragment "No Answer: mutisme/silence."

2 Though I borrow here the term favoured by the Situationists, there is no need to align the sort of city-building I am discussing, with its feet firmly rooted in reality, alongside the utopian New Babylon "city of play" advocated by Ivan Chtcheglov and Constant Nieuwenhuys. Still, there is something compelling about the vision of a city designed entirely for *homo ludens*, a city where, as Chtcheglov puts it in his manifests "Formulary for a New Urbanism," "[t]he main activity of the inhabitants will be CONTINUOUS DRIFTING." Chtcheglov promises an "aesthetic of behaviours" but also a "complete phenomenology of couples, encounters, and duration." Along the way, he reserves some choice words for Le Corbusier: "Some sort of psychological repression dominates this individual—whose face is as ugly as his conception of the world—such that he wants to squash people under ignoble masses of reinforced concrete, a noble material that should rather be used to enable an aerial articulation of space that could surpass the flamboyant Gothic style. His cretinizing influence is immense. A Le Corbusier model is the only image that arouses in me the idea of immediate suicide. He is destroying the last remnants of joy. And of love, passion, freedom." (See http://www.bopsecrets.org/SI/Chtcheglov.htm.) Chtcheglov first drafted the "Formulary" in 1953, when he was 19, under the name Gilles Ivain; it was published in the first issue of *Internationale Situationiste*. He spent five years in a psychiatric ward after being committed by his wife, and died in 1998.

3 A somewhat hostile review of my book *Nearest Thing to Heaven: The Empire State Building and American Dreams* (Yale, 2006) suggested that the claim there—namely, that the Empire State had in a sense "caused" the people of New York to construct it, given the logic of the "race for the sky," contemporary technological advances, and so on — was evidence of my having been "bamboozled" by fashionable French theory. No, just taking Aristotle seriously.

4 See Gilbert Ryle, *The Concept of Mind* (Hutchinson & Co., 1949).

5 The congruence between phenomenological theory and clinical psychological findings is a growth industry in academia. Just one example: a 2011 University of Notre Dame study found that doors and other spatial thresholds created "event boundaries" in episodes of experience or activity, prompting changes of consciousness that might, for example, present as changes of mood or, notoriously, temporary loss of memory. Hence the common experience, even absent dementia, of arriving in a room and not knowing what brought you there, or what you came to fetch. One of the study's authors offered this advice: "Doorways are bad. Avoid them at all costs." (Misty Harris, "Study Shows Doors Can Be Linked to Memory Loss," *The National Post*, November 9, 2011).

6 This is an extremely brief rehearsal of arguments that I make at length in *Concrete Reveries: Consciousness and the City* (Viking, 2008).

7 Pascal, *Pensées*, #348.

8 Aldo Rossi, *Architecture of the City* (MIT Press, 1982). It is worth noting that Rossi considers himself, after a fashion, a structuralist devotee of Barthes.

9 But for more theoretical discussion, see Mark Kingwell, "Monumental-Conceptual Architecture," *Harvard Design Magazine* 19 (Fall 2003/Winter 2004) and also *Nearest Thing to Heaven*, ed. cit., passim.

10 David Young, *Inexpressible Island* (Scirocco Drama, 1998), 116, 120.

WRITERS
AND WRITING

Prisons
Without Bars:
Of Lexicons and Lessons

"I have come here to chew bubble gum
and kick ass. . . . And I'm all out of bubble gum."
— NADA (Roddy Piper), in *They Live*

"STONE WALLS do not a prison make," Richard Lovelace wrote to the muse he called Althea in 1642, "nor iron bars a cage." Lovelace, Cavalier poet and friend of Herrick and Suckling, was in a Westminster clink for seven weeks. His crime: he wanted Anglican bishops, who had been ousted from Parliament by the Puritan power bloc, reinstated. His petition got him a jail sentence, but the physical bonds—he says—cannot contain his free thinking and frankly erotic dreams of the world outside. Althea, for her part, may or may not have been Lucy Sacheverell, a real-life Lovelace muse, girlfriend, and fiancée who, believing the dashing poet had been killed in battle at Dunkirk, married another man.

I prefer to take the metaphorical meaning. The name Althea has two possible roots, both from the Greek: *althainein*, to heal; and *aletheia*, truth. On this possibly fanciful interpretation, it is the healing truth that Lovelace addresses, and its message of spiritual defiance has offered solace to many prisoners down the centuries since. The poem, published seven years after its composition, is a distinguished entry in the powerful genre we might label Prison Plangent—the resounding expression of sadness, wisdom, or hope executed under conditions of utmost adversity. Koestler's *Darkness at Noon* and Wilde's *De Profundis* are thus joined to Boethius's *Consolation of Philosophy* and Plato's *Phaedo* and *Crito*. with countless memoirs and fictions in between: the voices of Gramsci, de Sade, Dostoevsky, Jean Genet, and Malcolm X—not to mention Humbert Humbert in Nabokov's *Lolita*. There is a peculiar freedom of mind possible only when one's physical freedom has been locked down. Paul Pennyfeather, in Waugh's *Decline and Fall*, notes with some satisfaction that he does not miss his daily newspaper while serving his sentence for trafficking in young ladies.

There is a clue here, because even more compelling than the actual prison that does not limit us, is the apparently free space that is, in fact, a mind-prison. And the most obvious of these is *work*.

Hannah Arendt famously distinguishes *work*, *labour*, and *action*— the three aspects of the *vita activa*—in her magnum opus, *The Human Condition* (1958). In this schema, labour operates to maintain the necessities of life (food, shelter, clothing) and is unceasing; work fashions specific things or ends, and so is finite; and action is public display of the self in visible doings. In our own day, work is obscurely spread across these categories. As a result, Arendt could indict the emptiness of a society free from labour—the wasteland of consumer desire—but could not see how smoothly the ideology work would fold itself back into that wasteland in the form of workaholism.

That ideology itself has a complex origin. We can blame the so-called Protestant work ethic, but structural forces of capital are clearly much more significant, creating the idea that one must work, and that one has no value if not working. The Marxist critique of this ideology is, perhaps surprisingly, of very little help here. Marx's idea that labour is a potentially noble and defining capacity of the individual, which has been sadly appropriated and hence alienating, actually reinforces the dominant ideology that work makes the man. Marx thus did not go far enough; he should have followed the lead of a more radical thinker, Aristotle, who argued that work, the realm of bare necessity, had no bearing on a meaningful and good life. Leisure, not work, was where humankind could taste its divine possibilities.

Of course, Aristotle's pupils would have had slaves to do all that dull work. So we must judge for ourselves how relevant his injunction against work remains. What is amply demonstrated is that work is today both inescapable and empty—a fatal conjunction. Consider this summing up by the Invisible Committee, a group of radical French activists who published their anti-manifesto, *The Coming Insurrection*:

> Here lies the present paradox: work has totally triumphed over all other ways of existing, at the same time as workers have become superfluous. Gains in productivity, outsourcing, mechanization, automated and digital production have so progressed that they have almost reduced to zero the quantity of living labor necessary in the manufacture of any product. We are living the paradox of a society of workers without work, where entertainment, consumption and leisure only underscore the lack from which they are supposed to distract us.[1]

It is perhaps no surprise that the Committee, viewing this superfluous majority as set off against the self-colonizing desire for "advancement" in the compliant minority, suggest that the current situation "introduces the risk that, in its idleness, [the majority] will set about sabotaging the machine."[2] The idler, that once-quiet figure of contemplative otherness and aesthetic cultivation of time for its own sake, is transformed by circumstances into an anarchist revolutionary!

*   *   *

In fact, this is not at all what has happened. Instead, in an inversion that has become so familiar it deserves a name—the Slacker Conundrum—any and all revolutionary energy is channelled back against its source in the form of irony.[3] In a sense, this is a version of Nietzschean *ressentiment*, because it visits psychic violence upon the agent whose desires are thwarted. The fox dismisses as sour the grapes he cannot enjoy, turning healthy longing into perverse soul-damage. In similar fashion, the signal texts of our current, profound enslavement to the ideology of work are not manifestos or calls to action but comic novels whose main effect is to leave everything as it is.

The novels themselves are full of incidental pleasures, which is part of what makes them such effective palliatives. Sam Lipsyte's novel *The Ask* (2010), which tangles its hapless protagonist in dark, funny skeins of corporate bafflegab, declining national confidence, and general cultural mendacity, is just the latest in a series of hilarious but nihilistic anti-morality tales. Ed Park's *Personal Days* (2008) neatly skewers the sick anxieties of cubicle culture, where the change in position of a stapler can call out squeaks of mortal dread. Joshua Ferris's *Then We Came to the End* (2007) does the same in Chicago rather than New York, in an insurance firm rather than a tech-publishing start-up. Both are indeed, as so often described, "darkly comic" and "caustic and hilarious." Lipsyte's more ambitious work, which follows on the savage comedy of *Home Land* (2005), a novel composed in imaginary class-note entries from a high school loser, indicts Bush-era fraud and geopolitics but its anchor remains the development office of a mediocre university in New York called, well, Mediocre University.

Much of the darkly comic caustic hilarity that runs through these books—and it does, it does—is a function of linguistic mangling characteristic of workplaces. Euphemism and doubletalk are the norm on the management side, countered by defensively clever slang on the wage-slave side. The paradigm here, of course, is Douglas Coupland's proto-workplace-nihilism novel, *Generation X* (1991), which went so far as (or felt the need) to include a running marginalia glossary of the neologisms the author was coining, from the now-famous *McJob* and *veal-fattening pen* (boring, indistinguishable entry-level employment and fabric-sided cubicles in open-plan offices, respectively) to the literally vaporous and forgotten *air family* (your enforced-proximity co-workers).

Along the way we get, among many others, *consensus terrorism* (the decision force in all offices), *dumpster clocking* (estimating the longevity of consumer durables, especially when made of plastic), *expatriate solipsism* (finding your cultural clones when travelling), *legislated nostalgia* (longing for a past you didn't experience), *option paralysis* (making no choice when offered too many), *paper rabies* (pathological dislike of littering), *power mist* (the diffusion of hierarchy boundaries under office conditions), *strangelove reproduction* (having children to compensate for a lack of belief in the future), *tele-parabilizing* (interpreting human action by way of comparison to television shows).[4]

Some of this is smart, some of it silly, all of it the mark of a writer who has exactly hit his stride with a series of deftly turned phrases. Coupland's achievement, here and in his other indisputably successful novel *Microserfs* (1995), is to nail a pattern of thought and speech with such thoroughness that his wordplay seems like eavesdropping. *Generation X* and *Microserfs* are less funny than the later books not because he is a less

talented writer but because, contrary to expectation, he is a more natu-
ralistic one. People in offices really do invent goofy terms to describe
their afflicted condition, especially if they are educated to the point
where, as an English writer of another generation put it, the work at
hand is at once beneath and beyond them. The same people do not, as
a rule, craft the nanosecond-reflex one-liners and layered punchlines of
Lipsyte, Park, and (less so) Ferris. That degree of creative liberty suggests a degree of personal liberty, the freedom of thought inscribed in all
real comedy, that they do not actually possess.

*   *   *

This is not meant as a criticism of the latter writers, really, only of their
seriousness in confronting the nihilism they espouse. Coupland's workplace books, especially *Microserfs*, which tracked the rise and fall of a
Silicon Valley "creative" firm, have been criticized for their soft-hearted
endings full of puppies and hope; but in fact, sentence for sentence, his
books are bleaker. You get a real sense of oppression as his characters
struggle to create a language equal to their oppression. They fail not
for lack of inventiveness but because of it: their cultural productions are
just what the situation expects of them, and we consume those productions just as they do, in the form of irony, second-order commodities of
an economy where the first-order commodity is the self. A mocking but
ultimately fond lexicon of new terms is a much more likely, but, for all
that, much more powerless response to wage-slavery than real satire or,
still less likely, real resistance.[5]

To be sure, both Coupland and his later heirs fail to fully enact the
nihilism they inaugurate. Without exception, the second half of the
Lipsyte, Park, and Ferris novels are inferior to the first, with the energy
of the briskly introduced comic situation rapidly fading into a dead-end
narrative. Park's book becomes a kind of bizarre ghost story about a legendary but shadowy fixer of corporate fuck-ups. Ferris shifts person and
perspective to focus on one worker's preparations for a cancer operation (a piece written before the rest of the novel was elaborated). And
Lipsyte's feckless semi-hero engineers a series of roughhouse confron-
tations with his past, his former friends, and his wife. The same issue
of structural bagginess dominates an even earlier example of the genre,
Don DeLillo's debut novel, *Americana* (1971), whose first line ("And

then we came to the end of another dull and lurid year") inspired Ferris's title. Not even DeLillo, with his already evident command of idiom and techno-cultural effluvia, can redeem the satire of his opening section, set in a Manhattan television-production office, with the rambling road-trip-to-Dallas meanders of the book's remainder. The downbeat satire of production meetings, the pretentious set-ups and constant resort to cliché (break bread, pick your brain, catch a big silver bird to the Coast; the sentence "I hear good things about you" acquires a special menace) give way to long pages of unbroken character braindump that will have most readers flipping the pages in irritation.

At this point in my argument, structural critics will take note of the salient point that the most accomplished television version of the work-idea fiction, *The Office*, had to resort to the classic comedic device of a wedding when it hit its doldrums.[6] Also that the tightly contained absurdism of Mike Judge's 1999 film *Office Space*, with its episodes of Y2K anxiety, supply theft, and pyrotechnics, works better than any of the novels

In part this is a matter of cultural inclination. North American intellectuals and novelists are rarely willing to follow the arguments about work and capitalist ideology to their logical conclusions. For real nihilism about the modern work-prison you have to resort to Michel Houellebecq's *The Elementary Particles* (1998), featuring a terminally bored high school teacher who becomes an insatiable sex addict, or J. G. Ballard's late novel *Super-Cannes* (2000), in which bored executives at a sleek French corporate park are advised by a company psychiatrist that the solution to their lowered output is not psychotherapy but psychopathology. Once they begin nocturnal sorties of violence on immigrant workers and prostitutes, productivity rates soar. Even Chuck Palahniuk, every Tool-fanboy's favourite dark hero, is a softie compared to the Europeans. His most successful book, *Fight Club* (1996; adapted as the 1999 film with Brad Pitt, Edward Norton, and Helena Bonham-Carter), is at best half-bleak, with some hawk-eyed ripping of reproducible culture and the boredom of life experienced as insomnia which, however, tails off into fantasy. The book, as Palahniuk himself has said, "was just *The Great Gatsby* updated a little. It was 'apostolic' fiction—where a surviving apostle tells the story of his hero. There are two men and a woman. And one man, the hero, is shot to death."

*   *   *

The Gatsby remark is revealing, though, because it is not simply at the level of theme that Palahniuk is channelling Fitzgerald. In a sense, all of these writers are struggling to write some version of *The Great Gatsby*, that wonderfully glamorous and moralistic soap opera of ambition and identity in America. The ambivalence that Fitzgerald, or more precisely Nick, evinces for both the lost-in-love Gatsby and beautiful, careless Daisy is less a sign of psychological complexity and more a matter of the American Dream's characteristic whipsaw effect, constantly shunting us from celebration to denigration, from surfeit to starvation, from possibility to failure. The work-prison novels of recent vintage are not really the dark side of the American Dream; they just are the American Dream itself in those many moments when it is working against you.

The central feature of the American Dream is not that hard work will triumph over lowly origins; it is that people stuck in negative-asset situations will forever believe they won't be there forever, and so will act against their own interests. In politics, that means a majority of people oppose a capital-gains tax even though capital gains are only ever declared by the very rich. Why? Because they imagine the day when they, too, will be so numbered. In fiction it means that all novels about work are the same novel, usually written by young men about young men who destroy themselves despite being given every advantage known to history and scripture. Why? Because as long as work remains essentially the preserve of the hapless, feckless, luckless individual—even a briefly successful, hard-working individual such as the former Jay Gatz—nothing structural, nothing *economic*, will ever change. On the contrary: every depicted failure is another success for the current arrangement, for the ways things are.

Now compare the following passage from *Americana*, its protagonist David Bell, a handsome and (yes) feckless twenty-something television executive, musing precisely on his relationship to the Dream: "But as a boy, and even later, quite a bit later, I believed all of it, the institutional messages, the psalms and placards, the pictures, the words. Better living through chemistry. The Sears, Roebuck catalogue. Aunt Jemima. All the impulses of all the media were fed into the circuitry of my dreams, One thinks of echoes. One thinks of an image made in the image and the likeness of images. It was that complex."[7] Later, the same point is made in a recorded conversation of McLuhanesque riffing about how a television commercial affects the viewer: "It moves him from first person consciousness to third person. In this country there is a universal third person, the man we all want to be. Advertising has discovered this man. It uses him to express the possibilities open to the consumer. To consume in America is not to buy; it is to dream. Advertising is the suggestion that the dream of entering the third person singular might possibly be fulfilled."[8]

The DeLillo narrator says "It was that complex" but nowadays I think we would be inclined to say: it was that *simple*. The simulacral nature of cultural experience, the infinite mirror-house reproducibility of images—this is where we start, not where we stop. Consider a cultural product suspended not quite halfway between *Americana*'s shadow-of-JFK 1971 and the millennial anxieties of *Generation X* and after.

John Carpenter's *They Live* (1988) features a quiet drifter named Nada (*nada* = nothing), played be former pro wrestler "Rowdy" Roddy Piper, who is looking for work in Los Angeles. In a complicated chain of events, he acquires a set of sunglasses that reveal the truth: a group of aliens has taken control of the Earth, with the aid of selected humans, and they rule the rest of us with a combination of subliminal messages and consumerism. Billboards that to the naked eye feature computers actually send the message *Obey*, and ads for a Caribbean vacation instruct us to *Marry and Reproduce* (biofascism being part of the larger consumerist ideology). Every bill of paper money shows, through the glasses, the obvious truth that *This is your God*. After an absurdly protracted alleyway fistfight with his friend Frank (possibly an inspiration for Chuck Palahniuk?), Nada enlists him as an ally and the two manage to infiltrate the alien conspiracy. With his last breath Nada destroys the television signal that is responsible for the generalized deception that enthralls the human population.

It's significant that Nada and Frank are construction workers, not office drones. Their plain virtue is equal to the illusions of the alien overlords, in part because to them a job is just a dreary necessity, not an ideology. *They Live* does not feature any signs saying *You Must Have a Job*, but it could have. But the message is so subliminal that it rarely even rises to the level of articulation, even in countercultural science fiction. In the world of *They Live*, culture itself is the prison, and work, like money, is just one of its instruments of comfortable delusion. *They Live* is goofy, but it is not comic. There is no inventive slang or witty repartee—unless you count the line I chose as my epigraph, a *bon mot* allegedly ad libbed by Piper when he was playing a scene in the film where Nada stumbles into a bank full of the aliens, and proceeds to lay waste to them with his stolen weapons.

Maybe the real limitation we sense with the post-*Gen X* comic novels is that all this linguistic invention, all the darkly comic talk of the lexicons and lessons, is part of the problem, not the solution. To appreciate a more radical option, I will end with the briefest appreciation of the greatest work story in the language, the granddaddy of them all, Melville's "Bartleby the Scrivener" (1853). When the pale copyist Bartleby begins his slow withdrawal from work, movement, speech, and, eventually, life, turning his face to the wall of his Wall Street law office in this story of walls, he needs to coin just one novel sentence: "I would prefer not to." The only words more affecting in the whole story are the ones he utters to his former employer when that worthy but ineffectual gentleman attempts to brighten up Bartleby's removal to a Manhattan debtors' prison, contained within the Halls of Justice, otherwise known as the Tombs:

> And so I found him there [the narrator tells us], standing all alone in the quietest of the yards, his face towards a high wall, while all around, from the narrow slits of the jail windows, I thought I saw peering out upon him the eyes of murderers and thieves.
>
> "Bartleby!"
>
> "I know you," he said, without looking round,—"and I want nothing to say to you."
>
> "It was not I that brought you here, Bartleby," said I, keenly pained at his implied suspicion. "And to you, this should not be so vile a place. Nothing reproachful attaches to you by being here. And see, it is not so sad a place as one might think. Look, there is the sky, and here is the grass."
>
> "I know where I am," he replied, but would say nothing more, and so I left him.

I know where I am: pleasant conditions do not make it any less a prison, just as flextime and casual Fridays do not change the conditions of wage-slavery. In the century and a half since Melville's odd, prescient story first appeared—1853!—Bartleby has been claimed as everything from an existential hero to an anarchist saint, an exemplar and an enemy of the state. The basic truth is simpler, and more disturbing: he is the bleak object lesson in the prison that is work, the inevitability of the condition we call, without irony, *being employed*.

There is the sky, and here is the grass. But like Bartleby, we know where we are. And we're all out of bubblegum.

Notes

1   *The Coming Insurrection*, anon. English trans. (Semiotext(e), 2009), 46.

2   Ibid., p. 49.

3   For more on the idler/slacker distinction and its political importance, see Joshua Glenn and Mark Kingwell, *The Idler's Glossary* (Biblioasis, 2008), passim (of course passim—what else?). My introduction was adapted as the essay "Idling Toward Heaven: The Last Defence You Will Ever Need," *Queen's Quarterly* 115:4 (Winter 2008): 569-85. The sequel was *The Wage-Slave's Glossary* (Biblioasis, 2011); a version of its introductory essay appeared under the title "Wage Slavery, Bullshit, and the Bad Infinite," *Queen's Quarterly* 117:2 (Summer 2010). We may be idle, but we are not lazy!

4   For a full list, see http://www.scn.org/~jonny/genx.html

5   You might think our *Wage-Slave's Glossary* (note 3) falls squarely into this category of futile or, worse, complicit gesture; we hope not, even if its satirical intent falls short of open call for revolution. By isolating the lexicon from its site and circumstances of origin, and allying this move to earlier defences of idleness, we aim to generate critical distance lacking in the defensive workplace use of workplace slang. Of course, we could be wrong.

6   I mean the U.S. version that debuted as a mid-season replacement on NBC in 2005. The BBC version (2001–2003), created by and starring Ricky Gervais, is appreciably nastier than its basically charming American cousin.

7   Don DeLillo, *Americana* (Houghton Mifflin, 1971), 130.

8   Ibid., 270.

Self-Made Men

EDUCATION has long been thought a site of renovation, or make-over, such that the unformed person or pupil enters a space of learning and emerges, some years and exercises later, with a refined sensibility. We call something "edifying" when it enhances the edifice of the person, or perhaps the soul. Education is, etymologically, a drawing out—*e-ducare* in the Latin root—but it is also a building up, adding new wings to the human house even as it remakes some of the existing rooms. From the point of view of a teacher, every person is a fixer-upper.

The benefits of this reno project, meanwhile, are considered to be more than mental. Education is supposed to open up new social or financial vistas as well as intellectual ones. Indeed, under the current market conditions of post-secondary education, where getting a degree has become inextricably connected to getting a job—even, or especially, when there are no such jobs to be found—the intellectual part of the equation may simply fall out. Students go to university as a planned return-on-investment project driven by statistics correlating degrees with lifetime earnings. That those earnings are actually diminishing across a generation, or that the degree itself comes burdened with punishing debt, is a less welcome renovation of the ideal of higher education.

When I was in graduate school, a sojourn from which I emerged unemployed but mercifully free of debt (I believe the technical economic term for this is "a wash"), I became fascinated with a small and almost forgotten subgenre of popular American fiction. In the reading room of the main campus library, which provided comfortable leather chairs and utter silence, I read through a couple of shelves of what I want to call the early-twentieth-century Ivy League bootstrap novel. These books, variants on the Horatio Alger waif-makes-good theme, featured clean but impoverished young men, usually from New York or Boston, whose highest desire was to attend Harvard, Princeton, or Yale.

The story was invariably the same: some hard work on the docks, plus maybe a secret benefactor, paved the rough road to admission, whereupon our hero, despite his manifest virtues, faced social awkwardness and condescension from the elegant young men who had entered New Haven or Cambridge on money or family connection—"legacies" is the term, then and still, for these sons (and since very recently, also daughters) of esteemed graduates. Undaunted, the upright exemplar of urban salt-of-the-earth integrity would try out for the football team, meet one or two others impressed by his toughness, and finally enter the inner sanctum of college society. At Yale at least, this would mean being "tapped" for one of the not-so-secret senior societies such as Skull and Bones or Scroll and Key, whose weird meeting-house "tombs" stand, mute and apparently doorless, along the streets behind Old Campus. The American Dream, by way of New Haven.

My favourite of these books are *Stover at Yale* (1911) by Owen Johnson, which continued the adventures of Lawrenceville prep Adonis John "Dink" Stover, pictured in the volume's frontispiece as a strapping, well-turned-out gentleman standing "all square to the wind"; and *Boltwood of Yale* (1914), by Gilbert Patten, a prolific writer of dime novels, here using the pseudonym Bert L. Standish. Patten, as Standish, was likewise the author, between 1896 and 1930, of some two hundred (!) books featuring sporting hero and amateur sleuth Frank Merriwell— including *Frank Merriwell at Yale* (1903).

Roger Boltwood is "a clean-limbed, square-shouldered young fellow." He is also the wastrel second-generation scion of a self-made family, going fast downhill after his mother's death. Two lazy years into a decadent stint as a Yale "high roller," a "blood," he crashes a sports car and is subsequently disinherited by his angry industrialist father. Forced to work for the first time, Boltwood vows to finish his Yale career even if it means living in a Harlem rooming house, giving up cigarettes and cocktails, and working on cars. After some displays of ingenuity and character, he rises rapidly in the world, returns to New Haven, boxes well, plays football even better, and makes up with his father.

Dink Stover never has to bootstrap. He goes to Yale with a solid prep-school reputation and aspirations for success on the gridiron and on Tap Night. But he meets some renegades—a real self-made man called Tom

Regan, and a budding writer called "Brocky" Brockhust—who together rebel against Yale's elitist hierarchy and teach young Dink about real democracy. "The biggest thing we can do is to reflect the nation, to be the inspiration of the democracy of the country, to be alive to the fight among the people for real political independence," an inspired Dink pontificates late in the book, under Brocky's influence. "We ought to get a great vision when we come up here, as young men, of the bigness of our country, of the privilege of fighting out its political freedom, of what American manhood means."[1]

Well, no. The Yale secret societies are still very much in place, and the Ivy League no more offers a democratic vision quest today than it did a century ago. "Places like Yale are simply not set up to help students ask the big questions," one contemporary critic has argued. "I don't think there ever was a golden age of intellectualism in the American university, but in the nineteenth century students might at least have had a chance to hear such questions raised in chapel or in the literary societies and debating clubs that flourished on campus."[2] That is, precisely one of the clubs, now defunct, at which Dink makes his impassioned plea for manly democratic virtue.

Nevertheless, these books (there are dozens of others) were wildly popular at a time when American higher education was indeed a privileged enclave even as social mobility, or anyway its promise, was changing American society. It would not be going too far to suggest that Stover, Merriwell, and Boltwood were essential in fixing Yale's position in the cultural firmament in the decades before the First World War as the place where young men of brains and brawn must aspire to be. Harvard was, for its part, too closely linked to Beacon Hill snobbery, and Princeton was considered too brainy.

The last perception would change briefly with F. Scott Fitzgerald's *This Side of Paradise* (1920), whose neurotic protagonist, Amory Blaine, the "romantic egotist" of the book's opening, Princeton-centred section, possesses none of the bluff, hale uprightness of the pre-war archetypes. Princeton was by this time a combination of jazz-age social club and literary hothouse—critic Edmund Wilson was a Fitzgerald pal—with all of the cleverness and social climbing but none of the juvenile concern with personal virtue that belonged to earlier (and of course much inferior) books. Despite having gone to the Newman school and Princeton rather than Lawrenceville and New Haven, Fitzgerald would later describe Johnson's

Stover at Yale as the "textbook of his generation." Fitzgerald was not exactly a bootstrapper, any more than Dink Stover: his father had been a Procter & Gamble man and offered Scott a comfortable middle-class life in Saint Paul, Minnesota. But he was a consummate self-inventor. It is no coincidence that the doomed hero of his greatest book, Jay Gatsby, is himself a distinguished *doppelgänger*, a made-up, made-over man.

Though they feature social movement and some satire of intellectual pursuits, the Ivy League bootstrap novels are thus distinct from certain close cousins with academic settings, such as the English "scholarship boy" novel, which tends to seethe with class resentment, and the comedic "campus farce" novel, which offers a parody of intellectual manners and academic eccentricities, usually with some illicit love affairs thrown in. Neither of these subgenres matches the Ivy League bootstrap novel for social influence; if anything, they make you *not* want to attend Oxford or Berkeley. And in both cases, Kingsley Amis's *Lucky Jim* (1954) offers the welcome endgame of the form, an unimprovable and savage aesthetic reckoning that takes place in a provincial university. In short, in the squat, angry, drunken figure of Lucky Jim Dixon the scholarship boy meets the campus farce, and both implode in a swirl of bitter, funny anger.

This truth, which should be more widely celebrated, has not stopped people from continuing to write campus farces, if not scholarship boy novels. In evidence I enter just three of the former, all of them pretty funny, to be sure, however pointless they may be conceptually, post-Amis: David Lodge's *Changing Places* (1975), which made literary theory a subject of easy fun via the Jamesian trope of American-English cultural differences; Jane Smiley's *Moo* (1995), which mocked midwestern land-grant universities in a manner not nearly as enlightening as Terry Castle's recent lesbian-abuse memoir, *The Professor and Other Writings* (2010); and Richard Russo's *Straight Man* (1997), which brought that writer's great sympathy for human weakness into an arena vastly less compelling than his beloved, benighted Mohawk Valley.

So much for that. Read these books if you like—I can't stop you!—but the genre they belong to is over.

* * *

What happened to the Ivy League bootstrap novel is more complicated, and offers the second kind of renovation worth our attention in the field (okay, the campus) of education. I want to suggest that this genre has been not so much subverted as inverted: it has generated its own uncanny twin.

The bootstrap novel is already about doubling, just as we could say that all education/renovation must be. That is, the trope of self-improvement is, in effect, one of self-creation, such that there are two Stovers and two Boltwoods in play: the pre- and the post-Yale (or "true" Yale). (This holds less in the Merriwell book, which is more a straightforward adventure.) The virtuous core is meant to remain, but the whole point of *wanting to go to Yale* is that a new person shall be formed out of the experience, a kind of superior replicant of the original who toiled on the Manhattan docks, dreaming of the Old Campus and the football field. It can be no surprise that the future of this genre, in the hands of a talented writer, should extend this replicant logic farther—so far, in fact, that the genre folds back on itself in creepy reverse.

My claim, then, is this: the natural successor to the Ivy League bootstrap novel, and its decisive inversion, is Patricia Highsmith's *The Talented Mister Ripley*. Published in 1955, it marks the creation and first adventures of an amoral genius of improvisation whose talents, while legion, all revolve around the very American desire to better oneself: to improve the person and find better social position.

Tom Ripley has not been to college, but he is, above all, a quick study. And, like Amis's Lucky Jim, his greatest hatred is reserved for boredom. The latter character, readers may recall, complains about a musical evening where he will be subjected to "some skein of untiring facetiousness by filthy Mozart" and then "some Brahms rubbish," followed by "a violin sonata by some Teutonic bore." For Tom, boredom has degrees. Here he has been chased down in a Manhattan bar by the father of his slight acquaintance, Dickie Greenleaf, whose uncanny *doppelgänger* he will soon become:

> His boredom had slipped into another gear. Tom knew the sensations. He had them sometimes at parties, but generally when he was having dinner with someone with whom he hadn't wanted to have dinner in the first place, and the evening got longer and longer. Now he could be maniacally polite for perhaps another whole hour, if he had to be, before something in him exploded and sent him running out of the door.[3]

It is this boredom that fuels his outbursts of violence—except, of course, when those outbursts are fuelled by a need to cover up earlier ones. In the film version of *The Talented Mister Ripley* (1999, d. Anthony Minghella), Matt Damon's version of Tom is driven to murder Dickie (Jude Law) only when the latter tells him he has become a bore.

In the book, Tom is more calculating from the start, and the tortured homoerotic aspects of the Tom-Dickie relationship are more muted. What is unchanged is Tom's version of an Ivy League bootstrap. He doesn't make his own way to college; he just pretends he has been there with Dickie. Tom says to Dickie's parents that he went to Princeton "for a while," a usefully ambiguous phrase, and then pauses to gauge their reaction. But he is not afraid of being found out. On the contrary:

> Tom waited, hoping Mr. Greenleaf would ask him something about Princeton, but he didn't. Tom could have discussed the system of teaching history, the campus restrictions, the atmosphere at the weekend dances, the political tendencies of the student body, anything. Tom had been very friendly last summer with a Princeton junior who had talked of nothing but Princeton, so that Tom had finally pumped him for more and more, foreseeing a time when he might be able to use the information.[4]

Tom has in fact attended two different colleges. "[T]here had been a young man named Don Mizell rooming in his Aunt Bea's house in Denver who had been going to the University of Colorado," the narrator points out. "Tom felt as if he had gone there, too." (In the film, Damon's Tom is shown acquiring specific fake tastes, like knowing Nina Simone is the female jazz singer who sounds like a man and Chet Baker is the man who sounds like a woman.)

Tom can imitate the Princeton grad, and that is just as good as being one. Unlike the Boltwoods of the world, he cannot hold down a manual-labour job in New York. "He had held the job less than two weeks, because he hadn't been strong enough to lift orange crates eight hours a day, but he had done his best and knocked himself out trying to hold the job, and when they fired him, he remembered how horribly unjust he had thought it."[5] But it doesn't matter—his sense of injustice is soon rescued by the opportunity of spending time with Dickie. When he kills

Dickie, it is only natural for him to assume his identity, social position, and bank account. Who needs Princeton?

But if Tom Ripley is the mid-century replicant who takes over from the Boltwoods of yesteryear, renovating the renovation of education, this is only possible because the Ivy League itself has been made over, by its own devices, into an upper-class finishing school rather than a hotbed of intellectual inspiration. We can note that the things Tom knows about Princeton—rules, customs, social mores—have nothing to do with education as such. And why not, since the value added by a name-brand college cannot be what you study there (anyone can study anything anywhere) but, instead, the small peculiarities that make a place what it is. The important thing is that you went there, or can pretend you did, not anything you did, said, saw, read, or learned during the time. The surest sign of this is the Harvard sticker that must be affixed to the rear window of your expensive car. These days, that sticker goes for about $200,000.

Thus the vaunted elite schools are really in the business of reproducing a ruling class, generating assembly lines of Wall Street and Beltway drones, simulacra of human beings. William Deresiewicz, a critic of the system who has worked within it, calls this the Ivy League's culture of "entitled mediocrity." Its main symbol is no longer the so-called "gentleman's C," which grade Yale legacy George W. Bush might have favoured like his father before him, but instead what we must call the whiner's A-minus: the inflated grade given for being there in the first place, without demonstrating any real intelligence or inspiration. In this culture we find no bootstrappers, nor even the louche opponents they faced, but lazy snobbery, overvaluation of analytic intelligence, inflated self-worth, and a strange kind of anti-intellectualism. Today's Ivy League would be unrecognizable to Boltwood not because Ivy football sucks (though it surely does) but because nobody in New Haven really takes ideas seriously. The whole point of being there is . . . well, being able to say that you were there. And then, of course, having said that, you can amble through the doors that having been there will open.

Given all this, it can't be any surprise that the American college novel has lately developed a new spur, neither the campus farce nor the genuine bootstrap novel but a kind of perverted, maybe we could say sexually renovated, young-adult soap opera. The two most prominent examples are Tom Wolfe's controversial *I Am Charlotte Simmons* (2004) and the sleazy but enjoyable *Prep* by Curtis Sittenfeld (2005).[6] The latter is set in an elite New England high school, but teaches the same lesson. Which is that the elite education system is really an extended social network whose main purpose is sex. People were shocked at the casual hookups that characterize Wolfe's Dupont University, which is a thinly veiled simulacrum of Duke, and the prep school in Sittenfeld's book, which is a thinly veiled simulacrum of either Groton (where she went) or St. Albans (where she taught). But they shouldn't have been. After all, what is college for when all the love of learning has been systematically removed?

I should say that my own experience at an Ivy League school differs in at least two respects from the scene depicted in these books. The students I taught were genuinely intellectual, and now include some of the colleagues I respect most. And the sexual hookups, when they happened, were typically reserved for end-of-term or even end-of-degree binges made necessary by how hard they all worked during classes. But that was in the late 1980s, when Ivy League tuition, while still high, had not outpaced inflation to the degree it has since then, making these degrees more and more obviously, almost exclusively, tokens of financial position.

$$*\qquad *\qquad *$$

The sad truth behind these economic and literary shifts is that, a century into the democratization of American higher education, there is no possibility of bootstrapping into an Ivy League education now. I don't just mean that the dime-novel conventions of work-ethic success have become tired, though that is true; I also mean that the very notion of social mobility on which these narratives rest seems decisively obliterated. If the Occupy movements of 2011 taught us anything, it is that the one percent is getting one-percenter all the time. The trope of the entrepreneur-hero, so dear to the minds of American dreamers, has entered its Bain Capital private-equity stage, where "success" is defined as making investment returns on the effort of others, without risking anything of your own, using their actual businesses and labour as leverage for your fun and profit. Of course profit. This is the Romneyfication of the entrepreneur-hero.

American democracy is unimaginable without the figure of the entrepreneur-hero. We could even say that the invention of this type, which moves decisively away from a long tradition of gentlemen and professionals disdaining trade and its associated filthy lucre, is another special bit of American genius, like jazz and baseball. The idea was a cornerstone of the post-revolutionary culture, defining an ideal of "the man who developed inner resources, acted independently, lived virtuously, and bent his behaviour to his personal goals."[7] This man disdained leisure, not trade; he abstained from whisky, not currency. He is related, in the cultural imaginary, with Emerson's self-reliant man—though close readers of the celebrated essay in praise of this man will hear sour notes of Nietzschean "strength" that anticipate some of the nuttier views of Ayn Rand.

It is really not until the late-nineteenth-century Golden Age, the period of prosperity and excess analyzed so deftly by Veblen, that leisure and its consumption would overwhelm the virtues of production, the heroism of the start-up. Even then, there would always be something slightly off, something too English or (worse) too French, about aristocratic tastes exercised in a democratic setting. That is why Henry James's protagonists, like their author himself, must abscond to Europe. And that, of course, is when you get a leisured, judgmental, exquisitely tasteful, poseur-creep like Gilbert Osmond in *The Portrait of a Lady*, who judges himself superior in all things on the unassailable basis of never having exerted effort in their pursuit.

The genius of the more recent American past has been to combine the myth of the entrepreneur with all the excesses of consumption: a final renovation. From this vantage Mitt Romney really is just a replicant of Donald Trump—that "bloviating ignoramus," as fellow conservative George Will has called him, a man who openly doubts that Barack Obama was born in the United States—with more acceptable hair. Carried interest and untaxed capital gains are the logical outcomes of a world where we have returned, by a roundabout and undemocratic route, to gentlemen who never get their hands dirty. And now virtue, which once meant public service and being morally as well as physically square to the wind, has retreated decisively into the purely private realm of the family or into the jingoistic display of martial might. These are two related forms of fascism, atavistic and close-minded assertions of value or "what it is all for." Both leave the rigged market of politics untouched, middle ground to be blithely bought and sold.[8]

And now the bootstrap novel, in both its basic and its Ivy League iterations, is remade into the biofascist market-manipulation novel. Jonathan Bennett's *Entitlement* (2008), Jonathan Dee's *The Privileges* (2010), and

Cristina Alger's *The Darlings* (2012) form a neat triumvirate of books that depict the family ties of people who manipulate financial and cultural markets in the service of reactionary kinship ideology, otherwise known as "building a legacy."

Alger's effort, about a Madoff-style ponzi scheme that ruins a marriage, is a page-turner, but notable mainly for the neat irony of that last name. And Bennett's book is slight but elegant, with Canadian content if you care about that. Dee's book is the best of the three, a defining novel of our moment, setting out without judgment and with the finest imaginable irony the life decisions and "epic love affair" (the phrase comes from a disaffected son, who half admires their predatory devotion) of Adam and Cynthia Morey. Middle-class in origin but gifted with looks, charisma, and infinite impatience about any obstacles to desire, Adam and Cynthia meet, marry, and make money. These are people who leave their birth families behind in order to create new heirs, who are predictably insufferable. Like their parents, however, they believe, without fuss or argument, that they are superior to other people because they have more. They are, after all, the Moreys.

The Privileges offers the perfect coda to the multiple renovations of the rags-to-riches narrative, with a new Great Recession frankness. Tom Regan and Roger Boltwood have to work and save to make it into Yale. Tom Ripley has to be an identity-switching murderer in order to complete his inversion of the Ivy League storyline. Even the ex-Yalie "masters of the universe" gamboling along Wall Street in Tom Wolfe's *Bonfire of the Vanities* (1987) are stricken by other social forces, including a flawed but functioning legal system, and punished. Adam Morey in *The Privileges* has no such scruples or debilities. *The Privileges* is not actually about inherited wealth or entitlement; it explores instead the bleak truth about real self-made men, the ruthless desire that churns beneath all the rosy American Dream narratives, now and always.

Adam dispenses with the social attractions of Yale in favour of a small liberal arts college. In New York, working in private equity—what else?—he lies, cheats, risks other people's money, and bulldozes lives without compunction; he harbours no doubts about any of this, and he never gets caught. He is, in short, the perfectly well-adjusted capitalist sociopath.

But identity theft? Murder? Why switch selves when you keep getting exactly what you want? Why murder people when you can just, you know, *buy* them?

Notes

1 Owen Johnson, *Stover at Yale* (Yale Bookstore, 1997), 265. .

2 See William Deresiewicz, "The Disadvantages of an Elite Education," *The American Scholar* (Summer 2008). The reasons for this intellectual deficit are various but one is relatively new: the overvaluation, at elite universities, of research as against teaching. "[T]he increasingly dire exigencies of academic professionalization have made [inspiring teachers] all but extinct at elite universities," Deresiewicz continues. "Professors at top research institutions are valued exclusively for the quality of their scholarly work; time spent teaching is time lost. If students want a conversion experience, they're better off at a liberal arts college."

3 Patricia Highsmith, *The Talented Mr. Ripley* (1955), in the Everyman's Library omnibus edition (Knopf, 1999), 9.

4 Ibid., 18.

5 Ibid., 39.

6 In the Strange Coincidence department I share the fact that, according to a *New York Times* report, *Prep* was part of the 2011 Occupy Wall Street library, a collection of books later trashed by New York's finest. A book I co-authored, *The Wage Slave's Glossary*, was also mentioned. I have no idea what this means; probably nothing. ("Inside the List," *New York Times Book Review*, October 7, 2011).

7 Joyce Appleby, *Inheriting the Revolution* (Harvard, 2000), 11. There is a good discussion of this trope of the entrepreneur-hero in Charles Taylor, *Modern Social Imaginaries* (Duke, 2004), chap. 9.

8 The roots of biofascism—the ideological celebration of the family—are deep in American political culture. So deep, in fact, that it is hard to imagine an American writing something like Frenchwoman Corinne Maier's controversial bestseller, *No Kids: Forty Good Reasons Not to Have Children* (Emblem, 2009). True, seven decades ago, Philip Wylie took aim at the cult of "momism" in his searing *Generation of Vipers* (1942); but the best anti-family arguments still come from France.

Compare this passage from *The Coming Insurrection* (Semiotext(e), 2009; orig. 2007), by the collective known as the Invisible Committee: "Everyone can testify to the doses of sadness condensed from year to year in family gatherings, the forced smiles, the awkwardness of seeing everyone pretending in vain, the feeling that a corpse is lying there on the table, and everyone acting as though it were nothing. From flirtation to divorce, from cohabitation to stepfamilies, everyone feels the inanity of the sad family nucleus, but most seem to believe that it would be sadder still to give it up. The family is no longer so much the suffocation of maternal control or the patriarchy of beatings as it is this infantile abandon to a fuzzy dependency, where everything is familiar, this carefree moment in the face of a world that nobody can deny is breaking down, a world where 'becoming self-sufficient' is a euphemism for 'finding a boss'." No Emersonian self-reliance there!

Serial Killers

"He was a guy who talked with commas,
like a heavy novel. Over the phone anyway."

— RAYMOND CHANDLER, *The Long Goodbye*

O WHERE HAVE YOU GONE, poor comma?
I behold the advance copy of my brand-new book, a collection of essays—yay!—and there, on the cover, in the subtitle, stands the word "CIVILITY" unadorned by the comma, the *serial comma*, that is meant to separate it from the final phrase of the three-part, admittedly somewhat stiff, subtitle: "ESSAYS ON DEMOCRACY, CIVILITY, AND THE HUMAN IMAGINATION."

Mine isn't an academic book, but have you ever noticed how many books and essays by academics have subtitles with three elements? I have. In fact, I have noticed it as a tic that often creeps into my own writing. And I think I know why it happens, beyond the natural Lawrence Welk rhythm of *uh-one, and-uh-two, and-uh-three*. The three-part subtitle usually goes with a main title that is a bold phrase and/or tortuous pun, the subtitle thus acting as a sort of earnest, apologetic, explanatory gloss on the title phrase. You know: *Torturous Pun: Dah, Dum, and Dee-Dee.* Or *Bold Phrase: The Blah, Bleh, and Blip of Whatever.*

There is thus a little dialectical void contained in the stacked full stops of those title colons, site of a struggle between what we must call the poetic impulses of the author and the reality principle of having to actually, you know, say what the damn book or article is about. "Dream On: The Desires, Limits, and Habits of Academic Prose."

But, but. If you are going to write titles that like that—and indeed do anything else in English that requires deployment of three distinct grammatical elements—you really need the serial comma. That's the comma that comes between Element No. 2 and Element No. 3. Also known as the Oxford comma and the Harvard comma, presumably because they are favoured by scholars at those two august institutions, the serial comma is preferred by that politburo of the academic written word, *The Chicago Manual of Style*. Fowler's *Modern English Usage* and Strunk and White's *Elements of Style* likewise support its maintenance. Most newspapers, commercial magazines, and wire services, by contrast, and presumably most informal writing, especially by younger writers, omit it: unnecessary, fussy, in the way.

Anyway, when the advance copy of the book arrived, there it was—or rather, there it wasn't. On the cover, after "CIVILITY," no comma.

The serial comma did appear on the inside title page, oddly enough, and elsewhere inside the book, on all the pages I had proofed. And yes, the words on the cover were stacked in such a way that "CIVILITY" was separated from "AND THE HUMAN IMAGINATION" and my meaning was clear. More embarrassing, at least to the publisher, was that the back cover of the book, down at the bottom left where the shelving information lurks, indicated that it was "FICTION." With this second error I have, at a stroke, answered all those people who wonder why I don't write fiction, the way other intellectuals do: Michael Frayn, Michael Ignatieff, Umberto Eco. There you are, friends: mission accomplished! I suppose it damages the credibility of my actual arguments, which were intended to be non-fictional and even factual, if not perhaps The Truth. But there you go: we are all at the mercy of words. We deploy them as the biddable vehicles of our meaning, but sometimes *they push back*!

Still, the loss of that serial comma—it rankles. I briefly entertained fantasies of applying minute brushstrokes of Wite-Out to any copy of the book I managed to get my hands on, rendering the correction the way I did with a mistaken version of some musical notation that appeared in the hardcover version of my book on the pianist Glenn Gould. Actually, that doesn't seem so crazy, now that I think of it, so if you see me unscrewing the cap of a little bottle during a signing or whatever, just know it's not for sniffing purposes.

You might wonder: What's the big deal? After all, the missing serial comma is not an actual error, like the missing sharp sign was in the Gould example.

A 2008 song by the band Vampire Weekend called "Oxford Comma" includes the line "Who gives a fuck about an Oxford comma?" The line is addressed by the singer to someone, presumably an ex-girlfriend, who has been snobby and deceitful, and about silly things to boot:

> Why would you lie about how much coal you have?
> Why would you lie about something dumb like that?
> Why would you lie about anything at all?

Good point. While it seems gratuitous to associate grammatical particularity with lying and other vices, I am prepared to believe there are people—maybe Oxford graduates—who conjoin them regularly, maybe as a matter of high-minded style. And it's true that defenders of the serial comma lay themselves open to the charge of preciousness, a kind of High Church dandyism.

So is this just one more case of grammatical fascism, another skirmish in the snobs-versus-populists war, the bullies against the liberationists once again? Is it a difference that doesn't make a difference, a matter of sheer preference? Those of us who stand by the serial comma will never consider it a matter of preference. We serial servants are staunch, and the progressive elimination of the little virgules from our prose, especially when done without notice (and in contradiction to the rest of a book), is akin to having a hangnail slowly torn back from a ragged cuticle. *That's* fascism!

There are instances where the loss of the serial comma actually threatens sense, and this is the final consideration when it comes to grammar and punctuation. Consider this notorious sentence from a biography of country-and-western star Merle Haggard: "Among those interviewed were his two ex-wives, Kris Kristofferson and Robert Duvall."[1] The want of a comma in this case not only cuts the mentioned number of people in half, but puts the remaining two in an unlikely position, perhaps wondering if they have legitimate alimony claims on Haggard.[2] A much-repeated though apparently apocryphal example is this book dedication: "to my parents, Ayn Rand and God."

Critics of the comma would retort, I imagine, that there is no genuine ambiguity in these examples, just willful misreading of obvious sense. Well, maybe. Most of the time, the serial comma is simply a matter of pace and elegance. The full title of my book, properly rendered, is this: *Unruly Voices: Essays on Democracy, Civility, and the Human Imagination*. The subtitle is accurate for all its stiffness, and it has a proper, thoughtful measure. On the subtitle's relation to the bolder main title—well, all I can say is that at least I'm fully aware that the colon is the sign, here, of my falling prey to A. J. Ayer's complaint in *Language, Truth, and Logic* (no subtitle for him, but nice use of serial comma in tripartite main title) that all non-empiricist philosophers are actually poets *manqué*. This is a category for whom, one imagines, the *manqué* part is just as important as, if not more than, the poet part. I feel no desire to write actual poetry but I guess I feel that a resonant title is better than a dull one.[3]

Punctuation, like writing more generally, is a always matter of style, and style matters. You, nameless designer of my book's cover, favour a forthright simplicity, comma parsimony. I think every comma is a breath, a minute pause or hitch in the flow of consciousness as it runs along the printed word. Every comma killed is a beat missed, a breath taken away.[4]

* * *

Every punctuation mark has its own peculiar vitality and personality, just as every letter-form does: they don't call them *characters* for nothing. Like the spaces between the words themselves, they are part of that universe we call the written word. An essential part of the economy of public discourse, they must be valued as such.[5]

The history of punctuation has been obscured by the dominance, in fact quite recent and arbitrary, of the nine marks (comma, dash, hyphen, parenthesis, semicolon, colon, space, and upper-case letter) that form the current available store. Nicholson Baker notes how these nine are "so pipe-smokingly Indo-European, so naturally suited in their disjunctive charge and mass to their given sentential offices that we may forgivably assume that commas have been around for at least as long as electrons" or that "the semi-colon, that supremely self-possessed valet of phraseology, is immutable."[6] Not so, of course—the semicolon's origins can be traced to a first edition "published two years after Columbus reached America," while the upward-migrating inverted comma that became the now ubiquitous quotation mark dates from circa 1714—and Baker is not alone in being a connoisseur of the once-common punctuation mark that has fallen into disuse.

I mean such things as the *double virgula* (//) that was once employed to separate sentences. Or the various *dash-hybrids* or *dashtards*, as Baker likes to call them, those marks (,— or ;— or :— or —,) that used to mark entry into, and exit from, parenthetical territory. Baker names these, respectively, the *commash*, the *semi-colash*, the *colash*, and the *reverse commash*, and notes that they were used by everyone from Thackeray, Carlyle, and Ruskin to the early Nabokov, but are now the preserve of eccentrics such as Salman Rushdie (who scatters them profusely in *The Satanic Verses*) and Baker himself (who sneaked one past a copyeditor at the *Atlantic Monthly*).

Or consider short-lived idiolectic printer's marks, such as the seventeenth-century fad for using, in place of the period, what Twitter now insists we call the *hashtag* (I was taught to call it either the *number sign* or the *pound key*), and the *punctus percontativus*, or backward question mark, which was used to close a rhetorical question and distinguish it from a direct query—a useful contrivance now sadly lost, like the typeface called *Ironics* demanded by H. L. Mencken, which was supposed to have letters slanting to the left rather than the italic rightward tilt.[7] The history of punctuation is one of "flourishing coralline tidepools of punctuational pluralism" that are now vanished from "our own purer, more consistent, more teachably codified, and perhaps more arid century."[8] (Nice use of serial comma there.)

It's not all purity-enhancing codification, either. Case in point: the shifting terrain of the hyphen. One of the most vertiginous parts of copy-editing my recent book was having one editor remove a bunch of my hyphens, then have a second re-introduce (reintroduce) them, with explanations and justifications. *Forward-looking* calls for a hyphen when used adjectivally, for example, but *ever-greater* does not because *ever*, used in the sense of more or always, is ever adverbial. I'm agnostic on the current general trend for removing hyphens, especially in academic copy—*postmodern* seems just as good as *post-modern*—though it has to be said that *hyperindustrialized* strains the eye a bit, as does *supererogatory*.

Baker's own struggles with the mighty mini-dash are instructive. An editor of one of his novels changed *back seat* to *backseat*, at a stroke rendering the intended, and correct, two-stress phrasing into slight but detectable trochee, like *baseball* or *touchdown*: BACKseat. (This is the way many Canadians pronounce the abbreviation for *television*: the TEEvee.) It can go the other way, too: I have a friend who consistently (mis)spells the word *nightcap* as two words—*night cap*—which I find inexplicably charming. Baker admits, even though he admires James Joyce's celebrated use of deliberate under-hyphenation—eye-stopping novelties such as *cuffedge*, *watchchain*, and (especially) *scrotumtightening*—that the word *pantyhose* (or *panty hose*, as his editor desired) might just be best rendered as *panty-hose*, that is, with a hyphen that "pull[s] the phrase together scrotumtighteningly at its crotch." (I prefer stockings myself.)

*   *   *

What no one disputes, in the world of punctles, is that they came about as a way to tame the wild thickets of *scriptio continua*, those blocks of undifferentiated letters that used to carpet the visual field of tablets and books. This writing, now to be seen only in cryptic fun-games or children's first stabs at writing (a significant conjunction), was the norm until very late in the history of the printed word. Medieval scholars inserted punctuation as they read a book, both to unlock the sense of the jammed letters, displayed in a way that constantly reminds one of the sacred difficulty of The Word, and to demonstrate the achievement of reading. (It was common practice to sign a block of text after reading it, to record the fact.) The spread of punctuation must therefore be viewed as a key part of the Great Demystification that came with the advent of moveable type. No longer was every clutter of letters a secret script, entombing its sense in marching lines of unpaused, unstopped, undigressed, and unemphasized word-strings.

Theodor Adorno, in a (for him) whimsical essay, interrogates the politics and poetics of punctuation under this sign of democratization of sense. His opening sentence, in the translation by Shierry Weber Nicholsen, is by no means a model of that sense, as was his elitist-lefty-academic wont: "The punctuation marks, taken in isolation, convey meaning or expression and the more they constitute the opposite pole in language to names, the more each of them acquires a definitive physiognomic status of its own, and expression of its own, which cannot be separated from its syntactic function but is by no means exhausted by it."[9] This is certainly true, though one might wish for a more straightforward opening: Punctuation marks help sentences make sense ("syntactic function") but they also each have a distinctive character ("physiognomy"). Thus the question mark looks like "a flashing light or the blink of an eye," the semicolon resembles "a drooping moustache," and the hungry colon "opens its mouth wide." There are notable variants between languages. "With self-satisfied peasant cunning, German quotation marks (« ») lick their lips." Awesome!

In this combination of visual personality and function, punctles make the music of the written word possible. More deeply, they can influence thought itself. The exclamation mark, Adorno suggests, "gave German Expressionism its graphic form," simultaneously a mark of protest against bourgeois conformity and an injection of energy. The dash—simple or compound—demonstrates the thought that thought is fragmentary, the notion of unity a fiction. But there are also dangers. Adorno warns us against the use, in political writing, of ironic quotations marks, so-called "scare quotes." (See? That's them there: the marks that indicate *mention* rather than *use* of a term, as we philosophers would say.)[10] These, he says, "violate the very concept of irony by separating it from the matter at hand and presenting a predetermined judgment on the subject."[11] Like emphasis, irony in writing should be, as it were, audible but not visible. (Adorno would presumably deplore Mencken's Ironics typeface.) Too many scare quotes can actually reverse the intended ironic effect, creating a new and unwelcome irony at the second order. "The abundant ironic quotation marks in Marx and Engels are the shadows that totalitarian methods cast in advance on their writings, whose intention was the opposite."[12] These marks are the seed from which grows, eventually, the double-talk of repressive political regimes.

Punctuation can also play. Sane people have doubtless grown tired of the old store of sideways emoticons. Baker calls them "vaguely irritating," which seems about right. I suppose one may still ironically employ the moderately witty ones, such as the winky-smiley face rendered with a semicolon:

;-)

or the face with tongue sticking out:

:-P

I also like elaborate inventions such as Santa Claus:

*<|:-)

and Homer Simpson:

~(_8^(I)

But Asian horizontal emoticons are kind of wonderful still, especially since they are so rarely seen in our texts. A few choice ones (with no comment on why angry and sad are the same face):

(x_x)	annoyed
(^^)//	clapping
(T_T)	crying
(>_<)	ouch!
\(^o^)/	wow!
(-_-)	angry/sad
(-_-)	zzz good night
(^ ^)	smiling
(*^_^*)	blushing
(^-^)	'Isn't it?'
(p_-)	magnifying glass
(^_^)	'Victory!'
(>_<)(>_<)	'No no!'
(@_@)	dizzy
((((((^_^;)	trying to leave
/(>_<)\	holding head in pain or irritation

What, you have removed my serial comma?	(>_<)(>_<)
Or do you, like me, love the little guys?	(^^)//
Or maybe you're bored of the whole question?	(-_-)zzz

*　　　*　　　*

There is, to be sure, a limit to the degree of consciousness one can bring to the matter of punctuation, indeed to the act of writing itself. Adorno concludes his own meditation on the subject by noting the "permanent predicament" of the writer: "if one were fully aware while writing, one would sense the impossibility of ever using a mark of punctuation correctly and would give up writing altogether." He advises parsimony. "In every punctuation mark avoided," reads the last line of his essay, "writing pays homage to the sound it suppresses."[13]

That great enemy of political double-talk, George Orwell, would surely have agreed with the merits of parsimony in writing, but would have noted the more general irony of Adorno's essay, which defends this very standard with a series of complex, multi-clausal, poetic, Germanic sentences. Indeed, with Orwell, aesthetics becomes ethics when it comes to written composition. The inventor of Newspeak believed passionately that a plain style—a puritanical style—created the impression of honest speaking. A reviewer notes of Orwell: "He remembers that early in his education he was blessed with an English teacher who insisted, with the same fervor as one might demand chastity from a daughter, on severe simplicity from her pupils."[14] Orwell himself would say the following: "Prose literature as we know it is the product of rationalism, of the Protestant centuries, of the autonomous individual."

As we settle decisively into the Twitter/txtng moment of our cultural narrative, it is worth noting that the restless evolution of language has thrust us into a post-Orwellian, maybe post-individualistic moment. The 140-character mini-universe of the tweet and the short-form wordlets of the text banish as impossible the evils of devious complexity which Orwell fought, bringing humour and a sort of found poetry back to daily communication. At the same time, distinction and elegant length, not to mention dialectical energy, are likewise gone. The Latin scholars who first started inserting punctuation into the great texts of Western literature and philosophy would have been, I think, both delighted and disturbed by this form of writing, with its swiftly emergent conventions of coding and decoding, its propensity for unintended hilarity via autocorrect, and, above all, its speed. All surface and no depth, it is nevertheless *writing* and so reminds us of the divine gift of intelligibility, the biggest riddle of them all, played out by billions every day.

"To be mistaken about the rhythm of a sentence," Nietzsche remarks in *Beyond Good and Evil*, "is to be mistaken about the very meaning of that sentence." The serial comma takes its place in the printed word's world of wonders by taking its place in sentences, making sense by marking rhythm and, so, creating meaning. It is a gift all by itself. Strike it out at your peril, dear editors!

Notes

1   Quoted in Robert Fulford, "Giving a F—k About the Oxford Comma," *National Post*, September 11, 2012; Fulford's column was also where I learned about the Vampire Weekend song mentioned here.

2 The title of Lynn Truss's popular tour of grammatical thickets related to punctuation—*Eats, Shoots & Leaves* (Profile Books, 2003)—plays on the larger significance of comma placement. Here is the joke from which the phrase is taken:

> A panda walks into a cafe. He orders a sandwich, eats it, then draws a gun and proceeds to fire it at the other patrons. "Why?" asks the confused, surviving waiter amidst the carnage, as the panda makes for the exit. The panda produces a badly punctuated wildlife manual and tosses it over his shoulder. "Well, I'm a panda," he says, at the door. "Look it up." The waiter turns to the relevant entry in the manual and, sure enough, finds an explanation: "Panda. Large black-and-white bear-like mammal, native to China. Eats, shoots and leaves."

We can note that a serial-comma purist would render the mistaken version as "eats, shoots, and leaves," not the way Truss's title does. (Of the ampersand we say nothing.) In fact, the whole book, while preoccupied with the so-called "grocer's apostrophe" ("potatoe's" and the like), simply omits the serial comma! Worse, as Louis Menand pointed out in his *New Yorker* review of the book, it contains dozens of punctuation errors, beginning with one in the dedication (see footnote 5 below).

3 I won't bore the reader of the main text with this point, but it occurs to me that another tic of my book titles is the recurring deployment of an *adjective-plus-plural-noun* formula. Thus: *Practical Judgments* (2002), *Opening Gambits* (2008), *Concrete Reveries* (2008), and *Unruly Voices* (2012). There was also *Marginalia* (1999), but I don't think that counts. I do think perhaps a future book, which will force me to address topics in analytic philosophy of language and mereology, will have to be called something like *Modified Plurals*.

4 It can matter a lot, to some people, whether the pause is the comma's beat or the semicolon's rest. In *Wit*, a 1999 play by Margaret Edson (rendered *W;t* in some editions and posters), an argument about how to punctuate a line by Donne is the central memory of a dying scholar. Should it be:

> And death shall be no more, Death thou shalt die.
> or:
> And Death shall be no more; Death, thou shalt die!

The poem, says the older party to the argument, "is ultimately about overcoming the seemingly insuperable barriers separating life, death, and eternal life." In the second version, "this profoundly simple meaning is sacrificed to hysterical punctuation." The comma version shows the proximity of life and death, the short breath of distance that at once separates and links them; the semi-colon implies a barrier that allows Death too much credit—precisely the opposite of Donne's meaning. "If you go in for this sort of thing," the senior scholar says, "I suggest you take up Shakespeare."

5 Lynn Truss dedicates her book of grammar scolding "to the memory of the striking Bolshevik printers of St. Petersburg who, in 1905, demanded to be paid the same rate for punctuation marks as for letters, and thereby directly precipitated the first Russian Revolution." *Everything is political!*

But strictly speaking there should be a comma between "St. Petersburg" and "who," since the rest of the sentence is a non-restrictive clause. Louis Menand notes that the book is "a wild downhill ride from there," and confesses he finds it "hard to fend off the suspicion that the whole thing might be a hoax." Menand's main argument is that attention to punctuation is meaningless given that the main value of writing is the mysterious quality we call "voice" or "music." See "Bad Comma," *The New Yorker*, June 28, 2004. But this argument seems *prima facie* invalid, since punctuation is part of what makes a sentence musical or not; compare Adorno, in footnote 9, below.

6 Nicholson Baker, "The History of Punctuation," in *The Size of Thoughts* (Vintage, 1997), 70.

7 We might consider the punctuation analogous to the baseball scorer's convention of using *K* for a strikeout, but a reversed *K* for a strikeout looking, i.e., where the batter does not swing at the third strike. For those keeping score at home, the *K* symbol was pioneered by sports journalist Henry Chadwick (1824-1908), who standardized many aspects of the box-scoring system; he apparently reasoned that, with *S* already taken to indicate a sacrifice, the last letter in "struck" would serve for strikeouts.

8 Baker, "The History of Punctuation," 88.

9 T. W. Adorno, "Punctuation Marks," Shierry Weber Nicholsen, trans., *The Antioch Review* 48:3 (Summer 1990), 300. On the same page, Adorno, the musicologist-turned-critic, will say this: "There is no element in which language resembles music more than in the punctuation marks."

10 The convention, in philosophical writing, is to employ single inverted commas when mentioning a concept or word, say as an example of something, and the standard double ones for its use. This difference ought to be observed for the execution of ironic mention also, but it is almost impossible to get copyeditors to accept the distinction. They prefer to double-quote throughout, which avoids ambiguity but unfortunately obliterates an important logical distinction. I note that this includes the copyeditors at *Descant*, who are otherwise perfection personified.

11 "Punctuation Marks," 303.

12 Ibid., 303.

13 Ibid., 305.

14 William H. Gass, "Double Vision: George Orwell's Contradictions," *Harper's Magazine* (October 2012), 79. Gass adds: "For Orwell, complexity was a weapon of the devious—though most issues had many sides. Language laced with Latin brought back the Middle Ages, but its loss cost us an entire repertoire of distinctions as well as the art of close reading." No benefit without cost, buddy.

Our Insidious Foes
and the Plot
Against America

T HE TERM "fifth column" was coined in 1936, during the Spanish Civil War, by the Nationalist general Emilio Mola. Asked by a journalist to estimate the strength of his forces, Mola replied that he commanded four columns of troops on the march to attack Madrid, then, he added, there was another column, a fifth column, of supporters among the city's population, who would act to undermine the government and deliver Madrid to the Nationalist side.

Immediately, and ever since, a fifth column has been any group of supporters, within a population, for the attacking enemy's cause. Within just a few years, the notion of a fifth column—and the fear of its reality—were so commonplace that U. S. president Franklin Roosevelt, in a fireside radio chat of May 27, 1940, could use it freely. The enemy he had in mind was not, of course, Franco's Nationalist force in Spain but the Axis force, which had supported them, especially Nazi Germany, whose Condor Legion had offered airlifts and terrifying Stuka dive-bomber attacks during the Spanish conflict. At the time of Roosevelt's broadcast, seventy-one percent of polled Americans reported that they thought a Nazi fifth column in America "likely."

Consider just a few of the reasons why. Charles Lindbergh was drawing crowds of thousands while speaking for the America First movement, the neutralist political interest group whose prominent members flirted with anti-Semitism, eugenics, and race superiority, and called for solidarity with the "pure blood" of European civilization. Lindbergh had written that certain races have "demonstrated superior ability in the design, manufacture, and operation of machines." Also that "[t]he growth of our western civilization has been closely related to this superiority." He claimed to admire "the German genius for science and organization, the English genius for government and commerce, the French genius for living and the understanding of life," and that "in America they can be blended to form the greatest genius of all." When Lindbergh refused to return medals awarded to him by the German government, Roosevelt questioned his loyalty. Lindbergh responded by resigning his commission in the air force reserve and slipping away to Europe. He returned to America a few years later and, after Pearl Harbor, asked to be re-commissioned; his request was denied.

Even more influential, perhaps, were the weekly radio broadcasts of Father James Coughlin, a Catholic priest in the Basilian order who hailed originally from Hamilton, Ontario. He attended the same undergraduate college I did, St. Michael's at the University of Toronto, and taught for a time at Assumption College in Windsor. Coughlin had started the broadcasts in 1926 in response to Ku Klux Klan cross burnings on the grounds of his church in Detroit. A decade later, his broadcasts were openly supporting Hitler and Mussolini and his weekly magazine, *Social Justice*, had, among other things, reprinted the controversial anti-Semitic propaganda piece "The Protocols of the Elders of Zion," which claims the existence of a global Jewish conspiracy.

In February 1939, an openly pro-Nazi group called the German American Bund held a massive public rally in New York, finally prompting Coughlin to distance himself from other American admirers of Hitler. The Bund, in a twist that will be familiar to any reader of today's discussion boards, claimed deep loyalty to American ideals, especially individualism and racial purity; they celebrated George Washington as "the first Fascist," a man who knew that unfettered democracy would bring only miscegenation and Jewish-directed financial ruin.

Given all this, it was easy enough for Philip Roth, in *The Plot Against America* (2004), to imagine a counterfactual history in which Lindbergh secured the Republican Party nomination, was elected president on a "vote for Lindbergh or vote for war" campaign, and proceeded to solidify American ties with the Axis powers. Roth's narrative recounts how the character Philip Roth watches as his beloved, benighted

Newark surrenders to routine bigotry. After being "Americanized" at a Midwestern exchange program for boys, his brother returned home to denounce his family as "ghetto Jews." Former columnist Walter Winchell, running against Lindbergh, is assassinated at a political rally. Only when the Lindbergh baby is kidnapped and Lindbergh himself disappears—events blamed on the international Jewish conspiracy but in fact orchestrated by the Nazis—do the American people settle on Roosevelt as an emergency presidential candidate. A few months later, Pearl Harbor is attacked and America's resistance to entering the war is shattered.

Certainly the routine anti-Semitism of Lindbergh was widely shared, as was the mostly unexamined belief in the superiority of the white race. For me, the character who embodies these attitudes best is Tom Buchanan, from Fitzgerald's *The Great Gatsby* (1925), the former Yale football star turned polo-playing East Egg millionaire. Buchanan's white supremacism is the stuff of casual conversation: at one point, he forcefully recommends a book detailing "proof" of the supremacy to Nick over lunch. Especially as played by Bruce Dern in Jack Clayton's 1974 film version of the novel, he is a formidable asshole, a worthy, manly equal to the challenge offered by Robert Redford's Gatsby when it comes to Daisy's narcissism and wavering passions.

In that film, if less so (or anyway more subtly) in the novel and other film adaptations, Gatsby is portrayed as a borderline-vulgar dandy, a man with too many clothes, an over-the-top mansion, and a cream-coloured luxury sedan. Tom's complaints against Gatsby are as much denunciations of the latter's excessively "European" style—too Jewish?—as they are aspersions cast on Gatsby's hazy social origins. "An Oxford man?" he exclaims, when told of Gatsby's tales of accomplishment. "Like hell he is. He wears a pink suit!" Tom, past master of the establishment Brooks Brothers and J. Press dress code from his New Haven days, knows that the pink suit is a sign of political and moral degeneration, not just aesthetic gaucherie: this is the sort of thing that happens when the Gatzes of the world get above themselves.

Gatsby's mountain of beautiful coloured shirts had brought Daisy to tears, but surely she will not, in the end, fall for these gaudy charms? By the 1970s, of course, the aesthetic code had shifted, as Fitzgerald perhaps hoped it would: Robert Amsel's drawn image of handsome Robert Redford sporting what may be American literature's most famous suit, certainly its most famous pink one, appeared on the March 1974 cover of *GQ* magazine. Buchanan's white supremacist certainties, meanwhile, were decisively out of fashion, at least in sane society.

*   *   *

In the 1940s, as Roosevelt knew, things were more uncertain and the films of the decade show it, albeit sometimes in odd form. Hitchcock's version of *The 39 Steps*, based on the 1915 John Buchan thriller and starring Robert Donat, was released in 1935. Employing source material from one world war even as it is poised on the brink of another, this might be considered the baseline fifth column film, or FCF—even though that same provenance makes the phrase anachronistic. The movie has everything: a mysterious female agent, urban and rural chases, trains and guns, and the essential scene of confrontation when the hero, in this case Robert Hannay (Donat), realizes a trusted member of society is in fact the mastermind villain.

In *The 39 Steps*, this villain, the apparently respectable Professor Jordan (Godfrey Tearle), is missing part of a finger, which makes the confrontation all the more dramatic. The plot in play here is theft: the design for a secret aircraft engine is being smuggled out of the country for an unnamed foreign power. It is foiled when—*spoiler alert!*—Hannay guesses that the London vaudeville showman Mr. Memory is the unwilling storage device for details of both the spy network ("The 39 Steps") and the engine design. Jordan shoots Mr. Memory as he begins to recite this information, eventually causing his death, but is himself apprehended soon after. (Trivia note for Canadians: in the Buchan novel, Hannay has returned to London from southern Africa, but in Hitchcock's film he has just come from Canada. The first time he sees Mr. Memory, in a performance at the London Palladium, he shouts out a challenge from the audience—three times in fact: "How far is Winnipeg from Montreal?")

With this template handy, directors and writers were free to start ringing changes on the fifth-column film. These include at least three more Hitchcock classics: *Foreign Correspondent* (1940), *Notorious* (1946), and *North by Northwest* (1959). By the time of the last, the insidious foe was communist rather than Nazi, but James Mason's portrayal of Phillip Vandamm as a suavely vicious master criminal is unimprovable: it effectively ends the competition for this part in the FCF genre. Like *Notorious*, it has Cary Grant starring as the good man in tricky circumstances, and both films contain scenes of high tension when the hero must venture into enemy-held territory in order to carry off the heroine. In *North by Northwest*, it is Roger Thornhill's daring single-person assault on Vandamm's cantilevered mansion near Mount Rushmore that saves Eve Kendall (Eva Marie Saint) from certain death. In *Notorious*, Grant (as T. R. Devlin) actually carries Ingrid Bergman (as Alicia Huberman) down a staircase and out of the house of her secret-Nazi husband, Alex Sebastian, played by Claude Rains.

All of these films feature the notorious MacGuffin, the desired thing around which all the action, sexual and political, is made to rotate: engine design, microfilm in an auctioned *objet d'art*, uranium stored in wine bottles, and what have you. In *Foreign Correspondent*, the MacGuffin role is played by a person, the Dutch diplomat Van Meer, who is variously imprisoned, drugged, impersonated, and assassinated—though it is in fact the impostor who is killed. The real Van Meer is made to divulge key information to Stephen Fisher (Herbert Marshall), ostensibly the leader of the Universal Peace Party but in fact a Nazi fifth columnist. In addition to the usual elements of romantic comedy that enliven all early FCFs—the hero, a reporter played with goofy bulk by Joel McCrea, falls in love with Fisher's daughter, Carol (Laraine Day), who has only admiration for her father's fake pacifist conviction—the film pushes back hard on American non-interventionist sentiment.

When the good guys are shot down over the Atlantic Ocean and rescued by an American vessel, they override the captain's objections and relay their story via radio. Later, back in London, McCrea and Day conduct a pleasing radio broadcast to America even as German shells fall on London—a clear homage to Edward R. Murrow's legendary "London Calling" CBS broadcasts during the 1940 Blitz, which always ended with his trademark salutation, borrowed from the stoic Londoners around him: "Good night and good luck." The word "blitz" is German for lightning, but the quickness was all in the speed of the bombing aircraft and the velocity of their payloads; the sustained raids on English cities began on September 7, 1940, and did not substantially weaken until May 21, 1941. During one period of 267 days, or almost thirty-seven weeks, London was attacked seventy-one times in volumes of high explosives totalling one hundred tons or more.

The implicit argument that the U.S. was already, in 1940, overdue to enter the war would become a minor theme of ensuing FCF activity, which creates the cinematic context for the dramatic events of 1941, which of course culminate in the December 7 surprise Japanese attack on Pearl Harbor; the United States would be in the war for good and all. Thus we have Powell and Pressburger's *The 49th Parallel* (1941), in which a gang of German sailors, stranded in Hudson Bay after their U-boat is sunk, attempt to reach neutral America by way of various Canadian obstacles, including an Inuit leader (Ley On), a Québécois trapper (Laurence Olivier), an eccentric academic (Leslie Howard), and a community of genuinely pacifist Hutterites. Raymond Massey, as a Canadian soldier who likes to box, makes an obligatory appearance, as do the Royal Canadian Mounted Police: they effect one of the key arrests of the fugitive Nazis.

On the other side of the border, there is the much less well-known *All Through the Night*, also from 1941, which mixes elements of standard film-noir crime caper with fifth-column paranoia. Humphrey Bogart plays Alfred "Gloves" Donahue, a New York bookie and sports promoter who is suspected of murdering a nightclub owner. In the standard crime-thriller tradition, in order to clear his name Gloves must find the real killer—but instead discovers an insidious Nazi plot against America! Using nightclubs as cover and led by another paragon of urbane menace, here played by Conrad Veidt, the fifth columnists have been infiltrating American social circles. Gloves, once a happy-go-lucky neutralist, is made to see the reality of rot from within.

*   *   *

Nor was all the activity on the silver screen. In the months before Pearl Harbor, Lillian Hellman's Broadway hit *Watch on the Rhine*—it ran for 378 performances—depicted an opportunistic, Romanian count advancing the Nazi conspiracy in Washington. (Roosevelt sent her a note of congratulation; her lover Dashiell Hammett would later adapt it for the 1943 Bette Davis film version.)

The FCF golden age can be extended a little on the far side of Pearl Harbor in order to include three excellent films that flirt with the basic conventions. *Casablanca* (1942) is not set in the United States and is not technically about fifth columnists, but it does reunite Bogart (as Rick Blaine) and Veidt, who here plays Major Heinrich Strasser, a fanatical, articulate Nazi with a taste for caviar and champagne who is on the trail of Resistance leader Victor Laszlo (Paul Henreid). Plus there's Claude

Rains, now not a secret Nazi but the cynical French captain of police, Louis Renault, and of course Ingrid Bergman, as Rick's long-lost love, Ilsa Lund. If there's any point, once again, *spoiler alert!*: Rick loses Ilsa again, but he shoots Strasser in the process, and he and Renault both decide that, when it comes to Nazis, it's time to stop being neutral. (For completists: Peter Lorre, who did some of the shooting in *All Through the Night*, here gets shot instead. Poor Ugarte! He can't even help himself! But Rick sticks his neck out for nobody . . .)

More in line with the basic FCF narrative is Hitchcock's neglected but compelling *Saboteur* (again 1942), which includes Dorothy Parker among the credited writers and offers one of the most thrilling cross-country chase narratives on film. A worker at a California aircraft-construction company, Barry Kane (Robert Cummings), is wrongly accused of starting a fire at the plant, the work in fact of fifth-column saboteurs. But, as so often with Hitchcock, clearing one's name calls for ever more desperate escapes from police and civilian custody. After a number of scrapes and narrow escapes, not all of them terribly plausible, Kane discovers that the root of the larger fifth-column plot, which embraces plans to blow up the Boulder Dam and the Brooklyn shipyards, among other targets, lies in New York upper-crust society. Here, at a party in the Sutton mansion, he confronts Charles Tobin (Otto Kruger), one of the leaders, who lectures him in grand Nietzschean style about power and its joys.

Kane escapes again, traverses New York by various means, and eventually confronts the actual saboteur, Fry (Norman Lloyd). The final struggle between the two gives rise to one of Hitchcock's most famous sequences. Kane, trying to save the falling Fry at the top of the Statue of Liberty, fails only because the latter's jacket tears at the shoulder, and he falls. As Gatsby would know, clothes maketh the man—and unmaketh the Nazi.

Finally for 1942, consider Leo McCarey's *Once Upon a Honeymoon*, a strange Cary Grant-Ginger Rogers hybrid that blurs the FCF lines maybe a little too much. It is a romantic comedy first, certainly, and yet contains dialogue references to Schopenhauer, Shakespeare, and Irving Berlin. Katie O'Hara (Rogers) is an American burlesque performer in Europe, masquerading as a socialite in order to marry an Austrian baron, Von Luber (Walter Slezak). Grant plays another straight-arrow foreign correspondent, this one called Pat O'Toole, and he is on to the baron's war-mongering and internal weakening of Vienna—later also Prague and Warsaw—in advance of the Anschluss. He poses as a foppish tailor in order to insinuate himself into the baron's circle, accuses O'Hara of Nazi sympathies, which she denies in favour of naked self-interest, and eventually turns her to the true cause. There are radio broadcasts here too, by O'Toole, that are initially pro-Hitler because he believes Von Luber has turned O'Hara over to the Gestapo. When he realizes she is free, he cleverly turns the broadcast against Von Luber, who is arrested instead.

But not for long. By the time O'Hara and O'Toole have boarded a ship bound for New York, he has managed to convince his Nazi bosses that the best place for him is America, there to continue the insidious plans for Nazi world domination. Again, *spoiler alert!*: there is a struggle and he falls overboard. Or is he pushed? Doesn't matter; he can't swim. Fifth-column plot foiled before it even reached the Hudson River docks. The real action in this film is the romance and comedy, anyway, which makes it either the perfection of the FCF or its endpoint—or both. By the time Orson Welles would come to make *The Stranger* in 1946, the Nazi in America is the one who is on the run, hiding secret war crimes instead of stealing state secrets.

In this case, Welles himself plays a New England schoolmaster, Charles Rankin, who has erased his past as a Nazi killer. He has been hunted down by Edward G. Robinson as Mr. Wilson, in a driven performance that acts as a sort of Simon Wiesenthal homage before the fact— incidentally bolstered by the fact that Robinson, born in Romania, was a Jew whose family had emigrated after suffering anti-Semitic violence in Bucharest. Among other tactics, Mr. Wilson will use graphic footage from the Third Reich concentration camps and details of genocide plans to convince Rankin's wife that he is guilty. The film ends (alert! alert!) with Rankin—in fact the ex-Nazi Franz Kindler—fleeing to the top the town's picturesque church belfry, and falling (or is it jumping?) to his death. Justice is done, after a fashion.

*   *   *

The FCF lived on, at least in outline, during the Cold War. But now paranoia, rather than pacifism or isolationism, is the force that is implicated politically. The Red Scare and McCarthy witch-hunt trials inspired, among other things, a Hollywood deft at creating political allegories in which space aliens, giant insects, body snatchers, or airborne toxic events stood in for the insidious invasion force of Soviet communism. The best of these, at least for me, was the short-lived (1967-68) television series *The Invaders*, whose memorable conceit was that the aliens were identifiable by an inability to close up their pinkies with their ring fingers, making them look as if they were forever drinking tea in a pretentious way—and, ironically, creating a deployment of digits just one space away from the Vulcan "Live long and prosper" salute.

There was also the looming spectre of brainwashing, most vividly depicted in John Frankenheimer's 1962 film *The Manchurian Candidate*. Laurence Harvey memorably plays Staff Sergeant Raymond Shaw, the apparent Korean War hero who is, in fact, a "sleeper" Soviet assassin being directed by his mother Mrs. Eleanor Iselin (Angela Lansbury), who also guides the political career of her idiot husband, and Shaw's stepfather, the McCarthyesque Senator John Yerkes Iselin (James Gregory). The height of fifth-column anxiety is thus achieved: the enemy agent whose effectiveness relies on his not knowing he is an enemy agent. But the plot against America is foiled by—yay!—Frank Sinatra as Major Bennett Marco, Shaw's former commanding officer and himself a victim of the same brainwashing (also, as it happens, of the female cruise; see "Hotel Bars and the Female Cruise").

The same funhouse-mirror logic of identity and doubt, whereby enemies may not know they are what they are, and in which the initially democratic society gradually, maybe inexorably shifts towards fascism, pervades the tortuous political plotlines of the *Battlestar Galactica* revision (2004-2009). Here, the Cylon cybernetic entities created by Earthlings acquire sufficient design skill to fashion versions of themselves indistinguishable from humans—well, if those humans are Tricia Helfer and Grace Park!—and sufficient intelligence to engineer a Pearl-Harbor-like sneak attack that destroys Earth civilization and scatters the human population. One of the many inspired subtleties of the series is the fact that the Cylons, who in their basic models are just machine-like killing machines, appear devoted to a monotheistic religion not unlike Christianity. The enemy within?

More recently, the phrase "a plot against America" can be heard uttered most often by Mandy Patinkin, in character as Saul Berenson in the riveting television series *Homeland*. America's insidious foes are now more shadowy than ever, Al-Qaeda or some similar Islamo-fascist group without nationality or uniform: not so much a fifth column as a non-column. The sleeper agent is another decorated war hero, Nicholas Brody (Damian Lewis), who may or may not be playing complicated counter- and counter-counter-espionage games with Carrie Mathison (Claire Danes), a brilliant but unstable C.I.A. analyst. The two develop a relationship, of course, because that's what returned Islam-converted assassins and their government-assigned watchers usually do in these circumstances. The series is nicely turned all the same, especially with Patinkin's gruff presence at its core. Needless to say, his character's virtues—consistency, loyalty, tracking the truth—will turn out to be liabilities in the pervasive paranoia that is the post-9/11 security state.

At one point, the series hung suspended between its second and third seasons. Season Two ended with Brody suspected of masterminding a deadly bombing, a charge of which he (probably) isn't guilty. He has fled to Montreal, because where else?—it's the only Canadian city that exists for a certain kind of American writer. Carrie, who seemed intent on entering Quebec with him—we love you here in Canada, Claire Danes!—has instead bid him farewell at the border and returned to Washington and the embrace of her now-rehabilitated mentor, Saul.

At this juncture, enemies and friends (even lovers) are entirely indistinguishable, one from the other, and the twisting plot is revealed as a kind of narrative grapevine, sprouting nodes of conflict and identity without resolution. *Homeland* is pervasive-paranoia television, where the plot against America is always already up and running and the presumed battle is between neo-liberal ideology, in the unlikely form of the C.I.A., and Islamic terrorists. The show's core message, consistent with its role in cementing the integrated version of Guy Debord's "society of the spectacle," is too disturbing to be articulated directly. Instead, it circulates in the form of digestible entertainment, a critics'-darling show among whose avowed fans is the drone-strike president himself, the bane of Bin Laden, Barack Obama.

Call it the final spoiler alert. When it comes to terrorism television, the plot is the plot: we have met the enemy—and he is us.

Saints, Sinners, and Exiles:

The End of Michael Arlen's Mayfair

H ERE's an involved literary-cinematic plot worthy of a Raymond Chandler novel. It involves a Raymond Chandler novel, in fact, and a literary character who has multiple identities even in his original form. Try to follow it like you would puzzle out the final-chapter summation of a tricky case as related by Philip Marlowe to Bernie Ohls.

"Now of this man who called himself Gay Falcon many tales are told, and this is one of them." So begins, awkwardly, a short story that appeared in a 1940 edition of *The Strand* magazine. Its author was then world-famous English novelist Michael Arlen and, despite the reference to many stories, it was Arlen's singular venture into the genre world of detective fiction.

The story introduced the world to a suave but shady character who may or may not be a professional thief, possibly a spy, certainly a man of mystery. "Your name is Gay Falcon!" the beautiful co-star of the story accuses him at one point. "I have others equally improbable," he replies smoothly. At a later stage, the police discover multiple passports in his possession. "Three passports," says Chief Inspector Poss, his Scotland Yard nemesis, "one for a man of independent means called Gay Stanhope Falcon, one for a soldier called Colonel Rock, who looks quite a bit like you, and one for a journalist with an address in Paris called Spencer Pott, who would be your twin brother but for his moustache."

Gay Stanhope Falcon is described as looking pretty much as you would expect. "He was tall, his clothes were as you like it for an old suit casually worn, his face was long and lean and dark, and his eyes were deep, hard shadows." Twice we are reminded of his "dark saturnine face" and those "deep" eyes. In another scene, for variety, the same eyes are labelled "hard, unsmiling." Of course they are! Arlen's Falcon is a stock creature, a warmed-over rehash of, among other forebears, E. W. Hornung's gentleman-thief Raffles, the "amateur cracksman" who began literary life in 1899, and Leslie Charteris's Simon Templar, the Saint, who first appeared in 1928 and lasted for more than fifty age-defying books. Inspector Poss takes his place alongside Arthur Conan Doyle's Inspector Lestrade, Agatha Christie's DCI Japp, and other stumbling professionals of the murder-mystery canon, forever doomed to be outwitted by gifted outsiders.

In this case, the man who called himself Gay Falcon foils an elaborate insurance scheme which involves society parties, purloined jewelry, and female cat burglars. There are a couple of murders, a run-in with a criminal mastermind, and of course the seductive female co-star, a lady with "famous blue eyes" who almost, but not quite, manages to get to the Falcon. Reading the story, one finds it impossible to say whether Arlen is fooling around with genre conventions, self-consciously paying tribute to Hornung and Charteris, or just running out of writerly juice. That final possibility is one to which we will return, like a loose end in the case file.

The Falcon's life, begun so casually, quickly blossomed into a complicated lineage. In 1941, the year after Arlen's story appeared, actor George Sanders, who would go on to (among other things) marry Zsa Zsa Gabor, was playing Charteris's character in a series of films. Sanders, nowadays probably best known for his portrayal of cynical theatre critic Addison DeWitt in *All About Eve* (1950, d. Joseph Mankiewicz), which won him an Academy Award for best supporting actor, has one of those faces we all know and a name most of us forget. In the 1940s he was a hard-working serial actor, and took what he could get. RKO, which had commissioned the Saint films, suddenly cast him and co-star Wendy Barrie in a new series of Falcon films. Charteris protested the switch, but RKO's lawyers pointed to the Arlen story as their source and cut him loose.

The Saint, who already had a radio life with the voice of Vincent Price, would of course be revived in a 1962-69 television series, starring a handsome, pre-Bond Roger Moore as the playboy adventurer. There were also other, less popular television versions, not to mention the wonderfully bad 1997 Val Kilmer film incarnation (d. Phillip Noyce), which features a number of implausible fake identities, awful foreign accents, and the goofy, beautiful Elisabeth Shue as a genius Oxford cold-fusion physicist.

Now as the man-about-town character Gay Lawrence, who enjoys a secret sleuthing identity as the Falcon, Sanders quickly did a number of films for RKO, from the original *The Gay Falcon* and *A Date With the Falcon* (both 1941) through to *The Falcon's Brother* (1942). The original character is killed in this last film, in part because Sanders was weary of the series and asking for more money than the producers of what amounted to a Saturday serial were willing to cough up. In the film, the Falcon identity is taken over by Gay's brother, Tom Lawrence, who goes on to further adventures. In a twist worthy of our story, Tom Lawrence, the new Falcon, was played by Tom Conway, who was George Sanders's real-life brother, to whom he bore a strong resemblance—but for a fashionable pencil-thin moustache.

It gets better. A sophisticated Falcon detective character was already in play when Arlen wrote his one-and-only story. Author Charles H. Huff, using the pseudonym Drexel Drake, because why not, had published *The Falcon's Prey* in 1936. The following year he released a sequel, *The Falcon Cuts In*, and then *The Falcon Meets a Lady* and "The Falcon Strikes," in *American Magazine*, both during 1938. Drake's Falcon had as his real name Malcolm J. Wingate. When his novels were adapted for radio in 1943—even as the RKO film series was running, with Tom Conway—the Drake Falcon was re-dubbed Michael (Mike) Waring. The show's producers concluded each broadcast with a clear reference to Drake as their source author, and yet the show's opening sequence featured an announcer saying "You met the Falcon first in his best-selling novels, then you saw him in his thrilling motion picture series. Now join him on the air. . . ."

If you're keeping score at home, you'll know that the bestselling novels were Drake's, and so was the radio series listeners were about to hear, but that the thrilling film series was in fact based on Arlen's Falcon.

Except that it wasn't. Not after the first two films, anyway. The third film in the RKO series was *The Falcon Takes Over*, also known, for some reason, as *The Falcon Steps Out*, and still featuring George Sanders as Gay Falcon. Watch it and you will quickly notice that the plot—a missing singer, her jilted husky ex-con boyfriend, a crooked clinician—has been ripped more or less intact from Chandler's 1940 novel *Farewell, My Lovely*, his second featuring Philip Marlowe. (The first was *The Big Sleep*, in 1939.) New York has replaced Los Angeles as the scene of the action, and the smooth Falcon takes over from tough-guy Marlowe, but the troubled big fellow at the centre of the action is still called Moose Malloy.

Bizarrely, this counts as the first film adaptation of a Raymond Chandler novel, even though it has none of the noir atmosphere one associates with Chandler. In 1944, a more proper adaptation of *Farewell, My Lovely* would appear, directed by Edward Dmytryk and starring, as Marlowe, crooner Dick Powell, who wanted to toughen his image and broaden his range after a series of light-comedy and musical hits. But it's not called *Farewell, My Lovely*; it's called *Murder, My Sweet* because the producers were afraid that the original title, combined with Powell's reputation as a singer, would suggest to audiences that the film was another song-and-dance picture.

For some Chandler fans, including me, Powell's Marlowe comes closest—yes, closer than Humphrey Bogart in *The Big Sleep* (1946) or Robert Mitchum in his versions of *The Big Sleep* (1978) and *Farewell, My Lovely* (1975)—to the flippant, tough, first-person tone of the books. The film adaptation does take liberties with the original plot, reversing parts of the action and shifting the weight of the narrative. Another fractured identity . . .

*   *   *

Meanwhile, what of world-famous English novelist Michael Arlen, source of our tangled story's original Falcon reference?

Well, let's start with the fact that Michael Arlen was not his real name, and he was not English. His real name was Dikran Kouyoumdjian, and he was born in Bulgaria to Armenian parents in 1895—an identity fit for a character in one of Eric Ambler's novels, if not one of Raymond Chandler's. In 1901 the family relocated to England, where young Dikran attended cricket-dominated Malvern College and, later, Edinburgh University. He stayed only briefly. "I, up at Edinburgh, was on the high road to general fecklessness," he would write in a biographical sketch. "I only stayed there a few months; jumbled months of elementary medicine, political economy, metaphysics, theosophy—I once handed round programs at an Annie Besant lecture at the Usher Hall—and beer, lots of beer. And then, one night, I emptied my last mug, and with another side-glance at Oxford, came down to London; 'to take up a literary career' my biographer will no doubt write of me."

Take up a literary career he certainly did. Arlen left Edinburgh in 1913 and found a London on the brink of a war in which he would serve for neither England nor Bulgaria, technically still his national home and allied with Germany. For several years he published reviews, essays, and stories under his birth name in obscure, ill-paid places. He had friends among the other writers not serving in the war for various reasons, including Aldous Huxley (eyesight) and D. H. Lawrence (German wife). Lawrence would say of Arlen at this time, in a letter to Lady Ottoline Morrel, "Kouyoumdjian seems a bit blatant and pushy: you may be put off by him. But this is because he is very foreign, even though he doesn't know it himself. In English life he is in a strange alien medium and he can't adjust himself."

That would change, though the background suspicions about Arlen's "very foreign" manner would never entirely dissipate. Lawrence used sombre, pushy Dikran as the model for one of the characters in *Lady Chatterley's Lover* (1928), the successful society playwright Michaelis, who is Connie Chatterley's first lover. "Connie really wondered at this queer, melancholy specimen of extraordinary success . . . Connie felt a sudden, strange leap of sympathy for him, a leap mingled with compassion, and tinged with repulsion . . . The outsider! The outsider! And they called him a bounder!"

In 1920 Arlen brought out *The London Venture*, a collection of biographical writings. From this time on, he signed his work "Michael Arlen" and, in 1922, with wartime suspicions lessened, he was naturalized as a British citizen and legally changed his name to Michael Arlen. His published work from this time includes *"Piracy"* (1922), a novel of manners complete with those scare quotes in the title, and a collection of linked stories, *These Charming People* (1923), that introduced a gentleman thief, "The Cavalier of the Streets," who might be considered a sort of foreshadow of Gay Falcon.

These books were mild successes. Then everything changed for Arlen. Still shy of thirty, he published *The Green Hat* in 1924. In one of those sweet-spot conjunctions of time and subject, this story of a fast young widow, Iris Storm, a woman with "a pagan body," rampaging through London's fashionable Mayfair, exactly captured the mood of excess then gripping 1920s London society. It was a massive bestseller on both sides of the Atlantic, projecting Arlen into instant fame and fortune. He, in turn, helped the success along by maintaining an impeccable social presence as a dandified, beautifully mannered imitation of an English man of means. His suits were cut by angels, his hair and moustache always minutely trimmed, and his cruising Rolls-Royce coloured a rich buttery yellow, than which there is no higher visible hue of *pukka* 1920s all-rightness. In a nice dandy's touch, Arlen had it registered in Manchester so that its licence plate would begin with the letters MA.

The Green Hat is a florid, sometimes sexy story of unexplained deaths and wild love affairs. Iris's late husband, Boy Fenwick, has thrown himself from a high window on their wedding night, no one is quite sure why. Lovely Iris is in a complicated pattern of self-recrimination and decadent release. She has more than a few suitors, and there will be shouting and crashing cars before the end. The dialogue is improbably excited, for English characters, but the combination of sex and death proved irresistible. The book was banned and bought with equal fervour.

It was also more than just a publishing triumph. There were successful Broadway and West End dramatic versions of it, and two film adaptations: one in 1928, starring Greta Garbo and John Gilbert, entitled *A Woman of Affairs*; and another in 1934, with Constance Bennett and Herbert Marshall, released under the title *Outcast Lady*. He was sketched for the *Tatler*, celebrated in poem by Osbert Sitwell, and, on May 2nd, 1927, a dapper and heavy-nosed Arlen made the cover of *Time* magazine, smiling wryly, confirmed in his status as a global literary celebrity.

But, as so often, early success released its own krakening demons into the personal world. Arlen would never match the success of *The Green Hat* again, even though he would go to produce similar Bright-Young-Thing satires of Mayfair life, including his sort-of sequel, *Young Men in Love* (1927), which in many ways is a superior book. His anxiety and restlessness with fame are evident on its pages, including several sly references to the evil presence of quick literary success writing about the romantic foibles of the rich and powerful.

The book's most likeable, and most hapless, character is the young author Saville, excessively worried that he is not taken seriously, who has "had enough of publicity" and is "tired of making a fool of himself," but who finds he is criticized for not continuing to write about "lords and champagne and lovely painted ladies." Readers find the serious Saville "very disappointing" and publishers accuse him of ingratitude. Saville is, naturally, especially desirous of the good opinion of gorgeous Venetia Vardon, a vague and careless beauty of the sort Evelyn Waugh would later render more cynical but just as dangerous. Ogden Goelet, writing in *The Harvard Crimson* of May 26, 1927, describes her as "the typical lovely creature of Michael Arlen, impossible yet plausible, stunning and elusive."

Goelet's review, even making allowances for Cambridge knowing-ness, captures the spirit of the mixed notices the book received. Its opening paragraph is worth quoting in full: "Arlen again, with his old characters in new names, dropped into a new book with the appropri-ate spring title *Young Men in Love*—that is all. It takes about a hundred pages of very, very polite conversation to get the plot tugged out of port and under way. Maxims are to be found at the beginning and end of each line, and one feels that Arlen is trying his hardest to impress us with his cleverness. I advise him to read some more Oscar Wilde and go back to Armenia." A jerk's double play: racist as well as dismissive.

There is no doubt that Arlen's fusion of his image with his work, abetted by a peculiar and easily mocked style, would work to undermine seriousness. The vivid, inflected manner, with its artfully omitted com-mas and fanciful images, was swiftly labelled *Arlenese* and was widely parodied. (Roger Abingdon's *The Green Mat: A Romance of Askew People* (1925), with an introduction by Arlen himself, is probably the best of these.) Here is a typical passage: "The moon made a great fuss of her all the way to a place called Great Neck. They had quite a party the moon and Marilyn. I left out had nothing to do but watch." And another: "The carpet of colours, on which the men were sprinkled like black smuts on a town garden, swayed between us and the doorway, but no crowd might hide that man, for he was as tall as a tree and his crisp yellow hair glared like a menace above the intervening heads and his frozen blue eyes petri-fied smoke, noise, and distance."

Arlen, like Saville, was right to worry that his swift ascent and super-ficial characters would doom his writerly future. After *Young Men in Love* he offered the world *Lily Christine* (1928), *Babes in the Wood* (1929), and *Men Dislike Women* (1931). None of them were either critical or financial successes, according to the standard biographies, and the 1929 market crash would count among its victims the sort of social romance Arlen had perfected. In 1936, P. G. Wodehouse would publish the appropriate Depression-era inversion of Arlen's steamy, overwrought romances, his title surely a sly reference to Arlen: *Young Men in Spats* is still about upper-class love triangles, but nobody takes Bertie Wooster and his twit-confreres in the Drones Club at all seriously—least of all themselves.

Arlen left England, first for Florence and Cannes, and then, after the Second World War, to the United States. He continued to write, producing a odd array of gothic, horror, science fiction and other miscast stories. But his moment was over. One critic recently compared his dated style to those of Ronald Firbank or E. F. Benson, other period writers whose stars have fallen, but Arlen is even less resonant now than they are, not as campy as the former nor as reliably funny as the latter. His writing career fizzled out: he published his last book, a sharp denunciation of Germany, in 1939. He then spent the last decade of his life under the heavy cosmic sentence of writer's block, moving from resort to resort up and down the American Atlantic coast, or tarrying in Manhattan, his lovely aristocratic wife, the former Countess Atalanta Mercati, ever in tow.

*　　*　　*

Also two children: a son (Michael John) and a daughter (Venetia). One of the saddest of the many sad stories to be found in *Exiles*, the warm 1970 memoir of Arlen written by his son, concerns a paper-wrapped parcel. The younger Michael, lunching with his still smartly turned out father one day in New York, notices he has under his arm a flat package, like a magazine or file. After lunch, he stops to affix postage and drop it in a mailslot. It is, Michael senior acknowledges, a short story that he is submitting to a magazine. The son is delighted: once-blocked father is writing again! But no, Michael senior confesses. It is an old story. He came upon it under a pile of papers, reread it, and found it not so bad. Why not send it on?

It never appeared in print.

To my mind, this is less a cautionary tale about the vagaries of literary fame than a terrifying parable of life in general, its heedless and cruel distribution of gifts. Our mortal span has an arc none of us can predict or control; and smooth narrative curves like those Aristotle identified in the *Poetics*, shaping everything from Sophoclean tragedy and Arlen's own melodramatic novels, rarely show up in actual human affairs. You may be raised high only to be dropped; or, worse, you may just glide imperceptibly down, like one of those weather-blinded pilots who, not trusting their instruments, spiral themselves into the ground, believing themselves level or even climbing all the while. Aviation people call this nightmare scenario "one *g* all the way down."

Flying not quite blind, let us consider some curious final entries in the case file of the man who called himself Michael Arlen.

In *The Atlantic Monthly* of October 1954, the critic Charles J. Rolo, an early American champion of Evelyn Waugh, offered a measured assessment of the writer who had, in effect, wrested the Bright Young Things from Arlen's grasp. "His style is swift, exact, almost unfailingly felicitous," Rolo notes of Waugh's prose. "His inventions are entrancing; his timing inspired; his matter-of-fact approach to the incongruous produces a perverse humour that is immensely effective." But he could, equally, lurch from luminous to trashy, especially when gripped by one of his many personal bugbears: religion, country houses, female desire. "Without the restraints of the ironic stance, his critical viewpoint reveals itself as bigoted and rancorous; his snobbery emerges as obsessive and disgusting; and his archaism involves him in all kinds of silliness." That, at least, had never been Arlen's problem.

Rolo also details some of the sources of Waugh's legendary social ambition. "At this time"—the mid-1920s—"he has said, he was a pagan and 'wanted to be a man of the world'—a well-rounded English gentleman in the eighteenth-century tradition. He joined in the whirl of Michael Arlen's Mayfair. He 'gadded among savages and people of fashion and politicians and crazy generals . . . because I enjoyed them'. But he was a worldling who could relish all this and still find it wanting." Thus, perhaps, the basic difference between Arlen's romances of that milieu and Waugh's more biting—and more lasting—satire: there was disapproval as well as desire in their author's heart. It is also notable that Rolo can use, without explanation, the phrase "Michael Arlen's Mayfair," knowing that *Atlantic* readers will understand its resonance. Arlen owned that world. In a sense that is here validated by the young climber Waugh, he created it.

Then, in February 1955, just four months after Rolo's s essay, a rival publication then known as *Harper's Monthly Magazine* added a poignant coda. This essay was called "What Happened to Michael Arlen?" and its author was Alec Waugh, Evelyn's older brother. The piece issues forth a strong whiff of the standard, disheartening Spinal-Tap, where-are-they-now-file odour of death, but with other, brighter notes also creeping in. Waugh details Arlen's rise and fame, his moves to Cannes and New York, the creation of a limited company in South America to protect his assets and avoid punitive British income tax. He notes with wonder the advances paid on *Lily Christine*, which totalled $85,000 in 1928 low-tax American dollars. He mentions the Savile Row suits, the pearl tie pin, the neat figure, the three martinis before lunch. Then the low sales, the questioning of his loyalty in Parliament during the Second World War, the lazy afternoons on the Riviera or strolling along Fifth Avenue, when it was so much easier not to write.

Waugh complicates the literary narrative, however. He may not be the soundest judge—one would like to hear brother Evelyn on the subject—but he finds the post-*Green Hat* books entirely worthwhile, *Men Dislike Women*, for example, "a delightful comedy of manners." They sold better than usually thought. Period critics were enthusiastic about the later, post-Arlenese books. J. B. Priestley, reviewing Arlen's dystopian fable *Man's Mortality* (1932), said "I did not think him to be a man of this mettle. Bravo." Of his last book, *The Flying Dutchman* (1939), Humbert Wolfe wrote: "Michael Arlen runs a serious risk of acclaiming himself a genius. For many years in point of sheer diabolical talent he has been unapproachable."

If sales of these last books were sluggish, the cause may have lain in public fickleness and superficiality. Waugh quotes a bit of doggerel that appeared in a London weekly magazine during the 1930s:

> *Mr. Arlen*
> *Was formerly Mayfair's darling*
> *But she raised a plucked and supercilious eyebrow*
> *When he went all highbrow*

Arlen himself, meanwhile, is portrayed as a paragon of middle-aged contentment. "I was a flash in the pan in my twenties," Arlen told a *New Yorker* interviewer at this time. "I had a hell of a lot of fun being flashy and there was by the grace of God a good deal of gold dust in the pan." He confesses to Waugh that he never liked writing, and was happy not to have to do it. He is lazy, he says; he prefers reading. "Of course I am happy," he tells Waugh, "any man should be happy who enjoys the patience of his wife, the tolerance of his children, and the loyalty of head waiters." The famous, elegant writer gathers a group of friends every noontime at the King Cole Room of the St. Regis Hotel in Midtown Manhattan. He laughs and talks, drinks the three martinis, orders a leisurely lunch. Later, Atalanta will appear and they will amble back to their spacious Park Avenue apartment. Hardly the picture of a tortured, blocked writer.

In fact, Waugh works hard to make of this lack of production not just a case of too-easy life but a sort of metaphysical position. Writing the later books, looking down at the ocean from his Cannes villa, the thirty-something Michael Arlen must have felt increasingly separate from that other, world-famous Michael Arlen, subject of endless romantic speculation, social envy, and undergraduate parody. Eventually, Waugh writes, "[t]he side of him that still might have cared to write was no longer Michael Arlen and he had no use for it. He can now be Michael Arlen more effectively by not writing. It is as simple as that."

That is hardly simple, though! If nothing else, all those ramifying Michael Arlens complicate this attempt to render Arlen as a sort of Glenn Gould figure, renouncing performance precisely because there was so much demand for him. The multiple Michaels are more like tokens without a type, simulacra of an identity that was always an assumed one. (For the record, Gould would continue to produce recordings at a furious rate after his celebrated "concert drop-out." His "silence" was actually replete with music.)

And yet, the vision of a happy, idle, sociable Arlen proves hard to resist. The *New Yorker* interviewer had described him this way: "Slender of waist, bushy of eyebrow, neatly sideburned, elegantly mustached, poised, urbane, resplendent in a pin-striped blue suit, the flourisher of a gold-banded Malacca cane, possessed of no demon whatsoever and apparently the world's best adjusted writer." Waugh adds his own summation, somewhat more florid but just as approving: "It has been a long road from Dvornok, Bulgaria, to that side table in the King Cole Room: a long and romantic road. Michael Arlen has fulfilled the destiny he chose."

You really want to believe it, the standard dark narrative salvaged by this late-life vision of pure, indolent, affluent happiness. Maybe we simply want there to be at least one person with a sane life after fame, contentment as a writer, and conjugal bliss—not to mention a slender waist into one's fifties. And it may have been so for Michael Arlen. But was it, perhaps, just another assumed identity, another role that sly, elegant Dikran Kouyoumdjian chose to play?

I keep thinking of that parcel under his arm at lunch with Michael John, the shrugged-off embarrassment of dropping that excavated story into the mail. In *Exiles*, Michael J. Arlen likewise recalls the rhythmic rumble of his father's pacing in the library at night, unable to write an acceptable word—a sound Alec Waugh could never have heard. Michael also relates how his father would hint that those boon lunchtime companions in the King Cole Room were often barely acquaintances, second-raters and hangers-on eager to pretend friendship with even a fading celebrity. *Second-rate* second-raters.

In any event, the elder Michael must have known by then that his days were numbered. In 1956—just sixteen months after Waugh's profile must surely have made him smile his wry smile—the man who called himself Michael Arlen ended his uneven romance with life. He died of cancer in New York on June 23rd.

Parties, Parties,
More Parties

I N A RAMSHACKLE HOUSE near Hillsborough, New Hampshire, not far from where Franklin Pierce, the state's only president so far, was born and raised, there is a treasure trove of what can't exactly be called antiques. These are not collectible items or hidden gems. It's not exactly a junk barn, but the place is stuffed with old records, beer steins, fishing tackle, campaign badges, and piles of rotting magazines and paperback books. There are gnarled leather ice skates that no human foot will ever again penetrate, boxes of obsolete ceramic fuses and defunct fasteners, piles of mildewed gut snowshoes and moth-eaten felt pennants from long-gone world's fairs and time-buried tourist attractions.

I visit this place, with my wife and her family, at least once a year, often twice: we go in summer, during a cherished annual August sojourn in the cool of the Connecticut River Valley, and every other year or so we also make the trek for the almost-guaranteed white Christmas to be had in the hills that rise on the Live-Free-or-Die side of that mighty artery that flows from Canada all the way to Long Island Sound. The antique house is one of a series of regular stops that cannot be skipped during these trips, the family-sanctioned imperative rhythm of blueberry picking, lake fishing, grilled hot dogs, fireworks, hiking, and porchside gin-and-tonics.

I have found my fair share of weird, wonderful jackpots in the house. One year, an old New York-published anthology of Stephen Leacock pieces, when he was arguably more famous south of the border than north of it, complete with a tipped-in yellowing newspaper review of the book written in the arch, breathless prose of the 1920s. Another time, a squat and barely worn silver plastic model of the Empire State Building, with green baize on the base, that dates from the 1940s, during the first wave of commercial replication of the building's iconic shape—about which I happened to be writing a book. Also on that visit, not far away on the same shelf, I uncovered an old hand-tinted postcard of the Woolworth Building. In 1911, when this tiny token of urban sophistication had made its way back to the farmlands and small towns of New Hampshire, the Woolworth was the tallest building in New York. The wavery fountain-penned message drew a line across the observation deck on the fifty-eighth floor, noting "Was up this last summer." The back mentions a sailing trip in the harbour of New York: good times recalled, from a century ago and more, the two-penny lifeline from the big city to back home . . .

On yet another occasion, my mother-in-law, who knows my tastes, triumphantly produced a brass-and-enamel cigarette case whose front depicts the lower half of Manhattan. The brand is marked inside as "Volupté USA," but there is no date on it. (The company was founded in Elizabeth, New Jersey, in 1926: my piece is probably mid-1940s.) Columbus Circle and Central Park, with both a cantering horse and a zoo-stuck elephant, appear on the left-hand side; the (now gone) Aquarium and Statue of Liberty decorate the far right. In between, on an abstracted grid that shows Fifth Avenue, Broadway, Thirty-Fourth Street, Fourteenth Street, and Wall Street, there are little cartoon icons of the Empire State Building, of course, along with the Chrysler, and Times Square, Rockefeller Center, Madison Square Garden, Penn Station, City Hall, Washington Square, and Sutton Place. Chinatown is marked with a blue-smocked, pipe-smoking figure wearing a coni-cal "coolie" hat. A prop-driven Lindbergian airplane is winging its way across the East River near the Williamsburg Bridge, not far from a leg-end pointing the way "TO WORLD'S FAIR," even as a barge steams up the Hudson near the Palisades. On the Lower East Side there is an organ-grinder figure in green and yellow, and another wielding some sort of wheeled contraption. "PUSHCARTS," the picked-out lettering says, a word that for some of us cannot help but invoke Jean Merrill's deathless chil-dren's novel of New York, *The Pushcart War* (1964), a future-look-back tale of plucky pushcarters who fought against oppressive downtown truckers using pea-shooters as weapons to flatten tires.

And finally, in the top left-hand corner of this little piece of gorgeous frippery, there is another antic figure, a little man in blue trousers, bright red topcoat, and a yellow top hat, who dances bandy-legged near an inscribed arrow and the words "TO HARLEM."

*   *   *

I thought of this minuscule dancing man when I secured the latest find from the rambling house, a novel by the almost forgotten literary and cultural figure Carl Van Vechten that is called, with studied sociological casualness, *Parties: Scenes from Contemporary New York Life* (1930).

The novel was published by Alfred A. Knopf. Van Vechten was just the third author this brave new house had signed, right after H. L. Mencken, whose trend-setting periodical *The American Mercury* (co-edited with George Jean Nathan) Knopf had been publishing since 1923. Knopf published over twenty books by Van Vechten, starting with the awesomely titled *Music and Bad Manners* in 1916, just the second year of their operations, and continuing well into mid-century. My copy of *Parties*, a bit foxed and loose in the binding, stained a bit here and there, carries the famous Borzoi (Russian wolfhound) colophon as an imprint on the back-cover cloth.[1] The book is also decorated on the cover with an embossed-silver impression of a little Cupid figure stomping grapes in some sort of birdbath, and marked on the flyleaf with a rubber-stamp imprint that says "NICKERSON DRUG CO., INC., HARWICHPORT, MASS., P.L. NICKERSON." Harwich Port is one of those tony vacation towns on Cape Cod, fronting on Nantucket Sound. How it got from a drugstore there to the house in New Hampshire is something we will probably never know. In short, this chunky little novel is a beautiful, flawed object that resonates with memory and the touch of human hands.

I almost didn't get my own hands on this book, which is partly why I now feel so strongly about it. I also knew nothing of Van Vechten until I read the novel, adored it, and began the usual rabbit-hole chase that seems to me so characteristic, and so wonderful, of literary infatuation. Unlike Michael Arlen, about whom I wrote in my last column, Van Vechten was never world-famous, nor was his decline and fall a matter of speculation and poignant wonder. He is, instead, a paradigm case of that most fascinating of literary sub-species, the Second-Rate Enabler of First-Rate Art.

But first, the story of the book. Last summer, wandering through the antique house, I had thumbed through a pile of paper ephemera and come up with a nice little find, a souvenir menu from a once-famous Manhattan fixture, the Brass Rail on Seventh Avenue, "An Eating Place of International Fame."[2] The menu notes that this large establishment ranged along the avenue from Forty-Ninth to Fiftieth Street, and had multiple floors. The front is decorated with an improbable colour illustration, by one Dorothy Winslow, of medieval pages and heralds, swinging long pennants or blowing clarions, as an armour-clad, lance-bearing knight rears his noble white steed back in . . . what? Chivalric salute for the culinary delights within, one imagines. And they are indeed delightful: chops, steak tartare, baked ham, lobster salad, corned-beef sandwiches. Little stapled-in bits of card with typed or letterpress messages indicate the specials: hot turkey sandwich with cranberry sauce, mushrooms and "candied sweets" (I know, me neither) for ninety-five cents; Blue Point, Cape Cod, or Lynnhaven oyster cocktails for twenty-five, thirty-five, and fifty cents, respectively; oyster stew in cream sixty cents; and—my favourite—the Gold Seal Vintage Champagne Cocktail, advertised on a gold card festooned with a crimson cocktail glass, for thirty-five cents. The back of the menu urges customers to visit "Our Four Restaurants on the Fair Grounds," which soundly dates this to 1939 and the very same world's fair indicated on my cigarette case.

A good day at the antique house, and I was about to wander back outside when, in a short shelf of miscellaneous books, I was struck by the acid-yellow cloth binding of a book. Oddly, it seems to me now, I picked up this book, which seemed to be about cocktail parties in New York during Prohibition, and *put it back*. This was not a matter of price, as I can now confirm: the proprietors of this Aladdin's Cave of cast-off cultural effluvia were asking something less than the cost of three 1939 Brass Rail champagne cocktails, namely, ninety-eight cents. I know, right? This was, if you can believe it, a first edition. (I later came to know that there was just the one printing.) And even given all this, I put the thing back on the shelf and left!

I can only plead temporary insanity, or buyer's fatigue, or something. Later, back at the family compound sipping a gin and tonic, I found that my momentary glimpse of this book was haunting me. I had to have it! But there was no time to revisit the Hillsborough house before departing for Canada and the new school year. Later, in Montreal, I called my father-in-law and tried, while he was distracted by a house party, to explain where the book could be found and how he had to secure it for me.

He had no chance, and then life intervened: it would be Christmas, four months later, before I would be back in New Hampshire. I had grown ill in a cabin near the old 1764 house that my wife's family have turned into a rangy family getaway, and could not make the trip to Hillsborough. I croaked out my best memory of where, exactly, the book was to be found; but imagine a house of many rooms stuffed to the rafters with unsorted stuff and you will appreciate my lack of confidence in anyone's ability to unearth this so stupidly discarded treasure.

The gods of literature grant wishes now and then, however. Late in the afternoon, as I sat listlessly watching the darkness creep across the hills, my wife's car crunched into the snow-covered drive. A few minutes later she came to the room where I was sitting, and produced the book. It had been exactly where I remembered; finding it had been the work of a moment.

*   *   *

The novel itself is one of several reliably witty narratives that Van Vechten published, and probably his best—though the wonderfully titled *The Tattooed Countess: A Romantic Novel with a Happy Ending* (1924) is a close second. The latter recounts the return of fifty-year-old Countess Ella Nattatorrini to her drab childhood home in Maple Valley, Iowa, after her husband has died and she has fallen into a disastrous, now failed, love affair with a much younger man, a caddish opera singer. "From the very beginning," we are told, "she had been vaguely aware that he was stupid, what the French call bête, that he dressed like a cabot, and that he had the habits and manners of a maquereau." The countess herself is described, in part, this way: "She was at that dangerous and fascinating age just before decay sets in." And she is indeed sporting some ink, the result of a bet: "a curious emblem . . . had been tattooed on her left arm just above the wrist: a skull, pricked in black, on which a blue butterfly perched, while a fluttering phylactery beneath bore the motto: Que sais-je?" Astute readers will recognize the motto as the same skeptical sentiment favoured by Montaigne in his *Essays*: "What do I know?" The countess also smokes cigarettes and wears makeup, things no more common and no more welcome in Maple Valley than tattooed middle-aged female skin.

Parties, for its part, consists of a series of sodden vignettes in which a cast of interlinked characters, of the sort familiar to readers of Evelyn

Waugh or F. Scott Fitzgerald, cope with flimsy marriages and the perils of urban life by way of music, dancing, adultery, and a great deal of alcohol. A very great deal of alcohol. When I used to write a cocktail column for a men's magazine I often lifted cocktail recipes from the references made to them in movies and books: Cary Grant's gibson on the train in *North by Northwest* (1959), the gimlets that figure so largely in Raymond Chandler's *The Long Goodbye* (1953). The first cocktail mentioned in *Parties*, as two of the main (male) characters struggle with their hangovers and vague memories that someone has been shot dead—this turns out to be true—is "a coupla drops of Pernod . . . and some Martell." Martell being a (very good) brand of cognac, and Pernod the anise-flavoured absinthe substitute well known for its syrupy consistency and blistering hangovers, I invite you to imagine what that resulting mixture might be like.

Here is Van Vechten on the scene, in his characteristic quotation-free prose style, with its superb ear for dialogue:

> With an unsteady hand Hamish poured brandy into a tall glass until it was half full and then added Pernod until the glass was brimming. Sitting up in bed, David gulped down this mixture.
>
> Better order a coupla sidecars, he advised. We gotta have a drink. Poor little Roy is dead. Poor little kid.
>
> Hamish drew a dressing-gown of mustard and white striped silk around David's shoulders. Rilda is dead too, he reminded David, a little reproachfully, but he rang the bell.
>
> So she is. Poor Rilda. He sighed and said to Hamish's man who appeared at the door, Give us a coupla sidecars, Boker. Probably Irene's dead too, he added, if you only knowed.
>
> There's music to that, Hamish commented.
>
> I know, David replied impatiently.
>
> Sidecars taste good after brandy, Hamish remarked, emptying the remaining contents of the Martell bottle into a glass which he raised to his own lips.
>
> Nothing like Pernod to put you on your feet, David responded.

If you're keeping score at home, note that the sidecar cocktail is made from brandy, lemon juice, and either Cointreau, Grand Marnier, or Triple Sec—so at least it matches the brandy of the other eye-opener. It also has a distinguished history as the hangover cure of choice for certain party-goers: in the 1958 film version of Patrick Dennis's bestselling novel, *Auntie Mame*, Rosalind Russell delivers a pitch-perfect order to young ward, Patrick: "Now, be a perfect angel and ask Ito to bring me a very light breakfast: black coffee and a sidecar."

David is a kind of shorthand version of the glamorous F. Scott Fitzgerald drunk-as-hero: *The Beautiful and Damned* had appeared in 1922 and set the type, perhaps crossed with a bit of Evelyn Waugh's Adam Fenwick-Symes, the up-and-down protagonist of *Vile Bodies* (also 1930, and likewise a cavalcade of champagne and cocaine). Everyone is in love with handsome David: women young and old, men, boys. He can't decide, between benders, whether he is really in love with his equally liquid wife, Rilda; at one point, he goes off to London and Paris to try and find out, along the way sleeping with various people whose names he cannot always remember. There are various recurring characters: a dashing bootlegger with a highly developed sense of honour; a German aristocrat bored of her European life, the Gräfin Adele von Pulmernl und Stilzernl, who becomes an incidental patron of parties; an outlandish flapper called Simone Fly, "a slender creature in silver sequins from which protruded, at one end, turquoise blue legs and, from the other, extremely slender arms and a chalk-white (almost green) face, with a depraved and formless mouth, intelligent eyes, and a rage of cropped red hair." A young man, addicted to cocaine, is the novel's central victim.

His death occurs during an altercation at a speakeasy in Harlem, and this detail marks what is of enduring interest in this novel, and in Van Vechten's career.

*   *   *

Born in 1880 in Cedar Rapids, Iowa, of all places, Van Vechten was, in the words of critic Choire Sicha, "one of New York's great narcissists . . . one of the Jazz Age's most hedonistic, screaming, drunken homosexuals. (He was also married.)" Indeed, he was married twice, the second time at least to a very long-suffering woman: they were together for five decades of his affairs and assignations. All through this time, in the words of biographer Edward White, Van Vechten "clung to the idea that . . . the world could be revolutionized one elegant cocktail party at a time." Sicha notes with some admiration that he marshalled his reputation carefully over the decades (he died in 1964), hoarding his notebooks, photographs, letters—even, if one can credit it, his neckties—for posterity. (The last are now held in the Museum of Modern Art. No kidding, it's true.)[3]

That marshalling of his legacy came later. In the early years, Van Vechten was just another young man on the make, a self-created dandy and sophisticate who had worked his way out of the backwaters of Iowa to mount the fashionable world's largest stages. After a few years writing largely fictional news stories for the *Chicago American*, in the Hearst chain, he moved to the *New York Times* in 1906. By 1913 he had become the paper's drama critic. He travelled to France to meet and cultivate Gertrude Stein, then returned to New York to edit a little magazine called *The Trend*, which featured Wallace Stevens, Mina Loy, and Djuna Barnes. His first book, published in 1915, championed the New Music of Schönberg and Stravinsky. He was also, by this time, the country's most vocal advocate of what was then known as Negro Music.

The Harlem Renaissance now seems like such an obvious good thing in the history of American music and culture that it is hard to recall how fraught with racial stress it actually was. Van Vechten's support for the emergent dance and jazz forms of the 125th Street vicinity of Manhattan was, along with that of other white taste-makers, essential to the dissemination of this most vibrant of subcultural movements. But dissemination was also domestication, a watering-down and assimilation of the primal forces into acceptable versions: the process that would be repeated, almost frame for frame, in the white acceptance of rock 'n' roll during the 1950s. Worse, Van Vechten's interest was, not singularly, a form of fetishism for the exotic.

Here is an unfortunately representative snippet from his 1920 essay called "The Negro Theatre" (and I ask forbearance from readers for quoting the N-word and other epithets here, but it is the point):

> How the darkies danced, sang, and cavorted. . . . Real nigger stuff, this, done with spontaneity and joy in the doing. . . . Nine out of ten of those delightful niggers, those inexhaustible Ethiopians, those husky lanky blacks, those bronze bucks and yellow girls would have liked to have danced and sung like that every night of their lives.

Ten years later, in *Parties*, the language is a little more muted by elegance, but the position is just as racist in describing a Harlem dance floor:

> Each dancer gave as serious an attention to this beautiful vocation as if he were in training for some great good game, and the colour of the participants, too, added attraction to the spectacle. This lithe African beauty, shading from light tan, through golden bronze, to blue-black, these boys and girls with woolly hair, these boys and girls with their hair ironed out and burnished, themselves imparted to their savage pastime a personal fascination which was a rich ingredient in its quality.

Carl, you slumming voyeuristic creep, we're only dancing!

All the same, Van Vechten's positive influence cannot be ignored. He helped stage Paul Robeson's first concert in Greenwich Village and ushered Langston Hughes into print. In the mid-1920s he wrote a series of *Vanity Fair* articles that lauded African-American theatre. Even in *Parties*, just before the passage quoted above, he spends some pages having his narrator trumpet the creative energy of black dancers, responsible for every major innovation from the Cake-Walk to the Lindy Hop, even as he dismisses the charge, common at the time, that these were nothing but tics until taken up by white society. Zora Neale Hurston would number Van Vechten among the essential group of "Negrotarians" without whom the popular spread of the Harlem Renaissance might never have occurred.

Gertrude Stein, as White reports, attempted to explain Van Vechten's negro fixation to himself, with her typical arrogance. Writing a year after the appearance of his novel *Nigger Heaven* (1926), a celebration of the happy middle-class "New Negro," Stein sent him the following missive:

> What are you doing, I know why you like niggers so much . . . Robeson and I had a long talk about it it is not because they are primitive but because they have a narrow but a very long civilization behind them. They have alright, their sophistication is complete and also beautifully finished and it is the only one that can resist the United States of America.

This strikes me as far too charitable. I am willing to bet that it *was* the primitive that fetched Van Vechten. That, and the range of African-American skin-hues about which he could never stop gushing.

Perhaps Van Vechten falls into that category of literary and cultural figures about whom it must be said that if he didn't exist we would have to invent him. He was a drunk, a preener, a self-promoting twerp. He was also a necessary chronicler of time and tide in the American twentieth century—as Choire Sicha puts it, "recognized as the connective tissue between Lincoln Kirstein and Gertrude Stein and Langston Hughes and the Fitzgeralds and H. L. Mencken and more." He was a passionate music lover and a distinguished critic of it, among other things introducing *Vanity Fair* readers to the genius of George Gershwin. He ranged far and wide in his enthusiasms, from neglected Herman Melville stories to the joys of erotic photography of the male form that would place him in a distinguished aesthetic line descending to Robert Mapplethorpe and beyond. As well as the bestselling and delicious novels, he wrote songs, churned out journalism, and penned biographies, pamphlets, and scholarly (if amateur) monographs. He also loved and respected cats, those "tigers in the house," about whom he wrote two books.

And still, to know all that about Carl Van Vechten is not yet to know him. "All the while," Clive Fisher has written,

> he attended hundreds of parties, his constant need for stimulus dictating involvement with a famous and flamboyant circle. But what the convivial cocktail crowd never knew, as he moved among them with white hair and walrus teeth, his shirts and ties provocatively contradictive, was the extent to which this apparently gregarious man, whose very trade was advocacy and espousal, guarded a personal reticence, his fears and longings clandestine, his generosity and love a fickle and elusive privilege.

For the two wives, who endured that succession of temperamental and sometimes dangerous male lovers, and for the cocktail-hour friends who might be summarily dropped in favour of a quick hookup with a black gigolo, there was only bafflement and, sometimes, heartbreak. He was fickle, mercurial, pleasure-driven, and self-centred. He resembled his cats, perhaps, as well as loving them.[4]

*   *   *

I began these thoughts about Van Vechten with the mundane mystery of that jumbled house in rural New Hampshire, so far from the Art Deco bar set-ups and music clubs of early-century Manhattan, one essential chronicle of which stood waiting for discovery by someone like me. I will end with another, smaller coincidence of the type that makes the bookish life so appealing year after year.

Searching for more Van Vechten, my appetite for his fiction (if not for his fetishism) aroused by *Parties*, I came across a listing for an illustrated reissue edition of the novel from 2010. Clearly I was not the only one interested in a minor Van Vechten Renaissance. A few keystrokes secured the order and, a week or so later, the package arrived. I opened the padded mailing bag with my usual greediness and the first thing I noticed—not clear in the online listing—was that this was the German translation of Van Vechten's novel. The title is still *Parties*, but the subtitle is delightfully Kantian-sounding in its spelled-out German pedantry: *Ein fulminanter Roman aus dem New York der "Roaring Twenties." Ein fulminanter Roman*—"a brilliant novel" is the obvious translation; but that unusual adjective *fulminanter* (instead of, say, the more common *gläzend*) also conveys other, less laudatory meanings: lightning-striking, sudden, flash-in-the-pan. And oh, those killer scare quotes around the phrase "Roaring Twenties"!

The second thing I noticed was that the illustrations—copious, from a brilliant cover and half-a-dozen full-colour interiors, plus blue-tinted headings for every chapter—were strangely familiar.

I checked the credit page. Yes, I *thought* I recognized that style, those lines and figures. There were by my friend Maurice Vellekoop, that ardent and witty observer of the gay life (in every sense). Here were the narrow waists and broad shoulders, the carved cheekbones, of Maurice's male figures; there the drop-waist dresses and long strings of pearls of his women; everywhere the cocktail glasses, cigarettes. Inside, a cornucopia of 1920s urban imagery: steelworkers fashioning high-rise girders, skyscrapers dancing on thin legs, steamships and cocktail bars and even one juicy scene of a naked (and well-endowed David) being fought over by two women—one of them naked herself—even as he fights a hangover in his London hotel room.

I hope you will believe me when I tell you that, just a few weeks before finally getting my hands on this gaudy version of Van Vechten's *Parties*, I met Maurice for a cocktail in one of my favourite bars, The Roof Lounge in Toronto (he lives on Toronto Island and I don't see him as often as I'd like). As well as catching up about work projects and mutual friends, he had brought along a piece of his artwork that I wanted to buy. It is a brilliantly coloured scene, from 2010, of two women sharing a drink. They are in a sort of space-age watering hole, not a deco scene. One has a pouffy-skirted dress, long long legs, and her hair in a sort of top-knot bun. The other sports harem-style pantaloons and a brunette bob. It is gorgeous, and I am looking at it right now even as I flip through my two copies of Van Vechten's *Parties*, one yellow and preserved from eight decades ago, the other bright almost to garishness and from the same year as my own cherished Vellekoop original.

And I am happy beyond telling.

Notes

1 Detail of interest to book-design geeks: it is considered a special honour when a designer for Borzoi Books, now part of Random House and its various corporate conglomerates, is asked to fashion a new version of the signature jumping hound. There are several dozen of them in existence from a range of excellent graphic designers such as Paul Rand, Chip Kidd, and Gabriele Wilson.

2 Not to be confused with various other incarnations of the Brass Rail, from an eponymous saloon that inspired a 1935 story by Don Marquis—he of *archy and mehitabel* fame—that was illustrated by James Thurber and complained of the entry of women into the bars after Prohibition, to the classy downtown Toronto establishment that features "adult entertainment" and has been visited by the likes of Alex Rodriguez, Samuel L. Jackson, and Charlize Theron. (Really? Charlize Theron? Wikipedia says so, so it must be true.)

3 Choire Sicha, "Off Color," *BookForum* (February/March 2014), 4. Sicha reviews Edward White, *The Tastemaker: Carl Van Vechten and the Birth of Modern America* (Farrar, Straus & Giroux, 2013).

4 For more, see Clive Fisher, "Burning Bright: The feline was more than a fancy for Carl Van Vechten," *BookForum* (April/May 2007). Fisher reviews—not very favourably—*The Homoerotic Photography of Carl Van Vechten: Public Face, Private Thoughts*, by James Smalls (Temple University Press, 2007).

ETHICAL
CONCERNS

Reading, Writing, and Consciousness:
The Future(s)

T HE ISSUE of reading's future is almost always framed, these days, as a question about technology. When will e-book sales render hard copies obsolete? Will print magazines and newspapers survive? Must I blog? Can I monetize my Twitter hashtags? Whither Kobo, Kindle, Kickstarter? Is there a living to be made when editors everywhere expect to get quality, on-time copy for the standard rate of zero cents a word? Above all, are we approaching the literary equivalent of the Singularity, namely the moment where every human being on Earth will, in fact, have written the book they have in them?

You will forgive me if I set these standard, and mostly boring, contemporary questions off to one side. It's not technophobic or Luddite to recognize that the techie questions are largely beside the point. The scope of their effects lies on a time scale that none of us can foresee, thus creating not genuine questions but opportunities for self-serving prediction. Those predictions are either wildly optimistic or comprehensively gloomy, depending on your interests, age, mortgage payments, and health plan. More importantly, these of-the-moment technology-driven concerns do not get us closer to the heart of reading, which is a matter of human consciousness.

I emphatically do not mean that technology is neutral here. Yes, you can use Facebook or Twitter for social activism as well as casual hookups, just as you can use a gun to topple a tyrant or to exact personal revenge. But a spectrum of possible uses is not the same thing as neutrality; all technologies have built-in tendencies, if not outright teleologies. You can use both a pillow and a gun to kill a person, but nobody sane would say that the pillow stands in the same relation to murder as does the gun. Guns don't kill people, maybe, but people with guns kill more people than people with pillows. Marshall McLuhan was correct: sometimes the medium really is the message.

McLuhan himself could be bold, sometimes wacky on the subject of reading. "As an extension of man," he said in a 1969 interview with *Playboy* magazine, the typeset codex-style book "was directly responsible for the rise of such disparate phenomena as nationalism, the Reformation, the assembly line and its off-spring, the Industrial Revolution, the whole concept of causality, Cartesian and Newtonian concepts of the universe, perspective in art, narrative chronology in literature, and a psychological mode of introspection or inner direction that greatly intensified the tendencies toward individualism and specialization."

That is all good fun, after its fashion—though it does raise the awkward question of which features of the modern world *wasn't* spawned by moveable type. Hoop skirts? Wigs for gentlemen? Monster truck rallies? Ambient techno? Martin Heidegger analyzes the question concerning technology with both more wisdom and more prescience. The task is not to understand the function of this or that tool, he argues, but rather to examine the way technology comes to dominate every aspect of existence. This *enframing*, as Heidegger calls it, which places everything within the ambit of possible use and disposal, is the real meaning of technology.

You could not hope to find a clearer example of this than the current debate about the future of reading. The first task, then, is to recognize how we ourselves are enframed. As long as we continue to think about reading in the context of technology, we will fail to see any deeper meanings, including the possible effects of our own self-imprisonment.

What are these alleged deeper meanings? Alas, here lurks another standard misconception of the question, which is that there is a single form of reading in question, and a single future for it. Current debates are overwhelmingly premised on the false idea that "reading" in its highest or best form means reading books, most often realist novels of the middle-class condition that have dominated the modern age. But reading has always offered us a host of experiences, from the mundane to the spiritual, and including the dipping, skimming, and hyperlinking that now seems to worry people so. The specific concern for the future of the bound-page book should be seen for what it is: a form of fond special pleading whereby a particular (how I like to read) masquerades as a universal (reading!).

I will hold off of my own self-serving predictions about all this until nearer the end, but for now I want to suggest a possible starting-point that takes seriously at least the last part of McLuhan's laundry list of effects. I mean the idea of "a psychological mode of introspection" that attends reading, which I will call inwardness, and the relation of that inwardness to individualism.

*   *   *

I begin by asserting the following metaphysical contradiction of late techno-capitalism: Our *present* condition is that we are (a) more networked than ever, and yet (b) we exhibit a growing deficit in that quality of fellow-feeling usually labelled empathy. The result is a strange doubled kind of individuality, one that is almost desperately narcissistic.

Evidence in favour of this assertion is available, if disputed. Researchers at the University of Michigan, in a 2010 study, found that American college students are 40 percent less empathetic than they were in 1979, with the sharpest dip—48 percent—marked in the past decade. According to the U.S. National Institutes for Health, meanwhile, the incidence of narcissistic personality disorder is nearly three times as high for people in their twenties as for the generation that is now sixty-five or older; fifty-eight percent more college students scored higher on a narcissism scale in 2009 than in 1982. These trends strongly correlate to the rise of online connectiveness.

Now, one could dispute the value of empathetic connection, as various psychologists have lately done. It has highly selective effects, for one thing, and can make for irrational allocation of resources. I will not try to answer that objection here, except to say that, while empathy may have limits, surely it is overall a good thing for human societies to be based on some degree of reciprocal regard for the other. Hobbesian competitive-interest accounts or Adam Smith's notion of private vice producing public virtue only go so far to underwrite social norms, and the behaviour that meets them. We have learned to be better than that.

Part of how we did so is indeed tied to reading's past, as McLuhan suggests. The rise of an educated reading public is linked inextricably to the emergence of democratic liberalism in the Western world. And the novel's emergence as a dominant literary form is likewise closely tied to the idea of open public discourse and rational-critical debate.

The philosopher Jürgen Habermas, examining the origins of the "rational public sphere," dwells at some length on the significance of Samuel Richardson's 1740 epistolary novel *Pamela*. The novel was a runaway bestseller, one of the first massive literary sensations in Britain. The novel relates the story of Pamela Andrews, a beautiful young maidservant who is repeatedly importuned and then imprisoned by her nobleman employer, who is infatuated with her. She must fend off his attempts at seduction, and indeed rape.

The novel, often read aloud in reading groups, entranced and shocked contemporary readers; it spawned critiques, imitations, parodies, unofficial sequels, and endless discussion in coffee houses, drawing rooms, and journals. The use of letters and journal entries as the raw material for the novel introduces the element of consciousness that strikes Habermas and others as so influential. We, the readers, are reading Pamela's private thoughts, with the page of her writing a kind of free interior space even when her movements are constrained; but, just for this reason, they are not private, though they were meant to be. In another twist, the master, known as Mr. B, is intercepting her letters as part of his campaign to break her will. We are then, as it were, reading over his shoulder.

Mr. B begins to admire Pamela's naturally noble character as well as good looks. She, for her part, enacts an early version of Stockholm Syndrome and falls in love with him. They make what we are meant to understand is an equitable marriage—thus the novel's alternative title, *Virtue Rewarded*—but even some contemporary readers found this happy consummation of upper-class lust a bit too neat.

If nothing else, the novel brilliantly enacts the process noted by Marx in which a "sentimental veil" of "human interest" descends over the economic realities of class, marriage, property, and procreation. The novel is, according to Terry Eagleton, a scene of "class collaboration," a romantic "pact between bourgeoisie and nobility" to smooth over the fact of wealth inequality. Absolutely. In back of that, though, lies the psychological interest that makes the novel's success possible in the first place.

In a manner now so familiar that we forget how revolutionary it felt in 1740, readers were able to substitute the consciousness of a (fictitious) other person for their own. This doubling and suspension of consciousness is, paradoxically, the essential ingredient for enriching one's own sense of interiority, or inwardness. For the first time, reading offers the heady experience of identifying with another, mirroring and reinforcing myself.

Hence its status as, in Eagleton's words, "a whole cultural event . . . the occasion or organizing principle of a multimedia affair." We might match it with Immanuel Kant's stirring claim, made some four decades later, that the motto of the Enlightenment should be a generalized version of Horace's imperative *sapere aude*: have the courage to think for yourself!

Once the ground is thus broken on literary inwardness and intellectual self-sufficiency, the gold rush is on. Jane Austen's supple irony about female existence begets Henry James's hyper-nuanced appreciation of aesthetic and cultural experience, then the high-water marks of Proust and Virginia Woolf in setting down the eddies and swirls of consciousness itself. Kant, meanwhile, would be the condition of possibility for Hegel on *geist*, John Stuart Mill on liberty, and Wittgenstein on language—to mention just the barest few.

What this kind of reading does, then, is something like this: it objectively summons a subjectivity that belongs to each one of us. This subjectivity is simultaneously suspended and sanctioned in the act of reading. The interiority thus revealed and reinforced is democratic in the sense that is available to anyone with the requisite tools of literacy and access to books. Public education addressed the first; public libraries and lending groups the second. Subjectivity was no longer a luxury good; we could all enjoy the benefits of inwardness, hence of individuality.

We might continue to argue about the relative merits of fiction over non-fiction, as the fictional characters in Austen sometimes do, but it is clear that the printed books and democratized culture of reading and publicity they enable are the most significant developments in human consciousness since, perhaps, writing itself.

One especially significant feature of this past is the discussion, sometimes acrimonious or endless, that attends reading. We may read aloud or in silence, together or alone; but we all know that the experience of reading—the mysterious sound of that other voice in your head—is just the beginning of a wider expansion of consciousness. This is why dictators and medieval monks alike feared the transmission of knowledge via books: more working critical minds were likely to put them out of a job.

To employ a contemporary reference, printed books were the MOOCs of their day, a technology of access to learning and pleasure that, suddenly and massively, exceeded institutional control. The monks would adapt to the new realities, more or less, which is why we still have universities where printed books are read and discussed. The dictators would survive, too, but the technology of widespread reading just made their jobs a lot harder.

*   *   *

So much for the present and the past of at least one kind of reading. What, now, of the *future*, or futures, of reading?

It has long been claimed by boosters of reading, especially reading in those subjects usually associated with the liberal arts, such as litera-ture and philosophy, that there is a strong connection between the act of reading and greater levels of understanding between individuals. The particular inwardness of reading, the argument goes, especially if it involves the revelation of human character, expands empathetic scope. I certainly number myself among these book-thumping cheerleaders, having made this argument often in both conversation and print.

In the standard version of this pro-reading position, the next rhetori-cal move is obvious: if online connection is lowering empathy, and read-ing raises it, then—books win! Turn off your computers, dammit, and get thee to the library! Of course, recent experience indicates that the most obvious feature of most libraries these days is the sight of row upon row of computer stations.

That's not the real problem with this argument, though. The prob-lem is that its premises are dubious, if not outright false; and so its pur-ported conclusion is invalid. At best, there is a confusion of necessary and sufficient conditions in the chain of inference.

Unfortunately, there is no evidence that exposure to literature reli-ably expands your moral imagination. Nor do the liberal arts make you a better citizen—a common variant on the basic claim. Nothing is more depressing to those of us who believe in the value of robust criti-cal thought and enhanced ethical imagination than to realize that some students can pass through years of forced ingestion of challenging texts without experiencing a glimmer of either.

You will want to reply that these students haven't *really* been reading the books. But that just begs the question by presupposing the very thing we need to demonstrate, namely the salutary effects of reading. Better to acknowledge that there are failures on all sides here; and seeing that is what keeps me and my dedicated colleagues coming back to the classroom with hope every September, looking to offer the things that students can't get by other means, no matter how fast their ISP connections. Even the failures do not, by themselves, diminish the value of liberal-arts education generally. But let us admit that such education does not guarantee good citizens; also, from the other side, that there are many exemplary citizens who have not attended a single literature class or read a word of Plato.

The very same fallacies of false necessity afflict the empathy argument. Reading *Sense and Sensibility* may give you a better appreciation of the joys and sorrows of love; but it need not. And even if it does, that appreciation may track only very unevenly or partially into your own dealings with others. You don't have to be a sociopath to find that prolonged exposure to the minds of fictional others, in the form of the modern novel, leaves you with just about the same level of regard as before.

Fiction gives us any number of vivid limit-cases of the point, as it happens. They are sociopaths, arguably, but still recognizably human for all that. The torturer O'Brien in George Orwell's *Nineteen Eighty-Four*, with his fine scholarly appreciation of human weakness, is, according to the philosopher Richard Rorty, a perfect illustration of what happens to intellectuals when devotion to an academic subject shades into obsession. The station chief in Ray Bradbury's *Fahrenheit 451*, meanwhile, is the one person in the novel who has read all the banned books. He is given to deft, apposite quotation and points out gleefully at one point how upsetting it is that books all say different things—a reaction familiar to my first-year philosophy students.

Literary exposure has not softened the hearts of these two villains, any more than exposure to Vermeer made Hermann Goering a nice guy. On the contrary, reading is precisely the foundation of their subtle psychic violence.

For some, the problem is precisely that the modern novel is so closely associated with a bourgeois form of existence, a mode of consciousness that we rightly ought to usher off the historical stage. The very same individualism that came with the rise of literacy, that experience of unique inwardness, has become a global blight, a vast network of rapacious desires and—yes—narcissism.

From this perspective, the current debates about the future of reading are merely the welcome death throes of individualism. The novel form is here transformed, by the likes of Tao Lin, Thomas McCarthy, David Mitchell, and Haruki Murakami, into a philosophical battlefield, with the forces of modern middle-brow conformity opposed by those of postmodern "networks of transmission."

Well, maybe. My feeling, as a reader rather than a writer of fiction, is that this is one more inside-baseball debate from which we will all benefit, just as we have from T.S. Eliot, James Joyce, Thomas Pynchon, and David Foster Wallace. In any case, it is time for me to conclude with my own set of self-serving predictions about the future of reading. So here goes, in a magic set of seven:

1. Long-form reading will be with us as long as there is such a thing as individual human consciousness. That consciousness is a complicated burden. There is stimulation and pleasure in consciousness, but also boredom, anxiety, frustration, loneliness, and grief. Books are my friends when nobody else can be; they offer a form of intimacy that no other experience does. They do not make me a better person, but they can offer respite from the incessant noise of existence. That market will never collapse.

2. That same consciousness will continue to exhibit a kind of narrative structure, which reading both illuminates and reinforces. We experience selfhood as a story, however haphazard, repetitive, and inconclusive; and while this hypothetical narrative of self may be an illusion, it remains a necessary one. You don't absolutely need reading to maintain this odd illusion of uniqueness, but it sure helps.

3. This peculiar experience of human consciousness will change. We know this because it is already changing. Individualism is neither woven into the fabric of the universe nor strictly necessary for human species survival.

4. But this won't happen nearly as fast as some people seem to think. Don't worry about it! Meanwhile, do worry about literacy rates. Literacy strongly correlates with higher life expectancy, political activity, and happiness; the United Nations considers it a human right. The global rate for bare literacy

is currently 84 percent, the highest in history, but 775 million people still can't read, the majority of them women. That's a bad thing, no matter what you think of the novel as a form.

5. Some people will be able to make a living as writers, others won't. Sorry about that! But writing will remain among the cheapest forms of cultural production ever, especially relative to its effects. A single person can do it. That's pretty amazing in an age where most narrative and intellectual efforts—films, television, conferences, video games, scientific research—demand elaborate infrastructures and payscales. Just don't take that as sanction for inflicting another bad novel on the world.

6. We will continue to argue about all this, just as Socrates and Phaedrus argued the relative merits of reading and speaking more than two millennia ago. The independent publisher Richard Nash wrote this to me when I asked for a judgment on the future of reading: "Yes, there is more reading, and what is being read will be as contested as it has always been. The power of reading is quite similar to the power of sex: everyone is doing it, but most public conversation about it consists of disapproving about how it is being done." Exactly.

7. In 2035, after a determined attempt to sideline it with a series of neurobabble TED talks, Radiolab podcasts, and facile *New Yorker* articles—not to mention that centuries-long glut of bourgeois novels, with its biofascist insistence on the importance of families and relationships and whatnot—critical philosophy will triumph as the most popular form of reading in history. I may be wrong about all the others, but I'm pretty sure I'm right about this one . . .

The Ethics
of Ethics and
Literature

I N COMMON with other debates that are at least as old as Plato, it is one that refuses to die a suitable philosophical death. Does reading fiction, being exposed to the fruits of aesthetic imagination, make you *as a person* better or worse? Each side has its distinguished advocates. Martha Nussbaum and Wayne Booth have argued, with great passion if not always matching precision, that reading fiction is an ethical pursuit, a matter of building empathy and character. Richard Posner, in his influential 1997 essay "Against Ethical Criticism," calmly demolished most of their arguments: empathy can be felt for the devil as well as the divine; only sly special pleading makes a list of books one that will improve character, and then only if such character is in the mood for improving. To evaluate literature on ethical grounds is transparently to commit a category mistake, and one that can only do a disservice to the literature in the name of ethics. In the words of critic Helen Vendler, "treating fictions as moral pep-pills or moral emetics is repugnant to anyone who realizes the complex psychological and moral motives of a work of art."

The implication here is clear: anyone who indulges in the pep-pill theory is, in effect, a bad reader, insufficiently sophisticated with respect to the experience of art. Such readers may be found in suburban reading groups, perhaps, complaining that they didn't care for a novel because they found none of its characters likeable, but we true readers of fiction know better. There is a moral dimension in play here, Vendler suggests, but it is some kind of higher or more refined notion of aesthetic morality, a morality that bonds writer and reader together in some manner irreducible to ethical instruction or, still more, parable-style bottom lines.

I am not unsympathetic to this line of objection; in fact, it strikes me as quite likely valid and needful, especially for challenging what might threaten to become a popular critical consensus in favour of edifying or uplifting narratives, the Oprah's Book Club "some improving book" school of appreciation. A more recent, and more winning, version of the position can be found, for example, in Jenny Davidson's delightful new book, *Reading Style: A Life in Sentences* (Columbia). "I've always been bothered by the notion that literature is worth reading chiefly for what it teaches us about life," runs the first sentence of this volume. "Of course we learn things about life from literature: it's self-evident that a book may make its reader wiser or more philosophical in some measure consequent upon the nature of the book itself. . . . But there is also something intolerably banal about the idea that the main reward of reading a novel by Leo Tolstoy or George Eliot should be my becoming a slightly better person."

There are important nuances in this declaration. Davidson does not sharply distinguish, though one could (Poser does, for instance), between becoming ethically better and becoming wiser. To learn about life is not at all necessarily to become a better person, even slightly. In any event, the suggestion that improvement of whatever kind might be the main reason for reading literature is "intolerably banal." Like Vendler, Davidson has another card to play: such banality about the reading experience misses a deeper, or higher, ethical point about immersion in fiction, "a form of intellectual play that seems to me ultimately as ethical as its lesson-driven counterpart." She herself focuses on literary *style*, in particular as conveyed in fictive sentences (hence the book's title). "By stripping literary language down to its constituent parts, I perversely gain a sense of transcendence, an emotional as well as intellectual liberation that comes by way of the most precise considerations of details of language." It may not be immediately obvious what is ethical about this precision, except that, soon after, we find Davidson explaining why she feels "furious" with the sentimentality or paranoia of a given novel: "this is one of the ways in which morality enters into even the most stringently formalist ways of reading."

Well, fine. One can appreciate this sort of aesthetic stringency as a kind of ethos, if not an ethical position, in the way we philosophers would use the concept. And I for one appreciate the close attention that Davidson brings to works high and low, teasing out of their basic building blocks a subtle, sometimes intoxicating beauty. But after all, Davidson is a professor of literature, and I am a professor too, one who writes and teaches about art as well as ethical and political theory. We both did doctorates at Yale, for crying out loud! We are, I might say, two dandies gathered together in a finely spun secret book club of the mind. Of course we are going to feel a *rightness* beyond mere correctness in making aesthetic judgments, and a sense of *importance* to them too. It has grown unfashionable, except in certain quarters, to view style as a mark of character, but we dandies know better. (One thing I must dispute: Davidson avers that she is "vehemently" against the Oxford comma— and indeed, there is one clangingly missing from the book's second sentence! She is clearly wrong about this, and it shows a shattering weakness of character. Perhaps she may be reformed over time.)

*   *   *

It seems to me, despite the various forms of self-congratulation one may indulge here, that this aesthetic-ethical flanking manoeuvre—or maybe, to switch metaphors, this kicking upstairs of the ethical stakes—does very little good in the overall dispute. It doesn't really confront the main issue, which is whether, or how, fiction is intimately connected to our lives as ethical beings. I believe it is so connected, despite the Posner-Vendler-Davidson objections, and I want to devote the remainder of this essay to saying how.

Several years ago, I was approached by my dean to take on a new seminar course. The University of Toronto has almost 34,000 undergraduates just on its main downtown campus; there are also two suburban satellites with another 23,000 or so students, and some 15,000 graduate students. Large classes, especially in first year, are an inevitability: I was myself, at this time, in the middle of more than a decade of teaching a 500-student intro philosophy course. The new seminar program would offer freshmen a credit where the class was capped at 25, guaranteeing at least one small-group experience in first year, and preferably with a full faculty member. Even though the teaching would be on overload, I agreed enthusiastically to do it. The other reason for my enthusiasm: the seminar was called "Ethics and the Creative Imagination." The idea was to broach ethical issues with fictional rather than philosophical texts as the primary source material.

Like many instructors in philosophy, especially intro, I have long included fictional material in my syllabuses: Jane Austen on virtue, say, or Doctorow's *Ragtime* as a drama of demanded justice. Fiction brings otherwise dry material alive; it gives texture and urgency to the abstract arguments of Aristotle or Kant. This ethics seminar would be an extended exercise in this technique, and I chose the novels (and some films) for the course with great pleasure. Over the years I taught the course we read, among others, Iris Murdoch's *The Nice and the Good*, Anthony Burgess's *A Clockwork Orange*, Margaret Atwood's *The Handmaid's Tale*, Ayn Rand's *The Fountainhead*, Graham Greene's *The Quiet American*, Edith Wharton's *The House of Mirth*, Henry James's *Washington Square*, Kasuo Ishiguro's *Never Let Me Go*, and Ian McEwan's *Saturday*.

I threw a few curves, or maybe sliders to mix it up with those perhaps obvious choices: Evelyn Waugh's *Vile Bodies*, Kingsley Amis's *Lucky Jim*, and Raymond Chandler's *The Long Goodbye*. And because they are friends and were willing to visit the class—a nice bonus!—but also just because I love their work, I included novels by the outstanding Canadian writers Miriam Toews (*A Complicated Kindness*) and Russell Smith (*Girl Crazy*).

Anyone familiar with even a few of these novels can likely see the shape of the ensuing discussions. All the novels are from roughly the twentieth century, with some marginal spillage on either margin. They all, in one way or another, see individuals struggling with issue of identity and obligation. There is war, religion, family, friendship, love, aesthetic commitment, technological change, and despair. Each week we met, with great mutual pleasure, to discuss the issues as the characters acted them out.

At first, and really for quite some time, I enjoyed this thoroughly. It was, in addition to everything else, a nice break from more rigorous philosophical work. And the students, who often came from science programs in search of their humanities breadth credit, were uniformly clever. One had the feeling that the seminar was making them more sensitive and nuanced readers, if not better people and not quite dandies in the sense sketched earlier. I never considered either of those outcomes— better moral agent, better disciple of style—at all likely, or even desirable, for the students. They had to decide on their own what the books, and the course, meant to them. But soon a different misgiving began to gnaw at me.

Was this way of going on, this subjection of novels to a rubric of ideas, however loose and in itself virtuous, a good thing? Was it ethical, in some important sense of that word, to treat novels as means to an end, rather than ends in themselves? This might sound pretentious, or perhaps deranged, but it began to seem to me that books, like persons, should not be instrumentalized. Some readers will recognize that the ends/means version of this unease is drawn from one articulation of Kant's categorical imperative. Was there, I thought, a duty to treat novels as *inherently inviolable*?

I don't mean, of course, that they can't be violated in all kinds of ways. One new twist in the development of this seminar is considering the issue of adapting a novel for a different medium, typically film: which raises another series of aesthetic and ethical issues. I mean rather to ask if there is something unseemly and wrong, not just intolerably banal (to use Davidson's quite sufficiently condemning phrase), about viewing novels as vehicles of moral instruction. This, it strikes me, is a genuine point of conflict within many readers, even the voracious natural readers whose lives would be made darker, if not desperate, without another novel to open. And so the misgiving must be worked through, not side-stepped. Doing so, I hope to reach what may be a familiar conclusion in an unfamiliar way.

*   *   *

A good deal, maybe everything, turns on what we mean by "moral instruction." Posner suggests that only someone holding a Socratic conception of moral psychology, where vice is simply a function of ignorance, can accept fiction as moral instruction. That is, the standard claims of enlarged empathy, knowledge of the other, and so on—bulwarks in the Nussbaum-Booth position—only run if acquiring such expanded consciousness necessarily entails improved action. Posner thinks it does not, because like Plato he knows that the soul is capable of self-deception, compartmentalization, weakness of the will, and a host of other avoidance mechanisms that make an expanded mind and a dark soul entirely compatible. Thus the proverbial music-loving Nazi; or, as Alexander Nehamas in his book on beauty, *Only a Promise of Happiness* (the title is drawn from a remark by Stendhal) writes: "beautiful villains, graceful outlaws, tasteful criminals, and elegant torturers are everywhere about us." Indeed. Hannibal Lecter adored, just as I do, Glenn Gould's 1981 version of *The Goldberg Variations*.

The error here, I think, is to imagine that Plato has the last word on moral psychology. It is he, after all, who is forever linked to the position that fictive art has a discernible ethical effect, albeit in his case a negative one. (The issue is complicated by the fact that the allegedly deleterious effect of fiction is a function of Plato's metaphysics, whereby imitations are necessarily deceptive and impoverished of reality.) Let us suppose for a moment that our moral natures are not fixed, but also not as prone to self-torture as Plato sometimes suggests. Yes, we *can* ignore or bracket the lessons of experience, whether in real life or as depicted in vivid aesthetic forms, but for the most part we do not. That is, we take seriously what we see and feel, and it affects how we see ourselves and the world. Even the most hardened criminal, Adam Smith averred in *The Theory of Moral Sentiments*, is not immune to the tug of empathy, the experience of another person's suffering.

In itself, I grant, this is thin soup; and the critics are right to note that there is no *necessary* entailment here. But the link between fiction and empathy is more than adventitious. Novels, at least those with the kind of supple, free-indirect narration that are the high-water marks of the realist tradition, offer an extended reply to the epistemological skeptic. On Cartesian principles, we cannot directly know the mind of another; but words printed on a page give us the best possible chance at coming close, better even than interacting with others. "We see person-like shapes all around us," Nussbaum writes; "but how do we relate to them? . . . What story-telling in childhood teaches us to do is to ask questions about the life behind the mask." And just as with other persons, reading novels as morally instructive is part of what it means to take them seriously, to treat them as ends in themselves. This is not an exclusive goal—we don't judge people just on their moral instructiveness, either— but it *is* an essential part of fiction's peculiar public-private contract.

Moral instruction is thus much more like a conversation than it is like an algorithm. On the Posner view, it would have to be granted— maybe he favours this conclusion—that works of ethical theory have no more ethical bearing on the people who read them than do novels. And of course it is a truism among philosophers than experts in ethical theory are hardly among the most reliably virtuous people. My own view is that this is correct—if by bearing we mean that they will directly change behaviour. No, they won't. But reading Kant on duty or Mill on general happiness give us insight into our moral worlds. They excite the imagination as well as reason. They are no more dispensable from the general discourse of how to live than the Ten Commandments or the Four Noble Truths. We may call such enumerations lessons or imperatives or rules, but they are really narratives of interior possibility.

So much more so, then, the great works of fiction. Not because they lay out coherent systems of effects, nor because reading them will make you or me behave better now, or tomorrow, or next week; but because this is one of the essential ways by which we humans reflect on our own possibilities—and failures. Attempts at strict formalism aside, a novel really is different from a sculpture or a painting. Reading a novel is the blessed burden of consciousness in action, two hopeful-monster souls communing via text, the evolutionary miracle of language enjoying one of its highest expressions. "Without good examples such as are preserved in literature," a young character muses in the course of Sebastian Faulks's 2007 novel *Engleby*, "there would be nothing to live up to, no sense of transcendence or of our lives beyond the Hobbesian." Engleby will soon murder this same character, a twenty-year-old Cambridge undergraduate: the novel is an elegant, appalling, and finally moving first-person narrative by a casually erudite psychopath who is fastidious about grammar and literary style.

Two concepts, somewhat surprising ones, gather all these thoughts together: (1) play; and (2) cliché. As Martin Amis has said, the war on cliché is not just a matter of stylistic vigilance, for there are also clichés of both the mind and the heart. The last of these is the most serious: falling into moral inattention. Great literature makes new skirmishes along all three fronts of this never-ending war. But it does so, even when utterly serious, using the free play of images, characters, and ideas. We might say, with Aristotle, that this contemplative mode of being is, rather than simple ethical action, the most divine part of ourselves, that which underwrites everything else. What could be more serious than that?

Can We Talk About Evil?

THE SCENARIOS ARE, by now, depressingly familiar. Crazed gunman enters classroom, parking lot, daycare, or cineplex, armed with multiple net-sourced weapons and several hundred rounds of ammo. He—and it is almost always he—is dressed in a long duster-style coat or some surplus black camo. He opens up on hapless kids, bystanders, or moviegoers. Bodies fall to the ground, expended shells litter the floor or concrete. There are pools of blood. Or the other narrative: mutilated female body is found in a dumpster, alley, or apartment, adorned with tortuous clues, a teasing rebus of hints and feints about what will come next. Then there is another body, another clue. He is playing with the police now, taunting law enforcement with a violent catch-me-if-you-can glee.

If aliens were to monitor our viewing habits, news and entertainment blurring, they would surely conclude that here is where fact meets fiction in a roster of resonant names and places: Littletown, Lecter, Bundy, Columbine, Sandy Hook, Gacy, Virginia Tech, Dahmer, Brevik, Bateman, Ripley—and, since May 2014, we must perhaps add Elliot Rodger, and Isla Vista, Santa Barbara. There is Whitman in the tower at Austin, the postal worker *going postal*. There are other notorious phrases whose origins are obscured by time and fading memory of the killers. Sixteen-year-old Brenda Ann Spencer, the rare female spree killer, shot two dead and wounded eight in an unmotivated attack on a San Diego playground in January, 1979. It was a Monday. "I don't like Mondays," Spencer said later, when asked to explain the deadly outburst of gunfire, the innocent dead. "This livens up the day." Reason not the need, normals! The resulting Boomtown Rats song refuses to entertain reasons but it does draw the correct conclusion: "School's out early and soon we'll be learning / That the lesson today is how to die." Adam Lanza's father, speaking to the media for the first time since his son rampaged through a Connecticut school in December 2012, killing twenty-six, simply called him "evil," expressing the wish that he had never been born.

Spree killers and serial killers, rampagers and rapists: these are the modern avatars of evil, the monsters among us. The absolute numbers are small, compared to deaths by automobile or household misadventure, and yet the impact is massive, as is the confusion about who, exactly, they are. Psychotic or psychopathic? Morally insane or suffering from brain-chemical delusions? Jared Loughner was delusional and tortured by inner compulsions when, in January 2011, he killed six people and wounded thirteen more, including Congresswoman Gabrielle Giffords, in a Tucson parking lot. This is known as reactive, rather than instrumental, violence. By contrast, the Columbine killers, Eric Harris and Dylan Klebold, were meticulous planners with every outward sign that they understood the difference between right and wrong. In 1999 the two students walked into their high school in Columbine, Colorado, and proceeded to kill thirteen, wound twenty-four, and then whoop with triumph before committing suicide. Serial killers John Wayne and Ted Bundy were psychopaths, but flesh-eating sexual predator Jeffrey Dahmer probably wasn't.

Not all serial and spree killers are psychopaths, in short, and most of the estimated 29 million psychopaths in the global population—some five hundred thousand adult males in the United States alone—are neither. People sometimes use the word sociopath as a cognate term, or a milder version of psychopathy, but that is incorrect. In fact, sociopathy has no rigid designation in medicine, psychopathy does not describe a single affliction, and, just to confuse things further, neither condition appears in the much-disputed handbook of psychiatric aberration, the *Diagnostic and Statistical Manual of Mental Disorders*, currently in its fifth edition (DSM-5). The DSM's "antisocial personality disorder" largely overlaps with psychopathy, but there are many diagnostic skirmishes along the borders.

It can be hard to track all these shades of difference, especially in the media coverage and moral panic that routinely attends the news of a spree or a captured serial killer, but the various cases are importantly different, as Dean Haycock writes in his measured account of the psychopathic brain, *Murderous Minds: Exploring the Criminal Psychopathic Brain: Neurological Imaging and the Manifestations of Evil* (2013). Most basically, a psychotic is awful but brute: the voices inside his head are not real. We might even, in considering the tortured experience of unwitting derangement, mitigate the psychotic's responsibility for his actions. A psychopath is, in some important sense, still living in the world the rest of us share, as Hervey Cleckley argued in his ground-breaking book, *The Mask of Sanity* (1941). He—and, again, it is overwhelmingly "he," by a factor of about twenty to one—is often intelligent, superficially charming, narcissistic, and cold.

Adam Smith, in *The Theory of Moral Sentiments* (1759), had argued that "pity or compassion, the emotion we feel for the misery of others" was to be found even in "[t]he greatest ruffian, the most hardened violator of the laws of society." Psychopaths are the counter-example; they just don't care about other people's lives or feelings, might even enjoy making those people suffer and die. In some cases, psychopaths literally cannot parse the signs of fear in another human face. In this respect, they are weirdly similar to the high-functioning androids in Ridley Scott's *Blade Runner* (1982), based on Philip K. Dick's *Do Androids Dream of Electric Sheep?* (1968), whose emotional flatness, measured by the retinal scans of the Voight-Kampff machine, is the only outward mark of inhuman status. When this lack of empathy gives way to criminal violence, we think it deserves, in humans anyway, the name evil—a word that dominates the subtitle of Haycock's book.

The words inside are less charged and more convincing. Haycock is a leading cheerleader for the use of neuroscience, especially functional magnetic resonance imaging (fMRI), in isolating the features of the brain that can be associated with psychopathy. His writing is coloured by a strong commitment to narrative, with almost every chapter opening with vivid stories of psychopathic violence or diagnosis, and he peppers his accessible discussion of brain structure with references to comic books, science fiction, Norman Mailer, the television shows *Boston Legal* and *The Sopranos*, and *The Lord of the Flies*. He is what Slavoj Žižek would sound like if he were a neuroscientist instead of a Lacanian theorist. Overall, the book offers an excellent account of the current state of play in mapping psychopathic behaviour with neuroscience, giving even-handed time to both the older school of assessment, which relies on interviews and a numerical scale of traits (lack of remorse, mendacity, sexual promiscuity, and so on), and the new cowboys of the fMRI. It should be required reading for anyone who wants to know more about the brains of violent criminals.

One of those fMRI rodeo kings is Kent Kiehl, who, along with James Fallon, makes several cameo appearances in Haycock's book. Kiehl's career straddles the shift from the textured face-to-face investigation of psychopaths to the current vogue for fMRI and other more objective instruments. He studied with Robert Hare, the dean of psychopathy researchers, at the University of British Columbia, and used Hare's canonical checklist of psychopathic traits, known as the Hare Personality Checklist-Revised (PCL-R), when he began to visit and interview incarcerated psychopaths as part of his doctoral research. He was a clever and sensitive interviewer, and wielded the PCL-R with a ninja's elegant subtlety. These interviews form the core of his own recent book, *The Psychopath Whisperer: The Science of Those Without Conscience* (2013)—though the main part of that title makes you wonder whether his editor suffers from the non-DSM condition of Limited Imagination Disorder.

The book is again considerably better than its cover. Kiehl is a fair writer and a likeable companion. His jittery scenes of confrontation with the inmates of a maximum-security prison on the lower mainland of British Columbia, practised and remorseless killers who regarded this wet-behind-the-ears grad student with a mixture of amusement and contempt, are excellent reading. One inmate, outraged at the psychopath label generated by his Hare scores, explained that the correct designation for him was, instead, "SUPERMAN." Kiehl endures all with humour and compassion. His explanation of the Hare Checklist, meanwhile, which scores out of forty—anyone in the thirties is likely a dangerous psychopath—is shot through with examples from history as well as the headlines: Charles Guiteau, who shot and killed President James Garfield in 1881, was almost certainly a psychopath; John Wilkes Booth, who took fatal aim at Abraham Lincoln in 1865, was not. (Kiehl doesn't mention it, but Booth's cry of *Sic semper tyrannis* as he shot Lincoln—roughly, *Thus always to tyrants!*—is the sentiment of a sane man, even if its misapplication in that instance was a mark of unbalance.)

The book shifts when Kiehl discovers the possibility of using fMRI scans to track psychopathy, and so shifts his research program over to a truck-mounted version of the resonance imaging machine which can be moved from prison to prison to amass more data on incarcerated psychopaths. He does not acknowledge the full extent of the controversy here: newer researchers have complained at length that the Hare Checklist is skewed too much toward criminal behaviour. Haycock tells the story of Hare's threats of bringing a lawsuit over a scientific journal article, which tells you more than you probably want to know about the personalities of academics. Kiehl's eyes are on the prize of prediction: we probably won't ever be able to prevent violent crime before it happens, he says, like the pre-cogs in *Minority Report* (PKD again!); but maybe enough collated fMRI data would allow us to track possible future psychopathic behaviour, maybe even prevent it. And what brain chemistry hath wrought may likewise be altered: could we, perhaps, heal psychopaths by, in effect, rewiring those parts of their brains that don't fire when the rest of us feel empathy or compassion?

Kiehl is, however, honest about the limits of this plan. "[S]ometimes psychopaths do things without reason, without motivation," he says of one case he studied at length, that of convicted serial rapist and murderer Brian Dugan. "The rest of us search for some logic, albeit a morally twisted logic, that we can use to understand why. I came to accept the fact that there is no logical answer to many of the crimes people like Brian commit—as disappointing as that might seem."

James Fallon, for his part, has become famous mainly for a TED talk in which he relates how he realized his own brain scan seemed to match those of confirmed psychopaths. Key areas of his hippocampus, amygdala, and orbital frontal cortex were "dark" on fMRIs, indicating a condition of psychopathy which is, in this case, non-violent or "prosocial." The resulting book, *The Psychopath Inside: A Neuroscientist's Journey into the Dark Side of the Brain* (2013)—and surely the better options for the main title were *The Psychopath Within* or *My Inner Psychopath?*—adds texture and some science to this story, but with many contentious claims about the so-called "warrior gene" as well as a surfeit of self-aggrandizing stories that begin to tax one's patience. He likes to mention his nights on the town and wine-sipping sessions in the California hot tub. (Kiehl also mentions his drinking, but mostly as a wind-down after interviewing imprisoned psychopaths all day.)

Fallon retails his childhood at some length and relives the myriad triumphs of his academic career. He comes off as blustering, self-important, competitive, vain, and intellectually pretentious. In sum, he is an example of an unfortunately common type, the Senior Academic Asshat. There is one hilarious section where he reports a poll he did, asking his "close friends" to express their views of him, and received a catalogue of vices that would make a more self-aware person sick with shame: "manipulative," "charming but devious," "an intellectual bully," "superficial," "cunning liar," "shameless," "blame others," "overblown sense of self-importance," "unreliable," "untrustworthy," "The Great I Am." As Sam Spade said to another pathological liar, Brigid O'Shaughnessy, "Well, don't *brag* about it."

The Psychopath Inside does us a service, though, in showing that the borderline or prosocial psychopath might pose a more proximate threat than violent criminals, who are statistically rare, or even those psychopathic "snakes in suits" who allegedly populate some portion of corporate boardrooms. The book is an extended exercise in Male Answer Syndrome, punctuated by Fallon's repeated claims that he is excellent company, a fascinating fellow. The biggest danger of the prosocial psychopath is thus not that he will torture and murder you, perhaps fashioning your flayed hide into a dress afterward. It is, rather, that you will be seated next to him on an airplane or in some corner of a cocktail party and, after two hours' bombardment of self-praising anecdotes, finally expire of boredom and rage. "Maybe this is my own narcissism speaking," Fallon says at the end of his book, "but I believe there's a sweet spot on the psychopathy spectrum. People who are twenty-five or thirty on the Hare scale are dangerous, but we need a lot of twenties around—people with the chutzpah and brio and outrageousness to keep humanity vibrant and adaptable—and alive. People like me." Memo to James Fallon: that *is* your own narcissism speaking.

*   *   *

These three books give us a useful illustration of why neuroscience is the discourse of the moment. They are lively and fascinating, and they throb with a compelling sense of scientific mission. Kiehl in particular is the kind of relatable guy whose enthusiasm for his project is infectious. He's driving around a tractor-trailer with an MRI machine on the bed. He can identify psychopaths. He can predict their future criminal actions. He thinks he might even be able to cure them. He's the Batman of neuroscience!

Of course, these books cannot do what they imply they can—or anyway what many people seem to want them to do. That is, they cannot explain evil. The problem is not the neuroscience itself, which advances and improves by the year; it is the old philosophical bugbear, the mind-body problem—now better framed as the mind-brain problem. The tools of neuroscience give us more and more precise pictures of our brain activity. These images can both localize and correlate that activity with various mental states. But they can't "get inside" those mental states any more than Cartesian mechanism or Spinoza's conatus could. Even the "inside" metaphor is misleading, in fact, because we are dealing with discursive realities, not physical ones. Conscience, intention, responsibility, empathy—these are all ways of talking about our sense of ourselves as persons in a shared world.

Whether or not these concepts *exactly match* physical states of affairs (they probably do), describing those states of affairs in physical terms is just an entirely different way of conceptualizing the realities under discussion. That's why, when taken as being in the business of explaining human personality, fMRI technology begins to recall the thought-experiment in which a scientist is asked to distinguish between two apparently identical objects: a urinal ripped from the wall of your local sports bar's men's room, and one that is signed "R. Mutt." Try as one might, no amount of microscopic investigation will reveal the relevant difference, which is the fact that the latter is a work of art by Marcel Duchamp, called *Fountain*, and the former is . . . well, not.

Neuroscientists understandably disdain this kind of talk—in part because, they say, it is merely talk. Most philosophers and almost all laypeople are agreed, Haycock notes, in thinking that consciousness is something distinct from brain function. "They rely on verbal arguments to defend this viewpoint," he notes. "They may be correct . . . [b]ut their arguments lie outside of the boundaries and limitations of science because they can't be tested convincingly and reproducibly in a laboratory." Pretty much every neuroscientist, by contrast, is a physicalist: to use Haycock's own definition, "anyone who believes that mental states and brain states are the same thing." He goes on: "If the physicalists are correct, then key underlying elements of psychopathy can be found ultimately somewhere in the structures that make up the brain and in the interconnections of its different regions. Somewhere in the neural circuits of the brains of [psychopaths] are answers that explain their aberrant outlook, behaviour and crimes."

A lot hinges on the choice of words. What is the force of "explain" in that final sentence? Localizing brain activity doesn't give us insight into human life. And what is the nature of that "belief" that mind and brain are identical? The identity is featured here as an assumed premise of neuroscientific investigation, which is fine as a working assumption for wielding the MRI machine. But physicalism is a philosophical position about the nature of what is real; it needs to be defended, not merely assumed as true. Neuroscience cannot exempt itself from its own standards of rational demonstration. More deeply, science is, after all, a discourse too—a way of talking. It is a principled (and privileged) way of talking about the material world, yes, but it is not the only way humans talk about themselves, nor is that the only world we inhabit. The concept of mind has irreducible explanatory power when it comes to making sense of personhood.

Again, this is where most neuroscientists would walk away, like interlocutors excusing themselves from the company of Socrates, maybe dismissing philosophy *tout court* along the way. But even a committed booster like Haycock must acknowledge the fundamental problem. Discussing the misleading depiction of neuroscientific evidence on a television show, he concedes that "there is no credible evidence showing that fMRI can be used in this way to 'tell how someone is feeling.' It shows blood flow patterns in the brain, which reflect brain cell activity. Neuronal activity in an isolated part of the brain is not the same thing as a feeling or an emotion." Nor do we always know what mental state the brain cell activity is matching. The most discussed feature of the brain, the amygdala, is, he notes, apparently stimulated by both fear and pleasure. "The fact is at this time neuroscientists understand too little about how brain structure and function regulate or influence motivation, emotion and behavior to convincingly establish a cause and effect relationship between brain scans and crimes."

One admires the scientific conviction the caveat language of "at this time" and "convincingly," but it may simply be that no such causal relationship could ever be established, simply because of the resistant human experience of self and world. The philosopher Colin McGinn, lately disgraced over allegations of the unfortunately common evil of sexual harassment of a graduate student, gets the basic issue right in his book *Ethics, Evil, and Fiction* (1997). "We might indeed eventually discover the neurophysiological basis of evil," he writes. "But . . . the explanation is at the wrong level to satisfy us: we want to know what it is *psychologically* that underwrites the evil disposition. Neural correlates cannot make sense of it in the way we would like." And so we might think to look at richer sources, such as Melville's *Billy Budd* or Shakespeare's *Othello*, where evil is provoked by pure resentment at the presence of good: Iago and John Claggart share the same quality of malevolent hostility to what they lack. Laclos's charismatic Vicomte de Valmont corrupts the virtue of Madame de Tourvel for what amounts to a bet that he cannot do so—though (spoiler alert!) in that case there is true love in the end.

*   *   *

Evil is a word we use too easily. It is a floating signifier that might attach to real-life serial killers but also to the maniacal world-domination fantasies of a James Bond villain or his pinkie-to-lip spoof-twin, Dr. Evil. We might think to contain evil by viewing it as a religious category only—the privation of good, as Thomas Aquinas tells us—but it has political bite too. In the days after the September 11 attacks on the World Trade Center and the Pentagon, it was impossible not to hear about the "evil" fanatics who masterminded the murder of innocents. But the attacks were neither inexplicable nor insane, and their targeting of civilian lives no different from the total-war doctrine laid out by Carl von Clausewitz more than a century earlier. One might invoke Nietzsche and view evil as ever the claim of denunciation against that which we most fear because it is at once within us and against us.

The popular entertainment of evil, meanwhile, fetishizes torture and murder in a series of television series and films where serial killers are portrayed as masters of some dark aesthetic, connoisseurs of calm violence. Hannibal Lecter is most people's idea of an evil man, a monster armed with a ceiling-scraping IQ and a penchant for surgical-strike murder, even as he appreciates the nuances of Glenn Gould's *Goldberg Variations* and tasty Tuscan reds. Lecter is terrifying but he is, finally, understandable because his motivations are fundamentally aesthetic, not ethical. Likewise Red John, of television's *The Mentalist*, an evil genius so manipulative he can convince people they are dead even as they live—the psychopath as artist of the mind.

Whether construed as perverted artist, satanic force, or self-obsession, these various common notions of evil are still forms of parsing human behaviour: they offer explanations for action. Far more troubling is the form of evil which involves cruel or violent action that has no evident motive except the pleasure it appears to provide to its enactor, nastiness without larger narrative. Perhaps, as the German concentration-camp guard notoriously said to Primo Levi: "*Hier ist kein 'Warum'* (Here, there is no 'why')." When it comes to the committed psychopath, perhaps there is no "why." In truth, we have not advanced our conceptual clarity much from the days of witch-trials and accusations of demonic possession.

Immanuel Kant noticed this lurking paradox of the evil person. It is, in effect, a limit-case of the tension between the doctrines of original sin and free will. The truly evil person is at once brutely given—beyond improvement, just "born that way"—*and yet* also fully responsible for his wickedness. Morally, it must be both; but logically, how can it be both? (Kant resolved the paradox by positing the choice of an evil life as a transcendental, *a priori* one, made "outside of time"; but that option carries a heavy metaphysical price.) This is the same impasse Haycock faced at the end of his book: if psychopathy is simply a matter of brain condition, about which none of us has any say, can we hold the psychopath responsible for his actions? The psychopath, once considered the paragon of planned wickedness, begins to resemble the pitiful psychotic, motivated by forces as mute and mysterious as demons.

And if we do not embrace that endgame of mental illness, the issue of moral responsibility remains murky. In Sebastian Faulks's 2007 novel *Engleby*, a casually erudite but unreliable first-person narrative delivered by a psychopath who is a stickler for correct grammar and good literary style, the issue is broached vividly during a trial. Engleby has been charged, many years after the fact, with the murder of Jennifer Arkland, a twenty-year-old Cambridge undergraduate with whom he was mutely, hopelessly in love. The prosecuting barrister forces the point. "He returned to attack the whole 'personality disorder' category," Engleby reports with his usual detachment and wry humour. "Schizophrenics are mad all the time; but people not suffering from mental illness—e.g., me— only get into Special Hospitals if they do something terrible. The murder is the thing that allows admission to take place." The prosecutor, Tindall, sums up the philosophical stakes: "How many psychopaths receive treatment *before* they commit a crime? Is psychopathy in effect no more than a fancy term for wickedness?" Genetic or brain chemistry aside, when is the judgment "mad" just an evasion of the old-fashioned "bad"?

But Colin McGinn is wrong to claim that what we need in evil-talk is more psychological texture. What is missing in almost all discussions of evil is an appreciation of its inherently social nature. It is not a coincidence or the result of the publisher's insistence that Haycock, Kiehl, and Fallon rely so heavily on narrative, including self-narrative, in their accounts of psychopathy. Psychopaths inflict suffering, not just pain: they are interested in rending the personhood of others, not just their bodies. We may call them predators, as if they were wolves among sheep, but they do not hunt to feed; they exploit vulnerability and fear. Their actions are, unfortunately, distinctly human, and instrumental violence requires keen imagination, even a twisted creativity. Richard Rorty noted that the torturer O'Brien, in Orwell's *1984*, is "a curious, perceptive intellectual—much like us." Hannah Arendt's related insights about the banality of evil are not always understood: it is not so much that Eichmann killed without hostility, or as an indifferent executioner; it was rather that an entire cultural and bureaucratic structure, together with the very notion of the "Jew" as alien species, allowed him to view his actions as *not about ethics*. They permitted a suspension of conscience— the social version of the psychopath's lack of brain function.

The true nature of evil is thus revealed only in our tangled relationships with the larger symbolic order. And that is one reason why Walter Kirn's vivid novelistic account of his encounters with the pathological liar, serial impostor, and convicted murderer he knew as Clark Rockefeller is an essential addition to the modern literature of evil. Kirn is a novelist, in fact, and his much-discussed book *Blood Will Out: The True Story of a Murder, a Mystery, and a Masquerade* (2013) has all the tension of a thriller, but studded with reveries about the strange vagaries of life. Kirn met Rockefeller in the oddest of ways: the eccentric New York millionaire needed someone to transport a dog from Montana to Manhattan. A friend of the family sending the animal, Kirn was a struggling writer whose marriage (to the beautiful daughter of actress Margot Kidder and writer Thomas McGuane) was becoming rocky. But the dog was severely crippled and barely hanging onto life. Sane people would have put it down—as Kirn's own mother urged when he stopped to visit her along the way—but this shaggy-dog story doesn't happen without Kirn's stubbornness about delivering the mutt, and Rockefeller's insistence that he do so.

Rockefeller will turn out to be selective in his devotion to canines: later events suggest he may have killed a dog over a dispute with a neighbour in New Hampshire. And of course, despite the club dinners and art collection he flaunts for Kirn in New York, he is no Rockefeller. He was, in fact, a German-born con man whose legal name was Christian Gerhardtsreiter.

Gerhardtsreiter is currently serving a life sentence in California for the 1985 murder of Jonathan Sohus, a neighbour in San Marino when Gerhardtsreiter was going by the name Christopher Chichester and claiming to be a film student at the University of Southern California. The murder was bloody, an extended attack of bludgeoning and stabbing, followed by dismemberment of the body into three parts that were buried in the Sohuses' yard. Sohus's wife, Linda, disappeared at the same time, and continues to be listed as missing. Sohus's remains were found buried in a shopping bag from the University of Wisconsin-Milwaukee, which Gerhardtsreiter had attended.

Gerhardtsreiter has argued that Linda was responsible for her husband's death and continues to maintain his innocence. Gerhardtsreiter is a stone-cold liar and killer who held a cookout and played a game of Trivial Pursuit on the shallow grave where Sohus's chainsawed remains were buried; he would later smile with evident pride when these details were read out in court, though doing so contradicted the argument of his lawyer, which was that Gerhardtsreiter is too clever to have wrapped Sohus's decapitated head in not one, but two, bags with labels traceable back to him. When he was reeling Kirn in, he dubbed himself a "freelance central banker" and hinted at ties to global finance titans and the Admiral of the Navy's Seventh Fleet; he claimed insider knowledge of an impending Chinese invasion of Taiwan and said he'd learned from "sources" that Prince Charles and the Queen had murdered troublesome Diana with the aid of crack commandos.

Crime writer James Ellroy, who befriends Kirn during Gerhardtsreiter's trial in Los Angeles, has no doubt either that Gerhardtsreiter committed the murders or that he is a psychopath, but his opinion is divided, at least on the second issue. Kirn's capacity for narrative identification with his marks suggests the twisted kind of empathy that some sociopaths appear to possess, but his book neverthe-less reads like an extended version of the Hare Personality Checklist. As Rockefeller, Gerhardtsreiter is an incurable, manipulative fantasist with a string of parasitic relationships and no sense of responsibility. He is gran-diose, self-flattering, and entirely devoted to his own needs even as he shows no emotional interest in anyone around him except insofar as they can meet those needs.. The full extent of Gerhardtsreiter's deceptions and violence emerged only after fifteen years of the Kirn-Rockefeller friendship—if that is the right word—and the book paints an unforget-table portrait of a man whom Kirn depicts as a real-life Tom Ripley.

Kirn says he "found [Gerhardtsreiter/Rockefeller] instantly annoy-ing; a twee, diminutive hobbit of a fellow whose level of self-amusement seemed almost delusional." In addition to all his other lies, he claimed degrees from Harvard and Yale and a seat in a tony New York trading firm. His Rockefeller relations were, conveniently, estranged from him and hence never in evidence. He hinted at friends in high places and inside knowledge about imminent coups and shifts in global markets. He was plausible, devious, and subtly manipulative. He raided the bank accounts of his two wives, who seemed stunned into obedience. He forced favours and demanded services, including the bizarre Travels-with-Charley dog road trip, without ever making good on promises. Kirn notes his tic of responding to all questions with the distracted phrase "Oh, that . . . ," a drawled delaying tactic that masked the lightning-quick improvisations he would then deliver in answer. In July 2008 he kidnapped his daughter and, after a dedicated police search, was arrested in Baltimore in August.

Kirn places Rockefeller in the American gallery of glib confidence men, from Melville's Budd and the Duke and Dauphin of Twain's *Huckleberry Finn* to the arch-dealmaker Milo Minderbinder in Joseph Heller's *Catch-22*. He will joke, during Gerhardtsreiter's trial, about pos-sible monikers for the shape-shifting killer: Hannibal Mitty, Gatsby the Ripper. And he tells his almost unbelievable story with a mixture of dry wit and moral outrage.

Clark Rockefeller's con was successful because he offered something Kirn wanted even as he pretended to despise it: proximity to fame and wealth, a seat at the big table, cocktails or sex with big literary names. And so the weird, willing suspensions of disbelief, the semi-conscious internal edits of the skeptical query. "What a perfect mark I'd been," Kirn writes.

"Rationalizing, justifying, imagining. I'd worked as hard at being conned by him as he had at conning me. I wasn't a victim; I was a collaborator." Kirn's final judgment on Gerhardtsreiter is that "he was worse than a murderer and dismemberer." Appropriating the dreams and desires of his marks or victims, he made them the raw material for crafting the shifting personae of his sick world. "He was a cannibal of souls," Kirn says, honing in on this vampiric capacity to suck the imaginative life-blood of others: a species of evil as vivid as anything in the psych literature, even if not as obviously violent as a Gacy, Klebold, or Shock Ritchie. A prison interview between these oddly entwined men, the writer and psychopath, delivers an even more complicated verdict, however. What is it, Kirn wonders, that allows him to manipulate people?

"I think you know," Gerhardtsreiter replies, teasing Kirn. Finally, pressed by his former friend, he answers: "Vanity, vanity, vanity." Sometimes, in another distinctly human action, we fall prey not to the predator but to ourselves.

'We Shall Look Into It Tomorrow':

Kierkegaard and the Art of Procrastination

"A book may have a title which makes you want to read it,
but a title can be so evocative, so personally appealing,
that you will never read the book."

— KIERKEGAARD, *Either/Or*[1]

I
N THIS LONG-DELAYED ESSAY, I argue that procrastination must be construed as a kind of psychic conflict, specifically a conflict between first-order and second-order desires familiar from Plato's moral psychology as well as more recent philosophy of action, such as Harry Frankfurt's account of freedom of the will. On this view of procrastination, we can compare it to other kinds of first- and second-order conflict such as *akrasia* (weakness of the will), addiction, and boredom. Kierkegaard's thought offers a particularly urgent and ethically freighted analysis of the apparently banal experience of putting things off. The paper concludes with a suggestion of how these everyday instances of psychic conflict can lead us to philosophy—albeit philosophy considered as a particular kind of self-understanding.

*　　*　　*

The subject of procrastination is best approached gradually, if not from behind, sneaking up. I want to examine Kierkegaard's special contribution to the philosophical literature on putting things off by a necessarily indirect route. I will start with Plato, move quickly forward to contemporary philosophy of action, and only then broach Kierkegaard's version of the art of procrastination—by which I mean not the art of doing it well, but the artful way it works its wiles upon us. Or, I should rather say, the artful way we work our wiles upon ourselves. This indirectness may, at times, look like postponement; I can only ask the reader to trust the truth of my claim that I will get where I mean to go—eventually. And so . . .

1. Leontius' Eyes: Psychic Conflict and Self-Recrimination

One of the most vivid depictions of psychic conflict in the Western philosophical canon appears in Book IV of Plato's *Republic*, where Socrates and Glaucon are considering the possibility (1) that a person may be divided within himself, or suffering disharmony in the soul; and (2) that, in such a condition, a person might exhibit signs of self-inflicted violence. Here is the relevant passage (Jowett's translation, with modifications):

> Socrates: The story is, that Leontius, the son of Aglaion, coming up one day from the Piraeus, under the north wall on the outside, observed some dead bodies lying on the ground at the place of execution. He felt a desire to see them, and also a dread and abhorrence of them; for a time he struggled and covered his eyes, but at length the desire got the better of him; and forcing them open, he ran up to the dead bodies, saying, 'Look, ye wretches, take your fill of the fair sight.'
>
> Galucon: I have heard the story myself.
>
> Socrates: The moral of the tale is, that anger at times goes to war with desire, as though they were two distinct things.
>
> Glaucon: Yes; that is the meaning.
>
> Socrates: And are there not many other cases in which we observe that when a man's desires violently prevail over his reason, he reviles himself, and is angry at the violence within him, and that

in this struggle, which is like the struggle of factions in a State, his spirit is on the side of his reason?

What strikes us most about this sad tale is, first, its commonality. Leontius is the ancient Greek equivalent of the so-called *rubbernecker*, the person driving past a highway accident who finds his or her eyes drawn to a gruesome spectacle, not despite its evident horror, but because of it. For most of us, this perverse desire is fleeting and only slightly troubling. We would not wish, perhaps, to *embrace* the desire to look at bloody bodies or tangled wreckage, but we can *own up to* such a desire without much cost to our overall mental self-regard. Yes, not the prettiest aspect of human psychology, we might say to ourselves, but not a crisis of faith concerning our general sense of self either.

Not so Leontius. He is wretched before his desire to look at the piled corpses—which, not insignificantly, lie outside the city walls, the place of barbaric absence of civilization. His struggle not to look is, we are told, protracted (it lasts "for a time"). And his conflicting desires are passionate, especially the "dread and abhorrence" he feels about the dead bodies. When this desire wins out over his (presumably more rational) desire not to look, his inner energy immediately turns outward, from struggle to violent action. He rushes to the corpses and, with some hatred, invites his betraying eyes to have their fill of the ugly sight which they nevertheless yearn after as if it were beautiful.

Socrates then suggests that this self-directed violence—somewhat exaggerated, we might think—is evidence of what has happened to his spirit, or will, in the struggles. First allied with reason against the perverse desire, once that desire has emerged victorious, Leontius's will (his "anger"), as it were, changes sides and rushes to condemn the failure. Thus the tripartite soul of Platonic orthodoxy is shown in living colour: the rational or wisdom-loving part (which enjoined Leontius not to look), the biddable and capricious desiring part (which experienced the ugly wish to look in the first instance), and the spirited part (which first sided with reason and, that failing, turned against the person). Poor Leontius! His soul is in disarray, unbalanced and at war with itself. And his eyes take the rap for a desire which he, as himself whole, could neither resist nor acknowledge. The eyes are figured here not as the window to the soul, but as a sort of synecdochic scapegoat. Thus do the conflicted curse their own limbs, or genitals, or organs of sense, for "betraying" the better parts of our nature.

Socrates' larger point is consistent with the general argument of *Republic* IV, that this kind of conflict, and the resulting picture of three aspects of the soul, can be transposed from the level of the person to the level of the state. Thus the three parts of the ideal city will, like the three parts of a given person's soul, need to achieve a harmony in which the rational part, aided by spirit or will, controls and guides the random and riotous desires which form a main part of any human undertaking, individual or collective. This argument need not detain us here, except to say that I will suggest, in a later section of the present paper, that societies, like individuals, can be in psychic conflict, especially when it comes to addiction.

For more proximate purposes, two points must be made. First, it is clear that Plato's moral psychology has significantly departed from received Socratic wisdom. (Compare this passage with similar ones in other dialogues: one thinks, notably, of the unforgettable image of the chariot and two horses found in *Phaedrus* 246a–254e.) Socrates was known to argue that ethical failure was always a matter of prior epistemological failure. That is, when one did wrong, it was because one had insufficient true knowledge of what was at stake. It was on this understanding of epistemological priority that he could claim that one never knowingly did wrong, that all wrongdoing was rooted in ignorance, and therefore that the main task of ethical reflection was to increase one's knowledge.

On the view now attributable to Plato, though articulated by Socrates in the dialogue, this is no longer the case. Given a tripartite soul and the evident, maybe even common, risk of conflict among the parts, one can do wrong *even though* one knows that it is wrong. Indeed, some ethical failures are seen to be rooted precisely in this conflict itself, such that the wrongdoing is not so much having a given desire as being unable to resist it. It is not really the wanting to look at corpses that is bad—desire is, in a sense, naturally wrought—but, rather, that I am unable to stop myself from looking when that is what I believe to be the right course of action. My moral failure is not perverse desire but lack of control.

This leads to the second point, which is that the story of Leontius may not necessarily warrant a Platonic moral psychology after all; or, rather, it may warrant a more neutral version of such a psychology that can dispense with the trappings of Platonic metaphysics. Let us recast the case of Leontius in the following way. He has (1) a desire, however perverse, to look at the corpses. I will call this a first-order desire, after recent philosophy of action, in that it is a desire concerning something external to the agent (the "object" of the desire) and concerns the action he eventually performs, namely looking at the corpses. But Leontius also has (2) an attitude with respect to this initial desire, namely that he is filled with dread and abhorrence concerning them and so not only wishes not to look, but wishes not to have the desire to look at all.

I further posit, perhaps a little controversially, that these feelings of dread and abhorrence concerning the corpses are not simply conflicting desires on the same level as (1), as if the two—look; don't look—were opponents on equal footing. I suggest, instead, that the dread and abhorrence constitute a second-order desire, a feeling in respect of experiencing (1) in the first place. They are second-order because their object is not something external to the agent, but rather prior feelings within the agent. That is, they are second-order because they are desires concerning first-order desires. Leontius wants to look; but he also wishes he did not want to look. Thus the presence of (3), the mental or psychic conflict he experiences, and the violence he inflicts upon himself in the figure of his own eyes.

I believe this is a valid construal of the story, though it is not precisely the one Socrates gives—or, to be precise, the story is very slightly ambiguous on whether the desire to look at the corpses is dreadful and abhorrent, or the sight of them itself is. Jowett's translation favours the latter, to be sure, but we know from Plato's general theory of appetite that he considers desire, in general, base, and lodges the better part of our natures in the reasoning part of the soul. In any event, it matters less whether my construal neatly fits Leontius than whether it accurately figures the common experience of *akrasia*, or weakness of the will. The weakness here is experienced as the result of conflicting desires. This conflict is either (1) between two first-order desires (look! don't look!), the latter of which the self disapproves at the second order but is unable to resist; or (2) it is a matter of the first-order desire (I want to look!) overpowering the second-order one (I don't want to want to look!). The attendant idea in both cases would be that psychic harmony, or happiness, is experienced if, and only if, one's first-order and second-order desires are aligned, when there was no conflict between them.

This notion of alignment immediately raises the linked questions of what status second-order desires have, what power they may or may not have over first-order desires (themselves conflicted or not), and what exactly we mean by "will" on such a view of desire.

2. Addicts, Wantons, and Bores

We find Leontius-style slippage in Frankfurt's now-canonical article "Freedom of the Will and the Concept of a Person" (1971), where there are, variously, conflicts between two first-order desires, conflicts between first- and second-order desires, and even (or especially) conflicts between second-order desires.[2] His particular interest in this argument is to link a special subclass of second-order desires—what he calls "second-order volitions"—to the idea of a free will. This free will is, in turn, a special feature of what we mean by calling certain entities, and not others, persons. "Now it is having second-order volitions, and not having second-order desires generally, that I regard as essential to being a person," he notes. "It is logically possible, however unlikely, that there should be an agent with second-order desires but with no volitions of the second order. Such a creature, in my view, would not be a person" (10-11).

This "creature" is something Frankfurt wants to call a wanton: an entity that acts and experiences both first- and second-order desires, but has no attitude specifically of willing, or endorsing with effective approval, any particular first-order desire. It is difficult to imagine such a creature, still more to imagine being one; whether they deserve to be deprived of the label of person is nevertheless controversial. I will not pursue that issue here, since it has been well worked over in the literature. More interesting, for my argument here, is another figure who is sketched in Frankfurt's account, namely the willing addict.

The standard sort of addict is unwilling, and indeed might be considered an extreme version of the case enacted by Leontius. This addict has (1) conflicting first-order desires, namely both to take and not to take the drug that figures in his addiction; but, significantly, he also has (2) a second-order desire not to have the desire to take the drug. He doesn't want to want the drug; but he does, and so there will be times when his will—now figured as the second-order desire not to want to—is insufficient to overmaster that desire in favour of the desire not to take the drug. The unwilling addict, Frankfurt says, "is not neutral with regard to the conflict between his desire to take the drug and his desire to refrain from taking it. It is the latter desire, and not the former, that he wants to constitute his will; it is the latter desire, rather than the former, that he wants to be effective and to provide the purpose that he will seek to realize in what he actually does" (12).

Now we might wonder, given the nature of addiction, whether it is accurate to speak of this second-order desire—that which makes him unwilling—as a volition, since it fails repeatedly to make the refraining desire effective. That is, if the addiction is severe, the first-order desire to take the drug has, in a deep sense, captured his will and he is, we might say, a slave to his addiction. He is not free, even if he remains unwilling in some attenuated sense. For Frankfurt, however, it is the wish to resist that constitutes freedom of will, rather than actually resisting, which concerns freedom of action. "When we ask whether a person's will is free we are not asking whether he is in a position to translate his first-order desires into actions," Frankfurt notes. "That is a question of whether he is free to do as he pleases. The question of the freedom of his will does not concern the relation between what he does and what he wants to do. Rather, it concerns his desires themselves" (15). In short, it concerns whether he wants to want the desire he has, rather than whether, as a matter of fact, that desire proves effective.

Thus the special interest of Frankfurt's third kind of addiction, after the wanton and the unwilling addict; namely, the willing addict. This blithe but benighted fellow is someone who has surrendered his will to a destructive first-order desire. He resembles Kant's happy slave in that he has, as it were, given away his freedom. (Kant will argue that a happy slave is no argument against the injustice of slavery: it is an offence to freedom of persons even if an individual does not feel the injustice.) If "[t]he wanton addict does not care which of his conflicting first-order desires wins out" (13), and so lacks a will, "the willing addict's will is not free, for his desire to take the drug will be effective regardless of whether or not he wants this desire to constitute his will. But when he takes the drug, he takes it freely and of his own free will" (19). This means that, unlike the wanton, the willing addict may be considered morally responsible for his actions, even though he has no effective wish to act otherwise than he does.

I dwell on this argument at some length not because I intend to settle the question of moral responsibility in respect of addiction, but rather, following Kierkegaard's lead, to raise that question in a different manner. Let us, then, consider some other cases of conflict between first- and second-order desires. These may also entail, or allow, conflicts between more than one first-order desire, but I suggest that the question of will—indeed, the question of selfhood—lies not so much in which desire is effective, or even which is endorsed, but instead in the dynamic relation between levels of desire. In other words, the experience of selfhood just is the reflective ability to form higher-order desires or attitudes about lower-order desires. As Frankfurt notes, there is nothing in logic to prevent this ordering from ascending to further levels—desires about desires about desires, and so on; but if the reflexive relation is the important thing, two levels are sufficient. And even if there are further levels, "[w]hen a person identifies himself *decisively* with one of his first-order desires, this commitment 'resounds' throughout the potentially endless array of higher orders" (16).

Earlier I used a language of "internal" and "external" about these two orders of desires. This is not language that Frankfurt uses, nor is it without its difficulties. But, accepting for the moment that we experience ourselves in some sense as a form of inwardness—the self as self-reflection—it will do to be going on with. The self is as the self desires, and one of the key things it desires is that I should not just want what I want, but should also *want to want* what I want.

To this point, we have examining cases—Leontius, the various addicts—in which the first-order desire is somehow abhorrent, harmful, or discreditable. But now consider a cluster of cases with a different resonance, that is, cases where the first-order desire is missing. The psychoanalyst Adam Phillips begins one his best essays this way: "Every adult remembers, among many other things, the great *ennui* of childhood, and every child's life is punctuated by spells of boredom: that state of suspended anticipation in which things are started and nothing begins, the mood of diffuse restlessness which contains that most absurd and paradoxical wish, the wish for a desire."[3]

The wish for a desire: it is not restricted to children, and though it may be judged absurd and paradoxical, it is nevertheless common and urgent. Human life, says Schopenhauer in *The World as Will and Representation* (1819), "swings like a pendulum to and fro between pain and boredom, and these two are in fact its ultimate constituents." Boredom is "anything but an evil to be thought of lightly: ultimately it depicts the countenance of real despair."[4] The reason for this despair is simple if we apply the two-order model of selfhood. A bored person is experiencing a psychic conflict, since the second-order desire (the wish) cannot align with a first-order desire (the desire), for the simple reason that there is no first-order desire in play. This sort of conflict, in contrast to the ones associated with addiction, may be called a *stall*. There is no desire to approve or make active, and the self falls into a hopeless struggle with itself that cannot resolve because there is no evident raw material on which to apply the energy of resolution. This is not weakness of the will but a dissonance between desire itself, at the two levels.

We are likely all too familiar with the experience: confronting the full refrigerator and yet complaining that there is "nothing to eat"; the enforced stillness of the long car journey with nothing to divert us from the unbroken vista out the window; the time spent waiting in queues, doctor's offices, or departure lounges; the long evenings that stretch out after one's lonely dinner without promise of incident or hint of pleasure. Boredom often, if not always, is experienced as a kind of temporal abyss, an acute awareness of time's passing; it is the existential variant of simple waiting, deepening that mundane experience into an apparently endless waiting-for-nothing that suffuses and dominates consciousness.[5] By contrast to these moments of quiet desperation, we might consider that the addict has it easy: even if he is powerless to solve it, at least he knows what his problem is!

I will suggest at the end of the present essay that boredom, like procrastination—the introduction of which, you may have noticed, I keep putting off—offers a profound opportunity for refection on selfhood, indeed for philosophical investigation more generally. For the moment, though, I wish to emphasize its negative features; also, of course, that boredom was a subject close to Kierkegaard's intellectual heart. "People of experience maintain that it is very sensible to start from a principle," he writes in the *A* voice of *Either/Or* (1934). "I grant them that and start with the principle that all men are boring" (227). The voice then goes on to offer a global theory of boredom that echoes Schopenhauer's lament from just fifteen years earlier:

> What wonder, then, that the world is regressing, that evil is gaining ground more and more, since boredom is on the increase and boredom is the root of all evil. We can trace this from the very

beginning of the world. The gods were bored so they created man. Adam was bored because he was alone, so Eve was created. From that time boredom entered the world and grew in exact proportion to the growth of population. Adam was bored alone, then Adam and Eve were bored in union, then Adam and Eve and Cain and Abel were bored *en famille*, then the population increased and the people were bored *en masse*. (228)

And there you were, thinking it was the love of money that is the root of all evil (1 Timothy 6:10)!

The *A* voice reflects further that, given there is no escape from this condition, there is no better strategy than 'crop rotation': the application of arbitrary decisions, the 'diverting' teasing of sensitive persons, and like divertissements. *A* makes a twofold mistake here. First, he fails to see that, though there are indeed boring people, boredom may also be in the eye of the beholder. Everyone's mother likely admonished us, at some point, that only mentally impoverished or lazy people find themselves routinely bored. This is not true, but it contains a germ of insight: sometimes the problem really is me, not you.

Second, though, and more seriously, *A* proposes to meet the condition of finding all men boring by substituting random or capricious desires for the desires, or interests, that he does not actually have. This is the essential error of boredom: thinking that the solution to the stall of lacking a first-order desire is to find some—any—desire to fill the first-order void. But the desire so found, or manufactured, will inevitably have an arbitrary or bogus aspect, a taint of the very desperation it seeks to deny. Moreover, such trumped-up desires will always fail really to satisfy the second-order wish, and so will fail to bring the happiness of psychic harmony. Instead, as experience often indicates, the restlessness of boredom is just continued by other means; we flit from desire to desire without being able to settle on any single one and endorse it as 'resounding' in the sense Frankfurt described. Boredom is not to be defeated so easily.

Judge William's reply to *A*, in *Either/Or*, makes a version of this point. He points out that only concrete ethical action will suffice to overcome the stall of boredom. This hints at the nature of Kierkegaard's views on procrastination also, as communicated in *The Sickness Unto Death* (1949)—about which more in a moment!—but in *Either/Or* the tension is, by design, never entirely overcome.

In part, this is a matter of Kierkegaard's longstanding antipathy to Hegelian dialectical idealism, which suggests that all conflicted states of mind, or spirit, are resolved into new *aufgehoben* syntheses. But it is also, or by the same token, a feature of Kierkegaard's notion of irony. Indeed, we find a complex insight about boredom in one of his earliest works, the dissertation he published *in propria persona* (as opposed to under one of his various pseudonyms) as *The Concept of Irony* (1841). There we find this emphatic claim: "*Boredom* is the *only continuity* the ironist has. Yes, boredom: this eternity void of content, this bliss without enjoyment, this superficial profundity, this hungry satiety" (302). This may be construed as presaging the "root of all evil" passage in *Either/Or*, but I prefer to read it in a more active, and positive, manner. The ironist risks boredom, but it is, we might say, an active boredom, a militant irony. In contrast to the empty boredom of merely negative irony, this yields action.[6]

But how? To answer that question, we must turn, at long last, to the art of procrastination.

3. Meaning to Get to:
Procrastination's Displacements

English poet Edward Young labelled procrastination "the thief of time," and the label has stuck because Young's characterization captures the temporal nature of the complaint. Like boredom, to which it can be usefully compared, procrastination is a kind of restlessness about the present's relation to the future: in neither case can I "settle" on a given desire, and execute its required action. Procrastination concerns something that I should (or might) be doing now, but am instead putting off or deferring, blocking completion of the given task. Again like boredom, therefore, procrastination is structured such that there is a missing first-order desire, an active will to do the necessary thing, combined with a blocked second-order desire recognizing that I want to want to do the thing, but can not or do not do it.

Both boredom and procrastination are thus matters of conflict between orders of desire. Unlike boredom, however, procrastination does not *stall*; instead, it *displaces*. A lower-priority desire steals into the space left open by the higher-priority, but for the moment ineffective, first-order desire. In this sense, procrastination is closer to classic Leontius-style *akrasia*, since the lower-priority task is, in a sense, a rival first-order desire to the one that is deferred or evaded.[7] It is therefore less paradoxical than boredom, if no less unsettling and, indeed, debilitating to consciousness. Indeed, it can often feel like the most severe form of addiction—perhaps especially when what is being put off is the task of ridding oneself of another addiction.

To see the texture of this displacement, consider a well-known passage from the writer P. J. O'Rourke:

> Usually, writers will do anything to avoid writing. For instance, the previous sentence was written at one o'clock this afternoon. It is now a quarter to four. I have spent the past two hours and forty-five minutes sorting my neckties by width, looking up the word "paisley" in three dictionaries, attempting to find the town of that name on the *New York Times Atlas of the World* map of Scotland, sorting my reference books by width, trying to get the bookcase to stop wobbling by stuffing a matchbook cover under its corner, dialing the telephone number on the matchbook cover to see if I should take computer courses at night, looking at the computer ads in the newspaper and deciding to buy a computer because writing seems to be so difficult on my old Remington, reading an interesting article on sorghum farming in Uruguay that was in the newspaper next to the computer ads, cutting that and other interesting articles out of the newspaper, sorting—by width—all the interesting articles I've cut out of newspapers recently, fastening them neatly together with paper clips and making a very attractive paper clip necklace and bracelet set, which I will present to my girlfriend as soon as she comes home from the three-hour low-impact aerobic workout that I made her go to so I could have some time alone to write.[8]

Here we observe the key features of the experience: (1) a clear but difficult task that the subject wishes to complete (writing); (2) a lack of external control or sufficient incentive; (3) a long list of possible displacement activities; and so (4) a possibly endless avoidance of the task at hand. In this protracted continuation of displacement, the mind's energy bent against itself all the while because, even as the subject completes various other tasks, he is ever aware that he is not completing, or even beginning, the one at hand. Hence the feelings of psychic conflict or personal disharmony.

We can distinguish various modalities of this displacement, as follows: (1) a small but onerous duty which is evaded because unpleasant (going to the dentist, completing a tax return); (2) a task which seems too large to begin, however desirable (writing a book, quitting smoking); (3) an important preparatory undertaking that nevertheless induces anxiety about future challenges (preparing a public speech, studying for an exam); (4) a necessary action that arouses fear (proposing marriage, asking for a raise, confronting a quarrelsome neighbour). We can also imagine subtler psychic evasions, such as (5) when I mitigate the psychic conflict by implicitly giving myself permission to avoid something, perhaps with a roster of reasons I consider sufficient to the case; or (6) those odd cases where I have a fairly firm intention of doing a thing at time T1 and yet find myself, at time T2, somehow not doing it—perhaps because I no longer feel the force of the original intention. (This can apply to both unpleasant and pleasant tasks: I might plan to see a movie later in the afternoon, and then find at a certain point that I have not left the house.)

All of these versions of procrastination—it is only a partial taxonomy; there may be more—are sufficient to cause displacement because the task is somehow experienced as overwhelming.

That feeling of being overwhelmed is like the visual blurring, or "aura," that signals the onset of a migraine headache. And once the feeling of being overwhelmed is in play, the first-order desire is displaced, and into the resulting vacancy can readily flow, almost any other desire/action, however trivial: sharpening pencils, sorting laundry, reading just one more book or article.[9] (This last is the particular affliction of procrastinating scholars, which helps to explain why there are so many such books and articles being produced despite much putting off of writing: the general demand for written scholarship's displacing power is sufficient to overcome the particular ineffectiveness of a given procrastinating scholar.)

Kierkegaard was well aware of these snares, of course. Once again in the *A* section of *Either/Or*, we find this "ecstatic lecture":

If you marry, you will regret it; if you do not marry, you will also regret it; if you marry or if you do not marry, you will regret both; whether you marry or you do not marry, you will regret both. Laugh at the world's foibles, you will regret it; weep over them, you will also regret it; if you laugh at the world's follies or if you weep over them, you will regret both; whether you laugh at the world's follies or you weep over them, you will regret both. Believe a girl, you will regret it; if you do not believe her, you will also regret it; if you believe a girl or you do not believe her, you will regret both; whether you believe a girl or you do not believe a girl, you will regret both. If you hang yourself, you will regret it; if you do not hang yourself, you will regret it; if you hang yourself or you do not hang yourself, you will regret both; whether you hang yourself or you do not hang yourself, you will regret both. This, gentlemen, is the sum of all practical wisdom. (53)

The mention of hanging nails the stakes here. The deep message of routine procrastination is a question: if this particular task, whatever it may be, seems not quite worth doing, then why is *anything* worth doing? Surely the task of going on living is the most overwhelming of them all? Why bother? And note that such despair can arise from too much fulfillment as easily as from too little. If life were a utopia where "pigeons flew about ready roasted," Schopenhauer wrote on the subject, invoking a standard image from the Land of Cockaigne, "people would die of boredom or else hang themselves."[10]

But would they really? The only salvation available here seems to be that summoning the energy sufficient to act on this procrastinatory endgame is itself subject to deferral. I can't see the point of going on; but I also can't see the point of making a decision to act on that lack of point.[11] In a very important sense, I can't be bothered. Dorothy Parker's poem "Résumé" (1926) makes one version of the point, with characteristic economy and wit: "Razors pain you; / Rivers are damp; / Acids stain you; / And drugs cause cramp; / Guns aren't lawful; / Nooses give; / Gas smells awful; / You might as well live."[12] Yes, *might as well* is about right.

Now it is of course true that most procrastination does not force us into such depths, nor is it always intractable. As in other forms of *akrasia*, procrastination can be overcome with sheer willpower. It can also be outsmarted, as when one, for example, breaks an apparently overwhelming task into smaller, more manageable bits; or imposes a series of deadlines on oneself, externalizing the will. These days, such externalization of the will can be in the form of an algorithm: various programs and applications—TaskTimer, Keep Me Out, Concentrate, Anti-Social—are available to block one's internet access for a set period, or to time-out a certain piece of work.[13] One can also sneak up on a task by beginning it without thinking too much about doing so—a psychic version of the Aristotelian *phronimos*, maybe, who can act ethically without deliberation, or the ace shortstop who doesn't allow thought to block his execution of the smooth throw to first base. My own version of this tactic, developed during the writing of my doctoral dissertation—a task with no certain deadlines and many feelings of being overwhelmed—was to switch on my computer on the way to the kitchen to make coffee. I was thus, in a sense, already working.

One can also use procrastination's displacements artfully, as in what philosopher John Perry has labelled "structured procrastination."[14] This means accepting the displacements of procrastination, but acting so that the replacement activities, albeit of a lower priority, are still valuable ones. Thus one can get a great deal done—and even, Perry suggests, enjoy a reputation as a very effective and timely worker—by doing things that one is not supposed to be doing, even as one evades the thing one is supposed to be doing. The beauty of structured procrastination is not just that one gets things done; it might even be the case, eventually, that the originally displaced activity becomes the replacement activity of some other displaced activity, and so one gets that done too. Of course, there is always *something* that is put off; the structural solution doesn't work otherwise.

Well and good. It must be noted, however, that structured procrastination is, despite its success, still a way of evading the existential stakes of the initial experience. It is, therefore, not unlike the desperate seeking after stimulus that many people fall into when they experience a hint of boredom, though it is more productive. Both are strategies of substitution; they keep the deep lessons of psychic conflict forever at bay, refusing to confront the abyss of selfhood. Kierkegaard himself would make the further point, in *The Present Age*, that certain social moments—ones that, like both his and ours, are an "age of advertising and publicity"— tend to facilitate this relentless drive for substitution and the endless stimulation of desire.[15]

One can also see how, in a world dominated by imperatives of work and production, procrastination could come to be viewed as sinful, just as boredom might be condemned as self-indulgent when there are so many forms of stimulus on offer in a hyper-mediated environment. Thomas de Quincey saw this danger as early as 1827, when he offered, in "On Murder Considered as One of the Fine Arts," the following playful inversion of moral failings: "For if once a man indulges himself in murder, very soon he comes to think little of robbing; and from robbing he comes next to drinking and Sabbath-breaking, and from that to incivility and procrastination."[16] (The sad footnote here is that de Quincey was himself a chronic procrastinator, often failing to meet deadlines, pay bills, or answer letters; he was thus that most tortured of souls: the procrastinating writer who must nevertheless write voluminously, and on deadline, in order to survive.)

Kierkegaard knew, like Schopenhauer before him, that these ordinary experiences of stall and displacement in fact sail close to the wind of despair. He also knew how inventive we are when it comes to finding reasons not to do things. Yes, we have finally arrived at the promised, much-deferred destination of the essay! Here is his penetrating analysis of procrastination, in a passage from *The Sickness Unto Death* (1849), using the voice of Anti-Climacus:

> [I]f a person does not do what is right at the very second that he knows it—then, first of all, knowing simmers down. Next comes the question of how willing appraises what is known. Willing is dialectical and has under it the entire lower nature of man. If willing does not agree with what is known, then it does not necessarily follow that willing goes ahead and does the opposite of what knowing understood (presumably such strong opposites are rare); rather, willing allows some time to elapse, an interim called: 'We shall look into it tomorrow'. During all this, knowing becomes more and more obscure, and the lower nature gains the upper hand more and more; alas, for the good must be done immediately, as soon as it is known—but the lower nature's power lies in stretching things out. Gradually, willing's objection to this development lessens; it almost appears to be in collusion. And when knowing has become duly obscured, knowing and

willing can better understand each other; eventually they agree completely, for now knowing has come over to the side of willing and admits that what it wants is absolutely right. And this is how perhaps the great majority of men live.[17]

Knowing, here, means our better natures, that which we know to be right—what I have been calling a second-order desire, to want to want the right thing. *Willing* may also be construed as second-order, since it is dialectical and has all of one's lower nature within its purview. The key to the conflict, however, is not the structure—though that is important—but rather the temporal dimension. The lower nature's power lies in stretching things out! This is exactly right, for it is into just that delay that the initial impetus falls, and is eventually lost. "We shall look into it tomorrow" is the first step on the pathway of avoidance.

Worse, though—and here we see again Kierkegaard's gifts as a psychologist—is that during the resulting delay, knowing loses its grip on the judgment of rightness, becoming vague to itself. Soon enough, knowing comes to agree with willing that perhaps the thing need not be done, or that some other thing might be done instead. This is the essence of self-deception, that one may come to convince oneself of just the opposite action that one once knew to be right—but delayed, even momentarily, in performing.

I want to call this kind of psychic inversion *ethico-theological procrastination*. Is it still *akrasia*? Not really, for it is not experienced primarily as a struggle that one loses. There is no Leontius-style anger here, however mistakenly directed at one's eyes rather than one's soul. Instead, there is a form of complicity, a sly and even comfortable slip into self-deception. In a sense, we have come full circle. Socrates argues that immorality was a function of ignorance, because we would always avoid what we knew to be wrong. Plato countered that one sometimes knows a thing to be wrong and does it anyway, out of weakness. Kierkegaard knows that sometimes failing to do right is indeed a matter of ignorance, but it is an ignorance we are ourselves responsible for producing. In ethico-religious procrastination, in other words, I pull the wool over my own eyes.

For Kierkegaard, the only solution to this deception, and the deeper condition it hints at, namely the despair one feels at having to be oneself—having to be a self at all—was to align oneself with a higher purpose.

Without denying the theological version of that claim, I want, in conclusion, to propose an alternative.

4. Philosophy Done Here

I mentioned earlier that both boredom and procrastination, now revealed as forms of despair, may nevertheless enable a welcome turn to philosophy. The former case is well known. *Langeweile ist der ursprung des philosophierens*, read a sign to be seen during the 1980s in Berlin's U-Bahn system. *Boredom is the wellspring of philosophers*. If boredom is the origin of philosophy in general, a condition in which one may, if one is brave, confront the nature of desire itself, then procrastination is the origin of philosophy of action. What makes anything worth doing? Why is doing something ever preferable to the not-doing of everything?

It is well known that Kierkegaard's attitude to philosophy was, to say the least, ambivalent. In its Hegelian guise he found it pernicious and prone to false claims of universal validity. Of traditional metaphysics he was as suspicious as anyone since Hume, and almost as much as A. J. Ayer. Here is a typical passage from the early pages of *Either/Or*: "What the philosophers say about reality is often as deceptive as when you see a sign in a second-hand store that reads: Pressing Done Here. If you went in with your clothes to have them pressed you would be fooled; the sign is for sale" (50).

This same parable has a reverse possible interpretation, however. Let us sharpen the point by modifying the sign. A young man in the grips of procrastinatory despair passes a storefront displaying a sign saying "Philosophy Done Here." Excited to learn the answers to his unsettling questions, eager for the wisdom that will console him, he rushes into the store—only to be informed that the sign is for sale. But this does not demonstrate the meretricious nature of philosophical promises; it illustrates the error of his thinking that philosophical answers—wisdom itself—are available for purchase, as in a self-help seminar. His is the very same error, *mutatis mutandis*, that Alcibiades makes when he plots to acquire wisdom by sleeping with Socrates. His shame when Socrates rebuffs his advance is the first glimmer of real wisdom—a glimmer that, in his case, is allowed to die rather than blossom into true flame.[18]

Philosophy is done here, but nobody can do it for us. The sign is not for sale; it is yours for free.

The *A* voice of *Either/Or* goes on to indict philosophy on another charge, namely that it is endless. "Experience has shown that it isn't at all difficult for philosophy to begin," he says. "Far from it: it begins with nothing and can accordingly always begin. What seems so difficult to philosophy and philosophers is to stop" (55). This is what makes philosophy "the higher lunacy," a kind of mental addiction that, once admitted, renders its victims into a species of slave.

It must be said that all of the philosophical addicts I have known (including myself) have been willing, if not exactly happy, ones. This is not, I believe, surprising. Pace Boethius, and contrary to the spirit of Kierkegaard's own complaints, philosophy is not consoling—and not meant to be. It is, instead, a kind of discipline that will not be denied: thought demanding to know the conditions of thought's own possibility. In this form, and once begun, philosophical thought proves irresistible. Can we call it, with appropriate caveats, the anti-drug, not just the logical outcome of boredom and procrastination but their psychic reversal.

Kierkegaard is correct that stopping, not starting, is now the problem with philosophy. "The real discovery is the one which enables me to stop doing philosophy when I want to," Wittgenstein remarks in his *Philosophical Investigations*. "The one that gives philosophy peace, so that it is no longer tormented by questions which bring *itself* into question."[19]

The "when we want to" is the crux here. Because, for some of us, this bringing-into-question is precisely the higher power with which we wish to be aligned. And we don't need to stop, exactly, just to pause now and then, in order to attend to other things. And if we are wise, we follow the standard anti-addiction advice and take this balancing of tasks one day at a time.

Easy does it.

Notes

1   Søren Kierkegaard, *Either/Or: A Fragment of Life*; trans. Alastair Hannay, (Penguin Classics, 1992 [orig. 1843]), 211. All subsequent citations are from this edition, given in parentheses.

2   Harry Frankfurt, "Freedom of the Will and the Concept of a Person," *Journal of Philosophy* 68:1, January 4, 1971, 5-20. All further page references are to this publication.

3   Adam Phillips, "On Being Bored," in *On Kissing, Tickling, and Being Bored: Psychoanalytic Essays on the Unexamined Life* (Harvard, 1993), 68.

4   Arthur Schopenhauer, *The World as Will and Representation* [Die Welt als Wille und Vorstellung, 1811, 1844], Vol. I, 313.

5   For more on this, see Lars Svendsen, *A Philosophy of Boredom* (Reaktion Books, 2005); and for some analysis on how boredom relates to work and leisure—a topic too large to discuss in the present essay, but most relevant—see Joshua Glenn and Mark Kingwell, *The Idler's Glossary* (Biblioasis, 2008) and *The Wage Slave's Glossary* (Biblioasis, 2011).

    One can compare Kierkegaard on the general point: "Whatever can be the meaning of this life? If we divide mankind into two large classes, we can say that one works for a living, the other has no need to. But working for one's living can't be the meaning of life; to suppose that constantly procuring the conditions of life should be the answer to the question of the meaning of what they make possible is a contradiction. Usually the lives of the other class have no meaning either, beyond that of consuming the said conditions. To say that the meaning of life is to die seems again to be a contradiction" (*Either/Or*, 49). Later, he will add this gloss: "Idleness as such is by no means a root of evil; quite the contrary, it is a truly divine way of life so long as one is not bored" (*Either/Or*, 230).

6   A good discussion of the point can be found in Gregor Malantschuk, *Kierkegaard's Thought*; Howard Hong and Edna Hong, trans. (Princeton, 1971), 205.

7   It should be noted that the deferral in question is distinct from Freud's notion of *Nachträglichkeit*, or "afterwardsness" (or, in Lacan's rehabilitation, the "après-coup"). In the psychoanalytic canon, what is deferred is a trauma, or sometimes just an experience of otherness, which manifests as neurosis only after the fact, thus obscuring its true origin. In the present discussion, the act of deferring is itself both the trauma and the thing obscured.

    Lacan and, later, Žižek offer an effective psychoanalytic deconstruction of desire, however, which might be relevant here. As Lacan argues, desire's "object" is always a *post facto* construction, retroactively (and misleadingly) granted the power to "arouse" longing, when, in truth, desire is constantly circulating, settling on objects only, as it were, for convenience. Žižek makes the point using Alfred Hitchcock's notion of "the MacGuffin," that obscure thing which everyone in a given film thriller must seek (microfilm, secret code, piece of technology, stolen cash). According to Žižek, "the famous MacGuffin, the Hitchcockian object, [is] the pure pretext whose sole role is to set the story in motion but which is in itself 'nothing at all'—the only significance of the MacGuffin lies in the fact that it has some significance for the characters—that it must seem to be of vital importance to them." See Slavoj Žižek, *The Sublime Object of Ideology* (Verso, 1989), 163

8   Despite having found numerous online sources for this quotation—and being drawn, as a result, into clicking on links for other O'Rourke quotations, retail sites

selling neckties, and discussions of Scottish history—I have not been able to confirm a print source. I'm working on it . . .

9   I discuss these features of procrastination in greater detail in Mark Kingwell, "Meaning to Get To: Procrastination and the Art of Life," *Queen's Quarterly* 109:3 (Fall 2002): 363-81.

10   Arthur Schopenhauer, *Parerga and Paralipomena* (1851), Vol. II, 293.

11   This is the bleakly hilarious conclusion of Geoff Dyer's *Out of Sheer Rage: Wrestling with D. H. Lawrence* (Macmillan, 1997), one of the best, and funniest, books ever written about procrastination. It should be noted that the book was supposed to be a book about D. H. Lawrence, but Dyer was unable to finish—or, indeed, start—that book.

12   First published in Dorothy Parker, *Enough Rope: Poems* (Boni and Liveright, 1926).

13   Is this the beginning of a slippery slope to accepting the redundancy of individual consciousness? After all, if I can offload part of my psyche to a program, why not all of it? On the other hand, one might regard the anti-procrastination aid as just a sophisticated version of the "extended mind," such as a note to oneself, left on the refrigerator, or indeed an alarm clock. For more on this, see Andy Clark and David Chalmers, "The Extended Mind," *Analysis* 58 (1998): 10-23.

14   Perry's original essay, "Structured Procrastination," was published in 1995 but it took him seventeen years before he produced a lively book on the subject, *The Art of Procrastination: A Guide to Effective Dawdling, Lollygagging, and Postponing* (Workman, 2012). The subtitle is misleading: dawdling and lollygagging are really forms of laziness, not procrastination. The procrastinator is not, in fact, lazy, only conflicted; for more on this point, see Kingwell, "Meaning to Get To."

15   Søren Kierkegaard, *The Present Age*, trans. Alexander Dru, (Harper Perennial, 1962 [orig. 1846]), 35. It is worth noting here that Dwight Macdonald's influential 1959 essay "Masscult and Midcult" closes with a lengthy quotation from *The Present Age*, on the debasing effect of publicity, followed by this sentence from Macdonald: "This is the essence of what I have tried to say." See "Masscult and Midcult," in *Masscult and Midcult: Essays Against the American Grain* (NYRB Books, 2011), 71.

16   Thomas de Quincey, "On Murder Considered as One of the Fine Arts," *Blackwood's Magazine* (February 1827).

17   Søren Kierkegaard, *The Sickness Unto Death* (with *Fear and Trembling*), trans. Walter Lowrie, (Oxford, 1941 [orig. 1849]), 94.

18   See Plato, *Symposium*, 216c - 223d.

19   Ludwig Wittgenstein, *Philosophical Investigations*; trans. G. E. M. Anscombe, (Macmillan, 1953), § 133.

WORDS ABOUT
IMAGES

In the Third Place

American Juggalo (2011, d. Sean Dunne, 23 min.)
Terminal Bar (2003, d. Stefan Nadelman, 23 min.)
Heavy Metal Parking Lot
(1986, d. John Heyn and Jeff Krulik, 17 min.)

I USED TO WRITE a cocktail column for a men's magazine, maybe the best part-time job in the world. What was, before, a slightly disreputable interest in bars and drinks was instantly transformed into research. I wrote off my bar tabs and liquor-store bills. I enjoyed films and novels exclusively for their use of drinks and drinkers. I was invited to gin tastings and brandy unveilings of awesome preciousness. The only downside was that I had to sample a lot of bad cocktails, but that was easily remedied by drinking a good one.

I mention this as a way to introduce a sometimes awkward fact without which you cannot appreciate this trio of short documentaries. Sure, you can clothe drinking and other vices in sophistication and connoisseurship. You can articulate your tasting notes, the caramel scents and spicy undertones, and list your fancy cultural allusions: Cary Grant orders a gibson on the train out of Grand Central in *North by Northwest*, and Philip Marlowe drinks the same in Raymond Chandler's *Playback*, but Marlowe drinks gimlets, not gibsons, in *The Long Goodbye*. That's all great, and I enjoy it, just like I enjoy the ambiance of a saloon right after opening time, when, as a character in the last novel says, "the air inside is cool and clean and everything is shiny and the barkeep is giving himself that last look in the mirror to see if his tie is straight and his hair is smooth."

But underneath all this clean glitter is a simple fact which accounts for the basic appeal of drink and drugs: humans like to get fucked up now and then. The burden of everyday consciousness can be a heavy load, and the hundredfold mundane challenges of being here, working and living and dealing with other people and the world, conspire to make that first hit, pull, snort, or shot look not only like a welcome respite from life but an affirmation of its possibilities. Stronger than an evasion; more like the *right idea*, a twisted sort of duty to self.

I think we all recognize this fact, even if we deplore it, or abstain from this intoxicant and that, or have witnessed up close the damage of "social drinking" and "recreational drug use," which too often mutate quickly into anger, meanness, neglect, and violence. Alcoholism and drug addiction are suicide on the installment plan. But it's the yearning I'm talking about, the ache for comfort and rightness. There's a reason for the euphemistic usage of "watering hole" to describe a bar, that oasis in the desert of life.

The people in these three documentaries are, most of them, pretty wasted. Some of them are destined to be, as Sheldon Nadelman says in *Terminal Bar*, "taken by the street." But I chose the films, and I think they belong together, to illustrate a second awkward fact that lies underneath the first one. And that concerns an even deeper ache than the one for bracketing selfhood's insistent demands. I mean the desire for communion with those who share the first yearning; and, even more important, for a physical place to answer the two needs together.

The sociologist Ray Oldenburg coined the term "the third place" for the space where this complex of desires can, sometimes, be answered. The third place is neither work nor home. It is not a space of motion or transaction, like a street or a store; it is a place simply to be, to enjoy. The list of these "great good places" between work and home includes bars, pubs, taverns, cafes, beer gardens, coffee houses, parks, even post offices and barber shops. They offer warmth and company, also solitude and anonymity; there is food and drink, gossip and intrigue, diversion and discourse. In some cultures, the place takes on an almost spiritual quality, beyond mere coziness or *gemütlichkeit*, approaching a transcendent serenity.

The third place is a public space, and hence also a public good, in the economist's sense of being non-exclusive on the outside (it is open to everyone) and non-rival on the inside (there is no competition for enjoyment). If you are lucky or rich enough to belong to a gentlemen's club or country club, that might be your third place; but the idea of gated membership is foreign to the spirit of the third place.

Which is not to say that officially open places may not turn out to be constrained; public houses in name only. English folk, culture from Tolkien to *Coronation Street*, idolizes the appeal of "the local"—going down to the boozer for a social pint or two—but anyone who has lived in Britain knows that entering certain pubs can cause a battery of cold stares to swing your way, or even lead to fisticuffs. Bars and cafes regulate clientele with messages far more subtle than just high prices or posted dress codes. The unfamiliar can be made to feel unwelcome.

Still, the ideal is one I think we all recognize, just like we recognize how the ideal speaks to human need, especially when it is enhanced by the self-selection around a cult artwork or a shared musical passion. I might not myself seek tribe by smoking dope in the woods with tattooed Insane Clown Posse fans. But I believe them when they say they would welcome me if I chose to come, maybe to join in some fucking chicken-fried steak, fucking collard greens, and fucking mashed potatoes. (Which actually sounds pretty fucking tasty.) The Juggalo campground is a moveable feast, a third place of the messed-up mind. Who can doubt that its claims to community are real?

Likewise with the loaded Judas Priest fans in Maryland who transform a parking lot into a festival surrounding a temple. I was more of a Clash fan than a Priest acolyte, but the convoy of Camaros and Chevettes, the profusion of centre-parted fluffy hair, the elbow-length rock 'n' roll T-shirts and bandannas, the suspenders, high-crowned ballcaps and cut-off jeans—well, it takes me back. And amid all the heavy-metal stylings, watch for the brief glimpse of a smiling blow-dried preppy in aviator shades and pink Lacoste polo shirt, collar popped, who clearly thinks he is in line to see Haircut 100. Or that awesome Valley Girl at the end, Kelly, who issues an ironic DUI warning and then pushes off the two lunging, hammered oafs: "Get away from me! Please!"

Tailgates deserve a sociological study all to themselves, from the sub-zero barbarian bacchanalias of Steelers and Bills games to the Range Rover and crystal-glass displays at the annual Harvard-Yale fixture known simply as The Game. Roger Ebert may have chosen to describe the *Heavy Mental Parking Lot* tailgate as "stoned worshipers at the shrine of their own bewilderment," but I think that's too condescending. This isn't bewilderment; it is, instead, one of the variform declensions of human joy. Those faces! Those stories! And where are they now, the sublime Priest fans of yore?

Which I guess brings me to the third awkward fact in play here, lurking in the shadows and yet in plain view whenever we want to get sideways in the company of others. The urge for the community, the human need to connect, has baseline limits. Compassion and fellow-feeling are fragile. More seriously, no matter how many friends we have, we all die alone. You could even say that, in a kind of paradox of human consciousness, it is precisely awareness of those limits that prompts the urge they limit. I mean what Martin Heidegger would call our "ownmost possibility": not the mere fact of death; rather, the fact that nobody can do our dying for us.

That awareness is mostly unconscious, and of course we contrive many ways to keep it at a distance. But there is no profit in despising these distractions and alterations of consciousness. They are human, all too human. Far better to reflect on the force of Sheldon Nadelman's hard-won Eighth Avenue wisdom: "When one person's lying in the street, *everyone's* lying in the street." Toast that.

Drawing Mies in Barcelona:

Shelagh Keeley's Photographs

IN THE FALL of 2014, the *Guardian*'s self-appointed "contrarian" art critic Jonathan Jones delivered a broadside that achieved its intended effect, at least partly: it got people talking about Jonathan Jones. (I, for one, had never before heard his name, but I suppose that's my fault for not following daily arts criticism from England.) Jones's argument was bold. Art photography, he said, "does not sing on a gallery wall." Proliferating electronic images are wonderful, luminous, and often moving. But, in his view, "it just looks stupid when a photograph is framed or backlit and displayed vertically in an exhibition. . . . A photograph is a flat, soulless, superficial substitute for painting."[1]

You might call this the art critic's version of the advice delivered by Dean Wormer to the Delta frat boy Flounder in *Animal House* (1978): "Flat, soulless and stupid is no way to go through life, son." Jones concluded: "Today's glib culture endlessly flatters photography's arty pretensions."

Predictably, and necessarily, the article spawned a barrage of counter-opinion, and even some counter-argument. Among the best of these was from another *Guardian* writer, Sean O'Hagan. After noting that the photography exhibitions Jones chose to mention were "eccentric," and making the obvious objection that a show of paintings—or any other medium—can be just as uninspired as any show of photographs,

O'Hagan set down the main point: "Several things are wrong about Jonathan's reasoning, not least that he still thinks painting is in some sort of competition with photography. How quaint. He also seems to think that all photography is derivative of painting. This is plainly not so."[2]

Further, and finally, Jones suggested that all photographs look better on backlit screens than on paper, when this is clearly false, and made no distinction between types of photography. And it's not a matter of technology: great artists can make great art using anything from Polaroids (Evans, Warhol) to digital phone-based cameras. "It's about a way of seeing, not technology." He finished with a plea for Jones to join him at a truly good photography show, with works by Awoiska van der Molen, where he might appreciate the "stillness and mystery" of the works, "so strong that everything on the walls around them seemed muted."

O'Hagan is on the side of the art angels, of course, not to mention of merely sane people everywhere; but the sad thing about the riposte was that it felt goaded, as if it had fallen into the original critic's poised trap. "If anything is anachronistic, it's the 'photography is not art' debate," he wrote at one point, and that really is the only rational response to an "argument" like Jones's. Getting drawn into the very assumptions that one should be rejecting outright—why are we comparing two mediums in the first place?—is the risk anyone takes when they respond to such things. I like to think myself among the sane and rational, and so maybe I should have ignored this little tussle myself, but it happened that I read the exchange while thinking about these superlative photographic works by Shelagh Keeley.

*   *   *

It is a valid commonplace of art that there is no subject unworthy of the artist's attention. Sometimes, as when the content is disturbing or violent, we may have to reiterate the argument before proceeding to appreciate the work. Less common, but just as troubling in its own way, is the inverse case, where the subject matter is already a supreme work of art itself. Mies van der Rohe's Barcelona Pavilion, built as the German contribution to the 1929 International Exposition in Spain, is a modernist masterpiece, one of the finest single buildings on the planet. Mies responded to commissioner Georg von Schnitzler's call for the building to give "voice to the spirit of a new era" in post-Great War Weimar

Germany by designing a building that is angular but flowing. Its open-plan concept, relative interior bareness—just the purpose-built furniture known as the "Barcelona chair" and the Georg Kolbe sculpture *Alba* ("Dawn")—was intended by Mies to provide "an ideal zone of tranquillity" for visitors.

The water features, open miniature vistas, and floating roof create a series of elegantly massed elements such that the Pavilion feels at once solid and about to levitate from the earth. Mies was extravagant with materials, using pure antique marble, travertine, golden onyx, and tinted as well as translucent glass to divide and order the building's spaces. Because the Pavilion itself was the entirety of the German presence at the Exposition, and served in part as a transition to other parts of the grounds, the Pavilion is in effect a large-scale Modernist sculpture executed in architectural forms. Designed by Mies in less than a year, it was always intended to be temporary: in 1930 it was demolished as planned.

Happily, in 1983 a group of Spanish architects, using archival photographs, plans, and contemporary accounts, reconstructed the building. The reconstruction was completed in 1986, and the Pavilion has since served as the site for art installations and interventions by, among others, architects Kazuyo Sejima and Ryue Nishizawa, who added interior walls made of spiral acrylic; and photographer Jordi Bernadó, who altered the various glass doors, effectively re-sculpting the interior space. Perhaps the most notable intervention was by Ai Weiwei, who refilled the building's two water pools with coffee and milk.

Shelagh Keeley visited the Pavilion in August of 1986, while living in Barcelona. The newly reconstructed building had not yet been opened to the public, and Keeley was able, with the help of fellow artist Antoni Muntadas, to view it "empty and austere." The plastic bag floating in one of the water features is the sole foreign object, a poignant little grace note. She has said that her inspiration was "the genius of Mies and the notion of the pavilion." The immediate connotation of pavilion is of a tent, or temporary structure, but its deeper etymology stretches back through Middle English and Old French (*pavillon*) to the Latin word for butterfly (*papilio*)—a metaphorical joining suitable to tents, but also to Mies's floating forms. Keeley's interest in architecture was already obvious. In 1985 she spent two months in Kyoto, Japan, studying the Zen gardens and temples, and making a two-hour Super 8 "essay film." In 1986 she did the same in Las Vegas, observing the decadence and decay of the American Dream's edgy playground. The engagement with the Barcelona Pavilion, a reconstruction of an architectural monument that was intentionally temporary, makes a sort of middle term in this exploration of the different kind of temples humans use to worship their deities.

The resulting work, like the more obvious artistic interventions, is a kind of collaboration—but without adding anything to the physical space. The images show the building as it would have appeared in 1929. The challenge here is to reveal, in the subtle textures of slides produced with an ordinary Olympus camera, something about what makes the building so spare and moving, so toughly perfect. And to do this Keeley had to use, contra the Jonathan Joneses of the world, the now-ubiquitous medium of photography. But there is, as always, the matter of who is wielding the camera. The works we see in this series are the result of scanning the original slides, which were developed in 1986 but never before shown, and then blowing them up to scale. "I love the grainy quality of slide film," Keeley told me. "No digital re-touching was done, or altering of the images with Photoshop. They are what they were."

Keeley has said that she views photography as really a kind of drawing: not the imitation of painting that so irks Jones, but rather a recognition that the medium of photography is just as much a matter of texture as it is of composition. This feature of her work can only be appreciated in the gallery-hung versions of these images, something that offers further evidence of the nullity of the anti-photography position. I can attest to this directly, since I first saw Keeley's Barcelona Pavilion images as backlit jpeg files which she had sent me, of course, via email. They were stunning, to be sure, revealing already to my eye the masterly sense of immediate familiarity in her relationship to the building. Their composition, capturing shadows and light at the same time as stone and water, was assured and revelatory. One immediately sensed here a version of Heidegger's notion of truth as disclosure, a combined revealing and concealing, the "clearing" of an open space that he calls, after the Greeks, *aletheia*.

This was just the beginning of the manifold gifts of Keeley's work, however. When one views them at the full, intended scale, and rendered on high-quality rag paper whose toothy surface is saturated with deeply injected pigment, the photographs take on a larger, more profound life. Another Heidegger resonance then, at least for me: his enthralled discussion of Van Gogh's celebrated 1885 oil painting, *A Pair of Shoes*. Here, Heidegger notes, in the heavily used and mud-caked work shoes of a peasant woman, we see revealed a world of her concern. She herself is absent—but fully, even painfully, present in her absence. The shoes are sweat-soaked, the leather gnarled like (we must imagine) the feet that struggle into their hardened shape each morning. They are also well-kept, however, because they must last. Heidegger saw the painting in Amsterdam in 1930, and this is part of his famous description, from his essay *The Origin of the Work of Art* (1935): "From the dark opening of the worn insides of the shoes the toilsome tread of the worker stares forth. In the stiffly rugged heaviness of the shoes there is the accumulated tenacity of her slow trudge through the far-spreading and ever-uniform furrows of the field swept by a raw wind. On the leather lie the dampness and richness of the soil. Under the soles slides the loneliness of the field-path as evening falls. In the shoes vibrates the silent call of the earth, its quiet gift of the ripening grain and its unexplained self-refusal in the fallow desolation of the wintry field."[3]

Later scholars, especially art historian Meyer Schapiro in *The Still Life as a Personal Object* (1968), demonstrated that the shoes had actually been purchased by Van Gogh himself at a Paris flea market, ostensibly for his own use, only to find that they did not fit. Facing the viewer as they do, Schapiro suggests, the shoes in fact execute yet another Van Gogh self-portrait.[4] But whatever their exact provenance, the shoes embody the materiality of Van Gogh's oils, themselves drawn from earthly materials, and make the essential connection between earth and the world of meaning that gives them place and identity. This is, we might say, the inversion of the glossy oils of official portraiture and still life which, as John Berger provocatively remarked once upon a time, exactly matches the glittering money of the *haute-bourgeois* and landed-gentry classes that were able to purchase them.

The same connection, maybe unexpectedly, is achieved via Keeley's use of everyday technical materials—high-quality rag paper, yes, but paper all the same; fine art inkjet printing, yes, but a process not all that different, technically, from the one available in most home offices. And yet, this can only be appreciated by standing in front of the printed works themselves. In their almost-abstract arrangements of colour, light, and form we feel, as well as see, the sense of place that is so important to her work generally. The graininess of enlarged film is executed just as the rough surface of a drawing would be, with carbon or pastel on toothy paper. The images capture the fleeting moments of liminal relations with space and place: the sense, achieved by a particular architectural "container" that one is *somewhere in particular*, grounded in one's physical embodiment and aware of being so. The images are phenomenological bracket-devices, isolating and concentrating our sense of the burden and blessing of consciousness.

*   *   *

This almost overwhelming sense of place—the properly scaled images are eye-filling, making the viewer feel a vertiginous inner squeak that Keeley might tip into the framed scene—is one of the aesthetic connections drawing her to this subject in the first place. Mies, justly renowned for the monumental skyscraper design evident in the Seagram Building in Manhattan and TD Centre in Toronto, is actually an architect of the intimate. (Hence his interest in furniture, one he shares with other masters of the interior detail such as Charles Rennie Mackintosh, Le Corbusier, the Eameses, Frank Lloyd Wright, Louis Khan, Ron Thom, and Frank Gehry.) But there is another essential affinity here, between Keeley's larger aesthetic practice and the Mies masterwork. I mean the very idea of a wall.

Walls are thresholds. They divide and join at once, creating insides and outsides, simultaneously part of both and neither. They create spaces and volumes that mark off the sites of life. Sometimes they bear loads, but they need not, and though the structural difference is all too real, the perceptual one is not. Above all, at least in domestic settings or other places where we spend a lot of our time, they are blank canvases asking to be decorated, covered, or papered. Mies lets his rich palette of veneers and glasses do the decorating in the Pavilion: the soothing minimalist aesthetic he favoured. Keeley cares about and draws on walls in another way altogether: she is a collage artist of playfully maximalist persuasion.

Since 1979 she has been making site-specific wall installations, executed in galleries in many parts of the world, that combine drawings and photography with a strong but elusive sense of interconnection. The viewer moves in and through the space created by the wall within the gallery, encountering the individual parts of the work, before stepping back and being struck by the whole. The works are also, of course, engaged in an aesthetic and physical exchange—not always comfortable—with the particular gallery spaces in which they are created. "You can't fight with architecture," she said of this process in a recent interview. "It's a dialogue with the space of the walls—the architecture of the space that I work in—and I respond to that. . . . It's not a framed drawing hanging on a wall. It's not a painting. It's directly on a wall, so it's a whole different discourse and a relationship for the viewer with their body in relation to the architecture."[5]

One thinks again, and not fondly, of Jonathan Jones and his aversion to the framed and flat image. His target was not drawing but photography; nevertheless, here the whole wall, the gallery itself plus the drawings and images affixed thereon, is the work. Keeley sees the installation itself as an extension of working with pigment and paper. "Drawing is a very physical act," she said in the same interview. "It's not just your hand and your wrist. It's your whole body—particularly with this method of working. It's the body, the head; your body is physically making the drawing. You can't do a huge wall drawing without involving the arc of your whole body. . . . I reclaim space through the gesture of drawing."

The Barcelona Pavilion images might seem to lie some distance from the physicality of the drawing gesture but we can still feel the hand of the artist here, the sense of their composition. There is also, in the two bodies of work, a linked reflection on the environmental psychologist James Gibson's idea of *affordances*: those elements of a physical space that answer to our embodiment and its many projects, large and small. A plane surface elevated above the floor is an affordance—a table. It allows us to place objects close to hand while we are upright, to sit and eat, to sit and write, and so on. The floor itself is an affordance, a most basic one, answering the needs of the organism, in this case a human one, to stand upon a surface that is (to use Gibson's language) nearly horizontal, nearly flat, sufficiently extended relative to human size, and of rigid surface. This floor *affords support*. "It is stand-on-able, permitting an upright posture for quadrupeds and bipeds," Gibson writes. "It is therefore walk-on-able and run-over-able. It is not sink-into-able like a surface of water or a swamp."[6] Walls afford division and conjunction, entertainment to the eye, and the deployment of equipment at rest, hung or shelved upon their vertical surfaces.

If the Barcelona Pavilion is a kind of essay in the negative capability of affordances, offering a sort of phenomenological bracketing of everyday spaces, the gallery-wall drawings are its necessary inverse, the wall itself brought into sharp focus. And though the Barcelona images are more conventionally hung upon the gallery wall, they are no less power-ful for being framed. On the contrary, and maybe paradoxically, they are set free to work their haptic magic upon the viewer. They take back space on the wall by glowing with an undiluted luminosity, the "stillness and mystery" that Sean O'Hagan found in Awoiska van der Molen's work, making the world around them seem mute. "I think that's what art does, right?" O'Hagan asked rhetorically in the final line of his article.

Rhetorical questions require no answer but let us offer one anyway, just for emphasis: Yes, that is right. And Keeley's Barcelona Pavilion photographs offer more beautiful proof.

Notes

1 Jonathan Jones, "Flat, soulless and stupid: why photographs don't work in art gal-leries," *The Guardian*, November 13, 2014; www.theguardian.com/artanddesign/jonathanjonesblog/2014/nov/13/why-photographs-dont-work-in-art-galleries

2 Sean O'Hagan, "Photography is art and always will be," *The Guardian*, December 11, 2014; www.theguardian.com/artanddesign/2014/dec/11/photography-is-art-sean-ohagan-jonathan-jones

3 Martin Heidegger, "The Origin of the Work of Art" [*Der Ursprung des Kunstwerkes*, 1935-7; 1950; 1960], in ed. and trans. Albert Hofstadter, *Poetry, Language, Thought* (Harper & Row, 1971), 15-86.

4 For a discussion of this difference between Heidegger and Schapiro, plus a related intervention by Jacques Derrida, see Scott Horton, "Philosophers Rumble Over Van Gogh's Shoes," *Harper's Blog*, October 5, 2009; harpers.org/blog/2009/10/philosophers-rumble-over-van-goghs-shoes/

5 Becky Rynor, "An Interview with Shelagh Keeley," *National Gallery of Canada Magazine*, September 5, 2014; www.ngcmagazine.ca/artists/an-interview-with-shelagh-keeley

6 James J. Gibson, "The Theory of Affordances," *The Ecological Approach to Visual Perception* (orig. 1979; rev. Lawrence Erlbaum & Assoc., 1986), chap. 8.

Worlds of Wonder:
Matthew Pillsbury's
City Stages

MATTHEW PILSBURY's luminous *City Stages* retrospective includes a selection of images from three previous bodies of work: "City Screens," "Hours," and "Screen Lives." What draws them together is a complex, haunted, not always reassuring sense of visual wonder. The images shimmer with the ghostly passage of time, their formal grace and careful composition everywhere undermined— and yet somehow also enhanced—by a spirit of transience.

We see rendered, with flawless classical technique, a series of places: apartments, museums, churches, theatres, reading rooms, railway terminals, bridges, parks, parades, boutiques, corner stores, handball courts, carousels, restaurants, and bars. The images take us to mostly canonical urban destinations—Paris, London, Tokyo, Venice, New York—but also San Francisco, San Diego, and Vancouver. In Manhattan alone, we visit the Highline, Lincoln Center, the Natural History Museum, the New York Public Library, Grand Central Terminal, Central Park, and Zuccotti Park during Occupy Wall Street. Each ordinary site of sitting or standing is revealed with an etched sharpness that does proper homage to the tradition of depicting the built environment, and its inhabitants, with black-and-white film: Atget, Brassai, Hines, Geoffrey James.

But this is the familiar made strange, even uncanny. The addition of wispy time-lapse traces of those inhabitants changes the aesthetic equation in subtle and profound ways. The fact of human occupancy in the halls and rooms is rendered delicate and finely spun, like evening mist pooling in low-lying ground. Look at these transient visitations haunting the

Victorian architecture of London's Natural History Museum (*Wyoming Diplodocus*, 2007), a New York concert auditorium (*Jazz at Lincoln Center*, 2011), or Venetian gallery (*The Unveiling of Titian's Presentation of Mary*, 2012). The people are spectres, auratic and insubstantial, present and absent at once. And so the framed scene becomes, like the parts of the natural-history museums where we see collections of apparently stampeding dinosaur skeletons (*Hordes, La Galérie d'Anatomie Comparée*, 2008) or an urgent elephant convoy (*Escaping Elephants*, 2004), a *wunderkammer* or cabinet of wonder, a sort of visual vitrine housing human life.

In many cases, what is on view in Pillsbury's images is itself a scene of *looking*: at artworks, at natural wonders, at public events or views, at television shows, computer screens, video games, and cell phone displays. For me, Pillsbury's images serve to illustrate Guy Debord's argument that spectacle is not primarily a projection or an event but a kind of relationship, of myself with others, of myself with the spaces around me. The screens and performances that bring these people together also work, paradoxically, to isolate them. There is a curious layering of effects when we spend so much time in this state of spectating. Not just our friendships and our spare moments, but our very identities, become mediated, virtual, processed, produced, and consumed.

Moving through these visual stages, we begin to sense the inarticulate urge that somehow links all the subjects who are semi-present here, their desire to be in place, chasing a desperate possibility of communion or authenticity—or maybe just seeking a diversion from the pressing anxieties of existence. Like all of us today, they are in the state of mind so intensely expressed by T. S. Eliot in "Burnt Norton": "Neither plenitude nor vacancy. Only a flicker / Over the strained time-ridden faces / Distracted from distraction by distraction / Filled with fancies and empty of meaning." To be sure, neither Eliot nor Debord lived to witness the heavy omnipresence of devices and media, the tablets and displays and phones, that Pillsbury's images convey so vividly.

So here are all the lonely people, dutifully visiting, and perhaps even seeing, the overdetermined Mona Lisa (*La Jaconde, Salle des Etats*, 2008) and Winged Victory (*La Victoire de Samothrace*, 2007) in the Louvre. There they sit, together and alone, playing video games and lazily watching the news of the day or banal, even bad, television shows: "Desperate Housewives" (*Desperate Housewives*, 2005); "CSI: Miami" (*Tanya & Santaj Gill*, 2004); "The Bachelorette" (*Alli & Deirdre Lord, Christine*

Matheis, et al., 2004). Meanwhile, the exposed light of the various screens glows with an extraterrestrial intensity, a kind of homing beacon or tractor beam that has brought them into this particular room or office. These luminous screens, in turn, fetch the eye of the unseen new viewer—you or me—who has been put into proximity with these acts of human desire, public and private.

Then, their entertainment or edification over for the moment, the human subjects exit the frame, leaving just traces of themselves. But for us, the questions they have raised must remain. Who were they? What mark did they make on this place, if any? What does it mean to be present, to be conscious and in place? Pillsbury's progression of images poses these unsettling questions again and again, with a quiet insistence that is only partly mitigated by their immediate, undeniable beauty.

"He was a good genealogist who made Iris the daughter of Thaumas," Socrates remarks in Plato's dialogue *Theaetetus*. The genealogy Socrates speaks of here turns on the fact that the sea god Thaumas, worker of miracles, is the root of the Greek word for wonder: *thaumazein*. Iris was a messenger of the gods, appearing in the form of the rainbow; she is herself a visual spectacle, hinting at the wisdom that mortals need to make sense of life. In place of a rainbow's spectrum, Pillsbury offers revelatory black-and-white images. The wisdom they reveal constitutes a heavy burden, the human one of individual consciousness, its many tangles and layers, especially its lurking, known-but-unknown finitude. Yes, tomorrow we die.

*   *   *

"The world is an astonishing place," the American philosopher Thomas Nagel has written. "That it has produced you, and me, and the rest of us is the most astonishing thing about it." Nagel's point is a large, metaphysical one concerning the staggering unlikeliness of a physical universe giving rise to entities like us. How did a world of brute physical forces produce human selfhood and all that it entails: our sense of unique identity, our worries large and small, the constant internal monologue that makes us who we are? It is somehow inconceivable and yet, at every moment, undeniable. Just think of one mundane version of this mystery, namely that you are right now reading these words that I have written, hearing them in your mind.

Pillsbury's photographs offer what is, in effect, a graphic representation of this astonishing feature of the universe—that we are here at all. Of course, we are only passing through. The traces of insistent human consciousness are sketched, in these images, in apartments and halls, on bridges and walkways. They create a sense of scale, like the tiny human figures that are sometimes included on architectural maquettes. They also, I want to say, perform a version of what a philosopher would call phenomenological investigation. That is, they remind us that places are real just insofar as we live, worship, play, and work in them. An architect or designer fashions an edifice, a span, a vaulted interior. But only the living presence of people makes the design intentions of built forms come alive. Pillsbury's art captures the mystery of that relationship of occupancy to its external conditions, poised precisely on the line between an abstract imagined space and a real, lived-in *place*.

Because the images are constructed with such evident care, the resulting effect is also, then, an extended meditation on the notion of *mise-en-scène*: the artful arrangement of things and bodies in an orderly pattern, the imagist's skill with meaningful deployment. Pillsbury is a master of this order. We might recall, here, André Bazin's theory of cinema, in which *mise-en-scène* means not only the arrangements of the set, but the movement of the players within the frame, creating and (sometimes) resolving narrative possibilities thereby. Pillsbury's images are still images that are, paradoxically, full of just this movement. And yet, because there is no narrative sequence, there can be no resolution. We stand forever on the threshold of significance, options laid open, hinted at, but never completed.

This is a kind of magic: not *legerdemain* but, instead, continued suspension, tension, or expectation that is never allowed to dissipate. The trick is never over; the illusionist never escapes his self-imposed bonds. The people whose traces we see caught in the images, like smoke in a bottle, may have experienced settled, comfortable moments in these rooms and halls. They made time to watch the news or to catch Woody Allen playing his clarinet at the Café Carlyle. They bought some candy or a toy dinosaur. They may have paused to admire the view across a river or over a skyline. They lived here; they said prayers and studied there; they lounged or stood or shuffled in that room, that concourse, that park.

In three of the book's most haunting images—*Self-portrait at Computer* (2003), *Self-portrait Contemplating Wapiti* (2004), and *Cell*

Phone on Venice Beach (2006)—we observe, arrested in single images, the combined sense of duration, sight, and singularity that marks so much of what we mean by the self. But also a feeling of pathos, a kind of suspension, a lingering question about what it means to be here.

And so now we, other selves who pause to look and reflect on these images, are caught by spectacle in another fashion. We are outside and inside at once. We can see only passage, not pauses. We cannot dwell in these places.

Time-lapse imaging is a straightforward method for depicting the passage of time with a still image. But Pillsbury's *City Stages* sequence does far more than that, I think. At their best, they hint at the mystery that underlies our experience of time, namely, that there is an experiencer—you and I and the others—present to feel time's passage in the first place. If the space/place dialectic is Pillsbury's version of the mind-body problem—how is it that a non-material conscious being like you or I can exist in an otherwise material world?—the implicit reflection on temporality is his version of a long-standing epistemological question about time. That is: is time a feature of the external world, or just part of the way my experience is structured? And how could I ever know the difference?

"Wonder is the only beginning of philosophy," Socrates goes on to say in the *Theaetetus*. Pillsbury's images are not philosophy, but they treat of the same questions of identity and meaning. Indeed, the resulting body of work is the complicated gift of a superb *thaumaturge*, a worker of wonders. I said that we cannot dwell in the results, because, despite their sharp detail, the living part of them keeps slipping away. But our delight is that we can spend time with them, immersed in the quiet, intimate astonishment of thinking about people and their places. Our places.

Faces of Chaotic Beauty:

Questions and Answers in Maya Kulenovic's Painting

"The face opens the primordial discourse
whose first word is obligation."

— EMMANUEL LEVINAS, *Totality and Infinity* (1961)

"It is no more possible truly to describe a
landscape than it is to describe a face."

— MADISON SMARTT BELL, *Straight Cut* (1986)

WHEN I VISITED Maya Kulenovic's studio to talk about her work, she was recovering from a short illness. It was a hot day and I was sweating after a long walk to reach her neighbourhood. Neither of us were at our best or most animated. We had not met before.

Despite all this, or somehow perhaps because of it, our conversation, as she showed me a series of recent paintings and sculptures, was laced with insights that would stay with me long after we parted and I was walking again along the sidewalks of our city. I had asked her about the relation between the haunting, uncanny human faces that feature in her work, portraits in anonymous emotion, and the buildings and houses to be found in other paintings. "After all, buildings have faces too," she said. The return of the repressed is experienced not only in the revenant human figure (zombies, mummies, vampires), or in the familiar strangeness of the almost-human (androids, puppets, Michael Jackson); it is also to be found in the fleeting glances that reveal faces—our own or those of strangers, faces not quite there but dimly outlined—in inanimate objects or non-living sites.

We use the language of faces with respect to buildings all the time— one speaks of a structure's *façade*, or discusses its plot-wise orientation in terms of which part faces the street—but the insight runs deeper than this form of metaphorical shorthand. The "face" of a building can speak to us via a form of *pareidolia*, that imaginative connection by which certain features of an inanimate object seem to take on human personality. The grille and headlights of a sports car appear to grin at us, intimating the joys of nimble speed. The grip of a bowling ball shows eyes and mouth circled open in wide surprise at its imminent violent journey down the lane. An upright rake has hair that stands wildly on end at the sight of the garden's weedy disorder.

Likewise, buildings exhibit eyes and mouths, indented heads and misshapen visages. They can look out at us in mute appeal, or retreat behind sly and devious glances. One thinks of certain houses in particular, often from unnerving, nightmarish experiences. There was an abandoned house at the end of the dirt road where I lived as a boy, one upper window boarded up to produce a palsied look, the lower cellar entrance looking like a loose, tooth-shattered mouth. Alfred Hitchcock was, unsurprisingly, a master of the effect: houses in *Psycho* and *The Birds* seem to acquire evil intent in the course of the action, exerting an active if immobile force in the narrative. They watch with silent malice as doomed characters make their way up paths or stairways; they conspire with the other characters, human or inhuman, to enact madness and mayhem.

This kind of association is fleeting and unreliable, a matter of *gestaltlich* duck-rabbit perception, as in the familiar optical illusion; but the experience of "seeing" a face or figure in an object is all the more uncanny for this fleetingness, showing a kind of repressed-but-returning tenacity, the insistent step of the revenant. A too-steady or overly obvious "face" association, after all, would risk feeling gimmicky or contrived. The matter-of-factness of Kulenovic's association between human face and built form is matched by the light, subtle, ever-returning version of pareidolic identification achieved in her paintings.

The human faces in her work, eerie presences based on found photographs (I want to say "caught" photographs instead, snatched imagistic moments), peer out at the viewer in a variety of complex attitudes. They are beseeching but menacing, challenging yet lost in thought. The dark palette of the backgrounds in these paintings make the faces seem to float in space, carved by shadows into a pattern of craggy promontories and deep cheekbone-overhang recesses. Seeing them this way pulls the metaphorical association back the other way, towards the natural world: we speak of a "rock face," for example; or, as in the title of Wallace Stegner's magnificent novel, an "angle of repose" detectable in a seam of silver or in a pile of granular material on the farthest verge of beginning to slide downward. These faces, fleshy and somehow mineral, stand poised on the edge of something unnamable.

Kulenovic's technique of scoring and scraping her painted canvases using solvent, brushes, or blades, is a risky play of alteration—what she describes as the deliberate introduction of a "chaotic element" to the work. This contributes deep texture and richness to the faces, a layering of material and hue that is not detectable in any reproduction. The faces have been, as it were, worked over; they are damaged, imploring, pre-haunted. Their mute appeals are without limit or end; they cannot be set aside or even answered. The figures that confront the viewer have an intensity and pathos, even a sense of menace, that sets them decisively apart from the superfluity of face images we encounter nowadays, in this age of Facebook, the posted "selfie" photograph, and the global celebrity visage.

One thinks, here, of Emmanuel Levinas's ethics of the face. Faces can express dark or mysterious presence, of course, and even hostile intention; but they also communicate welcome, joy, surprise, warmth, and recognition. In all cases, good and bad, the face of the other is at the centre of my experience of selfhood and obligation. The face of the other calls to me in a primordial way, in a manner that transcends any reaction of utility or disposal. The message of the face is as basic and as unconditional as that found in the Biblical commandment: *Thou shalt not kill*. But, as Levinas argues, the articulated forms of this commandment, and for that matter all the expressed strictures of morality, are really post facto reports or reminders of what the other's face commands without words.

"The face, still a thing among things, breaks through the form that nevertheless delimits it," Levinas says. "This means concretely: the face speaks to me and thereby invites me to a relation incommensurate with a power exercised, be it enjoyment or knowledge." The other's face holds me in its grip in a way that cannot be contained or transacted. The face can communicate many things, but above all it expresses its basic presence and the personal vulnerability of being here. The face is not merely the locus of sensory gathering, a compression of all five senses; it is also the main site of personality, that which lights up or darkens as moods come and go, the source of words, glances, smiles, kisses, and even rubs of the nose.

Thus, while we can sometimes recognize people we know from their body language, it is most often the face of the other that stands for their entire identity. And yet, the task of fully describing a certain face is liable to defeat even the most experienced wordsmith. We see family resemblances in faces, for example, features that are shared across a range of possible deployments but with no single feature, or even set of them, to be found in all members of the family. (Wittgenstein would argue that this perception of family resemblance confounds the traditional philosophical concept of the necessary condition in delineating related sets.)

In all cases, faces are deeply implicated in our experience of singularity in others—especially in the realm of assigning responsibility or blame. A particular face is caught, perhaps guiltily, on camera: That's the one! Or we spot the fleeing suspect's face in a crowd. Mugshots are used to pick out suspects, specifying a perpetrator or accomplice from within the volumes of captured gazes. No surprise, then, that the English slang term for a notable criminal, a celebrity hood, is a *face*. Nor that an anonymous or alienated person, lost in a crowd or floating without notable purpose, is sometimes described as *faceless*.

But the relations between particular and universal are even more complicated than that. For though it is naturally true that we come to recognize certain faces, and perceive specific emotions even in faces we do not yet know, the *ethical* nature of the face-to-face encounter is not, ultimately, a matter of particular physiognomy or even of physical presence. Levinas goes on: "To manifest oneself as a face is to impose oneself above and beyond the manifested and purely phenomenal form, to present oneself in a mode irreducible to manifestation, the very straightforwardness of the face to face, without the intermediary of any image, in one's nudity, that is, in one's destitution and hunger." I am not, nor are you, just the sum total of all the facial manifestations we express.

Levinas's notion of the face is not to be confused with the sociological concept of respect or social standing found in some Asian and

First Nations cultures and expressed as "face," for example, the Chinese notion of *diu lian*, the sort of face that can be lost when one fails at an obligation, experiences humiliation, or is insufficiently respected. There is perhaps a basic metaphorical association here, however, in that both ideas concentrate the essence and identity of the person, whether ethically or socially, in the visible locus of selfhood. It is worth noting that the English word *visage* is etymologically related to the words *vision* and *visible*, while the Latin-derived *face* is related to the cluster of words associated with the experience of *form* and, ultimately, with words having to do with making or presentation (fashion, e.g.). The face is, as it were, where a person is *made to be seen*.

And yet, even supposing we accept this ethical account of the face's call, where all value is rooted in face value, it remains essential that the other be encountered concretely: *this* face, here and now, with *this* expression and personality. The phenomenal or plastic realization of the face—yours as it becomes available to my experiences, mine to yours—is not reducible to a thesis or a feature of the moral code. It is sometimes, perhaps often, a matter of raw and immediate entreaty.

Thus the faces in Kulenovic's paintings, human and otherwise, begin to exert this kind of appeal. When we turn to the architectural images, the same techniques of imposed decay and deliberate chaos lend a living quality to the "faces" of walls and colonnades. But there is also something further, an echo of the soiled and spoiled film stock in Bill Morrison's *Decasia* (2002) or *Lyrical Nitrate* (1991), directed by Peter Delpeut. The frames of the painting take on the quality of frames in a moving picture, but with the colour and quality blurred and bubbled. They are parts of a film that no longer works, whose poignant, destroyed attempts at continuity and motions are now revealed in the singular beauty of the single "decayed" image.

The impression is strengthened by Kulenovic's own sense of the works: they offer, she says, a feeling of *interrupted series*, a sense of impending action. The progression of columns or windows is set in motion, as it were, but then arrested or deranged by some other element of the composition—which is, paradoxically, just as essential to the overall frame as the implied sequence. Thus, while the human-face works at first seem to have a persistent quality of stillness—sometimes an unnerving or dismaying stillness, to be sure!—the architectural façades are forever in a kind of arrested motion. And then, looking again at the faces, one perceives quivering possibilities, the visage caught between moods, on the way from one state of being—one frame of consciousness—to another. Stillness is ever an illusion, whether in an image or in a face: emotion and motion alike roil beneath the halted surface.

In her landscapes, meanwhile, Kulenovic deploys a mixed or transitional compositional style, with branches, sunlight, or small bodies of water working as the arresting feature, drawing the canvas to another kind of vibrant stillness. Here the palette is often lighter, featuring pale ochres and even silvery whites. The terrain seems bewitched, ensorceled, almost fantastic. Like the built-form works, there is an absence of figures. It is as if, in Kulenovic's imaginative world, the human form exists—or anyway is encountered—only in the form of the face. The rest is silence, and stillness; but they, too, call to us from their otherness, asking . . . what?

Asking to be seen, I think, with just the same care and shared sense of vulnerability that Kulenovic's faces arouse in us. The feelings excited by this remarkable body of work recall Mikhail Bakhtin's notion of "answerability." In the short essay "Art and Answerability" (1919), really a sort of manifesto, the youthful Bakhtin offered his first published words about what would become a lifelong preoccupation: the relation of art to life. "I have to answer with my own life for what I have experienced and understood in art, so that everything I have experienced and understood would not be ineffectual in my life," he urges the reader. "But answerability entails guilt, or liability to blame. It is not only mutual answerability that art and life must assume, but also mutual liability to blame."[1]

Whether it is at the face of the other or at art, just by looking we put ourselves in a position of responsibility. "Art and life are not one," Bakhtin concludes, "but they must become united in myself—in the unity of my answerability." Open your eyes, my friends, the other is calling. And there is no opt-out clause.

Notes

1   M. M. Bakhtin, *Art and Answerability: Early Philosophical Essays*, trans. Vadim Liapunov; (University of Texas Press, 1990), 1, 2.

Art's Unmediated Middles:

From *Ekphrasis* to *Ekstasis*— and Back Again

"For, to speak out once for all, man only plays
when in the full meaning of the word he is a man,
and *he is only completely a man when he plays*."

— SCHILLER, *On the Aesthetic Education of Man* (1794)

HEGEL was wrong about so many things—from the nature of consciousness to the flow of history and the supremacy of German culture—that it seems almost like piling on to note that his view of art is absurd. But, as with some other absurdities, his view opens up some new lines of thinking, albeit negative ones, that might be impossible to imagine otherwise. In the *Phenomenology of Spirit*, Hegel argues that art plays an important late-stage role in the self-realization of *Geist*, or Spirit, that flowering of the Idea of reason over time and in material conditions. Because art wants to speak the truth, it is a high form of spiritual activity; but because it is tied to sensuous form, especially the inherently limited fields of the visible and audible, it must, like the rituals and aesthetic trappings of religion, another near-contender, fall short of absolute knowledge.

Not surprisingly, that full expression will be found only in philosophy—and, as it happens, philosophy done in the German language, circa

1807, in Jena. Well, the barrage of Napoleon's artillery was audible as he wrote the lines, so perhaps some mitigation can be extended. As Walter Kaufmann has noted, Hegel "finished the book under enormous strain." Hegel's confusion is our gain, however, if we at once take seriously and overturn his basic dialectical method.

Art is neither a way station on the path to absolute knowledge, nor is it a momentarily stable synthesis of rival forces from a preceding moment of consciousness. It is instead, as contemporary tensions continue to reveal, an inherently unstable realm of refusal, where opposing forces are forever re-engaged in philosophical battle, a never-ending game of *Risk* that continually reforms alliances and power lines—and indeed, rewrites the rules of its game at will. This, I want to argue, is what endures in art: the serious playfulness of constant failure-as-success. Shards of this position may be unearthed in both Schiller's account of aesthetic imagination as the free play of ideas and the early Nietzsche's dynamic-tension account of warring Apollonian and Dionysian forces in aesthetic genius. But there is more to be said, and perhaps a couple of new elements-in-tension dyads to foreground—though they will prove to be not so new.

To substantiate these claims, allow me to contrast two pairs of opposites that might be thought to afflict the art world with a definitive choice, in what I hope is a novel fashion: (1) the question of beauty's meaning; and (2) the issue of art's parseability. Both offer us object lessons in an essential anti-dialectics of art, and an appropriate defence of free play for our times.

*   *   *

The first is more familiar and, therefore, perhaps less revelatory to a contemporary art world that may be presumed to be somewhat jaded and theory-weary. The conflict can be sketched as one between Charmides and Veblen; or, more precisely, between Socrates in praise of Charmides and Veblen in analysis of status goods. In Plato's eponymous dialogue, written in intimate first-person voice, Socrates returns to Athens after a violent military campaign. He inquires of his friends whether there are any young men of great beauty or wisdom—or both—to be met: fresh meat, in other words. Charmides is pointed out as the champion of the new crowd, and Socrates, gazing upon the handsome youth, makes a frank confession: "And all the people in the palaestra crowded about us, and at that moment, my good friend, I caught a sight of the inwards of his garment, and took the flame. Then I could no longer contain myself." Really? But Charmides isn't just a looker: his champion Critias says he is a philosopher and a poet as well. Socrates, feigning a headache, beckons the young man closer: a possible unique reversal in the literature of the usual headache/sex relation.

Further discussion between the interlocutors is directed—somewhat ironically, given Socrates' initial hot-pants reaction—to the virtue of *sophrosyne*, or self-control. Plato's trademark fast talk demonstrates that Charmides is more a charmer than a dialectician; but then, Socrates' own views are a little confused here: the dialogue meanders toward an account of *sophrosyne* without ever providing a coherent account of that virtue, or indeed its alleged relation to other desirable traits of the beautiful soul. Nevertheless, the dialogue is suffused by the conventional Greek view that external, physical beauty is closely allied with inner beauty, or psychic harmony. Beauty itself, moreover, is not pleasing merely to the eye, but also to the soul's desire for order. The beautiful man is also the virtuous man, if not quite simply in virtue of being beautiful then certainly because beauty is ever allied with other exalted traits. We needn't endorse Plato's metaphysics of transcendental Forms—not to mention his denigration of *mimesis*, or imitation, in the arts—to appreciate the force, maybe even feel some of the appeal, of this view. Charmides, for his part, lives on in culture as, among other things, the central figure of an epic 1881 poem by Oscar Wilde and the name of a cocktail that combines gin, absinthe, and ginger.

On the distant other hand, Veblen will argue in *The Theory of the Leisure Class* that the judgment of beauty is, with all due respect to Kant, neither universalizable nor intrinsic in any way. Veblen's tart sociological analysis finds only self-serving interests in the acquisition and display of art, which follows prevailing taste even in allegedly avant-garde choices, in order to exhibit and endorse the taste of its owner. The resulting reductive position drains substance from beauty, rendering it at best a relational property of the things I prize and you do not, which I own and you cannot. The cynical view of today's art world, where auction prices soar as one-percenters dispatch their agents to biennales and global art fairs, is just the logical economic extension of Veblen's anti-aesthetic.

So much is obvious. And yet, there is no doubt that beauty still fetches us, and even has the capacity, to use very old-fashioned language, to transport our souls. The proof of this bald statement is not to be found in revitalized Kantian philosophy, however; it is, rather, the negative argument that, if the function of art were only to confer status, there are many other things that would do just as well. Indeed, there are many such other things, from automobiles to wristwatches and one's place on the airplane seating chart. That some of these retain an element of the aesthetic, itself often praised in place of the status actually being claimed— look at how gorgeous the Hermès scarf is, how long and lean the lines of my Mercedes—is proof of two further truths: (a) people are as often self-deceived about their motives in acquiring things; and, more importantly, (b) there always exists an independent aesthetic surplus that may or not be part of a status good. You can get someone to buy an ugly suit or car because it is fashionable; you may even convince them to think, and say, that it is beautiful rather than ugly; but you cannot entirely collapse the distance between status and the claims of beauty. If Plato was wrong, because beauty often comes clean apart from virtue, so was Veblen, because it just as often detaches from status.

The most recent attempts to lay the beauty question to rest come from the dubious field known as neuroaesthetics: the study of brain activity as we respond to visual stimuli. Thus, there is empirical evidence that we exhibit more responses classed as "pleasure" when confronted by Ingres' *Odalisque* than when we view a work of fractured, twisted portraiture by Francis Bacon. But these claims fail on their face to explain the question of beauty. My brain might well register more "pleasure" in the simple experience of eating vanilla ice cream than in the complex challenges of a meal styled according to deconstructive molecular gastronomy, but this hardly proves a preference for the former over the latter—despite the fact that I, myself, would defend that preference! More pointedly, a neurological "preference" for the sight of the beautiful tells us almost nothing about the complex relationship between beauty and art, the textured pleasures of non-beautiful art, and so on.

*   *   *

One possible path out of, or at least away from, this impasse lies along my second artful tension of art, the one concerning paraphraseability. The basic problem here is as old as Plato: if the truth that an artwork communicates is detachable from the work, which might be considered itself unnecessary or even deceptive with respect to that truth, don't we do better to, as it were, cut to the chase? Why not bypass the aesthetic experience, in short, and get to the heart of the matter: what is the message of this or that work of art?

Now, before we dismiss this admittedly reason-centric line of thought, consider the possibility that poetic *ekphrasis*—the more nuanced, and therefore more respectable, rewriting of art—might offer a version of the same claim. *Ekphrasis* is the poetic style in which verse forms attempt to "read" a given visual work, usually a painting or sculpture, by rendering it into a verbal experience. Both W. H. Auden and William Carlos Williams write, for example, about the depiction of Icarus's fall that was once attributed to Pieter Brueghel (the provenance has since been questioned). In "Musée des Beaux Arts" (1938), Auden begins this way: "About suffering they were never wrong, / The old Masters: how well they understood / Its human position: how it takes place / While someone else is eating or opening a window or just walking dully along." Ploughman and sailing ship alike are indifferent to Icarus's plunge into nothingness, as imagined by the painter, and "the sun shone / As it had to on the white legs disappearing into the green / Water. . ."

Williams, in "Landscape with the Fall of Icarus" (1960), offers similar bleak wisdom, worth quoting in full:

> According to Brueghel
> when Icarus fell
> it was spring
>
> a farmer was ploughing
> his field
> the whole pageantry
>
> of the year was
> awake tingling
> near
>
> the edge of the sea
> concerned
> with itself

sweating in the sun
that melted
the wings' wax

unsignificantly
off the coast
there was

a splash quite unnoticed
this was
Icarus drowning

Other examples are perhaps less successful poetically but still compelling. Samuel Yellen's "Nighthawks" (1952), for example, after the Edward Hopper painting, begins with this rhyming *a-b-a-b* quatrain: "The place is the corner of Empty and Bleak, / The time is night's most desolate hour, / The scene is Al's Coffee Cup or the Hamburger Tower, / The persons in this drama do not speak."

The two most famous examples of poetic *ekphrasis* raise more difficult and illuminating questions than these. Keats's "Ode on a Grecian Urn" (1820—a year before the poet's death) is justly revered, and made memorable, by its much-quoted final lines:

When old age shall this generation waste,
Thou shalt remain, in midst of other woe
Than ours, a friend to man, to whom thou say'st,
'Beauty is truth, truth beauty,—that is all
Ye know on earth, and all ye need to know.'

The actual validity of these poetic claims is highly contestable, of course, if not simply *prima facie* false. Keats the poet is not interested in contesting them, however, and that would seem to be part of his point: art speaks to us in an imperative voice that brooks no rational contradiction. Beauty is not truth at all, nor truth beauty; and yet, the precious caught-in-clay antics of exuberance on the urn's curved sides—"What men or gods are these? / What maidens loth? / What mad pursuit? / What struggle to escape? / What pipes and timbrels? / What wild ecstasy?"—are not to be denied.

More troubling still is what I suggest is the pinnacle of *ekphrasis*, Rilke's "Archaic Torso of Apollo" (1908). Here the urge of the poet to paraphrase the meaning of the artwork, its *propositional content*— Brueghel is saying something about cosmic indifference, Hopper about mundane despair, the urn about fleeting youth and beauty—is neatly confounded by returning us, inexorably, to the mute work itself. Because the archaic torso is at once anonymous and partial, there is a poignancy we feel immediately. "*Wir kannten nicht sein unerhörtes Haupt / darin die Augenäpfel reiften,*" runs the first sentence of Rilke's German. In Stephen Mitchell's translation, my favourite, it is rendered this way: "We cannot know his legendary head, / with eyes like ripening fruit." Already the missing head is overwhelmingly present in its absence, the thing we *cannot* know—but long to!

Less able translations struggle with the adjective *unerhörtes*, always missing something of Mitchell's felicitous *legendary*. "We cannot know his incredible head," critic Sarah Stutt has written, burying the line's force in a word that has lost all its power through overuse. Another critic, H. Landman, has it as "We never knew his fantastic head," which merely sounds strange; while D. Paterson has unwisely chosen a second-person addressee in place of the first-person plural proper to *Wir*, creating an even more bizarre accusatory tone: "You'll never know that terrific head" (So there, losers!) And poet C. F. MacIntyre, struggling gamely, chooses a word that now carries an entirely unforeseen connotation: "Never will we know his fabulous head." That Apollo? *Fab*ulous head! But you'll never know it, girlfriend.

These variations give way to almost universal consensus concerning the poem's famous final line: "*Du mußt dein Leben ändern.*" You must change your life. You must. There is an imperative in the aesthetic experience, one that is both utterly particular to you, and to this moment, and entirely comprehensive in that it reaches into every corner and cranny of the unsatisfactory picture you present *to yourself* as you contemplate this shattered perfection, this headless messenger. *Your very life* is the question, and the answer is: Change it now! That, and that alone, is the message of beauty, even (or especially) beauty that has been compromised by time and decapitation. The torso alone is sufficient to its task!

And here, if I have not led you on too tortured a path, is where I think *ekphrasis* meets—or teeters into—*ekstasis*, and the apparently simple issue of art's paraphraseability reveals its full paradoxical nature. Because

Rilke writes simultaneously about a specific work and a class of works, all headless and anonymous, he is able to distill a potent insight proper to all art: we are drawn to beauty in art not for uplift or comfort, but precisely because it unsettles. The ravishing quality of the experience is essential to the message being communicated—this cannot be paraphrased—but there is a message. Not Keats' too-pat Romantic levelling of beauty and truth, but instead an ambiguous, unbalanced, indigestible bit of aporetic demand. Jacques Derrida has written that hope is that which lies beyond all dialectical enactment, the unresolved remainder of the gift that refuses to be reduced to transaction.

The gift of beauty is, to be sure, a complicated one—one, above all, we may sometimes wish we had not been given. *Ek-stasis* literally means to experience a state of derangement, an out-of-body experience. It can be far from pleasant, however much we might believe we desire ecstatic conditions. Art can bowl us over, but it is also sometimes a kind of spiritual assassin, sneaking up from behind the conscious mind's send of itself, slaying complacency with swift and delicate strokes. Either way, even as we might writhe in agonies of sense-making, it will finally, and forever, elude our attempts to bring it to the mat, to tame its energy.

I am once again conscious of using what might sound like old-fashioned language, and, worse, doing so in defence of what smacks of a neo-Romanticism about beauty and its place in art. But I want to take seriously here two insights the writer Henri-Marie Beyle (1783-1842), better known as Stendhal, offered his own version of the art world. Beauty was, he said, "only a promise of happiness"—a false promise, in other words, because happiness cannot be reliably delivered. Unlike Schiller, who concludes his *Aesthetic Education* with the claim that "[b]eauty alone confers happiness on all, and under its influence every being forgets that he is limited." Alas, Friedrich, not so. When it comes to happiness, beauty is all promissory notes and no cash.

Trading in happiness is, moreover, ever a dangerous business. Stendhal also recorded the most vivid incident of aesthetic *ekstasis* in the literature, describing a condition that now bears his name. In 1817, visiting the Basilica of Santa Croce in Florence—final resting place of Galileo, Michelangelo, and Machiavelli, among others—he saw for the first time the celebrated frescoes by Giotto. In his diaries, later published as a book, he describes his reaction this way: "I was in a sort of ecstasy, from the idea of being in Florence, close to the great men whose tombs I had seen. Absorbed in the contemplation of sublime beauty . . . I reached the point where one encounters celestial sensations . . . Everything spoke so vividly to my soul. Ah, if I could only forget. I had palpitations of the heart, what in Berlin they call 'nerves.' Life was drained from me. I walked with the fear of falling."

Recording such experiences became a preoccupation of those undertaking the nineteenth-century Grand Tour, a growing fraternity of those blessed with excessive sensibility. In 1979 the psychiatrist Graziella Magherini, who had observed more than a hundred cases of dizziness and fainting brought on by aesthetic stimulation, coined the term Stendhal's Syndrome, or *hyperkulturemia*, to describe this psychosomatic disorder. The usual symptoms are rapid heartbeat, dizziness, fainting, confusion and even hallucinations in the presence of art or, less often, natural beauty.

No clear ekphratic opportunity here, one might think, just pure unadulterated feeling. And yet, why? What is it in us that responds to beauty in this extravagant fashion, seeing it neither as virtue nor as status, but as something much more personal, and intimate? Could it be that we feel we must change our lives?

*   *   *

The question will not be laid to rest; lying to rest is just what it does not do. So: we now live in age in which the Schillerian imagination, once the preserve of intellectual play, has been colonized, assimilated, and commodified beyond all recognition. A philosopher in David Cronenberg's 2014 novel *Consumed* muses that the central challenge of personhood in our time is evading the depredation of the popular imagination, the media imagination, "which is quickly becoming the only imagination that exists." Constant, 24/7 wired meme-immersion, with its instant judgments and complex but fleeting intertextual jokes, its japes and gambols, has off-loaded the need for imagination just as Google and iPhones have done the same for memory and, indeed, learning of most kinds. It colonizes time itself by packaging every moment—even those spent asleep—for urgent consumption, hollowing out the notion of a *timeless* ecstatic moment, an experience beyond mere appetite or spending impulse.

Rather than capitulate to this condition, though, let us pause to consider the way Rilke's imperative might filter back through the present arrangement. The Situationist tactic of *détournement*, though much abused and derided, may serve here. The "turning" or "reversal" can indeed be reduced to the web-friendly acts of cultural mash-up and over-lay: parodies, juxtapositions, cartoonish redeployments. But Debord and the other Situationists knew assimilating counter-measures when they saw them: *détournement* isn't just empty bricolage, ripe for seamless con-sumption. It is, instead, just the kind of indigestible gift that lurks in the heart of an unsettling aesthetic experience. That is, *détournement* offers a "practical movement of negation in society," a "style of negation" that aims to contradict, or derange, whatever has been turned into an "official verity" in the general spectacle of culture (Debord, *Society of the Spectacle*, Theses 203-204, 206). "*Détournement*," Debord writes, "is the fluid lan-guage of anti-ideology. It occurs within a type of communication aware of its inability to enshrine any inherent and definitive certainty." Instead, it "founds its cause on nothing but its own truth as critique at work in the present" (Thesis 209).

Like language itself, beauty and art have often served the ends of the dominant paradigm, of course; but that is only so when *we* allow it to be, consuming forms without wit or resistance. The urging for some-thing else, the whisper of the necessity for change, for improvement, is ever-present. It cannot be fully parsed, only felt, in the serious play of a gift-game where the rules are always changing and there are never clear outcomes. But that may be enough, just enough. We are not really neo-Romantics; we are neo-Situationists. And this, this right now, is the situ-ation. Let's play!

MEDITATIONS
PERSONAL &
POLITICAL

Slack Enters
the System

KYLE has two very white front teeth that stand proud of their fellows, thinly outlined in black. Replacements, maybe. He smiles a lot so you see them; he is not self-conscious. The white gleams in his dark red face, the same red as the Popeye forearms and the thick sturdy legs of his not-tall frame. He played defensive tackle in college. He would have been hard to get around.

"I put one in the ground in front of him," he says, "but he kept on coming. So I had to whack him."

You think: *whack*. Gangland hit. Takedown. Sanction. The Gallatin Sanction.

He's talking about a black bear who encroached on his ranch, hungry for the good-food smells coming from the kitchen. Pulled pork. Grilled steak. Here he comes. But then: *blam*. Get off my lawn! And then: *whack*.

"What did you use?" Jules asks from the back. Jules is into guns.

"Ruger .338," Kyle tells him. "Fire-breathing dragon. Shoots real flat."

"They use that .338 as a sniper round in Afghanistan," Jules informs the car. "Just obliterates the target. One shot, one kill." He knows things like that.

"Actually my buddy has a .50-cal rifle he uses for hunting," Kyle says. "Now that's the real fire-breathing dragon."

You try to imagine a .50-caliber round, like from a B-17 gunnery mount. Seven inches long, shouldered brass cylinder with a top section tapering to a point, a hand-to-hand weapon in its own right. But in a hunting rifle.

"Have to use a tripod," Kyle says. "Big weapon."

"Must just take the animal apart," you say.

"Funny thing." Kyle chuckles. "I saw him shoot an elk with it once. Full metal jacket round. Went right through the body, clean, and sort of *sucked* all the guts right out the other side. Blood and intestines sprayed all over the snow. Most disgusting thing I ever saw." He's laughing.

You are going fishing. He is your guide.

*　　*　　*

The large winter snowpack, melting in the spring sun, was swelling the rivers into brown torrents. The Gallatin was impossible, high, fast, and dirty; the Lower Madison was a joke. "Worst I've seen it in thirty-seven years," one guy told you, looking at it. You would hear variations on this theme all week: worst in a decade, worst I can remember, worst in my life, worst ever. You caught one fish in two days, and it was a sucker.

So you decided to hire Kyle, who said he could put you on fish in the relatively clear Missouri, up north of Three Forks, where the Jefferson, Gallatin, and Madison combine. Little Prickly Pear Creek debouches into the Missouri just below Holter Dam, and there is a productive stretch of river more than thirty miles long. Even with high water, you should be able to drift nymphs and get some rainbows or browns.

"There is something refreshingly childish about the ever-renewed faith of the oldest fisher and something almost senile about the optimism of the youngest," essayist George Brennand wrote. He was right. Every day of fishing starts with the same conviction that this, this will be the day, the good day, the day of days. Hope is a line extended. But on the other side of this happy senility is the dark thought that each fishing day can likewise bring. Why do we do it? What is it for? Why are you here?

Maybe you are just hungover. There had been gin and tonics before dinner, wine with dinner, cigars after dinner. Yep, probably hungover. Norman Maclean says in *A River Runs Through It* that no angler minds a hangover: two hours on the water and the mind will clear, the spirit refresh. There is no better cure.

You guess he should know. But so far, three hours in, it is not working. You're thinking maybe a beer would be more effective than spiritual refreshment.

Or maybe the trouble is Kyle, whose guiding style combines aggression with sarcasm in a way that you would normally find amusing, but today . . . well, today you could use a little more support.

"Really like that Zorro-style hook-set you have there, Mark," he says at one point. "Sabre slash. Zip zip zip. Yeah. Like, hey fish, see this fly? Want it? No, you *can't* have it. Can't. Slash!"

It's a bad habit, left over from bad casting technique. Sidearm slippage. Your casting arm is oriented at about forty-five degrees to the water, not the purist's ninety. An instructor would make you tuck a newspaper under your arm to get it back square. So when the indicator dips and you want to strike the below-surface nymph rig, instead of hauling straight up—the quickest way to lift all line, no matter how it lies—you keep pulling back and to the right, taking the fly right out of the fish's gulping mouth. Back and to the right. Back and to the right. Sorry, fish: no fly for you.

You'll work on it. Also on the cast. Floating on the dark brown back of the Missouri, Kyle paddling from amidships and offering withering advice in the approved you're-paying-me-to-abuse-you manner, you're concentrating on flinging a mass of leader, weights, tippet, and the two-hook business-end into the drift. The line kinks and angles in the air, the nymphs popping out of the water on the back-cast in a way that hurls them straight for your head.

"Chuck and duck," Jules says from the front.

"Chuck and duck and *fuck*," Kyle offers. "Ha ha ha."

You think of a passage you just read, in an autobiography of Caresse Crosby, society girl and independent publisher, doyenne of Paris in the twenties. She and her husband, Harry, had leased a mill near Paris as their summer home, hosting parties and loose-end literary figures in a bucolic setting that had once been the residence of Jean-Jacques Rousseau. The surrealists André Breton and Valentine Hugo once came, and decided to go fishing.

"His leonine head and her fantastic headpiece etched the skyline hour after hour as they pontifically fished where no fish were," Caresse recalled. "[I]f ever there was a surrealistic conception of the gentle art it was there portrayed—and quite logically, these arch surrealists were the only ones who ever *did* try fishing at the Mill."

Fishing as surrealism: the logical end of fly fishing, fishing as performance art, a kind of dandyism whose categorical imperative is that *no fish shall ever be caught.*

"Jesus, hit that, Mark! Hit it!"

You look down and see that your indicator is submerged about six inches beneath the cold Missouri water. A fish is fooling with one of the flies down below, considering, wondering, debating . . .

You haul the nine-foot rod, a seven-weight, hard back—and to the right. The line pops free of the water, both flies surging overhead in a twinkling fish-free mass of tippet and leader. It flops on the off side, sadly spooled, slack.

"Jesus, Mark." Kyle is disgusted, and not in a guts-on-the snow way, either.

"I was looking at a magpie," you say defensively. Jules barks a laugh from the front. He had already landed two big-shouldered rainbows.

It's not so much the aggression as the joylessness, you think. Here you are, in one of the most beautiful places on Earth, floating in nature's glory, and you're supposed to have your eyes constantly glued to the little orange float, your rod tip pointed at it like a weird extended lesson in ostensive definition. *This, gentlemen, is a strike indicator.* You want to catch fish as much as the next guy, but surely . . .

"Hit that, Mark!"

This time, for some reason, you flow the rod smoothly back at a right angle to the water, and the slight bob of the indicator becomes a definite downward pull. The stiff rod bends right over and then the tip bounces, bounces again. Fish on.

Trout that run in the big Montana rivers, even specimens of modest size, will surprise you with their strength; they're as feisty as Great Lakes steelhead. This one is no exception. He takes you back and forth, diving for cover both to the bank and under the boat. The reel's drag is set hard—Kyle's idea of fishing. No long runs, no cat-and-mouse games of line and reel, no poetic silken-lines-and-silver-hooks seduction nonsense. You just spin the reel with your free hand to spool in the loose coils between your tight finger set and the tight drag, and then let the rod do the work.

Big sideways runs, deep deep pulls, your forearm and shoulder muscles taking the strain and the rod bends and springs. It's over too quickly, which maybe it always is, and the fish—a twenty-inch rainbow, a solid middleweight slugger—is netted, held, mug-shot, and sent back into the deep with expert efficiency.

When you sit down and pick up the rod again, your hands are shaking. Adrenaline. You realize you are breathing hard, and not just from the elevation. A wrestling match.

"Nice fish, Mark," Kyle says, showing the two white teeth. "You took the stink off the boat." He offers a big-mitt high-five that you return awkwardly, like Tiger Woods and his caddie that time at the Masters. Relief settles over the little boat in a fine, invisible mist. The first fish of the day—it makes all things right. There's the optimism, or the senility. Same thing, really, when you're middle-aged.

Disgrace averted. You realize you have been hunched with tension for an hour, your body clenched like a six-foot fist. You think maybe your hangover is gone.

*   *   *

A new day, another world. Close in miles only is a small spring-fed creek in the part of Montana south of Livingston called Paradise Valley. The creek runs alongside the Yellowstone which this spring is surging like all the other rivers, angry with brown run-off carrying trees and hapless campers and, downstream from here, a big pool of spilled oil. There is flooding further down the big system below the Missouri dams, into North Dakota.

The creek, though, is another story. The spring sluices clear cold water into a bed no wider than a two-lane highway, and it flows smooth and slow for three miles on one property, DePuy's, where access is limited to sixteen anglers a day. Large but picky browns lurk along the whole length of it, but this is the kind of fishing that rewards skill over muscle.

"Very technical fishing," Kyle says when you mention it. He is clearly not very interested. One of his buddies adds, with more candour, "Bunch of snobby faggots over there." Which about sums up what might be called the aesthetic stakes: stalkerish wading, precise casts, delicate presentation—not, uh, manly enough for some. A book in the ranch house, meanwhile, articulates another kind of caution. Spring-creek fishing in Paradise Valley, it says, offers "a lesson in humility for most anglers."

Size matters, for one thing. A lot. When you stop in at a shop near the creek, the clerk asks to see the smallest nymphs and dry flies you have. He laughs at what you show him. "All too big," he says and leads you to a rack of size eighteen and twenty pale morning dun (PMD) and crack-back nymphs. Also the secret weapon: bright red San Juan blood worm flies, little squiggles of felt like a tiny dribble of hot sauce. This is June fishing in Montana. The May hatches are even smaller: midges and blue-winged olives in twenty, twenty-two, twenty-four. You indulge a pang of regret for the salmon-fly and golden stone hatches you fished last year on the West Fork of the Bitterroot, where the bugs are so big you can use size ten or twelve hooks—the result a honking fly that one guy liked to call *the chicken*.

"You'll know there's something wrong if the fish nudges your fly aside to get to a natural," the clerk says, laughing. "Ha ha ha." Always with the laughing.

Match the hatch. You grasp a clump of three or four PMD dries in eighteen and wonder if you'll be able to tie one on with your half-century eyes and fingers.

DePuy's Creek is headquartered by a large house realized in some-body's idea of grand Southern-plantation style. Inside is a macabre col-lection of weird antiques, mounted hunting trophies, vintage fishing books, black-face lawn jockeys, and vast pictorial murals drawn from 1950s magazine photos of a lady angler in tight red sweaters and baggy waders. Someone who might be the real-life lady angler, Betty, now an ancient and crotchety oldster, takes your money after elaborate and baf-fling questioning and stony silences when credit cards are offered. Seems Betty doesn't hold with credit cards.

"Casa di Creepy," Jules says outside, glad to be free of the odours of old person and cat pee. "Welcome to the William Faulkner Southern Gothic serial-killer mansion."

The fishing is excellent, at least for the first part of the day, the creek as clear as tap water and arranged in a series of inviting pools and riffles with cute names: Annie's Run, Dick's Riffle, Narcissus, the PhD Pool. Clamping the bend of the tiny hook in your forceps you aim a sliver of tippet towards the eye and have one of those good-luck mini-moments when it goes through first try. A few spins of the tippet, aim the free end into the noose opening, back over once for the improved cinch, and seal the knot down with a lick of spit. Ready to fish.

You wade into a likely looking stretch of water—maybe it's Narcissus or thereabouts—and see the PMD hatch start to come off. Your rod here feels less like a weapon and more like a magic wand, a mid-flex five-weight that can lace its length of floating line anywhere you look. Kyle had said the water would be too cold for wet wading, but there you are, thigh deep in the middle of the stream wearing just wading boots, cargo shorts, and a pair of old long johns, the collar of your thrift-store cotton shirt flipped against the sun. Also battered, logo-free ballcap and insectoid polarized shades. Styling it old school. The water is cold but not uncomfortable, the air around your upper body hot and dry.

Fish are rising under the far bank, and so you shoot a cast upstream to drop the dry fly, treated with some floatant gel, into the top of the riffle. The minuscule PMD suddenly looks huge next to the naturals on the surface, and drifts downstream just a little too fast. Almost instantly the line creates midstream drag that you try to mend, flipping the line up and over. Two more casts, you're presenting the fly like a steak on a plate, and the fish are rising—next to it, behind it, around it. You matched the hatch; now, how about better presentation.

This is textbook fly fishing, the conventional pinnacle of the sport. One hook, one dry fly, catch and release. You need to lay that fly on the water as gently as a the bug it means to imitate. Argument no longer rages over the validity of any other kind of fishing, with adherents of the wet and dry schools known to cut each other on the streets of London or refuse handshakes in the House of Lords; but we all know that the cult of the dry fly still holds sway in the upper reaches of angling's class system. Nymphs or wet flies are still dismissed as "lures," a pejorative just a short ugly cast away from "bait-fishing bastards" excoriated everywhere. Purists will tell you the dry-fly skill is not just the cast, but reading the river and presenting the very bug—and only that bug—the fish are eating. And making them come up and get it, rather than dropping it on their noses. Everything else might as well be hand grenades.

*   *   *

Or so you would believe if you were drawn into conversation with a committed dry-fly cultist. Every sport has its class system, but fly fishing is maybe the only one that is premised on disdain: for spoons and lures, for worms and eggs, for jigs, rigs, and anything that doesn't give the fish the biggest chance of survival. Dry-fly bores are just at the far end of the notional spectrum of constraint. These western anglers like Kyle, with their two-hook nymph rigs and militant river tactics, are a weird sort of hybrid between high-toned purism and good-old-boy hammering of the water. They make it interesting, using small flies and light rods, but drifting with a two-fly nymph outfit and an indicator is really not so far away from trolling.

All choice of technique is about distinction, not success; the only difference is where you draw your lines. Every puritan is a dandy of his own convictions.

You're not sure you would try to argue this with Kyle and his buddies. Yesterday, in the truck, he pointed out the antelope who line the long valley fields near Helena, oblivious to the human traffic just yards away.

"See, it's like a river to them," he said. "The movement means no danger. If we stopped, they'd scatter."

"Guess that makes it hard to hunt them," you said.

"Nah. You get two guys in the truck. Slow down, passenger rolls out with a rifle, hides in the grass, truck rolls on. They startle, but then settle down when the traffic goes again. Bam."

There was a pause as you visualized this mobile tactical assault on the antelope.

"Seems kind of mean," you offered.

"We call it effective," he said.

This was eerily parallel to another exchange you'd had about that grizzly bear documentary where the freak-boy camper thinks he's befriended the bears and then they attack and kill him. "Kind of sad," you had commented.

"You thought that was sad?" Kyle asked. "I thought it was funny. *Oh, here is the noble mamma bear. I will call her Jewel.* Dude, she's the one who ate your head!"

Still, there is no art without constraint; it's the challenges you set for yourself that make success interesting. You're not a dry-fly bore, but you'll fish only dries today, just like you insisted on fishing for northern pike exclusively with this same five-weight rod and a leech "fly" six-inches long. That turned out right: you landed a thirty-four-inch pike, a cold-water monster, that made the rod bend and sing like a divining rod for half an hour.

Cast again, mend, drift the fly. A splash: you've turned one, and he showed you his back, thinking about it. Cast right back there. Your eyes watch the tiny fly move slowly along the surface, sometimes losing it in the hatch, picking up a natural by mistake. A fish slashes at a fly. It could be yours, so you hesitate a quarter-second and pull the rod back. Too fast on the hook-set and that fly will come right out of his mouth no matter what the sidearm angle.

Not this time. He's on and you can see the whole body now, a gorgeous brown trout flashing yellow and green to the sky. Western browns jump, unlike their east coast and English cousins, who prefer to bull down or swerve around. Jump! And another! You have him on the reel and there is nothing but clear water between his part of the river and you: nothing to snag the quick landing, nothing to foul your release.

You work him over, rod high over your head, and he slides right alongside, the tail meeting your wet left hand like a handshake. You hold him out of the water just for a second, to see that teensy PMD perfectly set in the right corner of his mouth, smaller than the smallest spot on his smooth eighteen inches of flank. A brown beauty, saluted and returned to the gin-clear flow.

You were lucky. You see that the parachute hackle on the PMD made it somewhere between a true, high-sitting dry and an emerger. Trout are effective predators because they max out the effort-to-calories conversion. You served up a meal that was easier to take than both a nymph and a hatched natural.

*   *   *

Catch and release may be the ultimate self-imposed constraint, one of those aspects of the sport that make anglers wonder what they're up to, the whole point of the outing lost in the mists of concentration—especially if the day is good. A bad day will make the questions pressing, and uncomfortable.

Is this just toying with the creatures of the earth for your selfish pleasure? Is it pointless and maybe even cruel? Well, it's certainly pointless if fishing is supposed to be about food, and the cruelty question can't be ignored. As a gifted writer once said about a lobster, it may not have desires or thoughts in the robust sense, but it certainly has *preferences*. Clearly a trout would prefer not to find that its mid-morning snack comes with a human attached to it, however well intentioned that human might be. You start to feel a grudging respect for those English anglers who routinely took their daily limit, spoke offhandedly of "killing" fish, and wouldn't dream of returning a catch except for lack of size.

This is an old argument, and an endless one. But there is more than just ethics involved, especially when the ethical objections can cut both ways—catch and keep is *killing*, but catch and release is *trifling*. There is the undeniable atavistic pleasure of being on the water, negotiating field and stream, landing what could be food *if it had to be*. There is a reason most anglers and hunters are ardent conservationists, and so aligned with green politics that are otherwise of the dreadlocked-vegan variety. You don't want agribusiness and real-estate developers to ruin the natural environment any more than some campus protester does. You love to be outdoors, away from structure and people and communication—away from *noise* in all its forms, so that the signal thrum of flowing water can be heard.

But there's something else again, something harder to define. Call it the happiness of skill, the satisfaction that comes from doing something rather difficult in such a way that it *works*. And then doing it again, doing it over and over under tricky conditions and with new learning every time. It really is more aesthetic than practical, at this far end, and maybe that's the point of the limits and constraints: to refine angling into the ultimate performance art. Breton's striking of poses, fishing where there are no fish, can start to seem like the next logical step from what you are doing right now.

So why? It's about slack and its opposite, you think, the fine firmness of dynamic tension. *Tight lines*, anglers wish each other at the start of a day or a season, meaning that exquisite feeling of success when you are hooked into a good fish. But it's not just about the fish taking in the slack of your laid-out line. Slack means looseness, lack of rigour. You ask someone to cut you some slack when you are feeling low, but you want to take in the slack to make a system or situation better, more squared away. Slack ideas, like slack dough, have too little body; they are excessively pliable. The slacker is shirking work, slacking off or skiving, not even idling in a free spirit of invention and joy. The slacker is still defined by that which he is not doing, namely work. He is lazy. An angler may be idling, but he is never slacking.

And so keeping the line tight after the gift of a strike is the business of angling, the shifting rod with tip lifted, the stripping in of line, the adjusted drag or palmed tension of runs and pulls. A slack line now means failure, a thrown hook. But too much tightness, as we all know, turns success into failure. The reel with too much drag, the first-burst fish run stopped by a line looped around the rod butt, the rookie angler who forgets that there is a reason rods are made to bend and holds his line instead—all of this creates the taut line trending toward breakage. Turns out, when that happens, the fish wins.

But the ghost of slack haunts the fly fisherman from the start, long before a fish is in the running to win or lose. Why are you so obsessed about the cast, after all? It's not a matter only of success. Yes, an accurate cast is a necessary condition of all fishing, but an ugly cast can be accurate. The beauty of the cast matters because the beauty elevates angling above utility, into that rarefied air of the art form. A slack cast is a dead cast.

"Unless you develop great line speed on the backcast," Bernard "Lefty" Kreh wrote, "you will push slack into the system as your rod-hand begins to move forward and your line-hand travels toward it. This slack must then be removed before you make the cast or your cast will die."

Slack enters the system. And the cast dies, losing its quickness and falling out of the air. You recall another guide, a salty-tongued Bahamian who abused you all day long for your shoddy casting in the hot sun of a Caribbean Christmas.

"People see a fish and their IQ drops forty points," he told you, adding that his best client was a blind angler who just answered his calls without hesitation—ten o'clock, forty feet; one o'clock, fifty—and bagged one bonefish after another. You got just one that day, in the skinny water of a mangrove flat, but not before the guide called sadly, more than once, "No, no, man—you're out of control now, you're out of control." And the slack-slain cast fell down, ugly like all dead things.

Line without tension is like the loose moment in a day, exposing the lurking futility of it all, of a day, a week, a life. The taut beauty of the good double-hauled cast, by contrast, the assured pull of the four-beat rhythm, suddenly looms larger than what it aims for, the sharp tightness of fish on. That loose-muscled happy feeling in the body is matched with the success of tension, like the smooth ease of a good golf swing or a home-run swat. The day acquires clarity, and that feeling of purpose we seek even when engaged in something pointless—beautiful and pointless.

*   *   *

Or maybe that's all just high-toned bullshit. The hatch is still coming off. You gather in the line and prepare to cast again, even as a savage wind kicks up, howling down the Yellowstone valley from somewhere upstream in the national park. Swallows push through the air above the creek, held stationary by the gusts, taking insects right out of the air.

The wind plays hell with your cast, and suddenly all the philosophical fun, the wizard-wand rod action, is gone. The gusts grab even a flat sidearm shot and slap it gracelessly onto the creek surface, sending the fly drilling into the water like no insect of nature's own devising. The line is pushed into drag without a pause, so the viable drift time shrinks from comfortable to urgent. You work back against the bank, trying to use it as a windbreak, but the bushes up top grab the backcast fly and tangle, forcing you to clamber up and free it. In a kind of shortstop's crouch you try to zip the line over and upstream, hoping for a decent drift even if the landing itself is a bit of a slam-dunk. The hatch is still on, the fish are still in there.

You will get one more brown before lunchtime, and that will be even better than the first. Not because it was bigger but because it was harder. If that's snobbiness . . . well let's just say, there are worse kinds.

On the Ausable

THE RUSHING WATER was about three inches away from my mouth, which doesn't sound so bad. I could move, so that was good. Unfortunately I was moving towards the water, not away from it, and that was bad. I had fallen and now I was life-trending in the wrong direction.

Also, to fall in such a way as to dislocate your shoulder. So that your right arm is useless because most of it is hanging a couple of inches away from where it joins usefully to the rest of your body, splayed across the boulder that did the damage there, you can only look at the water near your mouth and think about how it is, more or less, the same water that is even now filling your waders and that to die like a damn fool doesn't make you any less dead. Avidity in pursuit of a non-essential goal may be defined as the form of stupidity that is most honest, and hence noble. But it is still stupidity.

The Ausable is a tough river, though it looks tame enough in places. It starts high in the Adirondacks and has two branches that split at Ausable Forks, famous for little except that Rockwell Kent lived much of his life there, and, lower down, the combined river falls heavily into the Ausable Gorge, an imposing natural basin festooned with the usual tourist paraphernalia of the old school, non-theme-park variety, from bus-friendly parking lots to dilapidated motels. On the West Branch, between Lake Placid and a once-legendary Santa's Workshop in Wilmington, not quite in sight of the ski slopes on Whiteface Mountain, there are a couple of runs of flat, slow water followed by a linked jumble of boulders, shelves, and drop-offs. Together these fashion a precious few miles of little pools, rushes, and riffles offering some of the best, and trickiest, trout fishing in the northeast. This was destination fishing for the better part of the last century, then the river fell off with overfishing. It is now coming back with the help of artful stocking, barbless-hook regulations, and the righteous-but-right catch-and-release ethos lately in favour among most of the angling community.

The West Branch forms at the junction of South Meadow Brook and Marcy Brook, down from Mount Marcy, flowing north. About three miles east of Lake Placid, climbing a bit as you move away from the lakes and golf courses around the village, you cross the river on Route 86, then the trees thicken along the winding road and there are small pull-in clearings on the left-hand side. After a stretch of gravelly semi-rapids, the West Branch smoothes out. The water is welcoming here, but the fishing hard. I parked and opened the hatch of my girlfriend's car. I had dropped her off, together with her two teenage daughters, at a hotel in town. We'd driven all day to get here, the sun was already well down in the sky, and I had been thinking about the water every hour I spent behind the wheel, or in the passenger seat. Those three girls couldn't get out of the car fast enough for me.

The last time I managed to fish the Ausable I roused my girlfriend at dawn after arriving in Lake Placid too late the night before to get on the water. She shivered through a couple of luckless morning hours until I took pity on our future together and got back in the car to continue on our way to New Hampshire. For us, Lake Placid is always a stopover, not a destination. I glimpse this river coming and going, catching partial sight of wading, casting rivals with more time or different obligations. All fishing requires patience, patience entails time, and I never seemed to have enough of that. And still no fish on this river, legendary for its big browns and rainbows. Ian Frazier says you don't feel good about a river or lake, you're not really there, until you've caught at least one fish. Otherwise the day feels hollow, the water haunts and irks you.

Apostles of the Izaak Walton school like to emphasize the contemplative and hopeful side of fishing, the spirituality. But there's a reason "fishing expedition" is a term of abuse in legal slang, why angling for compliments or promotion is considered indecent. Fishing is competitive, deceptive, and importunate. Beyond angling's tiresome disputes between dandies and trout bums, grizzled vets and overgeared newbies, each obsessed with an exclusive norm concerning their own authenticity, there is a simple union of aim. Fishing is an invasion, and even catch-and-release anglers want desperately to fool fish, to win. These feelings, unfortunately, sometimes make for impatience. Thus the fatal fisherman's spiral, trying too hard to do something that depends on a finally mysterious combination of luck and skill.

I climbed and slid down the bank and into the water. This was an easy running section of river but the cold and, especially, the current of a mountain-born river are always a shock, however slow. The water came up to the edge of my hip-waders as I took a slow step across mulchy then sandy bottom. The waders are simple ones, with small metal hobs on the soles but no felt, and no lining inside. Like most anglers, I take peculiar and contradictory pride in my gear choices. Getting set to enter a river is at once the most exhilarating and exasperating part of fishing, the interlocking use-values of equipment revealing a complex world of desire and dream. How satisfactory to joint the pieces of your rod together, ferrule to stem, eyeing the guides for straightness, feeling the eager suppleness, the familiar grip of cork darkened with sweat, water, and fish guts from British Columbia, Ontario, New Hampshire, Wiltshire, and Cornwall. To pat down the pockets of your vest, checking for fly boxes and snips, leaders and line, cigars and whisky flask. To fix the reel to rod-butt, and loop the line along the guides. To noose-knot a number twelve or fourteen Ausable Wulff or Cahill with fingers controlled but impatient with longing, licking the tippet at the end to seal down the cinch.

I like to feel the water's chill. That's one reason I wear thin waders rather than Neoprene. Angling lore avers that ghillies in Scotland prefer to wade for salmon in bare legs, presumably as a natural extension of sporting the kilt. Norman Maclean, Stephen Leacock, Ernest Hemingway, and Teddy Roosevelt all waded in trousers, not bothering with the idea of dry legs. Getting wet was, for them, a feature of communion with the river. If you can take the cold, it makes more sense than waders. The close-fitting body suit, on the far side of the gear spectrum, almost negates the river. It makes sense to keep warm, but to me, fishing shouldn't feel like sitting around the house or driving a car. The Neoprene can also make you careless, since you figure the water poses no danger, and so it ends up hiking the risk of a fall. No filled waders, but you might hit your head and drown anyway. I realize it's not much of a theory.

The flat gave me a chance to spool out a few unkinking casts, rescuing the ten-to-two muscle memory buried by those hours in the car and the long off-season. I could wade out far enough to clear some back-cast room, and soon I was laying a few decent rolls up and across the water, mending the floating line with turns of the rod as it drifted down on the current. Drag is the river angler's great enemy. It makes your fly jerk unnaturally, spoiling the miniature game of deception that lies at the fine end of all this gear and technique. No matter how gorgeously fashioned and accurate, if a dry fly or nymph doesn't move like food, you're skunked. This was not promising water, mainly because the wide, smooth flow created few of the overhangs, drifts, and pools where fish feel comfortably sheltered. Brown trout are spooky anyway. I have caught respectable browns on similar stretches of the Grand River in Ontario, but mostly by sheer luck.

I threw another long one over the flowing water. There were tiny bumps on the line that might have been fish nudges or just the beaded nymph touching bottom as it drifted. I changed flies, which is what impatient anglers always do when in doubt, and got no further. A moorhen and six ducklings made their way upriver from my right, keeping well in to the bank there. As long as they were along, the fish would not be. The sun was lowering all the while, throwing long, purple shadows athwart the green hills on the far shore above me. The sound of the river water, nothing else.

I decided to move downriver out of the flats. I thought of getting back in the car and driving to save time but then thought the walk would allow me a better chance to judge my next spot. I realized my error soon enough, because the bank was far more thickly tangled with short trees, weeds, and spongy, precarious undergrowth than it looked from the road. I was sweating and cross by the time I broke back through the now-spilling and loud river, almost a mile from where I first went in. The sun wasn't getting any higher.

At the far end of the catch-and-release section of the West Branch is a hundred-foot dam and waterfall that marks a transition in the river. Downstream from this there is still fishing, including some good pools, but the river widens and deepens, impossible to wade, a flowing lake, favourable to spinning-rod anglers but less so to flies. The stretch above the waterfall is probably the best of the whole Ausable, though guides describe it variously as "challenging," "difficult," and "treacherous."

"The underwater rocks are so slick with gray-green algae that you have to grope along each one with your foot as you wade," Ian Frazier wrote of it, stoutly admitting that he once fished two full days on the Ausable without catching a thing. "The smooth granite of the big boulders, cool in the morning, warm on a sunny afternoon, does not give you much to grab on to when the current starts to pull." Writing in 1950, expert angler Ray Bergman said this: "A stream wildly fascinating, capable of giving you both a grand time and a miserable one; a stream possessing a Dr. Jekyll and Mr. Hyde temperament . . . . It is not a stream that will appeal to the timid, the weak, or the old. You like it best before you reach the age of forty. After that you wish you had youthful energy so that you could enjoy it as you did before the years of striving for existence had sapped your strength and made you a bit fearful of slippery rocks and powerful currents."

A few months before, I had turned forty-three.

*　　*　　*

Erwin Straus began his career as a physician but he never fully embraced the notion of clinical distance, whereby doctors minister to persons by treating them only as bodies. In Straus's native German there is a distinction, not matched in English, between *körper* and *leib*. The first means not our English *corpse*, though the common Latin root is obvious, but rather the body *considered as a mere thing*. *Leib*, by contrast, signifies the body as it is lived and experienced, the body in terms of experience, embodied emplacement, to use a recent formulation. When Straus grew interested in the phenomenological theories of Edmund Husserl, with their anti-Cartesian emphasis on the experience of experience, consciousness of and as place, he shifted his sense of the body from *körper* to *leib* and stretched the dominating medical model past the limits of its interest. Straus became a philosopher only by ceasing to be a physician.

Nevertheless, his most important intellectual work concerns the body, or rather the lived experience of being embodied. In 1966 he published a phenomenological paper, now canonical, called "The Upright Posture." The paper argued that "uprightness" is "the leitmotiv in the formation of the human organism," a central fact of human experience that structures and orders that experience. Our load of sensory inputs, especially sight and sound, is disproportionately concentrated in a head perched atop a five- or six-foot tower of ambulating tissue. In an experiential variation of prenatal gestation, our experiential ontogeny recapitulates phylogeny. Humans begin life with their bodies and faces low to the ground, fallen and helpless; they learn to walk in a moment widely noted as an achievement worthy of extensive video archiving; then they are off to whatever feats of destruction or innovation their brains can imagine. From the moment of walking, sense of self and engagement with world are comprehensively textured by the twin edges of standing and falling.

The metaphorical freight shifted by standing and falling is sublimely large. Uprightness, being upstanding, or a stand-up guy are morality made flesh. We stand for things, and stand up for friends. Standing for or standing in is even, we might say, the basis of all metaphor, all language, the logic of representation itself, moving meaning across and around the world.

We fall from grace, fall in love, fall asleep, take the fall, might be the fall guy, perhaps re-enact the Fall. Walls, buildings, cities, and whole empires have fallen, in Berlin, New York, Troy, and Rome, shaking their worlds. Night always falls even if the sky doesn't. Icarus fell from pride. The hymn tells us to fall on our knees. Prices and markets fall, sometimes crash. Appeals fall on deaf ears. Axes and responsibilities fall on necks or shoulders, deadlines and holidays fall on dates or days. Shadows fall on the future as well as the ground. Cenotaphs honour the fallen, who lately fell in, their tissue now destroyed in pursuit of politics. A few choose to fall on their swords. And we tackle issues, bring them to the ground, reveal a position to be on all fours with another.

Falls are funny, though not usually for the fallen. Pratfalls, trips, and stumbles are staples of vaudeville and its modern equivalent, home-video dignity purges where real people are shown getting hurt in hilariously stupid ways. It's funny because it's true! Falling can even achieve the layered genius of a postmodern *aperçu*: walking down the street with a friend who suddenly falls by slipping on, yes, a banana peel. Why is that so funny?

Already in *Civilization and Its Discontents*, published in 1930, Freud had noticed the importance of uprightness and falling. Human posture removed our faces from the ground, shifting the primary sensory array away from odour-heavy regions to the clarity of the air above. Smell still mattered to us, but often now negatively, in disgust. And those creatures still immersed in smell began to seem despicable to us. To call a man a cur, Freud notes, is to impugn his sensibility as well as his dignity. Dogs are contemptible as much for their shit-seeking noses as for their pack mentality, and humans keep their noses mostly in check, even in sex, where shame, as usual, effectively camouflages the actually overwhelming interest in scent. (Freud is silent on the more recent usage of "dog" to mean player, and by extension, as a variform synonym for pal, dude, or guy.)

Anthropologists have long underlined the evolutionary significance of *Homo erectus* on the road to *Homo sapiens sapiens*. Standing, as much as the opposable thumb, allowed us to begin our millennia-long streak away from all other species when it comes to intelligence, organization, and rapacity. But Straus reminds us that the intervention of phenomenology is to shift what seems obvious into new light, so that its very obviousness is revealed as something blocking insight rather than aiding it. We think we understand what it means to stand upright, but we obscure ourselves in that very thinking. Only a confrontation with uprightness can make us appreciate its world-ordering power. Like tripping on the absent step in Heidegger's famous staircase, we have to miss something to see that it is not there.

"Men and mice do not have the same environment, even if they share the same room," Straus writes. "Environment is not a stage set with scenery as the one and the same for all actors that make their appearance upon it. Each species has its own environment. There is mutual interdependence between species and environment. The surrounding world is determined by the organization of the species in a process of selecting what is relevant to the function cycle of action and reaction. Upright posture pre-establishes a definite attitude toward the world; it is a specific mode of being in the world."

We can go further: upright posture establishes our being *as a world*. A mountain-fed river in New York is an environment, but it is not a world until one of us world-making creatures ventures into it. There, as Straus says, we share the same room, but not the same environment, with mallards and beavers and, one can hope, brown and rainbow trout. "Environmental protection" and "natural resources" are misleading, even corrupt, phrases because environment, protection, naturalness, and resources are the wrong concepts when it comes to climate change, declining fish populations, and rising water levels. All four rank as contestable if not useless, endorsing despite themselves the centrality of human egomania. The issue is not the environment but the kind of *world* that dominates most of our experience of being here, a world ordered by order, abused by use, mastered by technology, held in reserve by what Heidegger called standing reserve: the world as available, out there, ours to consume. With us standing at its centre, the human surveillance tower ever extended up and out, measuring the distances and plotting the coordinates of mastery.

How many times a year does the average person past, say, the age of twenty—after contact sports and keggers but before canes and the fear of hip fracture—fall down? You might watch a football game one Sunday and see several dozen hits and tackles, the fallenness that stops play, without once reflecting on the violent sensory scramble that a fall creates. In Plath's *The Bell Jar*, Esther, struggling with a violent date, describes her fall as a feeling of the pavement rising up in a curl to strike her in the face. A knock sideways is not experienced as a movement, but as a flatspin whirl of helmet-cam overload. As the narrator of an Iris Murdoch novel notes of a fall, this one in the street: "The shock was not just the impact, but the awful sensation of falling iself, the utterly helpless movement through the air, the foreknowledge of being spreadeagled on the ground, smashed." Only when the picture comes back into focus do you have the chance to start processing the information: *I have fallen*. Then the whole-body security check, the consciousness autopsy. Am I hurt? How much?

*   *   *

I broke through the trees when the sound of rushing water grew louder than it had been all afternoon, and eased myself down the bank and into a pool. Ahead of me were boulders and stones ranging in size from balls of bread dough to small houses. Deep pools were nestled among the little rushes of white water. If I could reach them I could try some nymphs with the Leisenring Lift technique, which moves a sunk fly slowly up to imitate an emerger caddis or blackfly on its way from egg to surface. This is what anglers are doing when you see them standing in water and not casting but raising their rods slowly upward, apparently in mad supplication.

I waded further in and climbed over a rock about as big as me, slid down its slick surface, and wedged myself between two bits of stable granite under the surface. The river was nearly at my waders, so I braced my legs in an inverted vee and trailed out some slack on the line. I could see where I wanted to get the fly, but casting was harder than I expected. The natural line of my somewhat hingey sidearm throw was falling across a rock, snagging and dragging the line. Not for the first time I felt a powerful desire for some ninja mastery allowing me to cast at right angles or through solid objects, or to suspend myself above the water like Chow Yun-fat. The fly was landing in the pool but not staying long enough to attract attention, herked and lugged about immediately by drag. A few more fruitless rolls of the four-weight line and I knew I had to move.

Below me to the right was what looked like a possible route to a better vantage. I moved carefully across, feeling the river tug hard, and planted every foot with a tiny squirt of fear. One more step, a sideways hitch, and I'd be in full, clear view of a beckoning deep pool, hung over with trees but wide open and deep with the highly oxygenated water brown trout love to gill.

I took the step but didn't make the hitch. My foot slipped maybe two inches off and that was enough. I was falling. The forward momentum was a fraction too much, and even as I grabbed at the rock with my free left hand I knew there was no hope of stopping it. The fall carried me just a few feet forward and down but that was enough too. My chest and right shoulder slammed hard into a large boulder below where I'd been standing, my legs fell back behind, and the sprawl carried me down to hit another boulder, where I lay, spatchcocked on the wet granite, sucking for the wind the fall had knocked away.

I was alive and conscious. Was I helpless? I still had my rod in my right hand, which was excellent because it was an expensive one my girl-friend had given me for Christmas. But there was something not right in that arm. I slowly brought my left hand across in front of my face and felt for it. There was a gap of about two inches between the hard point of the top joint and the tibia, which hung loosely down and forward, the rod still gripped below. My stomach turned over and I felt the blood draining from my head in pursuit of the nausea.

Not a good idea to faint now. The water was close to my face, clear and cold, and I knew I had to get out of the river as fast as possible.

*   *   *

There is much to learn about pain in the modern American hospital. Signs in the emergency room, placed there with the blessing of the globe's pharmaceutical conglomerates, inform you of your right not to feel excessive amounts of it. Admitting nurses will ask you, on a scale of one to ten, to quantify your suffering. They want to get a hold of your pain, locate it on a grid, give it an identity.

"Three," I told the woman in the cubicle, standing before her, pale and sweating, right arm gripped with the left hand in a vain attempt to find a comfortable way to nestle the dangling limb. She cocked a skeptical eyebrow at me.

"I'd like to keep the higher numbers in reserve," I told her. "Like a figure-skating judge."

The guy who finally gave me a dose of my rightful analgesic—actually an amnesiac, a cutting-edge painkiller that causes a sort of mini-blackout—told me that, what with the river, the ski slopes, and the hockey practices, Lake Placid is pretty much the centre of the shoulder-dislocation world.

"Your shoulder is dislocated," he told me, looking at the X-rays. I knew that. "By definition that means the ligaments are torn." I didn't know that, though it made sense. "It's like fraying the edges of a buttonhole. From now on it will be easier for it to dislocate again." He seemed to derive some ghoulish satisfaction from this fact, or maybe from the way he'd communicated it. "You may also have torn the muscles in your rotator cuff." He smiled.

The shoulder is a dumb joint, considering how much of the body's work it has to do. Or, as medical researcher Stephen Levin puts it, it is "the least successfully modelled joint complex" in the human body. Its odd structure forces loads and stresses to strain the joint, causing pain and eventually damage, unless they are applied within a small range of angles. A major-league fastball, for example, reaching ninety miles an hour or better, can only be achieved by taking the shoulder—also elbow—right to the red line of joint failure: maybe sixty times in one starting pitcher's one-hundred-throw outing. Strapping the humerus to the body via the scapula and clavicle also puts strain on the upper back, one reason that many cases of back pain start at a keyboard. Awkward twists will blast the joint; so will sharp blows to the upper body when the arm is extended. Levin, a disciple of Buckminster Fuller, advocates a new joint design consistent with *tensegrity*, the principle by which systems are held together with just compression and tension—a spoked bicycle wheel, say. Unfortunately, the field of *biotensegrity* is, so far, mostly notional and we're all stuck with old-school friction and contact shoulders. I did wonder whether a bio-tensegral shoulder would have kept me out there fishing.

The amnesiac dulled the pain but I still fully remember the weird sensation of having my skeleton rebuttoned by the combined efforts of two large guys, one pulling the arm and the other pulling the rest of me by means of a towel around my torso. The *körpermeisters* at work, seeing the body as mere flesh. And thank god for that, on occasions like this. There is no sound, but the feeling is sort of like *slthuck*, the cap of the bone returning to its messy socket. Doctors call this reduction. I thought about how you twist the legs or wings off a roast chicken, the way the bone pops loose of its joint jacket. I would be in a sling and gobbling Advil for the next six weeks.

Gathering my wits had been one thing, gathering strength another. Pushing back from the boulder with my left hand I found I could, just barely, stand. The bank of the river seemed far behind and above me. I twisted around and made a small step to the right. Water was sloshing inside the waders as I moved but, heavy as they were, there was no full drag yet. If I didn't fall again, I could make it. If I did fall again I would have to count on going down to my left, at least, and once more not hitting my head.

Climbing and wading one-handed probably looks funny if you don't know what's going on, maybe as funny as the fall that made it necessary. I gained the bank and threw my rod up onto it with my left hand, then grabbed at long grass and half hauled myself out of the water. Sweat was pouring down my face from the effort. I crawled further up and got the waders off. Several quarts of clean, cold river water emptied onto the ground. I could not now get them back on. Through the trees was the road and, on the road, more than a mile back, was the car. I would have to walk.

In a meditative little book on human perception called *Things*, the philosopher J. H. van den Berg suggests the world is not made up of things at all, but of complex variable relationships at the level of self. Two-by-fours do not have a fixed length, despite their name; they are narrower at one end than at the other. Towers taper as they grow taller, their windows shrinking as well. Van den Berg recalls how furious he became, while hiking, with the regular kilometre markers he and a friend encountered near the end of a long trek. "The little poles at intervals of one hundred meters along the road bed seemed to be set too far apart; moreover, the distance between them was constantly increasing," he says. "The number five, like all numbers, is the number of one who is absent . . . only for those who are absent does the dimension of things remain constant."

It follows that for the length of a road to remain constant "the hiker should then be neither well-rested nor exhausted, neither happy nor sad, neither hungry nor satiated, neither lonely nor with others. But there is no such person. Hence our conclusion is that the road has a constant length only if no one travels it. But such a road is meaningless; there is no such road. If no one travels the road, then that road doesn't exist."

The road I was on existed, though I couldn't tell you how long it measured, except maybe in the numbers of the pain scale, and even they are no help. I considered abandoning all my gear until I could get medical attention and return, but it was almost dark now and I didn't care for the idea of my beautiful nine feet of rod lying there for any passing motorist to snap or steal. And the waders—well, dangerous or not, I like those waders, which have been with me in a lot of water. I strapped them together and slung them across my left shoulder. The rod and reel together weigh only a few ounces. I placed them back in my dangling right hand, climbed over the guardrail, and started humping barefoot down the blacktop, glad not to be dead.

The car is a standard, which I considered the funniest thing so far. By the time I got to it I was wondering if I was going to be able to stay conscious, let alone drive it with one hand. Dislocated shoulders don't compare with lots of actual serious injuries. They are obviously not life-threatening in themselves. Hockey players routinely suffer them, for example, though more often in fights than in hits. Assuming you don't want to let go, and the other guy is strong, that holding arm is going to blow out now and then. But make no mistake: dislocating your shoulder, especially the first time, when you tear the joint apart, hurts. It hurts a lot more than Mel Gibson makes it look in that movie about the crazy cop.

I stuck the waders and rod into the car and gained the driver's seat without further incident. Bare wet feet on the clutch and brake, I reached over with my left hand and turned the key, let out the parking brake, and put it in first. There was no traffic, so my occasional swerves across the yellow line as I leaned over to shift didn't threaten any pileups except my own. Another road that seemed a lot longer on the way out. Probably five miles as measured by the absent ones, all of it in second since the up and over of third was out of the question, and I was approaching town. I didn't know where the hospital was but this seemed like a good time to get over myself and ask somebody for directions.

The girl in the convenience store betrayed no interest in my pale, sweating face or grunts of pain, but her directions to the hospital were concise and, as it proved, accurate.

*   *   *

I first read Erwin Straus in a phenomenology seminar with Maurice Natanson, a great teacher of philosophy and a massive shambolic presence when I was in graduate school. He was not one those big men who move with surprising grace, if such exist anywhere outside of bad fiction. He shuffled and harrumped his way through the physical world, a world of wit and insight embodied in a clot of being with feet of lead, not clay. I was his graduate teaching assistant in a course on philosophy and literature. Camus's *The Fall*, that bleak meditation on human vanity, was on the syllabus. So was Tolstoy's *The Death of Ivan Ilych*, whose title character's fall from bourgeois grace is discussed in the following essay (see "Frank's Motel").

Natanson fell in this class. I mean, one morning, bending over to plug in the microphone he regarded as a personal enemy, he lost his heavy balance and pitched forward awkwardly onto the lecture-hall floor. I was sitting nearby but found, as sometimes happens, that an ice of embarrassment and shame had encrusted my will to act. There is no possible defense for this, but it was not callousness. I was twenty-three, two decades away from my own fall. I think somehow I didn't want to offer help if help would suggest weakness or pity. I didn't want to call attention to the indignity of it, the wrongness, as when you first witness your father failing at something. In an instant I lost the chance to do something—just like the narrator of *The Fall*, I thought later, who hears the splash of a woman jumping into the Seine and pauses, only to walk on again. Before I could reconsider, Natanson, unhurt in any serious way, had painfully regained his uprightness. His world reassembled, he was ready again to lecture on falls, near-falls, and those who do things properly.

Doing and not doing haunt us, that existential *esprit d'escalier*: what we should have done or said, now that it is too late. In a fishing guide to New York's rivers and lakes, the Ausable is singled out as "a river where you should never fish alone." But for some of us, the appeal of fishing is precisely its solitude, however risky. You may have buddies to swap stories with, even to share the journey with, but you must fish alone. And if you fall, you fall alone, no matter how many people are around. Fishing on a river is really a form of tourism, a pleasant and, ideally, respectful visit from within our upright world. We can't help but carry that world into the river with us, not least in the form of our desires and our equipment. Falling shatters that visit in the space of one misplaced foot and puts you on, or under, that river in a new, unworlded way. Not a targeted mission, now, but a wild search for one firm spot, one bit of sense, from which recovery of a sort might start.

"Inside of every long paper is a little paper trying to escape," Natanson wrote in a 1982 essay on Straus. "Liberated, the minuscule version looks homeward toward its full expression. I begin in an alternative way: here are a few pages in search of a larger statement." Substitute paper with life, so we all begin, and end too.

Frank's Motel:

Horizontal and Vertical
in the Big Other

I N THE SIXTH and last (also added—excessive) chapter of *Enjoy Your Symptom!*, Slavoj Žižek makes the excellent claim that if architect Frank Gehry had designed the Bates Motel from Alfred Hitchcock's *Psycho* (1960), the resulting structure of molten modernist and postmodernist forces would have obviated the violence of Norman Bates, who is torn by an embodied conflict between tradition and *heimlichkeit* in the Gothic (vertical) house of his mother, and capital venture and independence in the mid-century (horizontal) motel. In what follows I will pursue this figuring of conflict, not just in Gehry's architecture or even in architecture, but, with Žižek, in the many aspects of the symbolic order(s) established by Lacan's "big Other."

There are ten sections of analysis followed by one of suggestion. Yes, this essay's scheme of numbered sections *goes to eleven*. It will become evident later why that matters.

1. Norman

1.1 Mother

Norma's boy Norman is not normal. In pursuit of integrated personhood, the normative goal of modern life, he has come apart at the seams of his close-fitting crew-neck pullover sweater.

"If Norman starts to talk with the strange voice of his mother, it's not his fault," Žižek points out. "The price he has to pay in order to become 'really himself,' undivided subject, is total alienation, becoming an Other with regard to himself: the obstacle to full self-identity is the very condition of selfhood."[1] Norman is neither himself nor, in seeking to be so, his Mother. He is both, and neither.

1.2 Antic

Norman, as played by Anthony Perkins, is a slight and nimble figure, a flitting, twitching presence in college-boy clothes. Perkins figures Norman as campy, if not outright queer. There is something odd about him, as he greets Marion Crane (Janet Leigh) at this otherwise deserted roadside motel. The new, larger highway has diverted the flow of automobiles—and commerce, and life, and erotic potential—along a different channel. They no longer debouch into the motor court of the Bates Motel. There is a vacancy, indeed there are twelve of them. Norman feels the vacancy that the neon sign conveys in the rainy darkness. Indeed, Norman will act the vacancy out spatially, in his antics. "We all go a little mad sometimes," he tells Marion over their strained sandwich supper in the motel's office parlour, sitting amidst various stuffed birds. "Haven't you?"

"Another aspect of this same antagonism [between self and identity] concerns architecture," Žižek continues: "one can also consider Norman as a subject split between two buildings, the modern horizontal motel and the vertical Gothic mother's house, forever running between the two, never finding a proper place of his own. In this sense, the *unheimlich* character of the film's end means that, in his full identification with the mother, he has finally found his *heim*, his home."[2]

More on *unheimlichkeit* later. More on architecture later. More on modernism later. More on Norman's full identification with Mother now.

1.3 Standing

Norman becomes his mother in order to kill. Or rather, the violence of his identification with Mother—because of the attempt at integration, of wanting to be at home—splatters outward. In finding the victim, Marion, standing before him, arousing his sexual interest, Norman-as-Mother senses an opportunity to act out. The identification is figured, post facto, as a jealous message from Mother, in whose guise Norman will wield the knife that will cut the naked and beautiful Marion down in her shower. Mother herself has been dead for ten years, of course, victim of strychnine poisoning: an apparent remorse suicide committed after finding out that her lover was married and so poisoning him. This was perhaps the man who, as Norman tells Marion, hatched the plan to build the motel.

We might be forgiven, upon learning about his and Mother's deaths relatively late in the narrative, that events did not transpire quite as reported. It will take the film's psychiatric denouement to provide the real narrative: father's early death, disturbed son, clinging widow, new man on the scene, sudden arousal of violence. In any event, after the slashing murder of Marion, Norman will rush down from the house (as "himself") to discover the body, bundle it into Marion's car, along with her stolen $40,000, and push the car into the swamp behind the property: the swamp of repressed guilt. Marion's body joins two others, both subjects of outstanding missing-persons cases. Another, in the figure of Milton Arbogast (Martin Balsam), the private investigator looking for Marion and the stolen money, will soon join them.

Marion arrives at the Bates Motel along a horizontal trajectory, as all motorists do. But she has been playing with vectors all along.[3] The first glimpse we have of her is in a Phoenix hotel room, supine on a bed, as a voyeuristic exterior-interior shot brings us into the room. Her own illicit lover, Sam Loomis (John Gavin), a divorced man from another town, looks down at her and smiles.[4] They are both partially dressed, but in clear defiance of the Hayes Code, Gavin is shirtless and Leigh is in sexy white underwear. They also lie on the same bed together. It is evident that they have just made love. The hotel is an old-fashioned downtown establishment, rather cheap as befits the nooner they are just finishing in place of eating lunch, and their room is some stories high, as a window shot of the city outside demonstrates. Blinds on the windows cast bars of horizontal shadows across the two lovers.

The situation is compromising and confused: they are debating whether to break off their affair, or whether to be "respectable." The implication is that they cannot afford to marry because Sam is crippled by alimony payments to his ex-wife. Nor can they carry on their sexual relationship in the open. "Oh, we can see each other," Marion says. "We can even have dinner, but respectably—in my house with my mother's picture on the mantel, and my sister helping me broil a big steak for three." But Sam has other appetites still in mind, in a film that will turn out to be all about conflicts of desire. "And after the steak, do we send sister to the movies? Turn mama's picture to the wall?"

Events accelerate immediately after she leaves Sam in the room, still without his shoes on. Marion is already conventionally "bad," given her hole-in-a-corner affair with Sam, but she gets worse when she decides to steal that $40,000 house payment from her employer and sneak off to (fictional) Fairvale, California—Sam's home. What she images will happen then is not clear: will they use the money to get married? To flee together? What is clear is that she is a poor candidate for criminal genius. She sleeps in her car, arousing police suspicion, then hurriedly changes cars—even as the same policeman is watching, with a good view of the new California licence plate. Her arrival at the Bates Motel is the result of a wrong turn and the rain of a "dirty night," as Norman will call it as she is signing in. The rest is, we now know, more or less inevitable.

Marion's murder, in which, according to Hitchcock, the phallic borrowed knife is never shown actually touching her wet flesh—film nerds claim two frames show direct contact—reduces her to the irremediable horizontal of death. Hitchcock's camera lingers on this destruction of the upright posture, this final act of horizontal resolution. The famous lingering shot where the shower drain, washing Marion's lifeblood away, resolves into Marion's death-surprised, wide-open eye, emphasizes her final posture, cheek mashed into the hard tile floor of the bathroom—a word that Norman found he could not utter when showing her the amenities of cabin number one.

But Norman is not finished. Harried by the private investigator Arbogast, Norman, now wearing a title crew neck sweater, becomes twitchy and evasive; also touchy about women. Did Marion perhaps fool him? "Let's put it this way," he tells the suavely insistent Arbogast, "She may have fooled me but she didn't fool Mother." No indeed. And Arbogast is next to come under the knife, assaulted at the top of the house's main staircase. Stabbed and about to die, we plunge backwards down the stairs with him in one of the film's signature shots. Investigation over.

But now Mother must be moved into the cellar of the house, in case more snoopy visitors should arrive. She does not want to leave the rococo lushness of her bedroom. "I will not hide in the fruit cellar!" we hear her exclaim. "Ha! You think I'm fruity, huh? I'm staying right here. This is my room." Note the tangle of connotation here: fruity can mean crazy (fruitcake), but it also means gay (a fruit); these meanings may subsequently clump in Norman, but then there is also, less obviously, the sense of ripeness or fecundity. Of course Norman is the fruit of Mother's loins. And Mother's grave-stolen body is preserved, like an old apple, in a state of desiccation. Žižek has postulated elsewhere that Norman's carrying of Mother from upstairs to the cellar, which we observe from overhead in the twin of the shot initiating the fatal attack on Arbogast, is a shift from superego to id, performed by a conflicted ego. Marion's sister Lila (Vera Miles) will find her in the fruit cellar, and there, in a struggle with Sam, now pretending to be married to Lila, Norman's Mother identity will be ripped off, wig and all. "I am Norma Bates!"

Lila will later marry Sam for real. And, in writer Robert Bloch's sequel to the original novel version of *Psycho* (1959), rather cinematically entitled *Psycho II* (1982) even though its plot bears little relation to the inferior film *Psycho II* (1983, d. Richard Franklin), Norman will escape from his mental institution disguised as a nun, travel to Fairvale, and murder Lila and Sam.[5] He will then continue on to Hollywood to wreak havoc on the film industry, which he suspects of portraying him unfairly and glamourizing violence. Studio executives at Universal Pictures hated the novel—at least according to Bloch—and he was not involved in the film of the same name.

1.4 Poetry

The psychiatrist who examines Norman at the film's end, and pronounces the narrative conclusion of the case, is a modernist poet. We understand modernism here not as a period or a school, still less a style, but rather as what critic Gabriel Josipovici has identified as "the coming into awareness by art of its precarious status and responsibilities, and therefore as something that will, from now on, always be with us. Seen this way, Modernism, I would suggest, becomes a response by artists to the 'disenchantment of the world' to which cultural historians have long been drawing our attention."[6] Compare this to Roland Barthes's famous remark: "to be modern is to know that which is no longer possible."

Norman is thus a case study in what is not possible: that is, meeting the genre expectations (as it were) of "appropriate" filial feelings or "normal" sexual relations. And so here, the psychiatrist offers a narrative alternative to the enchantment of psychosis. That is, he is present precisely to perform, in smoothly delivered and authoritative words, a narrative resolution of Norman's violence, a settling of accounts between vertical and horizontal. But the narrative admits elements of contingency or doubt even as it attempts to reassure the various anxieties now in play, especially about sexual identity.

The same kind of sequence occurs in at least one other Hitchcock film, *Spellbound* (1945; screenplay by, among others, Ben Hecht), where Gregory Peck's extended bout of mistaken identity, amnesia, and doubling is "explained" through backward reference to a childhood accident and the resulting trigger of vertical lines arranged in a horizontal row! In its use of the celebrated Salvador Dali dream sequence, *Spellbound* teeters awkwardly between an extended apology for psychoanalysis as "scientific" modernity par excellence, here represented by the glibly Freudian Dr. Alexander Brulov (Michael Chekhov), and a surreal modernist aesthetic that is wilder, less resolved. The dream, with its vertiginous topography and undulating surfaces, is the site of this conflict.

The psychiatrist in *Psycho*, Dr. Fred Richmond, is played by Simon Oakland, a character actor best known for his depictions of gangsters, bosses, and thugs. Here, his rugged physiognomy, well-cut suit and brilliantined hair contain and deploy tensions of aggression and control. He is here to send a message to the audience of the film as well as to the assembled authorities and affected figures within the film. The message is simple: "Norman Bates no longer exists."

The simplicity is deceptive, however, as shown by the deliberate, nearly parodic jargon about split personalities, tangles of mutual jealousy, and repression that follows. The latent content (to use the Freudian term) is therefore more complicated: Norman is not, contrary to one policeman's suggestion, a transvestite. "A man who dresses in women's clothing in order to achieve a sexual change or satisfaction is a transvestite," Richmond explains. "But in Norman's case, he was simply doing everything possible to keep alive the illusion of his mother being alive. And when reality came too close, when danger or desire threatened that illusion . . . he dressed up, even to a cheap wig he bought. He'd walk about the house, sit in her chair, speak in her voice. He tried to be his mother. And, uh, now he is." He turns to Marion's sister, Lila, and sums up: "Now that's what I meant when I said I got the story from the mother. You see, when the mind houses two personalities, there's always a conflict, a battle. In Norman's case, the battle is over—and the dominant personality has won." His hermeneutic work done, Richmond then shakes loose a cigarette from the pack in his pocket.

Don't fear the psycho, at least he is not a cross-dresser! But it is Mother who, appropriately, has the last word—even if spoken from within the vaults of Norman's disturbed mind, in Virginia Gregg's superb (uncredited) voice-over, and repeating a line spoken earlier by Norman about Mother's harmlessness. "They'll put him away now, as I should have years ago. He was always bad. And in the end he intended to tell them I killed those girls and that man. As if I could do anything but just sit and stare like one of his stuffed birds. Oh, they know I can't even move a finger and I won't. I'll just sit here and be quiet just in case they do . . . suspect me. They're probably watching me. Well, let them. Let them see what kind of a person I am." He notices a fly crawling on his limp right hand. "I'm not even going to swat that fly. I hope they are watching . . . they'll see. They'll see and they'll know, and they'll say, 'Why, she wouldn't even harm a fly'." This last line intoned as Perkins lifts his head and smiles, looking directly at the viewer: a minuscule fourth-wall breach that chills the blood.

Final shot: Marion's car, still with the stolen money folded in a newspaper in its trunk, is recovered from the swamp behind the motel. Return of the repressed, with a heavy towing chain. Recalling the film's title sequence, the frame now dissolves into a series of horizontal bars, tearing the picture into strips, pulling it to shreds on either side of blankness . . .

2. Vertical

2.1 A-spire

Vertical reach is the premodern gesture par excellence: the church spire, the Tower of Babel, the surveillance tower, the tactical dominance of being above. Wider field of vision means wider field of fire. Religion and war share the same aspiration: to rise above. Architecture's history is, for the most part, a story of ascension: columns, lintels, arches, domes, gothic arches, groins. The ruins of these ancient achievements of uprightness retain their poignancy; in fact, they acquire that poignancy in ruin. "Perhaps the simplest lesson of antiquity is that, after a time, anything vertical—Doric, Ionic, Corinthian, whatever—commands attention," Geoff Dyer writes: "Ultimately, though, the lure of the horizontal will always prove irresistible. That's why the sight of the ancient vertical is always enhanced by a backdrop horizon of sky and sea. From their point of view—the point of view of sea and sky—[the ruin] was still in the early stages of a career of ruination which would end ultimately as desert, when the horizon would be undisturbed by any vestige of the vertical: the final triumph of space over time."[7]

To build is to defy the horizon, to create space within time. And this vertical aspiration is of course encoded in the human body itself, another site of uprightness destined for eventual ruination to the horizontal. The narrator of Russell Hoban's post-apocalyptic novel *Riddley Walker* (1980), in which Canterbury Cathedral has been destroyed by bombs but remains a stone forest of tremendous power, notes often the good feeling one has when coming into a declivity from higher ground. The primate's instinctive sense of tactical advantage. Building high, including the very cathedral that has been reduced to rubble, is the concrete manifestation of that instinct. Close to God, closer to judgment, closer to dominance.

But the desire to dominate from above is doomed to failure, not least because of the limitations of singular embodiment. The individual cannot encompass the whole, no matter how high he or she rises from the ground. In the debased English of the moments after apocalypse, Riddley muses on the matter this way: "If you cud even jus see 1 thing clear the woal of whats in it you cud see every thing clear. But you never wil get to see the woal of any thing youre all ways in the middl of it living it or moving thru it. Never mynd."[8] Never mind, sure—one must get on with life, living it and moving through it—but Riddley is reflective enough to know, in a primitive way, that the wish to see just one thing whole is what makes him human.

We keep trying.

2.2 Phallus

The skyscraper is not itself a modern form, but rather the transitional form dominating the endgame of premodernism. The first skyscrapers—in Manhattan, in Chicago—tried to solve the problem of density by creating height: vertical capacity. They did this with two essential technological advances: tempered steel and the elevator. Without either of these enabling conditions there can be no skyscrapers, first because the vertebrate interior structure of the very tall building remains impossible, limited by the crustacean, load-bearing capacity of exterior wall; and second because normal humans cannot routinely ascend more than five or six stories without mechanical help.

The resulting towers—paradigmatically, the Empire State Building, the Chrysler Building—resemble syringes, or rocket ships, or (of course) phalluses. Mankind and technology held erect. The thrusting skyscraper invites ridicule, perhaps. But its rigid longing is not despicable or foolish; it is understandable, even in its way admirable, however destined for mockery. Temples of the secular age—later versions to prove all too vulnerable, as we sadly know, to the slicing horizontal vectors of terror in the form of the hijacked airliner, the vehicle of transportation now weaponized.

2.3 LEGO

The god's-eye view is essentially childish. That is why children enjoy playing with models, miniatures, tiny representations of larger material realities: cars, buildings, airplanes. That is why there is LEGO. I mean old-style LEGO, where the small palette of uniform shapes were meant to be made into anything the player imagined; new-style branded LEGO, with its elaborate *Star Wars* vehicles and precise architectural renderings of famous buildings, has reduced itself to the status of by-the-numbers kit, rather than a field of open possibility. (There is now, however, the possibility of what artist Kim Adams calls *kit-bashing*: mixing and matching parts from various kits, against their stated instructions, to create something altogether new. Hybrid forms, monstrous and uncanny by definition because of their evident relation to the normal forms they are not, which they refuse.)

3. Horizontal

3.1 Stack

The essential form of modernism in architecture is horizontal: the cantilevered deck; the sleek, flattened line; the slab. There are very tall modern buildings, but their verticality is different—is a secondary, merely emergent property—from the soaring (a)spires of the premodern endgame. Ludwig Mies van der Rohe's Seagram Building in Manhattan, a bronzed and floating form so characteristically modern that it defines the so-called International Style and hence is replicated everywhere (Montreal, Toronto), is not really a tower at all. It does not seek to scrape the sky. It is, instead, a vertical stack of horizontals that together create a slab. It is a horizontal plane set sideways to the ground, not a vertical needle.

Look at the lobby of the Seagram, a glassed-in living room with the outside plaza setting off its ingenious foundation, which hollows out its join with the earth rather than emphasizing it, as the Empire State does, and you will feel the horizontal modern and its associated freedom. The Empire State is chthonic: made of earthly materials, especially the lovely cladding of Indiana limestone, it rises from the earth. The Seagram refuses the earth. It floats. The ground floor of the Seagram is not even a floor; it is empty volume, negative space. Squint and you will forget the heavy stories of stacked horizontals above you and imagine you are in Philip Johnson's Glass House in New Canaan, Connecticut.

3.2 Houses

The house, not the office building, is actually the signature modernist form. Le Corbusier's Villa Savoye. Frank Lloyd Wright's Fallingwater in Mill Run, Pennsylvania—still in transition with his organic roots but showcasing the massing of horizontal planes that will be his legacy, the prairie-style house elevated to conceptual perfection. The Glass House. Mies van der Rohe's own Farnsworth House in Plano, Illinois, is the most perfect realization of the modern aesthetic left to human view. It has no peer—though both it and Fallingwater may be built from a kit in LEGO.

3.3 Motels

The motel is the modernist house democratized. It is always a horizontal deployment of temporary personal spaces, arranged alongside the dominant horizontal line of the twentieth century, the car-generated highway. The two- or three-storey motel is a stack in the same manner as the Seagram Building, a stilted slab. It is never a hotel. The motor court accommodates the vehicles that brought it here, that will take us away. The swimming pool may even be in the middle of the same motor court, a sort of oasis of leisure precariously placed next to the highway.

Edward Hopper's painting *Western Motel* (1957) is the final aesthetic comment on modernism—and incidentally creates a miniature anxiety-of-influence loop, since the alleged inspiration for the Bates family home was Hopper's earlier gothic work, *The House by the Railroad* (1925). In *Western Motel*, qualities of meditative despair, the stillness of the parked car and the solitary figure ever implying a kind of restless movement, a stalled desire, open the way for postmodern thought. Notice the female figure's oddly strained posture, as if she were about to spring up. Her fixed gaze is apprehensive, perhaps slightly accusatory, but it refuses any final interpretation. The bag is packed, whether in arrival or departure it is impossible to say. The exterior landscape confesses nothing. We are the end of something, the beginning of something else. Go west . . .

3.4 Grid

But before the postmodern there is the grid. The grid is the ultimate modernist reconciliation of vectors. Mondrian is of course the grid's artist-in-residence. ("He gravitated towards the grid," Josipovici remarks, "because the grid implies that pictures have no beginnings and no ends, and no heroic or bucolic drama either, unless it is a factitious one introduced by the artist."[9]) The 1811 Commissioner's Plan imposed the grid, at least virtually, on the entire land mass of the United States. In practice it was Manhattan that achieved the only pure rectilinear realization, obliterating the confusions of Five Points and other messy, European-style convergences of streets. Even in Manhattan, though, the grid goes wonky at the edges and bottom of the sprawling island borough. Mini-grids are observable, lining up with the river's edge rather than the dominant street-avenue arrangement. The joins at the edges are faultlines rather than sutures: observe the erratic progress of West Fourth Street as it exits the logic of the grid and ambles slantwise toward the Hudson.

The grid runs north by northwest, in short; its apparent reconciliation of vectors is actually the imposition of a certain acquisitive madness, the mania for parcelling and control, on finally unruly topography: the land mass will always push back.[10] Recall that the opening credits for *Psycho*, as with its end, are executed with a long series of vertical and horizontal bars playing across the screen. They slice up the frame, sometimes the names themselves, but never resolve into a grid. It is as if they are fighting for visual supremacy in the open space of the visual field created by the camera. The title sequence for *North by Northwest* (1959), meanwhile, is executed as an apparently ordinary grid of lines that create spaces and—in a trademark sequence—resolve themselves into the glass-curtain windows on the side of a Madison Avenue office tower.

4. Celebration

4.1 Simulacrum

"In modernist works like *Psycho*, this split is still visible, while the main goal of today's postmodern architecture is to obfuscate it. Suffice it to recall 'new urbanism,' with its return to small family houses in small towns, with front porches, recreating the cozy atmosphere of the local community; clearly this is a case of architecture as ideology at its purest, providing an imaginary (although 'real,' materialized in the actual disposition of houses) solution to a real social deadlock that has nothing to do with architecture and all to do with late capitalist dynamics."[11]

The simulacral "authentic" is postmodern in the pejorative sense, of course. Consider the culmination of New Urbanism in the planned community of Celebration, Florida, built by the Walt Disney Corporation. Celebration, like its cinematic realization in *The Truman Show* (1998, d. Peter Weir)—actually filmed at another master-planned new urbanism enclave, Seaside, Florida—is a fake that is more watched than inhabited, a citation rather than a real place: a fact replicated explicitly in the present text, implicitly in Žižek's (which doesn't name it).[12] Celebration is, in a sense, always already Disneyfied. As in *The Truman Show*, the nested realities of life in the fake town are peeled back under the sign of suspicion and the deterioration of idiot happiness. But unlike the film, the "real" Celebration is not, finally, a spectacle with a determinate, if somewhat godlike director. (In the film this role is played by a smoothly creepy Ed Harris, sporting an intellectual's beret and patter of sub-Baudrillardian bafflegab.)

4.2 World

In short, the "real" Celebration offers no apocalyptic release on the order of the one enjoyed by Truman (Jim Carrey) who is able, literally, to climb out of his world at that world's edge. Thus, as so often, the cinematic postmodern is revealed as in fact a reactionary modern: a Cartesian return to the baseline of the real. Compare the *Matrix* film franchise on this point, especially its first installment, *The Matrix* (1999, d. Andy and Larry Wachowski). Although Baudrillardian traces are everywhere present, including a cameo appearance of one of his books, which is used as a hiding place—*Simulacra and Simulation*, here appearing as the book that is no book—the film's epistemology is, in the end, naively realist.

There is only one world-ending reveal, the scales of deception torn away once and for all. The character Morpheus (Laurence Fishburne) will intone in dread language what sounds like a postmodern sentiment— "Welcome to the real world!"—but all he really means is that reality kind of sucks compared to the dream from which Neo (Keanu Reeves) has just awoken. Worse still, both *The Truman Show* and *The Matrix* collapse into a form of fuzzy Christian, or at least theist, denouement.

The more troubling insight, namely that the world of deception does not end, that there is no possible reveal, is left untouched. But this is, of course, cinema, not reality. The symbolic order, as so often, works to repress the real, not to exhibit it.

4.3 Down

If Celebration, Seaside and other new-urbanist planned communities are clear examples of architecture as ideology, offering an imaginary solution to a real social problem, we have to go back one step in their development to see that problem clearly. Žižek merely notes the "late capitalism dynamics" in play here, but let us be more specific and name two concrete elements within those dynamics: the automobile and the single-family dwelling. Together these create the enabling conditions of the post-Second World War housing boom and the resulting exurban sprawl for which New Urbanism is seen as an alternative. In fact it is nothing but an affirmation of those conditions.

Again, the clearest view may be from above. Ross Racine's computer-generated artworks of imaginary suburban street plans, conceived as precisely ninety-degrees vertical, and showing no people or cars except by implication—the streets are arrayed this way precisely because of the people we cannot see and the cars which convey them from place to place—these images work to reverse the causal relations of the architecture on display. That is, we might say that the cars made us build the houses, and lay out the streets, in this manner. It is the cars who dwell here, not the people.

The car creates the motel. Marion changes cars while in flight from the scene of her crime, in one of the least successful fugitive actions on film. *Psycho* actually has two uncanny endings: Norman's final identification with Mother, and the dragging of the hidden car—the proof of Marion's absence—from the swamp behind her house, playing behind the final credits.

5. Frank

5.1 Crumple

A more ambiguous case of the same antagonism is the work of Frank Gehry [claims Žižek]. Why is he so popular, a true cult figure? He takes as his basis one of the two poles of the antagonism, either the old-fashioned family house or a modernist concrete-and-glass building, and then either submits it to a kind of cubist anamorphic distortion (curved angles of walls and buildings, etc.) or combines the old family home with a modernist supplement, in which case, as Fredric Jameson has pointed out, the focal point is the place (the room) at the intersection of the two spaces. In short, is Gehry not doing in architecture what the Caduveo Indians (in Claude Lévi-Strauss's magnificent description from his *Les Tristes Tropiques*) were trying to achieve with their tattooed faces: to resolve through a symbolic act the 'real' of social antagonism by constructing a utopian solution, a meditation between opposites?[13]

The mediation is fractal: it involves crumpled planes and unnerving angles, enabled by a design program that extends architectural possibility beyond the realm of flat, i.e., pencil-and-paper, design. *The Simpsons* episode including Gehry—he is brought in to design a "signature" concert hall in Springfield—shows him taking inspiration from a piece of crumpled paper on the sidewalk. The paper is rubbish, cast-off flatness which, in rejection, achieves dimension. The shot demonstrating the moment of inspiration is significantly vertical: the point of view is from sidewalk level, looking up at the giant figure of the designing man.

The concert hall, which closely resembles Gehry's design for the Walt Disney Concert Hall in Los Angeles, goes bankrupt on its first night. The building is acquired by Montgomery Burns, who repurposes the form as a prison. The resulting site of carceral normativity has an Escheresque resonance: a place to drive men mad. .

Gehry himself, meanwhile, has achieved the notable postmodern status of having been portrayed in cartoon on television. This form of celebrity enacts its own kind of resolution of the modern identity quest. Who is Frank Gehry? He is someone who has "appeared" on *The Simpsons*.

5.2 Dance

Just as often as the crumpled-paper, melted-skyscraper motif usually deployed on a singular site all its own, Gehry imposes a schizoid join with existing buildings or streetscapes. Consider the Rasin Building (or Dancing House) in Prague, the Starwood Hotel (Hotel Marqués de Riscal) in Rioja, the Peter B. Lewis Building at Case Western Reserve University in Cleveland, and the MIT Building in Cambridge, Massachusetts—four examples of the "dancing room" at the confused heart of his version of post-modernism. These buildings do not resolve; they shimmer and wobble.

5.3 Brain

"So here is my final hypothesis: if the Bates Motel were to be built by Gehry, directly combining the old mother's house and the flat, modern motel into a new hybrid entity, there would be no need for Norman to kill his victims, since he would have been relieved of the unbearable tension that compels him to run between the two places—he would have a place of meditation between the two extremes."[14]

The Lou Ruvo Center for Brain Health, in Las Vegas, may be this very structure. Norman has a fear of institutions, as we know from that late-night conversation with Marion over sandwiches. She suggested that perhaps he needed friends, or to get away from the dead-end motel. "A boy's best friend is his mother," Norman had replied, still in his sweet filial mood. But when Marion suggests that perhaps Mother would be better off "someplace" other than the house, Norman hardened into anger and a mist of vague threat descended on the creepy parlour. "You mean an institution? A madhouse? People always call a madhouse 'someplace,' don't they? Put her in 'someplace' . . . Have you ever seen the inside of one of those places? The laughing, and the tears, and the cruel eyes studying you? My mother there? Oh, but she's harmless! She's as harmless as one of those stuffed birds!"

Absolutely.

6. Falling

6.1 Fall

As we have seen, to fall is to lose, or surrender, uprightness. From Tolstoy's *The Death of Ivan Ilyich*: "Once when mounting a step-ladder to show the upholsterers, who did not understand, how he wanted the hangings draped, he made a false step and slipped, but being a strong and agile man he clung on and only knocked his side against the knob of the window frame. The bruised place was painful but the pain soon passed and he felt particularly bright and well just then." Not quite a fall, just a slip. Now and then Ivan, still going about his bourgeois business as an ambitious magistrate, felt "a queer taste in his mouth" or some "discomfort in his left side." But the mysterious injury worsens and nothing helps. He is dying, and for such a stupid reason too. Ivan Ilyich: victim of home decorating.

"Maybe I did not live as I ought to have done," Ivan thinks near the end. "But how could that be, when I did everything properly?" Tolstoy's moralism is heavy-handed—decorum and decorating equal death—but Ivan's anguish is vivid. He recalls a syllogism he learned as a law student, from Kiesewetter's *Logic*: "Caius is a man, men are mortal, therefore Caius is mortal." This, he notes, "had always seemed to him correct as applied to Caius, but certainly not as applied to himself."

In the end, we all fall down.

6.2 Sleep

Sleep is the other *petite morte*, the (usually) voluntary surrender of the upright posture into repose, to knit up what the poet called "the raveled sleeve of care."

It is mostly done in private—indeed, as sociologist Norbert Elias has suggested, the construction of the personal sleeping chamber, the individual bedroom, out of the common space of the dormitory or kinship hall, is the clearest material sign of modernity and the rising importance of the private individual.[15]

Thus to sleep in public is now, for us, a crime (the vagrant sleeping in a park), a radical gesture (a "sleep-in" protest) or else an embarrassment (dozing off during a musical performance or lecture). Christopher Alexander et al., in the monumental treatise on urbanism, *A Pattern Language*, offer this claim: "It is the mark of success in a park, public lobby or a porch, when people come there and fall asleep. In a society which nurtures people and fosters trust, the fact that people sometimes want to sleep in public is the most natural thing in the world." But of course this natural thing is mostly prohibited or disapproved. "In our society, sleeping in public, like loitering, is thought of as an act for criminals and the destitute. In our world, when homeless people start sleeping on public benches or in public buildings, upright citizens get nervous and the police soon restore 'public order.'"[16]

Note that the offended citizens are upright. The police acting on their complaint are the agents of public order. Norms of verticality are restored. Rest easy, citizens; just don't fall asleep—the way Marion did in her replacement car, only to be awakened and questioned by a stone-faced highway patrolman.

6.3 Master

The standard motel room is a simulacrum of what is sometimes called, in a home, the "master" bedroom. We know what goes on here: hetero-normative couples "sleep with" each other! But note just one specific resonance: in Hegel's dialectic of master and slave, the warring con-sciousnesses are preoccupied with bringing the other to his knees. In other words, with destroying the *gegenständlich* otherness of the vertical.

7. Fate

7.1 Geography

In "Network Theory, Plot Analysis," Franco Moretti dismantles the very idea of modernism, and hence of the modern poet, by reducing litera-ture to vectors of social relation, clustered not in plots but in networks. The correctness or interest of this claim is not our present concern. Instead, note this apparently offhand remark, made after Moretti notes the various peripheral characters in Hamlet indicate the world outside of Elsinore Castle: "These centrifugal threads—'tendrils,' as they are sometimes called—contribute to the uncanny feeling that Elsinore is just the tip of the tragic iceberg: geography as the hidden dimension of fate, like genealogy in Greek tragedy. Genealogy, vertical, rooted in myth; geography, horizontal, in something like the nascent European state system."[17]

Note that this feeling is precisely uncanny. The tragedy of Hamlet is a node in a larger network of emergent state intrigue in something called Europe. That network is, significantly, horizontal. The action at Elsinore is transitional, since it still involves family succession and adul-tery, if not incest or patricide. But the essence of the tragedy is not really genealogical or (still less) Oedipal; it is political. Sovereign succession, not blood relation, is the heart of the matter.

7.2 *Erfurt*

Moretti continues: "I may be exaggerating here, projecting onto the periphery of this diagram Napoleon's words at Erfurt on politics as the fate of the moderns. But Horatio's space—ambassadors, messengers, sentinels, talk of foreign wars, and of course the transfer of sovereignty at the end—all this announces what will soon be called, not Court, but State."[18] In other words, Hamlet's tragedy is that he is yesterday's man. Fortinbras is the harbinger of the modern, horizontal, political reality that has come.

As is well known, Napoleon's remark at Erfurt was made to Goethe, who met the emperor on October 2, 1808. By Goethe's own rather fawning account, it was a stiff conference in which Napoleon, after the manner of the rich and powerful confronted by an artist, proceeded to school Goethe in literary criticism. After meekly accepting a criticism of his own youthful *Stürm und Drang* sensation, *The Sorrows of Young Werther* (1774), which Napoleon claimed to find "unnatural" in places, Goethe ventures a defence of poetic licence: "But," I added, "a poet can be excused for taking refuge in an artifice which is hard to spot, when he wants to produce specific effects which cannot be created simply and naturally. The emperor seemed to agree with me; he returned to drama and made some very sensible remarks, remarks which could only have come from someone who had observed the tragic stage with a great deal of attention—such as a criminal judge might do—someone who felt very deeply how far French theatre had strayed from the natural and true."

Then we get to the crux: "He went on to talk about destiny plays, criticizing them. They belonged to the dark ages. 'Why these days do they keep giving us destiny?' he said. 'There's no destiny, only politics.'"[19]

The more famous version of the claim is expressed this way: *There is no fate but politics.* That is, on the current grid, the modern horizontal triumphs in the comprehensive reduction of life to the political. The statement is almost palinodic: there is no fate at all, only politics. Fate—the assumption that human outcomes are determined by the gods, inescapable and cruel, rather than by human will as it meets the contingencies of the world—is over. Thus, once again, a version of the disenchantment of the world that is the necessary condition of modernism.

Goethe's mild sycophancy paid off. The journal entry concludes this way: "The fourteenth. I received the Cross of the Légion d'Honneur."

7.3 Fate

The phrase "no fate" is a looping trope in the *Terminator* film and television franchise. Sarah Connor (Linda Hamilton) carves the words on a picnic table in *Terminator 2: Judgment Day* (1991, d. James Cameron). Her son is John Connor (Edward Furlong), the destined future leader of the human rebels who will battle the self-aware machines led by SkyNet, which has triggered a nuclear apocalypse on earth. John Connor's father, Kyle Reese (played by Michael Biehn in the first film), was sent back in time to warn Sarah of the imminent dangers—sent, indeed, by his beloved commander, John Connor.

John Connor, like the phrase itself, is trapped in a temporal loop. The young John, his mother now missing after an escape from a psychiatric hospital, sees the knife-carved words and recalls their origin:

> John Connor: No fate . . . No fate but what we make . . . My father taught me this . . . I mean, I made him memorize it as a message to HER . . . Never mind. Okay, the whole thing goes, "The future is not set. There is no fate but what we make for ourselves."
>
> Terminator: She intends to change the future.
>
> John Connor: Yeah, I guess. (shouting) Oh, shit!
>
> Terminator: Dyson.
>
> John Connor: Yeah, it's gotta be . . . Myles Dyson. She's gonna blow him away!

Myles Dyson (Joe Morton) is a hapless computer engineer busily enabling the emergent intelligence that will become SkyNet (presumably named in homage to Freeman Dyson, the former Bomber Command intelligence officer who became a distinguished physicist and outspoken opponent of nuclear weapons). Sarah Connor hopes that killing Dyson will avert the future, since it is not destined.

The Terminator to which John speaks here is the second, "good" Terminator (Arnold Schwarzenegger). Whereas in *The Terminator* (1984, d. James Cameron) he had come to kill Sarah, and so render John's existence impossible, here he is present to protect John from an even more advanced Terminator, the T-1000 (Robert Patrick, who is made of liquid metal that can assume any form). The Terminator, too, is trapped in a temporal loop. And so, significantly, is Norman Bates: he must keep on killing in order to manage the unresolved energy of his entrapment in bondage to Mother. There is no (sexual) release for Norman. He is fated to be a Terminator.

There is no fate but what we make. Nevertheless, some of us have no future, only an eternal return of the repressed.

7.4 L'avenir

The temporal tangles, the good and bad Terminators, the incessant dismantling of the future as a constructed reality, all suggest the end of *le futur*, understood as the specific future to which we turn our imaginations, our hopes, and our fears. We are left, instead, with *l'avenir*: what is to come. Walter Benjamin suggests that the human condition is one of *schicksalsverfallenheit*—inescapable submission to fate—induces melancholy. The Terminators suggest that submission may actually trigger a release, into the unconditioned future.

8. Uncanny

8.1 Heim

I am not at home. I am a monster to myself. The truly uncanny is not the doll or zombie but the *döppelganger*—the other me in the mirror, in the darkness of the mind.

Norman cannot contain himself.

8.2 Monster

All monsters are uncanny. Even the humanized Terminator remains creepy. Deep in the uncanny valley, past where doubles are cute or functional and become creepy, lies the reanimated human body or ambulatory human corpse: the zombie and the mummy. In these various undead figures we observe that the cessation of desire, which is death, figured as the final horizontal, has been repurposed, reanimated as relentless and endless desire—that is, figured as the never-ending vertical. This, too, is a potentially endless loop of identity and doubleness: recall the sheriff in *Psycho* saying: "If the woman up there is Mrs. Bates, who's that woman buried out in Greenlawn Cemetery?" Indeed, who?

Film, because it uses real objects in the world to create a false double, is by definition an uncanny medium, a zombie entertainment.[20]

8.3 Fast

"All manner of meanings have been and continue to be plastered on the zombie," critic James Parker notes. "Much can be made of him, because he makes so little of himself. He is the consumer, the mob, the Other, the proletariat, the weight of life, the dead soul. He is too many e-mails in your inbox, a kind of cosmic spam. He is everything rejected and inexpugnable. He comes back, he comes back, feebly and unstoppably, and as he drags you down, a fatal lethargy overtakes you."[21] Yes.

The slow zombie is canonical. "His slowness is a proverb, of course: his museum-goer's shuffle, his hospital plod," Parker writes. "Plus he's a wobbler: the shortest path between two points is seldom the one he takes." But this is the classical zombie, the staggering undead of modern apocalypse. The postmodern zombie is fast, an upgrade that is not a gain. In fact, the fast zombie may be considered an example of what the Germans call *schlimmbesserung*: the bad improvement.[22] In contrast to the original George Romero classics, these films feature the so-called fast zombie, which can move with the speed of a cheetah and materialize in seconds to begin a feast of the victim's brains.

But watching these speedy undead humans obliterates almost everything that is enjoyable about the original zombie movies: not just the agonizing chase scenes, with zombies slowly closing in on hapless, stumbling humans, but also the curious pathos of the slow zombies, their ululating cries of hunger and pain as they shuffle out of the cemetery and into our lives. The zombies are undead for a reason. Hell is full, they cannot rest, they have to eat brains! Fast zombies are just a generalized threat; slow zombies are individuals.

Fast or slow, zombies are not just speechless, they are cisgendered: no matter what their anatomy, they do not have fixed gender identity. They are a walking (staggering) virus. (In *The Matrix* the roles are reversed: Agent Smith (Hugo Weaving) sees humans as the virus; they disgust him.) They don't need to mate in order to reproduce, they just need to consume the bodies of other selves, of the sort they once were. Why, after all, do zombies eat us rather than the animal species that we blithely consume on a daily basis? Because we consume our selves, the zombie is the uncanny perfection of the self. Zombies are the self-infection of consumption run riot, spreading like the inexorable disease it is. A zombie outbreak will wreak destruction on human civilization, ironically as the highest expression of that civilization. Hence the traditional anti-capitalist zombie film, such as both versions of *Dawn of the Dead* (1978, d. George Romero, slow zombies; and 2004, d. Zack Snyder, fast zombies) that plays out the endgame in a shopping mall.[23]

Hurry! Time—and space for words—is short!

9. "Democracy"

9.1 Opaque

There is a political argument in these remarks, but it lurks like a mummy, staggers like a slow zombie—and may have to be found more fully developed elsewhere in the present book. 2011's Arab Spring and Occupy Wall Street—examples of so-called "horizontal" left politics, politics without leaders, hierarchies, or specific programs—were deployed under the sign of "democracy."[24] But democracy here functions as an opaque signifier: it means everything and nothing. That is its possibility, and its constraint.

9.2 Capital

Freud, in the essay on "The Uncanny" ("Das Unheimliche," 1919): "The negative prefix *un-* is the indicator of repression."[25] Zombies are, precisely, the un-dead. On this logic, capitalizing the phrases "Arab Spring" and "Occupy Wall Street" is to enact a return of the repressed, as if the label were able to convey meaning and impact. An avoidance ritual.

9.3 Come

All is not lost, however. This simply means that the only democracy is the democracy to come: seek *l'avenir* rather than *le futur*, what is to come rather than what is fixed in a bulldozing block of temporality.

10. Fugitive

10.1 Flight

Make yourself unavailable, flee consumption, even your own consumption of yourself.

10.2 Ge-stell

Enframing, as Heidegger calls it in "The Question Concerning Technology," is the enemy. You are not raw material or human resources. It is enough to know SkyNet wants you to think that you are. Resistance is not futile.

10.3 Slow

We finish quickly now in order to then go slowly. "This is how philosophers should greet each other," Wittgenstein says: "Take your time!" Also: "In philosophy the winner of the race is the one who can run most slowly. Or: the one who gets there last."[26]

Embrace idleness and repose. Lie down. Take a load off. Occupy.

11. Excess

11.1 Over

Our argument now goes to eleven: we are in a condition of excess. Excess text, excess thought, the thought of excess. The self of the modern condition is overdetermined, excessive, consumptive.

11. 2 Trans

Have we traversed the first uncanny valley and entered the second, the region of a trans-human future, a post-human identity? Or is this too much to claim? Trans-human identity is that which the other gives me, however. It was ever thus. This is not about technology but, rather, the conditions of selfhood. In the premodern world, necessity's despair was to lack possibility. The modern condition is thus one in which the poles are reversed: possibility's despair is to lack necessity. The tyranny of choice.[27]

11.3 Gift

Is it perhaps the postmodern condition, then, to reject this dichotomy between possibility and necessity, and so to dissipate the conflict, the dislocations of self, presumed by it? That dissipation of antic seeking-after-self may be the gift of horizontal and vertical when they are allowed to dance or crumple together. The excess of the gift is the unresolved remainder, what will not surrender to resolution in the symbolic order. The gift is precisely what is, and remains, unconditioned. It is always to come.

Not the promise of happiness, but the promise of a selfhood that Norman could not find in the house or the motel: embodied consciousness, comfortable in its own skin, untroubled by desire.

This, my friends, is the end.

Notes

1 Slavoj Žižek, *Enjoy Your Symptom! Jacques Lacan in Hollywood and Out* (first ed. Routledge, 1991; rev. second ed. Routledge Classics, 2001), 241.

2 Ibid., 241.

3 My thanks to Robert Nichols for discussion on this and other points in this section of the paper.

4 The name Samuel Loomis will later be attached, in deliberate homage to *Psycho*, to the psychiatrist character (Donald Pleasance) who tries to combat escaped serial killer Michael Myers in the Halloween slasher-movie franchise.

5 In the film sequel, which again starred Anthony Perkins as Norman and included Vera Miles once more as Lila, Norman is released after two decades of institutionalization and attempts to live a normal life. Soon, however, messages from Mother begin to appear. And then it gets complicated.

6 Gabriel Josipovici, "The Oracles Are Silent," in *What Ever Happened to Modernism?* (Yale, 2010), 11.

7 Geoff Dyer, "Leptis Magna," in *Yoga For People Who Can't Be Bothered To Do It* (Abacus Books, 2003), 193.

8 Russell Hoban, *Riddley Walker* (Jonathan Cape, 1980), 186. Images and reflections on oneness pervade the novel, which is driven by the destruction when the human desire for "clevverness" pulled the atom in two, creating the apocalypse now known as "the 1 Big 1." Hoban's inventive fracturing of language is an inspired realization of the meaning's fragility.

9 *What Ever Happened to Modernism?*, 140.

10 I discuss this point at greater length in Kingwell, *Concrete Reveries: Consciousness and the City* (Viking, 2008), passim. Robert Nichols tells me that, on the Canadian prairies, survey errors are concretely manifest in straight roads that juke left or right for no apparent reason, correcting to the true compass line.

11 *Enjoy Your Symptom!*, 241-2.

12 The point naturally calls for a specific citation itself. See Andrew Ross, *The Celebration Chronicles: Life, Liberty and the Pursuit of Property Values in Disney's New Town* (Ballantine, 1999). One notable feature of Ross's work is that he, at the time a scholar celebrated as a tricksterish postmodern poster boy, writes of the town with unironic sincerity and warmth.

13 *Enjoy Your Symptom!*, 242.

14 Ibid., 242.

15 See Norbert Elias, *The Civilizing Process* [Über den Prozess der Zivilisation], trans. Edmund Jephcott, (Urizen, 1978-82; orig. 1939).

16 See Christopher Alexander, Sara Ishikawa, and Murray Silverstein, "On Sleeping in Public," Sec. 94 of *A Pattern Language: Towns, Buildings, Construction* (Oxford, 1977).

17 Franco Moretti, "Network Theory, Plot Analysis," *New Left Review* 68 (March-April 2011); also published online at *litlab.stanford.edu/LiteraryLabPamphlet2.pdf*. Quotation is at p. 6.

18 Ibid., 7.

19 Johann Wolfgang von Goethe, *Mélanges*, Jacques Porchat, trans. (Hachette, 1874), *Annales de 1749–1822* ‡ 1822, 307-309.

20 There are exceptions (computer-generated films, for example). For more on this argument see Stephen Mulhall, *On Film* (Routledge, 2nd ed. 2008); also Mark Kingwell, "Beyond the Uncanny Valley of the Dolls," *Descant* 42:1 (Spring 2011): 186-98; reprinted in *Unruly Voices* (Biblioasis, 2012).

21 James Parker, "Our Zombies, Ourselves," *Atlantic Monthly* (April 2011).

22 Other examples: the VHS videocassette, the automatic transmission, polyester shirts, artificial football turf, the luxury VW Beetle, oversized tennis racquets, the aluminum baseball bat, the designated-hitter rule, and global capitalism.

23 Canadian researchers, modelling rates of infection and difficulty of eradication, determined in 2009 that an actual zombie attack would indeed destroy human societies in a very short time unless the counter-measures were swift and decisive. Significantly, they generated their models based on the traditional slow zombie, which is presumably easier to kill; an attack of fast zombies would likely be too virulent to counter. See P. Munz, I. Hudea, J. Imad and R. J. Smith? [the punctuation is part of his proper name], "When Zombies Attack! Mathematical Modelling of an Outbreak of Zombie Infection," in Jean Michel Tchuenche and C. Chiyaka, eds., *Infectious Diseases Modelling Research Progress* (Nova, 2011), 133-50. Small uncanny foot-footnote: Nova Publishers has been flagged as a vanity or otherwise bogus press. An academic zombie, in fact.

24 For an account of the vertical/horizontal in the Occupy movement, see Mattathias Schwartz, "Pre-Occupied: The origins and future of Occupy Wall Street," *The New Yorker*, November 28, 2011. "At times," Schwartz writes, "horizontalism can feel like utopian theatre. Its greatest invention is the 'people's mike,' which starts when someone shouts, 'Mike check!' Then the crowd shouts, 'Mike check!,' and then phrases (phrases!) are transmitted (are transmitted!) through mass chanting (through mass chanting!). In the same way that poker ritualizes capitalism and North Korea's mass games ritualize totalitarianism, the people's mike ritualizes horizontalism. The problem, though, comes when multiple people try to summon the mike simultaneously. Then it can feel a lot like anarchy."

25 A coincidence: the other Freud text mentioned in the current essay contains a signal "un": *unbehagen*, translated as "discontents" but also any of malaise, recession, slump, depression, dejection, dissatisfaction, displeasure, discord, discomfort, unpleasantness.

26 Ludwig Wittgenstein, *Culture and Value*, trans. Peter Winch, (Chicago, 1984), 80e.

27 Compare Giorgio Agamben, *The Coming Community*, trans. Michael Hardt, (Minnesota, 1993), 49: "Thus the glorious body of advertising has become the mask behind which the fragile, slight human body continues its precarious existence, and the geometrical splendor of 'the girls' [in stocking ads] covers over the long lines of the naked, anonymous bodies led to their death in the *Lagers*, or the thousands of corpses mangled in the daily slaughter on the highways. [. . .] To appropriate the historical transformations of human nature that capitalism wants to limit to the spectacle, to link together image and body in a space where they can no longer be separated, and thus to forge the whatever body, whose *physis* is resemblance—this is the good that humanity must learn how to wrest from commodities in their decline. Advertising and pornography, which escort the commodity to the grave like hired mourners, are the unknowing midwives of this new body of humanity." *Long live the whatever body!*

Democracy's Gift:

Time, Tradition, Repetition

"The motive power of democracy is love."
— HENRI BERGSON

"When we are all guilty—that will be democracy."
— ALBERT CAMUS

"Humour is the very essence of a democratic society."
— NUMBER 2 in *The Prisoner*

Prologue: Democracy's Gift

WHICH IS IT, then: love, guilt, or humour? Let me begin with this simple-sounding but of course quite vexing question: What exactly is the very essence, or motive power, of democracy, anyway?

Most philosophical answers to the question would not reference any of love, guilt, or humour—and perhaps so much the worse for them. They *would*, however, likely include reference to *forms or schemes of justification*, such as popular elections, representative assemblies, and plebiscites; or to *notions of philosophical legitimacy* that might be thought to underwrite and motivate the forms and schemes, that is, to ideas of individual equality and value that make the *demos* the proper locus of political power. Rule by the people, in short, both as a matter of procedure and in reference to the essential source of legitimacy. The simplest articulation of this combined standard notion of democracy might be the popular slogan "Nothing About Us Without Us"—itself a rhyming transliteration of the more euphonic Latin version: *Nihil de nobis, sine nobis*. Which is to say, no policy or regulation that affects a person should be decided in the absence of that person's consent, in some for or other, usually via elected representation or polled and summed interests.

I will not dwell, here, on the many pathologies that attend the working out of this noble ideal of political will.[1] Nor will I linger on the various kinds of hostility to the democratic impulse that haunt all politics. Summarizing his reactionary position, in 1796 the Catholic philosopher Joseph de Maistre, then ambassador to Russia, is supposed to have remarked to Czar Alexander I that "The principle of popular sovereignty is so dangerous that even if it were true, we would have to conceal it."[2] The remark was typical; as Terry Eagleton puts it, de Maistre "maintained that public order depended in the end on a single figure: the executioner. . . . Since he held that human beings were evil, aggressive, self-destructive, savagely irrational creatures in need of being terrified into craven submission by an absolute sovereignty, the public executioner played no mean role in his political imagination."[3] Two centuries after de Maistre's remark to the czar, the young Thomas Mann would opine: "As far as democracy in Germany is concerned, I believe completely in its realization: that is precisely what makes me pessimistic."[4] There are historical variants of this sentiment that are too numerous, and too depressing, to list; but the problem is not one that belongs only to the pre-democratic past.[5]

I am concerned, instead, to put into question an often-overlooked assumption in this standard view of democracy, namely that its presumed acts of justification take place in a timeless space of advice and consent, a place without a determinate past and a specific future—or set of specific possible futures—governing its inner logic. At an extreme, this assumption accounts for the curiously ahistorical tone of much democratic theory, which tends to enter into its discussions at a level of abstraction, and with dubious assumptions of homogeneity among citizens, divorced from awareness of particular social facts and narratives. These facts and narratives typically concern, to take just the most obvious, (1) cultural, regional, religious, and other identities; (2) the state of technology, including its uneven distribution within the target population; and (3) the intergenerational differences that produce tensions in all populations.[6]

Overly abstract democratic theory can thus easily leave itself open to the charge, levelled at thinkers at least since Locke, that the subjects of the state are comprehensively male, middle-aged, prosperous, articulate, and above all driven by forms of self-interest. Such individuals cannot help at least flirting with the toxic endgame of competitive identity vividly described by Thomas Merton:

> I have what you have not. I am what you are not. I have taken what you have failed to take, and I have seized what you could never get. Therefore you suffer and I am happy, you are despised and I am praised, you die and I live; you are nothing and I am something, and I am all the more something because you are nothing. And thus I spend my life admiring the distance between you and me.[7]

That condemning portrait of individualism is at one critical extreme, to be sure! A more proximate and common danger of the assumptions of ahistoricity and self-interest is the generation of "democratic" results that are driven exclusively, or almost so, by the summing of short-term individual interests. This in turn can generate an aggravated version of the familiar "tragedy of the commons."[8]

In the simple versions of the tragedy—collective action problems such as races to the bottom or collective self-defeat—we observe that the general pursuit of (rational) individual interests can lead to outcomes that are bad for everyone, as when the common pasture is destroyed by overuse. Such outcomes demonstrate, at a minimum, that collective interest is logically distinct from the aggregation of individual interests.[9] When a temporal dimension is added to the outcome metrics, the self-defeats may become actively unjust: depriving future generations of goods that we may ourselves enjoy short of self-defeat. One thinks here of environmental health, natural resources, and other likewise non-renewable goods. Exploitation of these goods can, as a matter of time itself, produce zero-sum games that nevertheless look, if viewed only synchronically, legitimate.

My concern in this paper, then, is to consider the temporal dimension of democracy, in particular its relation to the idea of tradition. But I will not be addressing the familiar liberal conception of tradition, which seeks to frame justification of a basic social structure amidst a plurality

of possible conceptions of the good, including ones that identify themselves explicitly as traditions.[10] I am interested, instead, in asking whether
democracy itself should be understood as a tradition. The motive question is not: What is democracy? It is, rather: What is the relationship of
democracy to time?

In what follows, I propose to analyze the notion of *fugitive democracy*
as the true meaning of the democratic ideal, once appropriately tem-
poralized.[11] This attempt at temporalization of the democratic entails
a critical engagement with the concepts of *tradition* and *progress*. And
so, to that end, I will suggest that the substance of democratic relations
must go beyond politics, punctuating normal sequences of events with
kairotic ruptures. These ruptures, in turn, work to realize an imperative of ongoing trusteeship—a kind of gift economy—at the heart of
democracy. What I mean by gift economy will emerge more clearly in
the succeeding sections but let me say something about it as part of these
prefatory remarks.

A gift is something freely given: that is, proffered without expectation
of profit or return. It is the opposite, even the negation, of a transaction.[12]
Our cultural gift-giving practices have devolved such that this basic distinction may no longer be so obvious. We give gifts at Christmastime,
for example, with a sense that we will also receive them. Lists are made
and checked off as the relevant goods are matched with their recipients.
Some families and businesses—also schools and voluntary associations—
striving to limit the economic burden of comprehensive transactional
gifts, adopt schemes such as "Secret Santa." Here a jumble of names
is sorted by an unseen hand and each person purchases a gift for just
one other, and receives one in turn, possibly from someone other than
the recipient of the first gift. Of course, in practice, such rather feeble
attempts to restore a gift economy in the thoroughly capitalized atmosphere of Christmas tend to backfire: gifters contact their recipients to
gauge desires, in turn creating a kind of indirect, or by-proxy, shopping
network barely distinguishable from simple transaction.[13]

Now I would not want to deny that there may well be much good fellow feeling in these exchanges. But they are not gifts in the pure sense.
They do not defy and even undermine the presumptive logic of transaction, which is what a genuine gift does. For the genuine gift creates
a scale of value that cannot be reduced to cost or benefit: it operates
beneath, or behind, the dominant patterns of tit-for-tat exchange. And

I want to say, any conception of political life that does not take account of the enduring value of gift economies in human affairs—Hobbes, for example—has made a baseline conceptual error about the subjects of its own theory. Humans are not fully human in the absence of some kind of free bestowal of their goods. A political theory of total transactional reduction is a philosophical non-starter.

When it comes to the subject before us, this is my central claim: democracy is itself a gift. Too often, of course, the idea of giving democracy has meant some form of cultural and political imperialism. We can think, here, of the Vietnam-era image of a bomb-spewing B-52 with the slogan "If you don't come to democracy, democracy will come to you." Or the cynical reporter in Billy Wilder's 1948 film, *A Foreign Affair*, which concerns American visitors (and love affairs) in occupied Berlin during the Second World War: "If you give a hungry man a loaf of bread, that's democracy," the character muses as his plane approaches the starved city's barely functioning airport. "If you leave the wrapper on, that's imperialism." (Significantly, the Berlin Airlift of 1948-49—a rolling operation begun around the time that Wilder's film was released—is considered by many to be a rare act of genuine giving in foreign affairs: food, personnel, and medical supplies provided without any consideration of recompense.)

The *gift of democracy* should rather be considered in terms of the phrase's double genitive "of." I mean the phrase's use of that same grammatically unstable "of" that creates ambiguity in phrases such as the *death of honour*. In such cases, the path of adjectival modification can flow in both directions: the phrase "death of honour" can mean both an honourable death OR the demise of honour itself. When we utter the phrase *the gift of democracy*, then, let us preserve the ambiguity rather than attempt to resolve it. Thus, the meaning of democracy's gift is BOTH the benefits that democracy bestows upon us AND our own acts of democratic bestowal.

At the conclusion of the present paper, I will try to answer the question concerning *to whom* the gift of democracy is given, and what kind of democracy that gift might be (section four). To begin the journey towards those conclusions—itself a kind of narrative of received benefits and forwarded trust—I turn now to some enabling thoughts about justice (section one); time and authority (section two); and tradition (section three).

1. Justice

The notion of democracy's gift may seem to raise immediately the cognate issue of intergenerational justice. The most widely accepted version of justice to future generations is found in John Rawls's magisterial *A Theory of Justice* (1971).[14] The basic orientation of his discussion is twofold. First: in the original position, where his hypothetical social contractors don't know who, in particular, they are—including to which generation they belong—a unanimous decision will be made for the fair synchronic, as well as diachronic, distribution of goods and services. In the event, Rawls argues that this distribution will follow his two principles of justice, namely, that there will be (a) equal access to life options, and (b) a "difference" mechanism that will guarantee that the least well-off will derive some benefit from any allowable social inequality. Second: the general claim that the site of justice is the "basic structure of society," to use Rawls's widely adopted phrase, seems to take sufficient account of persons both living and to come who will exist under that basic structure.

Rawls therefore argues that the original-position contractors agree on a *savings principle*, which is "subject to the further condition that they must want all previous generations to have followed it." He goes on: "Thus the correct principle is that which the members of any generation (and so all generations) would adopt as the one their generation is to follow and as the principle they would want preceding generations to have followed (and later generations to follow), no matter how far back (or forward) in time."[15] This conclusion is known as *just savings*, and while of course there can be no sense in which it is binding on factual previous generations, the principle is a part of just basic social structure because it is what the (present) contractors would have wanted from their forebears *had they been them*; and thus it is what they will (at present) bind themselves to, for the sake of those to come. The principle of just savings is therefore thought to be binding on all previous and future generations.

Like much of Rawls's theory of justice, the argument is both ingenious and somehow disappointing. The disappointment is not just of the standard academic variety, whereby flaws in the argument might be discussed—though there has been plenty of that.[16] I mean also the feeling that this conclusion, while possibly valid, seems without traction on our concrete inheritances from the past and our fraught decisions about the future. Nor does its sufficientarian logic ground a more comprehensive *trusteeship* conception of justice: the argument that we have not just a minimalist duty to leave some version of Locke's "enough and as good" to future people, but a responsibility to shift our basic position away from consumption (even curbed consumption) of goods and toward care of shared resources. I suggest that the notion of a tradition is a more viable way to plot a connection between the basic democratic principle (those who are affected must decide) and justice (there must be a valid distribution of resources, goods, opportunities, and potentials).

In his lively and clever book of popular Christian apologetics, *Orthodoxy* (1908), G. K. Chesterton had already addressed the issue of intergenerational injustice, using the trademark style of witty paradox. One result of this approach is that *Orthodoxy*, like Chesterton's *Heretics* (1905) before it, can be read with pleasure by believers and unbelievers alike.[17] But his arguments are not idle or facetious, and his attacks on willful comprehensive skepticism (a fashionable disease) and rampant materialism (a form of mania) are still worth attending to. He also, perhaps unexpectedly in a book on Christian belief, has much to say about democracy.

In the fourth chapter, called "The Ethics of Elfland," Chesterton offers this general statement: "[T]he democratic faith is this: that the most terribly important things must be left to ordinary men themselves—the mating of the sexes, the rearing of the young, the laws of the state. This is democracy" (43). (One presumes "men" might, even for him, eventually become "men and women," especially if mating and child-rearing are so terribly important.) He goes on immediately, in a crucial passage:

> But there is one thing that I have never from my youth up been able to understand. I have never been able to understand where people got the idea that democracy was in some way opposed to tradition. It is obvious that tradition is only democracy extended through time. It is trusting to a consensus of common human voices, rather than to some isolated or arbitrary record. (43)

Then, in a now-famous dilation on the point, Chesterton puts the matter in the following bold terms:

> Tradition may be defined as an extension of the franchise. Tradition means giving votes to the most obscure of all classes,

our ancestors. It is the democracy of the dead. Tradition refuses to submit to the small and arrogant oligarchy of those who merely happen to be walking about. All democrats object to men being disqualified by the accident of birth; tradition objects to their being disqualified by the accident of death. . . . I, at any rate, cannot separate the two ideas of democracy and tradition; it seems evident to me that they are the same idea. (43)

These are bold claims expressed in memorable language. No wonder both *democracy of the dead* and *small and arrogant oligarchy of those who merely happen to be walking about* have passed into the lexicons of many.

There is of course much to quarrel with in Chesterton's resulting discussion of social issues. He is too forgiving of the dangers posed by doctrine (96), too sanguine about the mechanism of democratic franchise (116), and too dismissive of the idea of social change (30-31). It might be thought that Chesterton emerges in this book as the answer to Kierkegaard's lamenting question: Among the Christians, is there a Christian? Yes, at least one; but he may also be the only one! Chesterton's humility and optimism are winning, but his notion of tradition is not sufficient on its face: it willfully ignores the evidence of traditions in practice, their tendencies to ossify, corrupt, and even oppress, not just on the basis of bare power or deception but *in the name of tradition itself*.

And so, despite some concluding protestations that Christian orthodoxy is "the only *logical* guardian of liberty, innovation and advance" (137), his presumptive conception of democratic tradition is too backward-looking. Guided by the idea of orthodoxy—meaning, whether Christian or otherwise, inherited ideas of right reason—such a tradition cannot take full account of the temporal dimensions of democracy. Yes, the interests of the dead, expressed in what they have left us, must indeed be part of the democratic conversation—including the conversation about democracy itself. Without an unwavering orientation in the other direction of the vector, however, we are likely to lose hold of our own duties to those who—notably, unlike the dead—have no way of expressing interests except via the exercise of our own imaginations.

It seems to me, then, that one crucial aspect of this imagination—the very same imagination that allows each of us as individuals to entertain a sense of self—must be a critical examination of the very idea of time. I have been speaking, consistent with both Rawls the political philosopher and Chesterton the Christian apologist, as if time is itself uniformly distributed, typically along a more or less straight line. But we know from our own temporal existences, in which we (among other things) live out memories over and over, and attempt to construct narratives of identity by recursively imposing present knowledge on past events, that time is neither uniform nor linear. I turn now to a brief discussion of two concepts of time—there may well be others!—that help us deepen our understanding of tradition, tradition as democracy, and democracy as tradition.

2. Two Concepts of Time, Two Concepts of Authority

In his brisk history of secular political consciousness and the public sphere, *Modern Social Imaginaries*, Charles Taylor remarks in passing on how different concepts of time, or time-consciousness, are necessary for the emergent modern political order. "The eighteenth-century public sphere thus represents an instance of a new kind: a metatopical common space and common agency without an action-transcendent constitution, an agency grounded purely in its own common actions."[18] This "metatopical common space" was, crucially, continuous and evenly distributed across its participants; that is why it could become the basis for what we now recognize as democratic civil society. Despite this continuity and equality, however, it was not considered to have originated *ex nihilo*: there are founding myths and moments which are considered to create the possibilities of public space. But these moments of origin, Taylor argues, "are displaced onto a higher plane, into a heroic time, an *illud tempus* which is not seen as qualitatively on a level with what we do today." And so, "[t]he founding action is not like our action, not just an earlier similar act whose precipitate structures ours. It is not just earlier, but in another kind of time, an exemplary time."[19]

The distinction Taylor suggests here has many forebears. One clear way of capturing its impact hinges on the fact that Greek has two words that both translate as "time": *chronos* and *kairos*. Chronological time is the time of measurement and portioning, the time that passes. In its modern manifestation, the history of chronological time is nicely traced by both Taylor and other, more radical thinkers such as Guy

Debord, in *Society of the Spectacle* (1967). This conception of time is crucial to the emergence of a shared public sphere—but also to the emergence of a work-world in which time can be subject to transaction. This is especially true in the special set of social relations that Debord calls "the spectacle," in which everything and everyone is a commodity. This is secular time, in the sense that it is "of the age": the space of everyday-ness, work, and exchange.

The visible sign of this time, as Lewis Mumford, among others, has noted, is of course the clock. The mechanism of keeping good time, once the holy grail of sailors looking to measure longitude, is here revealed as the enabling condition of capitalist labour relations. "The popularization of time-keeping," Mumford notes, "which followed the production of the cheap standardized watch, first in Geneva, was essential to a well-articulated system of transportation and production."[20] The clock keeps time by making its units identical and measured; it appears first as a shared community property in (as it might be) the town hall or church tower, matching the more ancient tolling of bells to a visual representation of time passing. Later, as technology advances, the mechanism of *chronos* time is bionically conjoined to the human frame in the form of the pocket watch and, eventually, the wristwatch. When I fasten on a wristwatch, in other words, I am signalling to myself and others my contract with the telling of time, expressing an agreement, in some sense, with the proposition that time is money. The same integration of technology and biology is essential to the logic of time-and-motion studies in factory production, as exemplified by the "scientific oversight" model of Frederick Winslow Taylor. "The enormous saving of time," Taylor writes in *The Principles of Scientific Management* (1911), "and therefore increase in the output which it is possible to effect through eliminating unnecessary motions and substituting fast for slow and inefficient motions for the men working in any of our trades can be fully realized only . . . from a thorough motion and time study, made by a competent man."[21]

We can summarize the qualities of secular, chronos time this way: it is (i) everyday, (ii) profane, (iii) homogeneous, (iv) linear, (v) horizontal, and (vi) egalitarian. We constantly encounter this time, measuring it and meeting its demands, by being on time, matching our movements and achievements to its punctums, saving time and spending time, each of us equally available to time, and having it available to us. Debord closely associates this time with the emergence of labour mechanisms and the bourgeois conception of society, taking time away from the more natural cyclical rhythms of seasonal agriculture and, before it, hunting-gathering to create a time-world in which production is potentially constant. Workers may now punch in to the line *twenty-four-seven*, as we would now say, making the relation to the time-clock explicit. Consistent with orthodox Marxist critique, Debord argues that this process is inseparable from the emergence of class, and so class conflict.

In a crucial middle section of *Society of the Spectacle*, "Time and History," Debord notes how time itself becomes a form of social distinction and conflict in the course of this triumph of *chronos* time:

> The social appropriation of time, the production of man by human labour, develops within a society divided into classes. The power which constituted itself above the penury of the society of cyclical time, the class which organizes the social labour and appropriates the limited surplus value, simultaneously appropriates the *temporal surplus value* of its organization of social time: it possesses for itself alone the irreversible time of the living. The wealth that can be concentrated in the realm of power and materially used up in sumptuous feasts is also used up as a squandering of *historical time at the surface of society*.[22]

Once measured and parcelled out, subjected to transaction in the form of paid labour, time immediately becomes a commodity with the potential, like any commodity, to support an upper-tier, luxury version of itself. Free time, leisure time, ample time, time off—these all immediately beckon as goods at the margins of a world ruled by time-as-labour and labour-as-time.

It is not necessary to detail here how the commodification of time creates the familiar pathologies of demented leisure characteristic of late capitalism: the living-for-the-weekend enthrallment that, with every reference to "hump day" or "TGIF" parties emphasizes the unshakable dominance of the work week.[23] Too often concealed is the persistence and bravery of those workers who demanded the regulated ten-hour, and eventually eight-hour, workday, and still later the two-day weekend.[24] Of more immediate interest, though, is the fact that those battles about time already accepted the premise of what time was. Both Taylor and Debord note that this secular, *chronos* time of labour and production-consumption achieves—one might even say *must* achieve—global reach. It is part of what Heidegger calls "the age of the world picture," the picture in which everything, including ourselves and our temporality, are in principle available for disposal: the comprehensive *standing reserve* or *enframing* (*Ge-stell*) of technology whereby everything, including human desire and possibility, is made fungible in the name of use.[25]

Debord joins other Marxist critics such as E. P. Thompson in noting the effects of this time: "With the development of capitalism, irreversible time is *unified on a world scale*. Universal history becomes a reality because the entire world is gathered under the development of this time. . . . What appears the world over as *the same day* is the time of economic production cut up into equal abstract fragments. Unified irreversible time is the time of the *world market* and, as a corollary, of the world spectacle."[26]

Thompson: "Indeed, a general diffusion of clocks and watches is occurring (as one would expect) at the exact moment when the industrial revolution demanded a great synchronization of labour." Thus a new ethos of punctuality and efficiency is born: "In all these ways—by the division of labour; the supervision of labour; fines; bells and clocks; money incentives; preaching and schooling; the suppression of fairs and sports—new labour habits were formed and a new time discipline was imposed."[27]

And compare Charles Taylor: "A purely secular time-understanding allows us to imagine society horizontally, untouched by any 'high points,' where the ordinary sequence of events touches higher time, and therefore without recognizing any privileged persons or agencies, such as priests and kings, who stand and mediate at such alleged points. This radical horizontality is precisely what is implied in the direct-access society, where each member is 'immediate to the whole.'"[28]

Now, Taylor may be thought too sanguine about this larger temporal development in modernity, even though he does allow that there are persistent local verticalities even in the comprehensively horizontal world of the secular: uneven access to goods, disjointed proximity to glamour or celebrity, corruptions of power. But Debord's sense of the dominance of spectacle in a society in which cyclical time has been lost, while accurate enough, may seem to invite a kind of nostalgia or romanticism about the time-out-of-time. One may accept the value of Debordian Situationism's tactics of *dérive* and *détournement*—drifting and repurposing through the byways of the spectacle-dominated city, rather than resisting in some pre-doomed alternative organization—but still detect an odour of charming failure in the analysis. One of the aims of the present paper is to restore vitality to the Situationist project without inviting any new moments of romance; more on this in the final section.

The larger point about both the benefits and the costs of secular time is politically significant. Even as it invited commodification and disposal, the achievement of egalitarian secular time was a necessary condition for the emergence of popular sovereignty in full force. Without a sense of immediate access to a non-hierarchical present, however attenuated or subject to doubt, there can be no conviction that we, the people, are the creators of our social order, nor that, to use Taylor's words, popular elections—not bloodlines, transcendental access, or historical precedent—are "the only source of legitimate power." He goes on: "But what has to take place for this change to come off is a transformed social imaginary, in which the idea of foundation is taken out of the mythical early time and seen as something that people can do today. In other words, it becomes something that can be brought about by collective action in contemporary, purely secular time."[29]

This cannot be done purely through action at the level of secular time, however. Not only will a *narrative of origin* continue to prove necessary to the development of democratic society, it will also be necessary to keep open the ever-present possibility of an *eruption of justificatory argument* concerning legitimacy. This kind of argument is distinct from the day-to-day business of collective action, still more from the policy-making and regulatory business-as-usual of politics.

The narrative of origin is familiarly sketched in the various versions of contractarian thought-experiment that come down to us in the liberal tradition: Hobbes's state of nature, Locke's pre-social order, even Rawls's original position—though the last does not indulge in a dubious appeal to history or human nature that undermines our respect for the early modern examples. Rousseau, notably, who sounded such a strong keynote in *The Social Contract* about man being born free but living everywhere in chains, would chide Hobbes for not stripping away enough of the accretions of social contagion in his conception of natural man. The humans for whom pre-social existence was "solitary, poor, nasty, brutish, and short," were, Rousseau argued, already highly socialized beings trained to pursue their own competitive self-interest. This criticism, though well aimed, does not, however, thereby lend more credence to Rousseau's alternative, which invites the parallel objection that it is a species of special pleading. Rawls's atemporal version of a justificatory scheme, with the original position framed as a thought experiment that one might undertake at any time, draws fire concerning what, precisely, must be excluded by the veil of ignorance in order to generate a unanimous outcome. The political narrative of origin will always be controversial.

The eruption of justificatory argument, because it is grounded in actual rather than imagined history, seems more promising. Such an eruption might be discerned in historical narratives of democratic process, such as Bruce Ackerman's magisterial account of the American republic, in which the Founding plays the originary role, including sometimes heated appeals to the Founders' intentions, but which is open to returns to originary discourse at times of crisis: the Reconstruction after the Civil War, the New Deal in the wake of the Depression. Ackerman argues that the truly democratic republic, no matter how atavistic its self-narrative, can never foreclose on the option of returning to the democratic drawing-board.[30] To be sure, Founders' Intent remains itself a disputed property, both in everyday judicial argument and in returns to constitutional first principles. More darkly, the same return to originary framing can be glimpsed in Carl Schmitt's notion of the *exception*, that which is decided upon by the sovereign; and in Walter Benjamin's rejoinder about the *violence* in all acts of political establishment.

The contrastive term for secular time gives us an insight about what this complicated narrative of origin and legitimation might look like: the tradition that is distinctively democratic. That is, we are now in a position to characterize the useful diacritical opposite of *chronos* time, namely *kairos* or transcendental time. It is (i) mysterious, (ii) divine, (iii) eternal, (iv) infinite, (v) vertical, and (vi) hierarchical. In many cases, of course, precisely this kind of time—the time of divine intervention or communion with the eternal realm—is familiar as part of an anti-democratic social order, in which privileged access, or anyway claims thereto, keeps a steeply hierarchical class division firmly in place, ostensibly as part of a Great Chain of Being or Divine Universal Scheme. The forerunner here might be, of course, the Platonic Theory of the Forms, with realms of knowledge and reality arranged in rigid order. The upward ascent of the self-freed slave of Plato's Cave, struggling through blindness and pain toward the sun's light, is an ascent to eternity as well as reality—for they are the same.

But these towering religio-philosophical edifices have their less grandiose analogues even in our own world. I mean, for example, the sense of time beyond time that still marks genuine leisure, play, and idleness, the *skholé* of Aristotle even now to be found in our aimless games and blissful moments of "flow"; or the true holiday, where the usual tyranny of work and use-value is suspended in the name of carnival or sabbath.[31] The common desire for what the Germans call *freizeit*—time free of obligation—is united with the transcendence of time available to almost any North American urban dweller in a baseball game, say, where time is told only in outs and innings, in a pastime that is played in what is usually called a park. (The cognate game of cricket arguably offers even more in the way of time out of time!) In his paean to baseball, Milton scholar and commissioner of baseball A. Bartlett Giamatti references *Paradise Lost* (IV, 434-5) as an expression of Aristotelian leisure, which he calls "the ideal to which our play aspires." From the poem: *Free leave so large to all things else, and choice / Unlimited of manifold delights.* "But in fact, the serpent is already there," Giamatti notes, "and our sports do not simulate, therefore, a constant state. Rather, between days of work, sports or games only repeat and repeat our efforts to go back, back to a freedom we cannot recall, save as a moment of play in some garden now lost."[32]

I will suggest later that these and other *ludic episodes* to be found within everyday existence are portals to the gift of democracy, for they remind us of the resistance to transactional reduction that grounds the most valuable features of our common life. The question for present purposes must be this: Is there a sense of *kairos*, or transcendent time, that can exist as a proximate option for a democratic tradition? In order to advance the argument that there is, once more lodged squarely in the idea of democracy's gift, I will now sketch another useful distinction, between two kinds of social authority.

We can associate two kinds of claim, both indispensable to democratic thought, with the two notions of time I have here contrasted. As Taylor notes, the linear secular time of the modern world-picture is a necessary condition of a political world in which *everyone* feels capable of meaningful action. We are at once de-centered and enabled. The voice of authority that addresses itself to secular time is that of a wisdom tradition. The claims of such a tradition are typically (1) conservative,

(2) continuous, and (3) linked to the past. This is the species of authority we associate with scriptural reference, for example, or embodied rituals passed from generation to generation.

The "wisdom" in question need not always be of world-shaking profundity. The traditions of games such as cricket or baseball, with their "laws" and prescribed behaviours, a spirit of continuity that good players and fans come to respect and honour, demonstrate this kind of authority. The claim is not "It shall be done this way because it has always been done this way," but rather "It shall be done this way because we acknowledge the accumulated fitness and rightness of doing it this way." Origins are not lost in time, but they are recognized as essential to our current projects, whatever they might be. The wisdom tradition of democracy is acted out in, for example, the various iterations of the Westminster model of parliamentary democracy, the rule of common law, and even such detailed inheritances as the writ of *habeus corpus* and the chancery court. We may debate these details, as when we seek to reform unbalanced first-past-the-post elections, say, but we will do so in the terms set out by the tradition.

This voice of authority, though it ought to be respected, cannot close off even more radical ruptures in the fabric of social life. The authority of *prophetic intervention* must likewise be recognized, a kind of eruption of new energy that rends the time of everyday life and exposes a harsh light of higher responsibility. This voice, then, is (1) radical, (2) discontinuous, and (3) linked to the future. The prophetic voice need not be utopian, however; it may be hortatory or even scolding of our complacency and laziness. It is the voice that condemns the money-changers in the temple and called out the Pharisees for their hypocrisy. It is, as Terry Eagleton notes with some relish, "the sour unreasonableness of a document that admonishes us to yield up our lives for the sake of strangers that is most striking, not its diffusion of sweetness and light. There is nothing moderate or middle-of-the road about the scandalous extremity of its demands, as a theologian like Kierkegaard was aware."[33] In a non-Christian context, we might detect this voice in the lately mocked but actually stirring *soixante-huitard* and Situationist slogan: "Be reasonable: demand the impossible." It is the voice that demands that we occupy Wall Street.

The common ground of these two voices is language, the shared discursive space of democratic politics. Human history, Hegel said, was carried in language, transmitted from one epoch to the next in history and philosophy. This is the sense of discursive immersion that Heidegger refers to when he says, provocatively, language speaks us—not the other way around. Language is the house of Being. Heidegger was no democrat, as we unfortunately have cause to know; even so, his infamous "Rektoratsrede" on "Die Selbstbehauptung der deutschen Universität" (1933) is itself, necessarily, a discursive intervention which we can even now examine and criticize. Democracy never sleeps when language is present. And, while we listen to the voice of authority and its claims to both the horizontal vertical temporalities of shared social space, we can never abandon the individual responsibility which is the condition of granting legitimacy—a responsibility, as both tradition and prophecy would agree, can never be bought or sold. *Nihil de nobis, sine nobis*, indeed.

3. Living Traditions?

Let us now, with these thoughts in mind, turn to the question of tradition. "A real tradition is not the relic of the past that is irretrievably gone," Igor Stravinsky argued: "it is a living force that animates and informs the present."[34] Stravinsky was thinking specifically of music, of course. What is a tradition in the political sense? Can we speak meaningfully of a *real tradition of democracy*, or is the very idea mired in confusion? I will dwell here on a vivid example of the problem, one drawn from fiction but nevertheless rooted in real social movements and events. Evelyn Waugh offers some typically effective mockery of the notion of tradition in a minor part of his second novel, *Vile Bodies* (1930), which is also seriously concerned with the question of culture and its demise—about which more in a moment.

First, the mockery. The male protagonist, Adam Fenwick-Symes, is attempting to earn a living as a newspaper gossip columnist known as Mr. Chatterbox. Working under a "black list" injunction that certain society people, suing his proprietor's newspaper, shall not be mentioned in the column, Adam resorts to invented subjects. Among these is the dashing Captain Angus Stuart-Kerr, who, unlike most big-game hunters, "was an expert and indefatigable dancer." But, as with several other characters, including a sculptor whose work is so in-demand it cannot be purchased and a fashionable couple quickly claimed as everyone's best friends, Adam's invented Scotsman is all too real. A rival gossip sheet begins to mention the deeds of the captain: spotted at a point-to-point meeting, known as the hardest rider in the Hebrides.

Adam decides to put a stop to this appropriation and so writes this in his next column:

> Some people [he wrote] are under the impression that Captain Angus Stuart-Kerr, whom I mentioned on this page a short time ago, is a keen rider. Perhaps they are confusing him with Alastair Kerr-Stuart, of Inverauchty, a very distant cousin. Captain Stuart-Kerr never rides, and for a very interesting reason. There is an old Gaelic rhyme repeated among his clansmen which says in rough translation "the Laird rides well on two legs." Tradition has it that when the head of the house mounts a horse, the clan will be dispersed.

To this bit of foolery, the narrator adds a footnote, also worth quoting in full:

> This story, slightly expanded, found its way later into a volume of Highland Legends called *Tales from the Mist*, which has been approved to be read in elementary schools. This shows the difference between what is called a "living" as opposed to a "dead" folk tradition.

Tales from the Mist indeed!

Without wanting to blunt the edge of Waugh's irony, let us note that the episode nicely explodes the use of a living/dead distinction—one which, at the beginning of the current essay, seemed still to retain some power. That is to say, if a "living" tradition is one in which a fabricated story, plausible only because sufficiently silly *prima facie*, could be taken up and folded into the "lore" of a culture, then perhaps one's tradition is better off dead. The Scots, in this rather elaborate joke, are no better or worse than middle-class personages who seek proximity to glamour by reading the gossip pages in the first place. The limits of invention are also shown in the novel: when Adam attempts to influence male fashion, he first succeeds (black suede shoes for formal wear) and then fails (bottle-green bowler hats for town—a fiction that only one sad aging beau attempts to emulate by badly dying his existing headgear).

Waugh has a more serious point to make here than just poking fun at those who grasp after culture. *Vile Bodies*, like *A Handful of Dust* (1934) and, especially, *Brideshead Revisited* (1945), sounds a young fogey's lament for the disappearing country-house culture of Edwardian England. The suggestion is that the devastation of the First World War must be seen to include a way of life that is quintessentially English, and which has been replaced by a harsh modernity of industrialization and democratization. Tony Last, in *A Handful of Dust*, is seen as indeed the last of a breed, and ends his days the casual prisoner of a Dickens-loving madman. The estate of Brideshead and the Anglo-Catholic Marchmain family symbolize, in Waugh's greatest novel, the generational and cultural tensions of the slide into another world war.

These tensions become the essential springwork of Waugh's fictional and moral vision. A large section of the conclusion to *Vile Bodies* offers an unabashed, almost sentimental celebration of the aristocratic order, complete with exchange of gifts and good wishes between the social orders and carolling waifs given punch by a faithful servant. The background fact—that Adam is there with the daughter of the house, Nina Blount, pretending to be her husband—is remarked only by the neighbouring rector, who has previously decided that Adam is mad. Nina's father, Colonel Blount, is in effect suborned to adultery under his own ancestral roof.

Already another war is coming. (Recall that this novel was published in 1930.) Adam will end up on the front lines, carrying a pocket-sized "Huxdane-Halley bomb (for the dissemination of leprosy germs)"—an especially nasty, but very Waughian detail. The shadowy Father Rothschild S.J. is the sole character in *Vile Bodies* who seems to sense this impending conflict. He is also the voice of moral judgment about the generational demise of traditional culture represented by the Bright Young People who are the book's ostensible heroes. In fact, Waugh's attitude is complex.

In a discussion of the younger generation, the Rt. Hon. Walter Outrage M. P., then briefly prime minister (he alternates the position with dizzying swiftness with a certain Lord Throbbing), complains thus: "I don't understand them, and I don't want to. They had a chance after the war that no generation has ever had. There was a whole civilization to be saved and remade—and all they seem to do is to play the fool." Fr. Rothschild is less damning: "Don't you think," he says, "that perhaps it is all in some way historical? I don't think people ever *want* to lose their faith either in religion or in anything else. I know very few young people, but it seems to me that they are all possessed with an almost fatal hunger for permanence. . . . And this word 'bogus' they all use. . . . They won't make the best of a bad job nowadays." Rothschild goes on to suggest that the motto both of his church and of the older English generation might be something like, "If a thing's worth doing at all, it's worth doing well." Whereas the Young People say "If a thing's not worth doing well, it's not worth doing at all." He concludes that this inversion "makes everything very difficult for them."

Another party to the discussion, which may be considered the centre of Waugh's novel, Lord Metroland, is less sympathetic. "Anyhow," he complains, "I don't see how all that explains why my stepson should drink like a fish and go about everywhere with a negress." Fr. Rothschild acknowledges the problem: "I think they're connected, you know," he says, taking his leave for further behind-the-scenes business of state. "But it's all very difficult." Indeed.

The link between the recurrent slang term "bogus," flagged by the Jesuit, and the various inventions and deceptions throughout the novel seems significant to me. In the usage, a thing is bogus if it is boring, or tiresome, or done by someone else with too-serious intent, or simply unpleasant. Like more contemporary versions—"lame" would be one recent favorite—the judgment is vague and all-purpose, but no less effective for that. And it is clear that any association with truth or authenticity is long broken: bogus decidedly does not mean fake or insincere. Quite the reverse, since these traits are among the amusing non-bogus features of the comedy—which is admittedly quite black. Two rather harmless young characters, one a penurious nobleman and the other a carefree flirt and party-girl, die suddenly in the course of the action, the first by suicide and the second through madness. Waugh is already, pre-conversion, familiar with the wages of sin, including the uncomfortable knowledge that sometimes those sins go unpunished even as others die.

We may seem to have come a fair distance from the question of tradition, but I suggest in fact not, especially since this twisting of "fake" and "bogus" nicely captures the central problem of tradition, namely, how to carry something on in a manner we regard as authentic—even as, perhaps, our ideals of authenticity themselves are ever put in question, and found unreliable. It may be that the very concept of authenticity, not just its various iterations, is found to be incoherent. Or it may be that the once-valid reasons for doing or cherishing something are no longer present, leaving a carapace of ritual obedience reflexively justified as tradition. (A character in Richard Powell's novel *The Philadelphian* (1956), musing on social convention in that most status-conscious of American cities: "We do something for a reason, and then the reason vanishes, but we keep on doing it because by that time it's a tradition."[35])

In such cases of defunct reason or conceptual emptiness, I suggest we have at least three options: (1) an aggressive "traditionalist" retrenchment; (2) a desperate rootlessness; and (3) what we might call the Nietzschean option, the *sprezzatura* of cool celebration. Here, to use Eagleton's words, "one's beliefs are more like one's manservants, to be hired and fired as the fancy takes you, than like one's bodily organs"; or, varying the metaphor, "as costumes one can don or doff at will ... as with kilts and cravats, it is aesthetic considerations which govern the donning and doffing."[36] (Kilts again!)

Eagleton regards this last option as "cavalier," and seems to deride its "modernism" in favour of a principled postmodernism—and yet, it is the latter conception that is most often attacked by the stalwarts of option (1). I will prefer to call option (3) *fugitive*, in the sense that its energy comes from the combined freedom and responsibility of self-invention. But our acts of self-invention are never entirely aesthetic (in the pejorative sense detectable in Eagleton's characterization) nor are they without grounding in the concrete practical realities of shared social life. That is, our circumstances allow for a range of options in framing our life narratives, but the range is not without limit: it is, as Bernard Williams put it, not a real option for *me* to live *my* life as a samurai warrior, still less (one might add) as a Klingon battle commander—though I may well act out these aspects of my desire-world in fantasy, online games, cosplay, and the like. We can say, after Mill, that these are "experiments in living." By their very nature they stand opposed to reductive claims of tradition, especially those that are revealed as bogus, such as some parts of Scottish clan identity, and those that are actively harmful, such as the ethnic nationalism and bloodline dominance to be seen in Hutu-Tutsi hatred, religious intolerance of homosexuality, or Nazism.[37] Tradition becomes ideology—typically with violent results.

The gifts of option (3) are not just individual; experiments in living create a milieu in which further, and sometimes more radical, experimentation is possible. This milieu, in its trans-temporal existence, is what I mean by the democratic tradition. It is an imperfect standard, but let us say for the nonce that there is a valid possible distinction between *open* traditions and *closed* ones. The democratic tradition, by virtue of its structural combination of conservation (the present as a gift of the past, the future as a gift of the present) and innovation (we must each invent ourselves as we go on) strikes to correct balance to achieve openness. There is, to be sure, a democratic version of what Harold Bloom called "the anxiety of influence" operative here. How, indeed, could there not be? The freedom to self-invent is, as noted, importantly conjoined with responsibility. Every successful experiment is a bequest to future democratic generations; every failure is a cost that they will be made to bear.

The closest non-political analogy to the open, anxious, free, responsible, conservative, and innovative features of this tradition is, it seems to me, the tradition(s) of scholarship. There may be very closely held standards of responsibility here, as in science, where the byword is "creative destruction" of results in the form of testing and reiteration. But even in less strictly policed regions of scholarship we find constraints and standards that compel practitioners to go on in a certain way. And that way is forward-looking—wanting to generate new results, new interventions, new interpretations—even as it is guided and governed by a vast inheritance. This, then, is a trans-temporal discursive community, whose members are in an endless conversation about what is right, good, or simply interesting. Some ideas will reign for a time, only to be rejected, perhaps even reviled, later. Once dismissed, results may come into new favour. The only overarching rule of the process is that everyone who possesses the wherewithal to contribute to the conversation acquires, just in virtue of that wherewithal, the authority to do so.

In the democratic tradition, there is one clear difference: no credentials are demanded for inspection at the threshold of the discursive arena. You do not need a PhD to be a full member. Indeed, there is no means test except the basic existential one; just being here is enough.

4. Fugitive Democracy

Too many accounts of tradition, positive and negative alike, rely on contrastive force, so that tradition is defended (or condemned) as against modernity, progress, change, or some similar forward-facing value. I hope I have shown in the previous sections that the notion of a demo-cratic tradition, if there is any valid version thereof, cannot be defended in this manner. For one thing, no account of democracy could rely on an unchallenged notion of such anti-traditional values.

Progress, for example, has been the cover and clothes of the worst depredations against human spirit and freedom, not least in its aspi-rations to an ideal state. Walter Benjamin is suitably chastening in his "Theses on the Philosophy of History" (1940):

> A Klee painting named Angelus Novus shows an angel looking as though he is about to move away from something he is fixedly contemplating. His eyes are staring, his mouth is open, his wings are spread. This is how one pictures the angel of history. Its face is turned towards the past. Where we see a chain of events, he sees one single catastrophe which keeps piling wreckage upon wreck-age and hurls it in front of his feet. A storm irresistibly propels him into the future, to which his back is turned while the pile of debris before him grows skyward. This storm is what we call progress.[38]

Benjamin's image here is reflected in the small Paul Klee work *Angelus Novus* (1920), which Benjamin carried with him in his flight from France to Spain as the Nazi forces entered Paris. The words above were written in January of that year; fearing repatriation to Nazi Germany, Benjamin committed suicide in September in Portbou, Spain.

One needn't be such an obvious world-historical victim to see the force of Benjamin's argument, which indicts the logic of materialism and never-ending social change as a nightmare of instrumental ratio-nality. One might think, here, of another famous artwork, Francisco de Goya's etching *El sueño de la razón produce monstruos* (1797-99). This image is plate forty-three of the eighty etchings that comprise Goya's satirical album *Los Caprichos* ("Caprices").[39] It shows a sleeping male figure, his head slumped upon a work desk scattered with drawing instruments, beset by a rising flock of bat-like flying creatures, some that resemble owls, as a large cat, reminiscent of a sphinx, looks on. The title is usually translated as "the sleep of reason produces mon-sters," and the full epigraph reads this way: "Fantasy abandoned by rea-son produces impossible monsters: united with her, she is the mother of the arts and the origin of their marvels." This gloss suggests a benign Apollonian-Dionysian union, in controlled art, of constraining reason and rampant imagination, which would otherwise spin itself off into nightmarish vision.

But another interpretation offers itself, turning on the linguistic ambiguity that has the Spanish word *sueño* meaning both "sleep" and "dream." Suppose that reason, rather than a helpful curb, is itself a generator of monstrous visions when it is allowed to run unfettered in human life. The original meaning captures Goya's *ars poetica*, perhaps, and executes a kind of self-satire in a series of works that mock pretension and excess in contemporary Spanish society. The inverted interpretation sounds, in addition, a subtle warning message for the age about to unfold, in which reason will gather into its hands the reins of everything, including social order—and the results will be monsters that fly into the darkness from our dreaming, world-dominating minds.

Well, perhaps that is itself a flight of fancy. For a more grounded version of the point, compare Chesterton on the question of anti-traditional manias for change. "It is true that a man (a silly man) might make change itself his object or ideal," he notes. "But as an ideal change itself becomes unchangeable. If the change-worshiper wishes to estimate his own progress, he must be sternly loyal to the ideal of change; he must not begin to flirt gaily with the ideal of monotony. Progress itself cannot progress. . . . Change is the hardest and narrowest groove that a man can get into."[40] One could add the basic logical point that there can be no such thing as change unless and until there is something that is *not* changing. Change is a contrastive force. Consider: the paradox of Theseus' ship does not make us pause to question the idea of identity over time in the absence of some notion, or at lease the *desire* for the notion, of the one and only ship that belongs to Theseus.

Even worse than a mindless devotion to change for its own sake is the peculiar stasis observable in "presentism," the perverse instantaneity in which everything seems to happen now and seems to demand a response even earlier.[41] The very same social media that allowed for near-instant connection to coordinate resistance in Tahrir Square can effect, in New York or London, a radical disconnection and a generalized feeling of ephemerality. This shrinking of time is a blight on the democratic body, even a sort of *zombie virus* in which we consume our own consciousness at a pace just beyond our ability to process the world.[42] This never-ending preoccupation with the tyranny of the now, which can be neither completed nor overcome, renders individuals incapable of framing long-term interests of their own, let alone attending to the trusteeship responsibilities we the living bear to those who are still to come. It has been the case, historically, that democracies have defined themselves diacritically against tyrannies, the freedom from oppression of arbitrary rule.[43] We should see that a tyrant of one's own devising, internalized as a dominant part of one's self, is just as harmful to genuine freedom as one whose force is enacted from without.

A self lived under the tyranny of the now is not capable of taking proper stock of its own history. Sheldon Wolin, an avowed "progressive" thinker, argues that one key factor in the emergence of "managed democracy," and its attendant threat of "inverted," or soft, totalitarianism, is the speed of social change:

> Today, thanks to the highly organized pursuit of technological innovation and the culture it encourages, change is more rapid, more encompassing, more welcomed than ever before—which means that institutions, values, and expectations share with technology a limited shelf life. We are experiencing the triumph of contemporaneity and of its accomplice, forgetting or collective amnesia. Stated somewhat differently, in early modern times change displaced traditions; today change succeeds change.[44]

A casualty of that shift is the very idea that "progress" might have the power to realize our desires for social justice. Early champions of progress "believed that while change might result in the disappearance or destruction of established beliefs, customs, and interests, the vast majority of these deserved to go because they mostly served the Few while keeping the Many in ignorance, poverty, and sickness."[45] The logic of this dialectic has, however, since vanished, because there is nothing for the forces of "progress" to push off against. Meanwhile, our sense of time has become compressed and distorted; the outcome of such time is "the tyranny of efficiency" and so the subversion of democracy's demand "that time be defined by the requirements for deliberation, discussion, reconciliation of opposing viewpoints, all of which suddenly seem 'time-consuming.'"[46] This, we might say, is the final, but alas self-consuming, victory of *chronos*-time.

Nor does the damage end there. This condition of relentless change-upon-change leads, in turn, to a neglect of anything that stands in relation to that self as a public trust or a common good. Social change without direction, instead of leading to desired general goods, merely raises the spectre of empty narcissism. "With postmodernism," Terry Eagleton argues, rather recklessly using a blanket label,

> history is reduced for the most part to commodified cultural heritage, an ever-present repertoire of inherited styles and a "presentist" approach to the past. . . . History is too brutely given for a culture which delights in an endless array of options. It is an unwelcome reminder that our freedom in the present is constrained by the irreparable fatality we know as the past.[47]

Under these conditions, postmodern thought is revealed as "depthless, anti-tragic, non-linear, anti-numinous, non-foundational and anti-universalist, suspicious of absolutes and averse to interiority."[48] Quite a catalogue of vices! We should, of course, be careful to distinguish our reactions to this denunciation from a thinker whose hostility toward postmodern thought is sometimes more vivid than reasoned. In concluding the present paper, I suggest *pace* Eagleton that one can—indeed must—retain suspicion towards universalism and foundationalism, a variform version of Lyotard's "incredulity towards metanarratives," without sacrificing interiority, tragedy, and a sense of history.

And yet, society is changing so fast that sometimes the tug towards both presentism and the bad forms of postmodern restlessness seems irresistible. In previous democratic moments, social change was itself a motor of political aspiration, not stasis. As Zygmunt Bauman has argued, "The considerable speeding up of social change" was seen by reformers as a necessary condition for the creation of "historical consciousness." And this consciousness was in turn "duly reflected in the . . . novel sense of history as an endless chain of irreversible changes, with which the concept of progress—a development which brings change for the better—was not slow to join forces." The resulting notion of constant progressive change, or perfectibility, "paved the way for utopia."[49] We have seen that this utopian impulse has its considerable downside risks, even assuming that such a thing as "constant progressive change" was possible—as Chesterton, for one, denies.

The answer is not, however, a decline into anti-utopianism, whether of the Fabian sort or, worse, the disengagement and cynicism that characterizes too much of the electorates in Western democracies, especially among young people now experiencing income levels lower than their parents and record levels of under- and unemployment, even when highly educated.[50] Is there, perhaps, a form of anti-anti-utopianism that can keep alive the very idea of democratic aspiration without courting the dangers rightly associated with ideal outcomes? This is the crux of the concept of fugitive democracy. In our initial analysis, the fugitive quality of democracy seems like a disadvantage, an escaped prisoner on the run. This, Sheldon Wolin suggests, is itself the legacy of a long-held but erroneous identification of democracy, and the political more generally, with a form of electoral politics and centralized government. "Institutionalization marks the attenuation of democracy," Wolin notes:

> leaders begin to appear; hierarchies develop; experts of one kind or another cluster around the centers of decision; order, procedure, and precedent displace a more spontaneous politics: in retrospect the latter appears as disorganized, inefficient. Democracy thus seems destined to be a moment rather than a form. Throughout the history of political thought virtually all writers emphasize the unstable and temporary character of democracy.[51]

This initial analysis prompts two urgent questions for democrats: "Why is it that democracy is reduced, even devitalized by form? Why is its presence occasional and fugitive?"

In a way, the answers are obvious. Such institutionalizations of the political are further evidence, if any was needed, of Robert Michels's so-called "iron law of oligarchy," which decrees that the emergence of an oligarchy, or non-circulating elite, is an unavoidable consequence of the "tactical and technical necessities" of democratic politics, especially in systems of electoral representation.[52] Michels: "It is organization which gives birth to the dominion of the elected over the electors, of the mandataries over the mandators, of the delegates over the delegators. Who says organization, says oligarchy." Nor, argued Michels, is this a chance development in some cases rather than others. "Historical evolution mocks all the prophylactic measures that have been adopted for the prevention of oligarchy," he said; and the stated purpose of democratic movements, namely to *eliminate* elites, cannot but generate them through the very attempts at elimination. Like Oedipus, their every move away from social elite formation creates the tragic outcome of creating a political elite—which becomes itself social. This rule by an elite in the name of the *demos* is oligarchy; worse, joining the iron law with Chesterton's oligarchy of the living might be seen to raise the problem to a second power. (Michels was true to his conclusions: in his native Germany he was a vocal socialist; he later emigrated to Italy and joined the socialist wing of Mussolini's fascist party.)

Put in less structural terms, we can say that the devolution to organized, hence corruptible politics, is just the inevitable development of a socialized citizenry, all of whom view themselves as either aspiring to or shadowing the trappings of bourgeois material comfort. Georg Lukács put it in the following terms, which reflect also on the changing nature of time and space under late capitalist conditions: "Bourgeois society carried out the process of socializing society. Capitalism destroyed both the spatio-temporal barriers between different lands and territories and also the legal partitions between the different 'estates.'" Lukács concludes: "Man becomes, in the true sense of the word, a social being. Society becomes the reality for man."[53] In toxic versions, this combination of aspiration and shadowing congeals into a comprehensive ideological myth—the American Dream, perhaps.[54] In Wolin's own measured words, "The democratization of 'advanced industrial democracies' comes down to this: the labor, wealth and psyches of the citizenry are simultaneously defended and exploited, protected and extracted, nurtured and fleeced, rewarded and commanded, flattered and threatened."[55]

One could be far more incendiary than this, and denounce the managerial capture of democracy in more rousing language. But such cries tend to dissolve quickly, or else devolve into a cynicism that edges always towards apathy. A better course is to work constantly to free democracy of its institutional shackles and return citizenship to the centre of political life—even if only for rupturous moments at a time. Thus does the fugitive transform from a prisoner on the run into a guerrilla warrior in the democratic cause. "Democracy is not about where the political is located but how it is experienced," Wolin notes.[56] And later: "Democracy needs to be reconceived as something other than a form of government: as a mode of being which is conditioned by bitter experience, doomed to succeed only temporarily, but is a recurrent possibility as long as the memory of the political survives."[57]

I take particular note of the *temporality* embedded in this revitalized notion of fugitive democracy ("the memory of the political," "recurrent possibility"); and likewise its invocation of *authority* ("conditioned by bitter experience" and "doomed," but nevertheless doomed "to succeed"). This, I suggest, is precisely the living tradition of democracy. Though its orientation to future possibilities marks it as akin to some recent politico-theological conceptions of democracy, such as Derrida's "democracy to come" or Agamben's "coming community," it is rooted in the deep soil of inherited social life and concrete obligation to those both before and after us.[58] Unlike them, it does not ask for a vague "infinite responsibility" towards those who are yet to come, but it *does* enjoin a real infinite, namely the infinite demand to renew and revitalize democratic legitimacy, here and now (and again).

We might think, in this connection, of Gilles Deleuze's notion of *repetition*: that infinite miracle of singularity, the uniqueness that lies beyond law, equivalency, and transaction, but which can be encountered again and again. "Repetition as a conduct and as a point of view concerns non-exchangeable and non-substitutable singularities," Deleuze says. "If exchange is the criterion of generality, theft and gift are those of repetition."[59] That is: only that which can be stolen can also be given, and vice versa. "Repetition belongs to humour and irony," Deleuze continues; "it is by nature transgression or exception, always revealing a singularity opposed to the particularities subsumed under laws, a universal opposed to the generalities which give rise to laws."[60] Repetition is festival, excess, rupture. In its democratic possibility, it is where you and I are citizens together, returning to our shared locus of trust, equal not in the sense of being exchangeable but precisely in respect of our infinite difference. Jacques Rancière makes the connection vivid in one of the few optimistic formulations in his *Hatred of Democracy*. "Democracy is neither a form of government that enables oligarchies to rule in the name of the people, nor is it a form of society that governs the power of commodities," he writes there. "It is the action that constantly wrests the monopoly of public life from oligarchic governments, and the omnipotence over lives from the power of wealth."[61]

The possibility of repeating the democratic demand is the gift bequeathed to us by our forebears. The making of it, in the service of our own needs but also in trust to those who will come after us, is the gift we bequeath to them. That is to say, democracy is a gift that we must give to ourselves—so much is obvious—but is also a gift of insight, that we the people are far more than an electorate, a voting bloc, a population. It is, then—to offer another double to match the double genitive of my opening section—a gift in time: that is, one which is both received and given across *and* that must be given without delay if its benefits are not to be squandered in cynicism or complacency, frozen into institutional attenuation, stolen by the monied interest, or otherwise wasted.

Notes

1 The seeds of the present essay may be found in Mark Kingwell, "The End of *The End of Democracy*," *Descant* 42:4 (Winter 2011): 204-17; adapted as "Incivility, Zombies, and Democracy's End," Introduction to Kingwell, *Unruly Voices: Essays on Democracy, Civility, and the Human Imagination* (Biblioasis, 2012), 11-26.

2 Maistre's proximate target was Rousseau, in particular the latter's ideas of natural freedom, emancipation, and the general will, as set out in *The Social Contract, or Principles of Political Right [Du contrat social ou Principes du droit politique]* (1762). Maistre's considered objections to popular sovereignty can be found in *Against Rousseau: On the State of Nature and On the Sovereignty of the People* (McGill-Queen's, 1996).

3 Terry Eagleton, *Culture and the Death of God* (Yale, 2014), 25-6.

4 Thomas Mann, *Reflections of a Nonpolitical Man [Betrachtungen eines Unpolitischen*, 1918] (Frederick Ungar, 1983), 354.

5 See, for example, Jacques Rancière, *Hatred of Democracy [La haine de la démocratie]*, trans. Steve Corcoran (Verso, 2006). I discuss some of Rancière's ideas in "Throwing Dice: Luck of the Draw and the Democratic Ideal," *PhaenEx* 7:1 (Spring/Summer 2012): 66-100; reprinted in Kingwell, *Unruly Voices*, 103-130.

6 A good critique of this general tendency may be found in John O'Neill, *The Missing Child in Liberal Theory: Towards a Covenant Theory of Family, Community, Welfare, and the Civic State* (University of Toronto, 1994).

7 Thomas Merton, *New Seeds of Contemplation* (New Directions, 1961), 48.

8 For the canonical statement of the problem, see Garrett Hardin, "The Tragedy of the Commons," *Science* 162 (1968), 1243-48.

9 There is a voluminous literature on the topic of collective action problems, but an especially clear overview, in the context of urban planning, can be found in Henk Voogd, "Social dilemmas and the communicative planning paradox," *The Town Planning Review* 72:1 (January 2001), 77-95. See also Mark Kingwell, "'Fuck You' and Other Salutations: Incivility as a Collective Action Problem," in D. Mower and W. Robison, eds., *Civility in Politics and Education* (Routledge, 2012), 44-61; reprinted in Kingwell, *Unruly Voices*, 149-68.

10 See, for example, Will Kymlicka, *Liberalism, Community, and Culture* (Oxford, 1989 and 1991).

11 A seminal work here is Sheldon S. Wolin, "Fugitive Democracy," *Constellations* 1:1 (1994): 11-25; see also Wolin, *Democracy Inc.: Managed Democracy and the Specter of Inverted Totalitarianism* (Princeton, 2008).

12 Here I follow the analysis of Lewis Hyde in *The Gift: Imagination and the Erotic Life of Property* (Vintage, 1979).

13 In a variant sometimes known as Thieving Secret Santa, participants contribute wrapped gifts and then take turns, either opening a gift and keeping it or "stealing" an already-opened but abandoned gift. This game is also known as the white elephant gift exchange, Yankee Swap, Dirty Santa, Devil's Santa, Nasty Christmas, Snatchy Christmas Rat, Chinese Christmas, or the Grinch game—all names that suggest that, while the game preserves a more genuine gifting culture in being anti-transactional, it is also considered competitive, if playfully so.

14 See John Rawls, *A Theory of Justice* (Belknap Press, 1971 and 1999), especially section 44; Rawls, *Political Liberalism* (Columbia, 1993), 274; Rawls, *Justice as Fairness: A Restatement* (Belknap Press, 2001), especially sections 49.2 and 49.3.

15 Rawls, *Political Liberalism*, 274; *Justice as Fairness*, 160.

16 I won't attempt to cite the body of criticism here. A telling early response was Kenneth J. Arrow, "Rawls's Principle of Just Saving," *Swedish Journal of Economics* 75:4 (December 1973): 323-35; compare the later concerns expressed in Thomas Schramme, "Is Rawlsian Justice Bad for the Environment?" *Analyse & Kritik* 28 (2006): 146-57.

17 Chesterton was an indefatigable controversialist—his own age's Christopher Hitchens, perhaps—and he cannot resist jibes at contemporaries. My (unfair) favourite: "Surely one might pay for extraordinary joy in ordinary morals. Oscar Wilde said that sunsets were not valued because we could not pay for sunsets. But Oscar Wilde was wrong; we can pay for sunsets. We can pay for them by not being Oscar Wilde." G. K. Chesterton, *Orthodoxy* (orig. 1905; Hendrickson, 2006), 53. All further quotations are taken from this edition.

18 Charles Taylor, *Modern Social Imaginaries* (Duke, 2004), 96.

19 Ibid., 97.

20 Lewis Mumford, *Technics and Civilization* (Chicago, 2010), 17.

21 F. W. Taylor, *The Principles of Scientific Management*, in *The Early Sociology of Management and Organizations, Vol. 1: Scientific Management* (Routledge, 2005), 129. Compare Rem Koolhaas, *Delirious New York: A Retroactive Manifesto for Manhattan* (Monacelli, 1974), which relates Taylor's time-motion ideas to the spectacular rise of first-generation skyscrapers in Manhattan, especially the Empire State Building; I expand on this latter point in Kingwell, *Nearest Thing to Heaven: The Empire State Building and Americans Dreams* (Yale, 2006).

22 Guy Debord, *Society of the Spectacle* [*La societé du spectacle*] (orig. 1967; Black & Red, 1983), sec. V:126.

23 But see Mark Kingwell, "The Work Idea: Wage Slavery, Bullshit, and the Good Infinite," in Todd Dufresne and Clara Sacchetti, eds., *The Economy as Cultural System: Theory, Capitalism, Crisis* (Bloomsbury, 2013), 127-40; reprinted in Kingwell, *Unruly Voices*, 181-96 and as the introduction to Kingwell and Joshua Glenn, *The Wage Slave's Glossary* (Biblioasis, 2011).

24   Witold Rybczynski's *Waiting for the Weekend* (Viking, 1991) tells a gripping version of this story, set against the Babylonian origin of the seven-day week itself.

25   Martin Heidegger, "The Age of the World Picture," in William Lovitt, trans., *The Question Concerning Technology and Other Essays* (Harper & Row, 1977).

26   Debord, *Society of the Spectacle*, sec. V:145.

27   E. P. Thompson, "Time, Work-Discipline, and Industrial Capitalism," *Past & Present* 38 (1967), 69, 90.

28   Taylor, *Modern Social Imaginaries*, 157.

29   Ibid., 110.

30   Bruce Ackerman, *We The People, Volume I: Foundations* (Belknap, 1991) and *Volume II: Transformations* (Belknap, 2000).

31   See Mark Kingwell, "Idling Toward Heaven: The Last Defence You Will Ever Need," *Queen's Quarterly* 115:4 (Winter 2008): 569-85; also the introduction to Kingwell and Joshua Glenn, *The Idler's Glossary* (Biblioasis, 2008).

32   A. Bartlett Giamatti, *Take Time for Paradise: Americans and Their Games* (Summit Books, 1989), 44.

33   Eagleton, *Culture and the Death of God*, 136.

34   Igor Stravinsky, *The Poetics of Music in the Form of Six Lessons* [*Poétique Musicale*], Charles Eliot Norton Lectures 1939-40 (orig. 1942; Harvard, 1947 and 1993), chap. 3.

35   Mrs. John Marshall (Carol) Wharton, the wife of an aging, respectable lawyer, says these words to a young colleague of her husband with whom she is contemplating a love affair. Richard Powell, *The Philadelphian* (Scribner's, 1956), 218. The novel was later adapted in film as the Paul Newman vehicle *The Young Philadelphians* (1959, d. Vincent Sherman).

36   Eagleton, *Culture and the Death of God*, 193. He adds: "The left-wing historian A. J. P. Taylor once informed an Oxford Fellowship election committee that he had extreme political views, but held them moderately." This suggests the valid question whether moderate political views, held extremely, might offer a better course.

37   The standard attack on spurious Highland clan identity is Hugh Trevor-Roper, "The Invention of Tradition: the Highland Tradition of Scotland," in Eric Hobsbawm and Terence Ranger, eds., *The Invention of Tradition* (Cambridge, 1983). But, as critics have noted, the distinction between "invented" and "initiated" traditions, particularly in the case of nation-states (a particular concern of this volume), can be difficult to hold without committing its own kind of special pleading. A better approach to the trappings of nationalism is, arguably, the one taken by Roland Barthes in his *Mythologies* (orig. 1957; Annette Lavers, trans., Paladin, 1973), which examines specific bits of cultural effluvia—steak frites, the Citröen motorcar, a *Paris Match* magazine cover—in order to reveal their ideology-driven fabrication.

38   Walter Benjamin, "Theses on the Philosophy of History" [Über den Begriff der Geschichte], Harry Zohn trans., in Hannah Arendt, ed., *Illuminations: Essays and Reflections* (Shocken, 1968).

39   In a curious and controversial inversion of the standard anxiety-of-influence aesthetic tradition, the British artists Jake and Dinos Chapman purchased several

prints from Goya's *Los Caprichos* series and then drew on them. According to Dinos Chapman, these acts of defacement did not constitute vandalism because the altered works *actually rose in value*. "You can't vandalize something by making it more expensive," he said. In 2005, the Chapman Brothers' "revised and improved" versions of *Los Caprichos* were selling for $26,000 each in the White Cube gallery, London. For an account of vandalism, value, and renewed gift economies in discarded or rescued art, see Ben Lerner, "Damage Control: The Modern Art World's Tyranny of Price," *Harper's Magazine* (December 2013), 43-49.

40 Chesterton, *Orthodoxy*, 31.

41 For a brisk journalistic account of the details, see Douglas Rushkoff, *Present Shock: When Everything Happens Now* (Penguin, 2013). It has to be said that this book, while valuable as a diagnostic, itself suffers from a measure of discursive breathlessness, leaping from topic to topic with the speed of the very virus it wants to analyze.

42 For more on the trope of zombies in democratic life, see Mark Kingwell, "Frank's Motel: Horizontal and Vertical in the Big Other," in Joshua Nichols and Amy Swiffen, eds., *The Ends of History: Questioning the Stakes of Historical Reason* (Routledge, 2013), 103-26.

43 For example, in the Declaration of the Rights of Man and of the Citizen (Paris, 24 June, 1793) we find these words offered in defense of the French Revolution: "in order that all citizens . . . may never permit themselves to be oppressed and degraded by tyranny." The same language is present in Robespierre's (rejected) Declaration of Rights (24 April, 1793), though it does not appear in the (accepted) 1789 Declaration.

44 Sheldon S. Wolin, *Democracy Incorporated*, xviii.

45 Ibid., xix.

46 Ibid., 233. Wolin is particularly worried by the combination of such anti-democratic instantaneity with a misguided reverence for the past in the form of "originalism" concerning "Framers' Intent" and the U. S. Constitution.

47 Eagleton, *Culture and the Death of God*, 188.

48 Ibid., 188; see also Terry Eagleton, *The Illusions of Postmodernism* (Blackwell, 1996).

49 Zygmunt Bauman, *Socialism: The Active Utopia* (George Allen & Unwin, 1976), 18-19.

50 For some alarming statistics concerning defection from electoral politics among young Canadians—dubbed Spectators—were reported by Michael Valpy, "The Young Will Inherit a Future They See as a Sham" *Toronto Star*, December 8, 2013; Valpy in turn drew on an analysis by David Herle, "The Spectators," *Policy Options* (November 2012), 19-20. News reports suggest the situation similar, if not worse, in other developed "democratic" nations.

51 Wolin, "Fugitive Democracy," 19. In support of the last claim Wolin cites Plato, *Republic* VIII: 557e-558a and *Laws* III: 693d.

52 Robert Michels, *Political Parties: A Sociological Study of the Oligarchical Tendencies of Modern Democracy*, trans. Eden Paul and Cedar Paul, (orig. 1911; The Free Press, 1915).

53 Georg Lukács, "What is Orthodox Marxism?," in *History and Class Consciousness: Studies in Marxist Dialectics*, trans. Rodney Livingstone, (MIT, 1972), 19.

54 I explore the reach of this particular version of ideological conditioning in Mark Kingwell, "The American Gigantic," *Unruly Voices*, 41-56.

55 Wolin, "Fugitive Democracy," 16.

56 Ibid., 18.

57 Ibid., 23.

58 See Jacques Derrida, *Rogues: Two Essays on Reason*, trans. Michael Naas and Pascale-Anne Brault, (Stanford, 2003) and Giorgio Agamben, *The Coming Community*, trans. Michael Hardt, (University of Minnesota, 1993). Derrida is consistent in maintaining that all political thought, including the radical injunctions of deconstruction, speak out of a tradition. For a clear overview and critique, see Ernesto Laclau "'The Time is Out of Joint,'" in *Emancipation(s)* (Verso, 1996 and 2007), 66-83.

59 Gilles Deleuze, *Difference and Repetition*, trans. Paul Patton, (Columbia, 1994), 1.

60 Ibid., 5.

61 Jacques Rancière, *Hatred of Democracy*, 96.

Acknowledgments

With one exception, the essays in this volume were all published between 2012 and 2015 (the outlier essay was first published in 2008 but seemed right for inclusion here). Most were commissioned by editors with whom I have worked for some time, plus a few new ones, and I offer thanks to them all here: Boris Castell at *Queen's Quarterly*, Natasha Hassan at the *Globe and Mail*, Lauren McKeon at *This Magazine*, Russ Lumpkin and James Babb at *Gray's Sporting Journal*, Andrew Potter at the *Ottawa Citizen*, Evan Goldstein at the *Chronicle of Higher Education*, Tatum Hands at *LA+*, Daniel Simon at *World Literature Today*, Meeka Walsh at *Border Crossings*, Deirdre Foley-Mendelssohn and Jeremy Keehn at *Harper's Magazine*, and above all, Karen Mulhallen at *Descant*. This last superb quarterly, recently demised, has been an intellectual and creative home for me over several happy decades. I regret its passing and thank Karen for the decades of stimulation she and the magazine offered me and so many other readers.

Thanks, too, to Jeet Heer, Emily Donaldson and Tracy Pryce for editorial advice on the complete manuscript, and to Dan Wells at Bibilioasis for once more taking on a book project with me. Several of the essays in Section D were arranged with the individual artists, and so I thank Shelagh Keeley, Matthew Pillsbury, and Mira Kulenovic for the invitations to write about their work. It was not feasible to include images of the artworks in this volume, but clearly the texts included here are incomplete without them; please consult the sources listed overleaf, or visit the artists' online sites, to get the full picture. Thanks also to the Jackman Humanities Institute, where a faculty fellowship in 2011-12 allowed me to work out many of the ideas found in the book's final two essays. A number of these pieces were also delivered as public lectures in Canada, the United States, France, Holland, Qatar, and Australia, and I thank all the inviting institutions for the chance to test these thoughts and arguments in speech before committing them to the relative fixity of writing. As always, love and thanks to Molly Montgomery.

Parts of the introduction were previously published in the *Globe and Mail* and *This Magazine*. "The Barbed Gift of Leisure" and "Bright Stroll, Big City" were first published in *The Chronicle Review*. "Walking Downtown" was published in *Harper's Magazine* and "Urban Pleasures" in *LA+*. "Hotels Bars and the Female Cruise" first appeared in *Descant*; for those keeping score, it is the 2008 essay mentioned above. "Building Cities, Making Friends: A Meditation" was published in *Kuwabara Payne McKenna Blumberg Architects* (Basel: Birkhäuser) and in *Queen's Quarterly*.

"Prisons Without Bars: Of Lexicons and Lessons," "Self-Made Men," "Serial Killers," "Our Insidious Foes and the Plot Against America," "Saints, Sinners, and Exiles," and "Parties, Parties, More Parties" all appeared first in *Descant*.

"Reading, Writing, and Consciousness: The Future(s)" was published in the *Ottawa Citizen* and, revised, in *Harper's Magazine*. "The Ethics of Ethics and Literature" was published in *World Literature Today*, while "Can We Talk About Evil?" was commissioned by *Harper's Magazine* but in the event appeared in *Descant*. "'We Shall Look Into It Tomorrow': The Art of Procrastination," commissioned by my colleague Abrahim Khan, was first published in the *Toronto Journal of Theology*.

"In the Third Place" was published as guest curator's notes in the *DOXA Documentary Film Festival Guide*. "Drawing Mies in Barcelona" was published online as a Circuit Gallery Catalogue Essay (http://www. circuitgallery.com/exhibitions/keeley-barcelona-pavilion/mark-kingwell-essay/). "Worlds of Wonder" was published as the introduction in Lesley Martin, ed., *Matthew Pillsbury: City Stages* (New York: Aperture). "Faces of Chaotic Beauty" was commissioned by the artist and is pending publication as of this writing. "Art's Unmediated Middles," meanwhile, appeared in *Border Crossings*.

"Slack Enters the System" and "On the Ausable" were first published in *Gray's Sporting Journal*; the former also appeared in *Descant*, while the latter was published in *Queen's Quarterly*. A version of "Frank's Motel: Horizontal and Vertical in the Big Other" was published in Joshua Nichols and Amy Swiffen, eds., *The Ends of History: Questioning the Stakes of Historical Reason* (New York: Routledge), while "Democracy's Gift: Time, Tradition, Repetition" was published in revised form as

"Fugitive Democracy Narratives: A Gift in Time," *Narrative Matters 2014 HAL Univ. Diderot* (http://hal-univ-diderot.archives-ouvertes.fr/hal-01069114).

Final note: both of these last two essays are available as illustrated stand-alone pamphlets at *Blurb.com*. Please see http://www.blurb.com/b/5190878-frank-s-motel and http://www.blurb.com/b/5157548-democracy-s-gift, respectively.